SHAKESPEARE ON SI

Several hundred films based on Shakespearean material were made in cinema's 'silent' era. What economic and cultural ambitions combined in order to make Shakespeare such attractive source material for the film industry? What were the characteristic approaches of particular production companies and of particular national film industries? How were silent Shakespeare films marketed, distributed, exhibited and received? Through a series of close readings, and drawing upon a wealth of fresh primary research, this engaging account tells an evolving story that both illuminates silent Shakespeare films already known, and brings into critical circulation other little known films not yet commercially available. Subjects covered include nineteenth-century precursors of silent Shakespeare, the film industry's transitional era, the many Shakespeare films of the Vitagraph Company of America, films of the 1916 Shakespeare tercentenary, silent films of *Hamlet* and Asta Nielsen and Emil Jannings as the stars of German Shakespeare films of the 1920s.

JUDITH BUCHANAN is Senior Lecturer in Film Studies at the University of York and the author of *Shakespeare on Film*. With a background in early modern literature, she now writes on silent cinema, on literary and biblical adaptation in the cinema, cinematic authorship, bodies on film and cinema's material legacies. She provided the introduction and voice-over commentary for the British Film Institute's *Silent Shakespeare* DVD.

SHAKESPEARE ON SILENT FILM

an Excellent Dumb Discourse

JUDITH BUCHANAN

CAMBRIDGE
UNIVERSITY PRESS

CAMBRIDGE UNIVERSITY PRESS
Cambridge, New York, Melbourne, Madrid, Cape Town,
Singapore, São Paulo, Delhi, Tokyo, Mexico City

Cambridge University Press
The Edinburgh Building, Cambridge CB2 8RU, UK

Published in the United States of America by Cambridge University Press, New York

www.cambridge.org
Information on this title: www.cambridge.org/9781107403727

First published 2009
First paperback edition 2011

A catalogue record for this publication is available from the British Library

Library of Congress Cataloguing in Publication data
Buchanan, Judith.
Shakespeare on silent film : an excellent dumb discourse / Judith Buchanan.
p. cm.
Includes bibliographical references and index.
ISBN 978-0-521-87199-0 (hardback)   1. Shakespeare, William, 1564–1616–Film and
video adaptations.   2. English drama–Film and video adaptations.   3. Silent films–
History and criticism.   4. Film adaptations–History and criticism.
I. Title.
PR3093.B775 2009
791.43´6–dc22   2009006846

ISBN 978-0-521-87199-0 Hardback
ISBN 978-1-107-40372-7 Paperback

for Maureen, aunt and friend

I cannot too much muse
Such shapes, such gestures, and such sound, expressing –
Although they want the use of tongue – a kind
Of excellent dumb discourse.

The Tempest

[In these silent films] it struck me that I was witnessing a dead art, a wholly defunct genre that would never be practiced again. And yet, for all the changes that had occurred since then, their work was as fresh and invigorating as it had been when it was first shown. That was because they had understood the language they were speaking. They had invented a syntax of the eye, a grammar of pure kinesis ... It was thought translated into action, human will expressing itself through the human body, and therefore it was for all time ... They were like poems, like the renderings of dreams, like some intricate choreography of the spirit, and because they were dead, they probably spoke more deeply to us now than they had to the audiences of their time. We watched them across a great chasm of forgetfulness, and the very things that separated them from us were in fact what made them so arresting: their muteness, their absence of color, their fitful, speeded-up rhythms. These were obstacles, and they made viewing difficult for us, but they also relieved the images of the burden of representation. They stood between us and the film, and therefore we no longer had to pretend that we were looking at the real world. The flat screen was the world, and it existed in two dimensions. The third dimension was in our head.

Paul Auster, *The Book of Illusions*

Contents

List of illustrations	*page* ix
Acknowledgements	xi
List of abbreviations	xiv
Preface	xvii

Introduction: wresting an alphabet   1

1   Shakespeare without words: the nineteenth-century
legacy   23

2   Biograph's pioneering film of *King John* (1899)   57

    King John (BMBC: W.K.-L. Dickson and Walter
Pfeffer Dando, 1899)

3   Conflicted allegiances in Shakespeare films
of the transitional era   74

    The Tempest (Clarendon, 1908), *Otello* (FAI, 1909)

4   Corporate authorship: the Shakespeare films of the
Vitagraph Company of America   105

    Vitagraph's *Julius Caesar* (1908), *Macbeth* (1908), *Romeo and Juliet*
(1908), *Othello* (1908), *The Merchant of Venice* (1908), *A Midsummer
Night's Dream* (1909), *King Lear* (1909), *Twelfth Night* (1910);
Georges Méliès' *La Mort de Jules César* (1907); Cines' *Brutus*
(1910); Thanhouser's *A Winter's Tale* (1910); Film d'Arte
Italiana's *Re Lear* (1910)

5   Pedigree and performance codes in silent films of *Hamlet*   147

    Hamlet (Gaumont-Hepworth, 1913), *Amleto* (Rodolfi-Film, 1917)

Contents

6   Shakespeare films of the 1916 tercentenary   190

The Real Thing at Last (J.M. Barrie), *Macbeth* (Triangle-Reliance),
Romeo and Juliet (Fox), *Romeo and Juliet* (Metro)

7   Asta Nielsen and Emil Jannings: stars of German
    Shakespeare films of the early 1920s   217

Hamlet (Art-Film, 1920), *Othello* (Wörner-Filmgesellschaft, 1922)

Afterword: 'No tongue, all eyes! Be silent': performing
wordless Shakespeare today   252

*Filmography   (a) Commercially available Shakespeare
                   films of the silent era*   260
*   (b) General filmography*
Bibliography   279
Index   299

Illustrations

I.1 Frederick Warde in *Richard III* (James Keane, 1912)   *page* 14

1.1 Magic lantern slides of Ophelia from Briggs'
'Shakespeare Illustrated' series, 1890s   37

2.1 Stills from *King John* (BMBC, 1899), *The Sketch*
(27 September, 1899)   65

3.1 Stills from *The Tempest* (Clarendon, 1908)   83

3.2 Pathé advertising poster (1910)   89

3.3 Stills of exteriors in Venice: *Othello* (FAI, 1909)   92

3.4 Stills of interiors in Cyprus: *Othello* (FAI, 1909)   97

4.1 A title card and still from *Julius Caesar* (Vitagraph, 1908)   117

4.2 Stills from the Vitagraph *Macbeth* (1908) and *Romeo
and Juliet* (1908)   120

4.3 Still from *Julius Caesar* (Vitagraph, 1908)   122

4.4 Still from *Julius Caesar* (Cines, 1914)   123

4.5 Still from *King Lear* (Vitagraph, 1909)   124

4.6 Stills from *A Winter's Tale* (Thanhouser, 1910)   128

4.7 Stills from *A Midsummer Night's Dream* (Vitagraph, 1909)   134

4.8 Still from *Twelfth Night* (Vitagraph, 1910)   140

4.9 Still from *Twelfth Night* (Vitagraph, 1910)   142

5.1 J. Glulick's charcoal drawing of Forbes-Robertson as
Hamlet in the Farewell Season Souvenir Programme   153

5.2 *The Play Pictorial* (June 1913), front cover   154

5.3 Amerigo Manzini, *Ruggeri* (1920), front cover   165

5.4 Frontispiece and line-drawings from Gustave Garcia,
The Actors' Art (1880)   176

5.5 Frontispiece and line drawings from Charles Aubert,
The Art of Pantomime (1901)   177

5.6 A commemorative postcard of Forbes-Robertson as *Hamlet*   180

5.7 Commemorative postcards of Forbes-Robertson, painting
and relaxing by a fire   182

6.1   Publicity shot of Theda Bara as Juliet   204
6.2   Still from *Romeo and Juliet* (Metro, 1916)   208
6.3   Still from *Romeo and Juliet* (Fox, 1916)   209
7.1   Stills from an early film fragment of
       an unidentified *Hamlet*   222
7.2   Asta Nielsen as Hamlet, Lilli Jacobsson as Ophelia.
       Tie-in star card   226
7.3   Stills from *Hamlet* (Art-Film, 1920)   237
7.4   Stills from *Othello* (Wörner-Filmgesellschaft, 1922)   244
7.5   Stills from *Othello* (Wörner-Filmgesellschaft, 1922)   245
7.6   The murder of Desdemona from *Othello*
       (Wörner-Filmgesellschaft, 1922)   249
8.1   Paata Tsikurishvili in *Hamlet ... the rest is silence*
       (Synetic Theater, 2007)   258

Acknowledgements

For a valued research leave term from the AHRC, pump-priming funding from the Department of English at the University of York and a short-term Folger Fellowship that enabled me to spend time with the Robert Hamilton Ball Collection at the Folger Shakespeare Library in Washington DC, I am extremely grateful.

Bill Sherman, Richard Rowland, Pat Palmer, Mike Cordner and Chris Hogg have each kindly read draft sections of this book and provided invaluable suggestions of which I have made grateful use. I am particularly grateful to Russell Jackson and Luke McKernan for their responses to the entire manuscript: the book has benefited from these in both its detail and its drift. Terry Borton, Mervyn Heard, Mo Heard, Stephen Herbert, Richard Manwaring Baines, Ken Rothwell, David Williams, Dorin Gardner Schumacher (granddaughter of film star Helen Gardner) and Ned Thanhouser (grandson of film pioneer Edwin Thanhouser) have each kindly answered questions that have helped with my research. Betsy Walsh and her reading room staff, Erin Blake (Curator of Art and Special Collections) and Richard Kuhta (Eric Weinman Librarian) at the Folger, Rosemary Hanes at the Library of Congress, Robert Bearman from the Records Office of the Shakespeare Birthplace Trust, Vicki Principi, Curator of Special Collections at Princeton University Library, Barbara Galasso and Karen Everson at George Eastman House, Jo Ellsworth at the Theatre Collection of Bristol University, Francesca Angelucci at Il Centro Sperimentale di Cinematographia in Rome, Signior Cocchi at the Cineteca di Bologna, the reading room staff in the Berlin Filmmuseum, the British Film Institute and the study room of the Theatre Museum, Covent Garden have all provided invaluable assistance. Paata Tsikurishvili and Nathan Weinberger of the Synetic Theater Company kindly met with me to discuss their extraordinary wordless theatrical Shakespeare productions, prompting me to consider contemporary perspectives on this performance tradition. A heartfelt individual thank you goes to Zoran

Sinobad of the Library of Congress's Motion Picture, Broadcasting and Recorded Sound Division, who shares my interest in this material and who, while we collaborated in preparing a lively public screening of rare silent Shakespeare film prints from the LOC archives in April 2007, also kindly helped me track sources and procure images. Huw Llewellyn-Jones and Matthew Gaughan provided technical assistance in the preparation of images. Stephanie Buchanan kindly lent me her unsparing editorial eye before submission. Sarah Stanton and Rebecca Jones at CUP have guided me through the publication processes with wisdom and patience. I thank them all warmly. Colin Buchanan's suggestions for excision when I was over words were both generously offered and finely discriminating. Christopher New's gently framed questions about the detail, and specific encouragement about the whole, made for a delightful correspondence. I am pleased to acknowledge my considerable personal and professional debts to both. Any outstanding errors or clumsiness are, needless to say, fully my own.

Parts of this book have previously appeared in other forms. Several sections had a first, less detailed outing in *Shakespeare on Film* (2005). Sections of the Introduction appeared in an earlier instantiation in the Introduction to the December 2007 special issue of the British Shakespeare Association journal *Shakespeare*, which I guest-edited. Sections of Chapter 3 appeared in an article ('In Mute Despair') that came out in that same special issue. A briefer version of Chapter 5 appeared in the June 2006 issue of *Shakespeare*. All appear here reworked and with permission.

Having the opportunity to go through the notes and unpublished catalogue cards of the diligently systematic scholar Robert Hamilton Ball has been tremendous. Nothing could replace his invaluable book *Shakespeare on Silent Film* (1968) and this book does not intend to try. I do, however, consciously make use of his legacy to further the enquiry that he began, in tune, I hope, with his voracious appetite for detail and nimble capacity to convert detail into story. In this work, therefore, I warmly acknowledge my debts to his pioneering scholarship.

Meanwhile Kostja has, as ever, kept things together with wit and generosity, while Douglas and Frederike have been happening up around us in their chirpy, individual ways. I thank all three for cutting me enough slack to write the book, for relocating cheerily to Washington when there was research to be done there, and for their regular and infectious injections of hilarity into the business of life.

I first sampled the pleasure to be had in considering the performance implications of a Shakespeare play a quarter of a century ago, when my mother helped me plan an 'O' Level essay on *Macbeth*. I caught the bug then and have since been fortunate enough to be able to convert this particular pleasure into a professional interest. I therefore take this opportunity to thank my Mum for getting me started (and for much more besides).

Abbreviations

AFI	American Film Institute
AMBC	American Mutoscope and Biograph Company
Ball Collection	The Robert Hamilton Ball Collection, held at the Folger Shakespeare Library, Washington DC
BFI	The British Film Institute (London)
BFK	Bundesarchiv-Filmarchiv, Koblenz
BL	The British Library (London)
BMBC	British Mutoscope and Biograph Company
BUFVC	British Universities Film and Video Council
CSC	Il Centro Sperimentale di Cinematographia (Rome)
CNPG	Cinema News and Property Gazette
FAI	Film d'Arte Italiana
fps	frames per second
Folger	Folger Shakespeare Library, Washington DC.
GEH	George Eastman House, Rochester, New York
ILN	Illustrated London News
ISA	International Shakespeare Association
KLW	Kinematograph and Lantern Weekly
LOC	Motion Picture and Recorded Sound Division, Library of Congress, Washington DC.
MLS	The Magic Lantern Society
MPM	Motion Picture Magazine
MPW	Moving Picture World
NFTVA	National Film and Television Archive, London (now the BFI National Archive)
NY	New York
NYPL	New York Public Library

NYT	New York Times
PRO	Public Records Office, London (now the National Archives)
SB	Shakespeare Bulletin
SQ	Shakespeare Quarterly
Theatre Museum	The Theatre Museum, Covent Garden, London

Preface

Shakespeare and silent cinema do not strike the casual observer as natural allies. For all the apparent oddity of the match, though, nearly three hundred silent Shakespeare films were made between 1899 and 1927.[1] Even some of those involved in their production were struck by the disconcerting nature of the project. While filming his *Hamlet* in 1913, for example, the famous English classical stage actor Sir Johnston Forbes-Robertson is said to have stomped through a wood in frustration at the 'capped' nature of the performance he was required to give in this context, shouting at the cameraman, 'Lines, damn you, give me lines!'[2] Two years earlier, on 27 February 1911, at a showing of Herbert Beerbohm Tree's *Scenes from Shakespeare's King Henry VIII* at the Palace Theatre, London, a gentleman in the audience had allegedly taken it upon himself to represent the crowd when he jumped to his feet minutes into the projection to call out, 'I say, you know, we can't hear a thing.'[3] This genteel heckler simply could not, it seems, credit that anyone would have the *sangfroid* to perform Shakespeare without the words.

Audiences today tend to agree. For many, the most noticeable characteristic of these films is the thing conspicuously missing from them. In its muting of Shakespearean drama, silent Shakespearean cinema cannot but seem self-negating, the result of a senseless act of stripping away of all that is nuanced, beautiful and meaningful in the inherited source.

---

[1] The use of the term 'silent' for films of the era is conventional. The word, however, is misleading since films were never, of course, silent at the point of exhibition. Though they typically lacked integrated sound, they were always exhibited with live musical accompaniment, and sometimes also, as discussed in the Introduction, by live vocal commentary and/or other sound effects. The number of 'silent' Shakespeare films is also discussed in the Introduction.

[2] Paul Dehn, 'The Filming of Shakespeare', in John Garrett, ed., *Talking of Shakespeare* (NY: Hodder and Stoughton, 1954), pp. 49–72 (50). Forbes-Robertson's desire to speak the lines for the camera is part of movie legend. See, for example, Iris Barry, *Let's Go to the Pictures* (London: Chatto and Windus, 1926), p. 97.

[3] Dehn, 'The Filming of Shakespeare', p. 50.

Unsurprisingly, perhaps, this body of films has typically been considered too flimsy, too silly a project perhaps, to merit critical discussion of the sustained type that, by contrast, has been generously lavished on Shakespeare films of the sound era.[4]

It was not in such terms, however, that these films were principally understood on first release. The story about the heckler at the Palace Theatre may have its basis in fact, or may simply be a piece of retrospective myth-spinning. If the latter, it is of interest for expressing a subsequent moment's desire to visit its own prejudices back upon a time yet itself to assume these particular concerns. And if the former, this picture-goer might either have been articulating his genuine puzzlement about the technology (though it was, of course, not new in 1911), or might simply have been a wag making a satirical interjection to entertain the crowd. Real or hypothesised, earnest or ironic, however, the outcry should not be taken as indicative of a general anxiety about silent Shakespeare films in the early cinema period. The quantities of primary materials that come under scrutiny in this book show that of all the many things for which Shakespeare films of the pre-sound era were lauded and/or castigated, the languagelessness of the performances was far from dominant.[5] A detailed trawl through the trade papers, 'fanzines' (as they would subsequently become known) and other relevant journals of the period[6] reveals that Shakespeare films were, by contrast, repeatedly commended for their pictorial qualities, engaging performances, pleasing use of location scenery, narrative clarity, passion, humour, delicately employed special effects, fluency in cutting between

[4] Scholars whose work has proved the exception to this include Jon Burrows, Anthony Guneratne, Russell Jackson, Luke McKernan, Roberta Pearson, Kenneth Rothwell, Emma Smith, Lisa Starks, William Urrichio, and, above all, Robert Hamilton Ball whose immense, charming and minutely researched *Shakespeare on Silent Film: A Strange Eventful History* (NY: Theatre Arts Books, 1968) remains the invaluable point of reference for all in the field.

[5] The primary materials examined for this book include scripts, film-makers' and actors' reminiscences, screen acting manuals, writers' manuals, company logbooks, distributors' account books, exhibitors' catalogues, theatre programmes, press books and other marketing materials, reviews and moving picture gossip – what James M. Welsh aptly calls the 'mass of shifting and disintegrating evidence' of the period in his article, 'Shakespeare with – and without – words', *Literature/Film Quarterly* v.1 (1973), 84–8 (84).

[6] The principal British trade papers and film periodicals of the period were: *The Biograph*, *The Kinematograph and Lantern Weekly* (*KLW*), *The Cinema News and Property Gazette* (*CNPG*), *The Optical Lantern and Cinematic Journal*, *The Pictures*, *The Illustrated Films Monthly*. The principal American publications were: *The Moving Picture World* (*MPW*), *Film Daily*, *Motography* (*The Nickelodeon*), *The Motion Picture Magazine* (*MPM*), *The Motion Picture Classic*, *The Motion Picture Story Magazine*, *Exceptional Photoplays*, *Variety*. Other contemporary newspapers and journals covering the pictures to which I refer include *The Picturegoer and Society*, *The New York Times* (*NYT*), *The New York Dramatic Mirror*, *The Era*, *The Illustrated London News* (*ILN*).

planes of action, edifying social and educative aims, appealing showcasing of popular stars and even for their sensitivity in interpreting Shakespearean dramatic moment and poetic force. Since there were plenty of non-linguistic aspects of the films to which critics could profitably attend, they only rarely needed to carp about the missing language in order to fill copy. If the pictures were excused the requirement to *be* Shakespeare, they could, more simply, be invited to operate in interesting proximity to his work. And if they were allowed the space to be autonomous entertainments in their own right, critics could equally be excused the obligation to disapprove of them out of some moral mission to protect Shakespeare from dilution or pollution. The films, that is, could be accepted, and judged, on their own merits rather than being held to account for the thing they self-evidently were not.

Resisting the temptation to define silent Shakespeare films principally by lack has the advantage of making it easier to discern the things that these maverick films delightfully and tellingly *are*, both as film industry products and as performance readings of Shakespeare. Accordingly, this book will explore what these moving pictures can reveal about technical, interpretive and institutional developments in the film industry during the silent era (1895–1927). And it will also ask how these films illumine the ways in which Shakespeare was being read, received and transmitted in this period. Even in its necessarily selective interpretive approach to Shakespeare, silent film can, after all, render some aspects of 'the Shakespearean' with aplomb. In his essay 'Lear, Tolstoy and the Fool', George Orwell wrote:

Lear can be imagined as a puppet show, a mime, a ballet, a series of pictures. Part of its poetry, perhaps the most essential part, is inherent in the story and is dependent neither on any particular set of words, nor on flesh-and-blood presentation.

Shut your eyes and think of *King Lear*, if possible without calling to mind any of the dialogue. What do you see? ... a majestic old man in a long black robe with flowing white hair and beard ... wandering through a storm, cursing the heavens, in company with a fool and a lunatic. Presently the scene shifts, and the old man, still cursing, still understanding nothing, is holding a dead girl in his arms while the Fool dangles on a gallows somewhere in the background. This is the bare skeleton of the play.[7]

---

[7] George Orwell, 'Lear, Tolstoy and the Fool' (first published in *Polemic* 7 [March 1947]) in Orwell, *Collected Essays, Journalism and Letters* v.4 (1945–1950), Sonia Orwell and Ian Angus (eds.) (London: Secker and Warburg, 1968), pp. 287–302 (293).

Images from *Lear*, Orwell argues, are imprinted so deeply upon our collective visual imagination that it is possible for the play to be evoked in its skeletal form as a series of cameo pictures. Part of its *poetry* (to claim the offered licence) is inherent in the story implied by this sequence of pictures. Broadly understood, the drama's identity is not, therefore, exclusively dependent on the specificity of its words. Needless to say, it is the words that have inspired the series of extra-linguistic expressions that now form part of the broader *Lear* legacy. However those non-verbal expressions have also taken on a life of their own, no longer merely the derivative and lesser cousin of the words that first authored them. As such, they have come to constitute an analogue life for the drama, and it is partly in this parallel, pictorial form that the drama latently resides in our individual and collective imaginations.[8] This culturally prevalent and yet only half-consciously acknowledged series of images emerges from a remembered composite elision of edition illustrations, Shakespearean paintings and well-known cameo moments from the play's performance history. *Lear* is not unique in this respect. Each of the plays has its own parallel life as a sequence of pictures from which iconic moments stand out: Romeo scaling the balcony, Portia addressing the court, Malvolio cross-gartered, Ophelia drowning in the brook, Othello murdering Desdemona, Macbeth reaching for an air-drawn dagger, Prospero conjuring a sea-tempest.[9]

A silent Shakespeare film can act, more or less consciously, as a conduit to this communally owned pictorial 'version' of a play by trading upon, or even quoting, the series of images conventionally associated with each. Equally, it can diverge from established pictorial expectations by reconfiguring the play in terms that defy the conventionalised pattern of Shakespearean tableaux we have come to expect. Both when adhered to and when eschewed, the set of culturally prevalent images associated with

---

[8] The paintings, drawings and engravings that contribute to the iconic force of the image of Lear in the storm include: Poussin's 'Landscape with Storm' (1651), Romney's 'Lear in the Tempest tearing off his Robes' (1762), Reynolds's 'Lear' (before 1762), John Runciman's 'Lear in the Storm' (1767), Alexander Runciman's 'King Lear on the Heath' (*c.*1767), Mortimer's 'Head of Lear' (1775), West, 'King Lear in the Storm' (1793), Wilson's 'David Garrick as King Lear' (1754), Dyce's 'King Lear and the Fool in the Storm' (1851). All reproduced in Jane Martineau *et al.*, *Shakespeare in Art* (London and NY: Merrell, 2003) and/or in Stuart Sillars, *Painting Shakespeare: the Artist as Critic 1720–1820* (Cambridge University Press, 2006).

[9] For a discussion of the iconicity of Lear in the storm and of other celebrated moments in Shakespeare, see Sillars, *Painting Shakespeare*, particularly pp. 83–93.

each drama necessarily forms part of the interpretive lens through which we view the films.

Orwell is not alone in reminding us that well-known dramatic literature is a more complex concatenation of formal elements and cultural forces than merely a set of scripted words awaiting performance interpretation. W. Stephen Bush, for example, is worth heeding on this score. As a regular, and thoughtfully zealous, contemporary commentator on moving pictures in the American trade paper *Moving Picture World* (*MPW*), Bush waged an ongoing campaign to establish the artistic credibility and moral standing of the early cinematograph industry. His interest lay particularly in pictures made from reputable literary or theatrical sources. In an article for *MPW* in 1911, he approvingly quoted theatre critic Clayton Hamilton on the subject of rendering theatrical material on screen:

The kinematograph bereaves the drama of the spoken word; and it must be surprising to the literary theorists to learn how much is left – how vividly the essential elements of action, character, and setting may convey themselves by visual means alone. Pantomime has been recognized for many centuries as a legitimate type of drama: but it is safe to say that the variety and the extent of its adaptability as a means of story telling were never fully understood until the invention of the kinematograph demanded of it an unprecedented exercise.[10]

Hamilton's words have a sustained relevance in relation to silent Shakespeare films. The question 'how much is left' when cinema 'bereaves the drama of the spoken word', however, starts from a premise that presupposes a finite and stable starting position from which only loss is then possible in subsequent adjustment. There are other ways of viewing this transaction and, therefore, other questions to ask. How is translated expression found for ideas inherited from a source? How are emphases clarified or adjusted in the transmediating processes of excision and selective concentration? What new considerations are introduced both through cinema's proper absorption in its own emerging presentational codes, interpretive priorities and commercial imperatives and also through the cultural-historical moment in which the particular interpretation is being wrought? This book seeks to uncover 'the variety and extent of [the] adaptability' of Shakespearean 'pantomime' in moving pictures, and by doing so, to learn not only 'how much is left' when the drama is bereft of the spoken word but also how much is rethought, recast and remade in the process.

---

[10] W. Stephen Bush, 'Signs of a Harvest', *MPW* v.9 n.4 (5 August 1911), 272.

Before pursuing the book's analytic and historical agenda, however, a brief prefatory word about the personal experience of living intimately with these films while preparing this book. In the course of these preparations, I have viewed and reviewed the films in any number of modes: at full speed, in slow motion, frame by frame, forwards, backwards, occasionally upside down (when I have accidentally mis-fed a print), on Steenbeck viewers in archives in Britain, the US, France, Germany and Italy, with live improvised and live scored musical accompaniment, with brilliantly appropriate and grimly inappropriate canned musical accompaniment, animated by actors speaking the lines, in eerie silence, as a series of stills, as archived paper deposits, projected onto the exterior walls of the Globe Playhouse in London, on domestic screens, while leafing through star cards to identify a player or through a Shakespeare play to pin a dramatic moment, while giving simultaneous commentary on them at academic conferences and at public screenings, or while simply sitting back alone to let them unspool uninterrupted for my private pleasure. As I have wondered at the verve, variety, eccentricity and ambition of these pieces of cinematic history, the single aspect that has affected me most significantly, staying with me after the cans of film have been returned to cool storage or the DVD to its shelf, has consistently been the simple presence of the individual actors. The muted, gesturing figures rendering both grand Shakespearean moment and inconsequential pieces of linking business in mimed action, often drained of their intended colour in the surviving prints and vulnerable to ridicule by being exhibited at an inappropriate projection speed, tell a story that is not only their own but that of their moment more generally.[11] As seen now, that tale can play out as one of figures marooned in time, earnestly (and sometimes skittishly) playing to a world that has moved on without them, to a spectatorship that now finds them curious, antiquated, stylised and in one way or another *too much*. But they were not always poignantly stranded in the wrong moment. As they were first committed to celluloid, they were the lords of time, occupying the moment with touching confidence, and often playing to considerable acclaim. The seeming remoteness of the actors can certainly estrange the contemporary spectator unaccustomed to the screen acting conventions informing those performances and the

---

[11] For a useful account of projection speeds in the era, see Kevin Brownlow, 'Silent Films – What Was the Right Speed?', in Thomas Elsaesser (ed.), *Early Cinema: Space, Frame, Narrative* (London: BFI, 1990), pp. 282–92.

shooting conventions employed to film them. However, it is also this seeming otherness that then renders more arresting those moments in which the sense of removal falls away and a piercingly recognisable truth-fulness in the performances cuts across the divide between then and now, between the long-gone actor and the contemporary spectator, between their world and ours. In renewing our collective acquaintance with some of these films, this book hopes to reconnect us also with some of the actors who occupy and animate them.

Wresting an alphabet

Thou shalt not sigh, nor hold thy stumps to heaven,
Nor wink, nor nod, nor kneel, nor make a sign,
But I of these will wrest an alphabet
And by still practice learn to know thy meaning.
Titus to Lavinia, Titus Andronicus III.ii.42–45[1]

In the course of Shakespeare's early tragedy, *Titus Andronicus*, Titus's daughter Lavinia is rendered mute: her tongue is cut out and, as if this were insufficient, her hands too are hewn off. Despite these evident impediments to communicative performance, Lavinia's gestural eloquence is the subject of comment and admiration by other characters. When faced with his brutally muted and mutilated daughter's exquisitely tormenting sighs, winks, nods and kneelings, Titus commits himself to learning the meaning of her signs, to 'wrest[ing] an alphabet' from the silent gestures whose significance is initially, and frustratingly, lost on him.

Titus's urgent desire to draw meaning from Lavinia's elliptical and codified performance is matched by his recognition that it may not yield up its secrets without study on his part. His words are considerably affecting on both counts. They also bear usefully on subsequent wordless performances whose specific import may not be immediately self-explanatory. In terms directly borrowed from Titus, therefore, the project of this book is, similarly, to seek to 'wrest an alphabet' from silent Shakespeare films and the performances they contain, to tease out their mysteries and to lay their eloquence before the reader.

The number of Shakespeare films made in the silent era may surprise. Between 1899 (when the first Shakespeare film was made) and 1927 (when the first properly commercial sound film was released), a total of between two hundred and fifty and three hundred films adapted from

---

[1] All Shakespeare quotations from Stanley Wells and Gary Taylor (eds.), *William Shakespeare: The Complete Works* (Oxford: Clarendon, 1988).

Shakespearean sources were made by the British, American, French, Italian, German and Danish film industries.[2] As is the case for so many films from the silent era, however, large quantities of them have since gone missing, or been destroyed, or have disintegrated beyond the point of possible restoration. The cellulose-nitrate stock onto which all films before the 1950s were shot makes them liable to combust spontaneously or, like all polymers, simply to decompose irrevocably. Nitrate film is equally vulnerable to damage from moisture in the atmosphere as it is to slight increases in temperature. The arrival of the sound era in the late 1920s quickly despatched silent film to the status of 'yesterday's thing' and, as a result, the cans containing gently crumbling or spontaneously combusting prints of silent films were not a mainstream archiving priority for some time.[3] As a result of a combination of neglect, loss, disintegration and wilful destruction, of the three hundred silent Shakespeare films originally made, only approximately forty now survive.

Some of the losses incurred are acute. There is, for example, no surviving print of Georges Méliès' innovative 1907 film, *Le Rêve de Shakespeare* (*Shakespeare Writing Julius Caesar* in its English release), nor of Vitagraph's updated and culturally translated 1912 film, *An Indian Romeo and Juliet*, which reconceives of Shakespeare's doomed love story as that between a Mohican princess and a Huron brave. In a curious piece of theatricality that self-consciously displayed the combustibility and impermanence of film, the prints of the 1911 Herbert Beerbohm Tree/William Barker *Henry VIII* were all publicly and ceremonially burned by Barker himself specifically to increase their market value ahead of the scheduled blaze.[4] The 1916 Fox big-budget *Romeo and Juliet* starring screen vamp Theda Bara (playing a Juliet who was, as she herself expressed it, 'no Sunday-school girl') is lost,[5] as is the 1916 *Macbeth* that ambitiously attempted to combine a fast-moving Hollywood action picture with the acting talents of the English classical stage actor Herbert Beerbohm Tree. Of all the many films missing, disintegrated or destroyed, the one I personally most

---

[2] The Filmography lists all films discussed, including the current status of each (lost or extant, commercially available or held in archive preservation prints).

[3] A significant number of film archives were, however, founded in the mid-1930s partly to arrest the effects of the destruction of silent film prints. See David Bordwell, *On the History of Film Style* (Cambridge, Mass. and London: Harvard University Press, 1997), p. 24.

[4] This was a marketing ploy, announced ahead of time, to generate publicity (and revenue), making audiences feel the urgency of seeing the film during its limited six-week run before the prints were all recalled and destroyed. See Robert Hamilton Ball, *Shakespeare on Silent Film: A Strange Eventful History* (NY: Theatre Arts Books, 1968), pp. 80–2.

[5] Theda Bara, 'How I Became a Film Vampire', *Forum* 62 (July 1919), 83–93 (92).

regret not having seen is James (J.M.) Barrie's 1916 cinematic pastiche *The Real Thing at Last*. This film wittily differentiated between, and unsparingly lampooned, British and American styles of performing Shakespeare by juxtaposing contrasting hypothetical productions of *Macbeth* from either side of the Atlantic (see Chapter 6). That such films should be unrecoverable is as significant a loss for those with an interest in early twentieth-century Shakespearean performance as it is for those concerned about the preservation of early cinematic material more generally. Given the attrition rates for silent film in general, however, the fact that, losses notwithstanding, a not inconsiderable forty silent Shakespeare films *have* survived is testimony as much as anything to the staggering numbers initially made.[6]

The imprecision of the tally of silent Shakespeare films merits a gloss. The most significant challenge is to decide how 'Shakespearean' – how close in plot, character, structure, theme, setting and/or quoted language – a film needs to be to qualify as a 'Shakespeare film' for the purposes of enumeration. Amongst the many and varied cinematic skirmishes with Shakespearean material in the period, there is inevitably some latitude in defining the terms of such an enquiry. The approach I have taken tends towards the generously inclusive to incorporate inconsequential flirtations with Shakespeare's plays and characters as well as more earnest cinematic adaptations. The films included in the count therefore range from the fully earnest to the gleefully parodic, from the stultifyingly theatrical to the confidently cinematic, from the period adaptation to the imaginative update, from the studio picture to the location shoot, from live action to animated cartoon, from the picture intended for projection as part of a theatre-based show to that intended for autonomous film exhibition, from the one-reel memorialising performance record to the full length, big budget feature, from the picture commended for its Shakespearean charm to that censored for its gore or disapproved of for its sexual explicitness. It includes films produced by major multi-national film companies and by smaller independents, in the US and across Europe and starring actors of such prestige, profile and range as Herbert Beerbohm Tree, Sarah Bernhardt, Georges Méliès, Ermete Novelli, Dante Capelli, Julia Swayne Gordon, Florence Turner (the 'Vitagraph Girl'), Florence Lawrence (the

---

[6] David Francis, former Head of the Motion Picture, Broadcasting and Recorded Sound Division of the Library of Congress (LOC), estimates that only 10 per cent of the films produced in the US before 1929 still exist. If this figure is symptomatic, the survival rate for silent Shakespeare films is slightly above average for the era. The cultural capital associated with Shakespeare might help to account for their slightly enhanced survival rates.

'Biograph Girl'), Charles Kent, Maurice Costello, Francesca Bertini, Frank Benson, Frederick Warde, Johnston Forbes-Robertson, Francis X. Bushman, Theda Bara, Ruggero Ruggeri, Asta Nielsen and Emil Jannings. It includes films which court a high seriousness of tone and films which glory in their own idiocies. The silent Shakespearean filmography is, that is, eclectic in both material and approach.

The only previous book-length study to take on this eclectic body of films was written in the late 1960s by the meticulous American scholar Robert Hamilton Ball. Those of us who come after owe a weighty debt to Ball, who made it his labour-intensive business to produce a comprehensive survey of the field as it then appeared.[7] Ball's book distils the findings of more than a decade of entrepreneurial research, makes for delightful as well as densely informative reading and is *the* invaluable resource in this area. However, the sheer extent of the book's coverage necessarily prevents Ball from giving sustained attention to any individual film or even cluster of films.

My approach is more selective. While alluding to the wider body of other films that form the background to, and useful comparators for, each film under discussion, I select a smaller number for detailed discussion. Some of the films I consider were also known to Ball; others – such as Herbert Beerbohm Tree's 1899 *King John*, Thanhouser's 1910 *A Winter's Tale* (all prints of which were believed to have been destroyed by a fire in 1917) and the 1912 Frederick Warde *Richard III* – have come to light since. Other films simply proved impossible for Ball to locate in the very different research world of forty years ago. Prints of the 1908 Vitagraph *Julius Caesar*, the 1909 Film d'Arte Italiana *Othello* (*Otello*) and the 1909 Cines *Macbeth* (*Macbett*), for example, are now archivally catalogued and so possible to trace in ways they were not then.

The commercial release of films in reviewable formats has also transformed the critical landscape into which I write in comparison with the one Ball knew. His readership would rarely have had the opportunity to see many, if any, of the films he discussed. I am writing for a readership for whom some of these films will already be well known through the four currently available DVDs: the BFI's *Silent Shakespeare* (featuring seven silent Shakespeare films), Thanhouser DVD's *Thanhouser Presents Shakespeare 1910–1916* (featuring three Thanhouser productions), Kino Video's 1912 *Richard III* (produced in association with the AFI) and Kino's 1922 *Othello* (which also features four supplementary shorter

---

[7] Ball, *Shakespeare on Silent Film*.

silent Shakespeare films).[8] With regards to coverage, this book therefore has a twin objective: first, to develop the debate about films that may well already be known to readers, and second, to bring into critical circulation some films not commercially available and so, as yet, scarcely known, if at all. In the examples I choose, I attempt to keep a balance between these two pools of material. Films I examine which are currently only available in archival prints include releases from early Italian production companies Cines and Film d'Arte Italiana (FAI), from the early American producers Vitagraph and Thanhouser, and three separate films of *Hamlet* – starring Sir Johnston Forbes-Robertson (1913), Italian classical actor Ruggero Ruggeri (1917) and Danish film star Asta Nielsen (1920). Most of the films discussed are extant, but some are only recoverable through the paper trail of scripts, catalogue descriptions, review and production reports they leave behind. All case-study films (extant or not, commercially available or not) are chosen for their capacity to illustrate with particular clarity, grace or piquancy some of the symptomatic issues raised by silent Shakespeare films as a more extensive body.

*

From a contemporary perspective, silent Shakespeare films seem oxymoronic in conception. The collaboration of this dramatic material with this medium of expression might even be considered a liaison of antithetical forces: one imaginatively evokes the image through the suggestive power of the word, the other does not just erode the power of the word by its privileging of the image, but all but evicts those words from its playing space. As if in acknowledgement of the contradictions inherent in the match, the resulting films themselves often pay homage to multiple masters: stage and screen, word and image, textual fidelity and filmic autonomy, inherited iconographies and vital performance, high culture and popular culture, heritage and topicality, 'author' and market, acts of memorialising and acts of making new. They are, therefore, frequently both burdened and enriched by competing agenda.

Being caught between worlds has not typically endeared them to the critical establishment. For some Shakespeareans, silent cinema could bring only loss and intolerable dilution to Shakespeare's dramatic poetry, generating little more than a husk of frantic and undignified gesturing from

---

[8] For publication details of these commercially available DVDs, and a list of their precise contents, see the Filmography.

its engagements with the world's greatest dramatist. 'There was little point in tackling Shakespeare seriously until the movies could speak,' wrote Laurence Kitchin in 1966. The Shakespeare films that were made in the pre-sound period were, he continued, 'half piously theatrical and half frivolous'.[9] Roger Manvell considered the films 'absurd little charades'.[10] Robert Hapgood maintained it 'hard to see' the attraction of silent Shakespeare films which, he claimed, could only possibly be of interest 'as a curiosity'.[11] And even Ball referred to the films as 'inadequate' and 'ridiculous'.[12] Most damning of all was Jack Jorgens' summary account of the phenomenon:

First came scores of silent Shakespeare films, one- and two-reelers struggling to render great poetic drama in dumb-show. Mercifully, most of them are lost.[13]

Jorgens' celebration of the loss of these films makes difficult reading. If a mercy *is* to be identified in this history, it is surely not, as Jorgens would have it, that most early Shakespeare films are lost, but rather – given the fate of the majority of films of the era – that not quite all of them are. For Jorgens, however, these were shadows whose innate capacity to offend could, it seems, only be 'mended' by being razed from the history.

Principally considered risible aberrations in the history of Shakespearean performance (when considered at all), they have scarcely fared better in the history of the film industry. Here they have fallen prey to charges of paralysing textual fidelity and a medium-inhibiting reverence for stage practice. At root, they have struck cineastes as inherently anti-cinematic, burdened by the memory of a literary wordiness that they cannot slough off even in silence and, as a result, unable fully to embrace the cinematic resources on offer. Writing in 1915, the American poet and early film theorist Vachel Lindsay made the case emphatically for cinema to distance itself from a trammelling theatrical heritage:

the further [the motion picture] gets from Euripides, Ibsen, Shakespeare, or Molière – the more it becomes like a mural painting from which flashes of lightning come – the more it realizes its genius.[14]

For cineastes, therefore, Shakespeare came to epitomise the theatrical burden that was inhibiting the cinema from realising its own potential.

[9] Laurence Kitchin, *Drama in the Sixties: Form and Interpretation* (London: Faber, 1966), p. 142.
[10] Roger Manvell, *Shakespeare and the Film* (London: J. M. Dent, 1971), p. 17.
[11] Hapgood, 'Shakespeare on Film and Television' in Stanley Wells (ed.), *The Cambridge Companion to Shakespeare Studies* (Cambridge University Press, 1986), 273–86 (274).
[12] Ball, *Shakespeare on Silent Film*, p. 302.
[13] Jack Jorgens, *Shakespeare on Film* (Bloomington: Indiana University Press, 1977), p. 1.
[14] Vachel Lindsay, *The Art of the Moving Picture* revised edn. 1922 (NY: Liveright, 1970), p. 194.

Lev Kuleshov spoke for many cinephiles in 1918 when he called upon film-makers to reject the alleged charge of being 'not literary enough' and 'not dramatic' and to embrace the idea that 'the cinema's language [should be] cinematographic!'[15] Inherited literary and dramatic values had, in this characteristic articulation, become the inappropriate import that was stifling cinema's own uninhibited engagements with its own 'language'. In the face of antagonism from both directions, the position of silent Shakespeare films is not just that of an idiosyncratic curio: it is awkwardly and provocatively liminal – caught between a Shakespearean world and a filmic one and apparently wonderfully well placed to disappoint both.

In the chapters that follow, I take account of the weight of criticism the films have attracted from both Shakespearean and cineaste camps. I consider the contradictory charges of textual violation and of stultifying textual reverence. I also, however, attempt to see beyond such limited and limiting readings to the ways in which the films' divided allegiances can illuminate a range of issues: the aspirations of both theatre and cinema as institutions, the tonal register of performance styles, the status of stars, the priorities of production companies and of national film industries, the history of Shakespearean performance and even, at times, the nature of the plays themselves. It will be part of the project to delineate the lines of tension created by the encounters and contests to which the films play host and to show how expressive the resulting dissonances can be about the inherited material, the medium of adaptation and the complexity of the cultural baggage that attends the union of the two.

It is salutary and right to begin this study by remembering that, despite their considerable numbers and richly individual virtues, the indecision of their medium allegiances has mostly debarred silent Shakespeare films from forming more than a quirky aside in film history and an idiosyncratic corner in the history of Shakespearean performance. They are far from central to either. Positioned at the peripheries of two intersecting histories in this way, they present a particular challenge for anyone seeking to give a just account of them. The challenge is this: how to pay due attention to this curious body of films without in the process distorting the balance of the broader dramas in which, with a few exceptions (notably including the two *Romeo and Juliet* films that caused a market stir in 1916, the aesthetically striking 1920 Asta Nielsen *Hamlet* and the grandly overblown

---

[15] Quoted in David Bordwell, *On the History of Film Style*, p. 27.

Emil Jannings 1922 *Othello*), they have only ever been considered merely bit-part players? The simple fact of writing a book-length study on silent Shakespeare film might be thought an attempt to draw in this material from the edges of other stories into a more privileged position at the centre of its own. This is not my intention. I am interested in these films partly *because* of the discrepancy between their prevalence and individual merits on the one hand and the fringe position they occupy in relation to other, more dominant histories on the other. That fringe position, as critically determined, is in itself illuminating about cultural hierarchies and how history privileges some tales, or some modes of telling tales, over others: I would therefore be loath to lose the sense of roguish marginality from the account. It forms a necessary part of the contextualising backdrop to the appeal of the films themselves.

CRITICAL REPUTATION ON FIRST RELEASE

The first audiences for silent Shakespeare films certainly did not struggle to find viewing pleasure in them. Indeed, the standard critical response on release was broadly, and often warmly, enthusiastic. There were, of course, those who felt it incumbent upon them to express suspicion about the value of wordless cinematic Shakespeare *per se*. Even the self-declared sceptics, however, usually confined their cautious comments to their introductory remarks. More often than not, such remarks then served simply as the ground-clearing precursor to making an exception in the case of the particular film currently under discussion. Three film releases of the 1916 tercentenary provide a useful source of examples for this critical tendency.

In the British trade paper *The Cinema News and Property Gazette* in November 1916, an anonymous reviewer began his account of Fox's *Romeo and Juliet* with a general consideration of what was at stake in adapting Shakespeare for moving pictures:

It is well-known that the beauty of Shakespeare's work lies in his complete mastery of language ... The problem the producer has to face in placing Shakespeare on the screen is, Can he incorporate into his actions Shakespeare's flow of words?[16]

Having thus established his own cultural legitimacy as someone who valued literary worth, the reviewer concluded his thoughts about the adaptation process by conceding that so long as there was no direct pretence to *be*

---

[16] *CNPG* v.II, n.215 (23 November 1916), 16.

Shakespeare, Shakespearean moving pictures could achieve much. In the Fox *Romeo and Juliet*, for example, he wrote:

the eye feasts upon a riot of action and a bounty of beauty, which is almost immeasurable ... As a spectacle, the Fox show is supreme ... The action of the play follows faithfully the drama ... After all, Fox is very wise. He is not playing Shakespeare; he is screening Shakespeare ... We think that many a cinemagoer will turn eagerly to the pages of Shakespeare after seeing this successful presentation. The beautiful pictures, the high-standard acting, bring the world-old story as vividly to the mind as any producers could.[17]

The picture was thus received as a beautiful allusion to Shakespeare (as, perhaps, a ballet or a painting might also be), as a lively vehicle for storytelling and as an advertisement for Shakespeare, tempting picture-goers towards the real thing by means of an appealing 'taster' experience. The following week, the same paper once again declared the impossibility of adapting Shakespeare successfully for the screen, only then to announce that the impossible had in this case been achieved:

To convert the spirit of Shakespeare into a silent form that will register clear and true, without seemingly missing a single important line in the brief, would seem next to impossible, *yet it has been done.* (my emphasis)[18]

Both *MPW*'s review of the Metro *Romeo and Juliet* and *Variety*'s of the 1916 Thanhouser *King Lear* adhered to the same critical formula:

We have all heard it said that the works of the Bard of Avon are not for the screen – that the 'upright stage' robs them of their matchless dialogue. The Metro production measurably disproves the assertion. Elaborate use has been made of the text. Artistically and clearly presented are these gems of the world's best literature; there is no possibility that their images will be marred by those who are 'capable of nothing but inexplicable dumb-shows and noise.' ... 'Romeo and Juliet' ... will possess a distinct double appeal – to the eye and to the mind.[19]

The value of Shakespearean plays upon the screen is questionable and in most instances in the past such photoplay productions have not proved box office magnets. But judged from an artistic standpoint the Thanhouser (Pathe-Goldrooster) five-reel production of "King Lear" is deserving of almost unlimited commendation ... Frederic [sic] Warde in the title role contributed an interpretation of the part that can, without fear of contradiction, be set down as a classic.[20]

An acknowledgement of the problems considered innate to the venture, followed by a sweeping aside of the identified problems with an

[17] *Ibid.*   [18] *CNPG* v.11, n.216 (30 November 1916), xxvi.
[19] George Blaisdell, Review of Metro *Romeo and Juliet*, *MPW* v.30, n.5 (4 November 1916), 685.
[20] 'Jolo', Review of *King Lear*, *Variety* v.45, n.6 (5 January 1917), 25.

appreciative account of the exceptional virtues of the particular film discussed became, in fact, a recognisable critical response. Although it was accepted as a truism in some quarters that adapting Shakespeare for silent film was misguided ('It is well known that ...', 'We have all heard it said that ...'), in practice, as first released, these films were far more frequently the cause of pride, admiration and congratulation than of embarrassment or incredulity. Sceptical commentators were comfortably outnumbered by those who declared themselves impressed by the cultural, artistic and commercial potential of the endeavour to bring Shakespeare to the screen for the appreciation of the masses.

Individual aspects of the films' production, marketing, distribution and exhibition practices will be discussed as they become relevant in the pages ahead. However, there is one exhibition convention of the early cinema period – the use of a live lecturer during the projection – that bears so directly upon the idea of what silent Shakespeare films *were*, and how they were received, that it merits a separate note ahead of time.

LIVE LECTURERS

Between 1895 and 1913/14 (when the practice mostly fell into abeyance), a more or less expert, more or less charismatic showman-lecturer was laid on at some exhibition venues to accompany the picture show with a live recitation or talk. This figure was in many respects a direct continuation from the magic lantern tradition. At lantern shows, the lanternist himself, or a specialist lecturer imported for the purpose, would either extemporise or give a scripted reading to enliven and explain the projected images. Introducing a comparable figure to moving picture shows tempered the impression of cinema as an entirely pre-packaged phenomenon whose formal characteristics were all fully determined ahead of time.[21] As Norman King has argued, a live commentary included as part of the exhibition 'actualised the image and, merging with it, emphasised the presentness of the performance and of the audience', so encouraging 'a sense of immediacy and participation'.[22]

The usefulness of such an accompanying lecture for Shakespeare films was clear. W. Stephen Bush hired himself out as a guest lecturer for the

---

[21] On the similarities and differences between lantern and moving picture lectures, see Richard Crangle, '"Next Slide Please": The Lantern Lecture in Britain, 1890–1910' in Richard Abel and Rick Altman (eds.), *The Sounds of Early Cinema* (Bloomington: Indiana University Press, 2001), pp. 39–47 (45–6).

[22] Norman King, 'The Sound of Silents', *Screen* v.25, n.3 (May-June 1984), 2–15 (15).

American exhibition of 'quality' films in this period.[23] As he explained in an article for *MPW* in December 1908, he had delivered the accompanying lectures for the presentation of Shakespeare films 'in various theatres in different portions of the country' and was, therefore, 'in a position to speak from actual observation' about the way in which these films were received. With his credentials thus established, Bush wrote that, in his experience, not only had Shakespeare moving pictures 'been enjoyed by all who ever had any acquaintance with Shakespeare at all', but also that 'many persons who had never read a line of Shakespeare have come away delighted after seeing the pictures *and hearing them competently explained*' (my italics).[24] Bush's partisanship about this is not in doubt. In a piece published in August of that same year, he had even expressed disapproval for those exhibitors who presumed to show a Shakespeare film *without* live vocal accompaniment. Picture-goers, he wrote, would be 'bewildered' if left to make sense of the images for themselves: appropriately addressed, by contrast, they could instead be 'thrilled and delighted with a proper presentation of [Shakespeare's] work'.[25] 'Proper' in this case clearly meant a presentation that included a lecture. Bush's position was not without foundation: the presumption in 1908 was, as by 1914 it had ceased to be, that Shakespearean moving pictures were in need of supplementary explication for the story to be fully intelligible to those unfamiliar with Shakespeare.

Despite Bush's proselytising enthusiasm, however, the role of the moving picture lecturer was never a given in the way that of the lantern lecturer had been, and there was an ongoing debate in the film industry trade press about the variable quality of those offering their services as such. In February 1909, the British trade paper *The Bioscope* made this contribution to the debate:

There is much to be said in favour of the lecturer if he is competent, if speaking to pictures is with him more of a hobby than a duty, and if he has a sympathetic voice. But there are plenty of lecturers who are calculated to make any audience feel very ill in bed, and the supply of good men is by no means equal to the demand. [26]

---

[23] See David Robinson, *From Peepshow to Palace: the Birth of American Film* (NY: Columbia University Press, 1996), p. 87. Bush advertised his services in the *Dramatic Mirror*. See Charles Musser, 'The Nickelodeon Era Begins: Establishing the Framework for Hollywood's Mode of Representation', in Thomas Elsaesser (ed.), *Early Cinema: Space, Frame, Narrative* (London: BFI, 1990), 256–73 (273, n.15).

[24] W. Stephen Bush, 'Shakespeare in Moving Pictures', *MPW* v.3, n.23 (5 December 1908), 446–7.

[25] W. Stephen Bush, 'Lecture on Moving Pictures', *MPW* v.3, n.8 (22 August 1908), 136–7.

[26] *The Bioscope* (25 February 1909), 3.

A lecturer, depending on his competence or otherwise, evidently had the potential to mar as well as make a picture show. In 1911, *MPW* published an article entitled 'Lecture it Right or not at all' that complained about lecturers who obscured the sense of a picture and confused the audience.[27] In 1912, a German academic, Professor Dr Sellmann, sat through a screening of an (unidentified) film of *Othello* in Berlin, faithfully transcribing everything the lecturer said, and then published the full transcript as part of an essay entitled 'Literatur und Kinematograph' in *Eckart – Ein Deutsches Literaturblatt*. The lecturer himself was evidently a gruff Berliner who made no effort to elevate his colloquial tone. His commentary was delivered in a thick Berlin accent (which Sellmann conscientiously notated) and punctuated by proverbial sayings and asides to the audience as he attempted to retain some crowd control. The final section reads thus:

Now just look at how the black watches his pretty wife in this bit. You can see that – (gentleman in the front right there: smoking's not allowed in here, so would you mind . . .?) – so, where were we? Oh yes, that the jealousy of the Moor has reached boiling point, which bears out the old adage: jealousy is a passion which seeks out its own suffering. So now he just lets rip at her and drags her out of her sweet slumber. Look now – she's protesting her innocence. But what does the black monster do? (I have to insist on silence for this gripping section of the drama. If you want to giggle, I'd thank you to go over to Luna Park.) So what does he do? He strangles the loveliest creature the world has ever seen. Don't miss this bit: one last spasm, see, and now she's dead.[28]

As an accidentally entertaining side show, or means of lampooning the film, such a lecture might well have had its appeal. As a potential aid in drawing out the poetry or pathos of the moment, however, it may have left something to be desired.

The following year, in May 1913, Robert Grau was pleased to announce that, in his opinion, the standard of lecturing in the US had recently improved. The 'boomer', he wrote, had finally:

given way to the man of real intellect, possessed not only of the necessary showmanship, but also of literary talents that will enable him to give the amusement-loving public a conception worthy of the amazing progress in the photoplay.[29]

[27] *MPW* v.8, n.17 (29 April 1911), 943.

[28] The 1912 lecture-transcript is quoted in full (in 'Berlin-German') in Steffen Wolf, 'Geschichte der Shakespeare-Verfilmungen (1899–1964)', in Max Lippman (ed.), *Shakespeare im Film* (Wiesbaden: Deutsches Institut für Filmkunde, 1964), pp. 15–32 (19–20). Between 1903 and 1933, Luna Park was the largest amusement park in Europe.

[29] Robert Grau, 'High Grade Exploitation of Photoplays', *Motion Picture Story Magazine* (May 1913), 115.

Frederick Warde, the famous stage classical actor and star of two Shakespearean film productions – *Richard III* (Shakespeare Film Company: James Keane, 1912) and *King Lear* (Thanhouser: Ernest Warde, 1916) – turned himself into a moving picture lecturer as part of the high-profile promotion for *Richard III* (see Figures I.1a and b). He delivered a live commentary to accompany screenings in various film theatres around the US in 1913 ('During the showing of the pictures he explains the situations') and during reel changes he additionally gave 'a dramatic recital of famous passages in the play, elucidating them at the same time'.[30] An editorial in the *Augusta Chronicle* in January 1913 declared the 'lecture-interpretation by Mr Warde' an 'immensely instructive feature of the attraction'.[31] It seems reasonable to assume that hearing Frederick Warde recite and comment on Shakespeare would have been a different order of experience from hearing the Berlin lecturer's comically brutal alert to Desdemona's death spasm. The particular screenings for which Warde supplied the commentary were, therefore, not only not silent (as, of course, no film exhibitions were), but were specifically and richly worded by nuanced and engaging Shakespearean recitations delivered *in situ*.[32]

There were plenty of venues, however, unable to afford a celebrity lecturer and either not able or not inclined to 'make do' with a cheaper but potentially ear-offending 'boomer'. In such venues, Shakespeare films were, therefore, projected without vocal addition. Post-1902/3, when title cards were introduced to films, a few lines of plot summary or a sprinkling of Shakespearean quotations would appear on screen intermittently to help orient the audience about the progress of the plot and/or flag the

---

[30] A *NYT* review (n.d.) quoted in the programme for the Olympic Theatre, Broadway (22 March 1913). LOC *Richard III* copyright deposit file no. CIL 1299 (9 September 1913). Warde's role as moving picture lecturer is also briefly discussed in Kenneth Rothwell, *A History of Shakespeare on Screen* (Cambridge University Press, 1999), p. 19.

[31] Editorial, 'Illustrated Dramalogue RICHARD III', *Augusta Chronicle* (12 January 1913) – in response to Frederick Warde's in-person appearance at the Prince Theater. LOC copyright deposit file CIL 1299. For more on lecturers, see André Gaudreault, *Du Littéraire au filmique: système du récit* (Paris: Meridians Klinksieck, 1988). For more on the film, see Warde's own autobiographical account in *Fifty Years of Make-Believe* (NY: International Press Syndicate, 1920), in Thomas Elsaesser (ed.), *Early Cinema*, pp. 256–73.

[32] Early picture theatres sometimes also employed actors to stand behind the screen and speak lines of dialogue in synchrony with the pictures. See Musser, 'The Nickelodeon Era Begins', in Thomas Elsaesser (ed.), *Early Cinema*, pp. 256–73. In screening early silent Shakespeare films to contemporary audiences, I have sometimes emulated this practice, using live actors voicing the relevant lines to correspond precisely with the on-screen action. This has transformed the effect of the films upon an audience. Precedents in relation to other films suggest that this must sometimes have been done specifically for Shakespeare films during their early exhibition runs. However, no specific documentary record of this has yet surfaced.

Figure I.1a and b. Richard Duke of Gloster (sic) (Frederick Warde) woos the
Lady Anne (Violet Stuart) and then slaps his thigh with glee at the impudence, and
success, of his suit in *Richard III* (James Keane, 1912).

'Shakespeareanness' of the production with a little authentically imported
language. However, even where such interjections were absent, or merely
token, the officially 'wordless' status of the exhibition might still have been
pleasurably compromised for some sections of the audience. For some

spectators, then as now, Shakespeare's words would not have needed to be uttered to be potently present in a scene: they were embedded in, and clearly evoked by an image of, for example, Juliet on her balcony, Puck laughing at mortal folly, Hamlet holding a skull, Othello extinguishing a bedroom candle. The pictures themselves would have conjured the words.

The ubiquitous profile of Shakespearean language in this period was specifically recognised in 1908 by Bush, who, in addition to being a film lecturer, was also the leading commentator on 'quality' pictures in the American trade press:

> Pick up any book or newspaper, listen to any conversation, and you will be astonished how often, consciously or unconsciously, the words of the great poet are quoted. They have indeed in the most literal sense become household words.[33]

Early twentieth-century audiences might, in fact, have been better placed to call to mind Shakespearean words than were audiences later in the century. Lawrence W. Levine, for example, has documented how, by the middle of the twentieth century, Shakespeare had been sidelined into being a part of 'polite' American culture whereas in the nineteenth century, he had been the people's 'familiar ... part of *mainstream* culture' (my italics). 'Shakespearean phrases, aphorisms, ideas, and language,' he argues, were an 'integral part of the nineteenth-century imagination'.[34]

The widespread penetration of Shakespearean language, acknowledged in the cinema trade press at the time and by cultural historians since, cannot but have infused the reception of the films. Though silent Shakespeare films were largely unworded at the point of projection,[35] for many audiences who had grown up in a time in which Shakespeare was a required part of the school curriculum and a significant cultural force, they would not have been so in the intricate space of individual reception;[36] the associated dialogue, triggered by the imagery (and the supplementary verbal prompts on title cards, where offered), would have been silently supplied – more or less accurately, more or less completely – from the

---

[33] Bush, 'Shakespeare in Moving Pictures', 446.

[34] Lawrence W. Levine, *Highbrow/Lowbrow: The Emergence of Cultural Hierarchy in America* (Cambridge, Mass: Harvard University Press, 1988), pp. 31, 37–8. On how well Shakespeare was known and how frequently quoted in nineteenth-century America, see also pp. 27–8.

[35] There were attempts to integrate recorded sound into the presentation of Shakespeare moving pictures in the sound era – including Clément Maurice's 1900 duel scene from *Hamlet* starring Sarah Bernhardt, and a 1913 Edison Kinetophone scene from *Julius Caesar* briefly exhibited in New York. The experiment did not, however, prove widely commercially exploitable. See Ball, *Shakespeare on Silent Film*, pp. 24–5, 162–3.

[36] For a discussion of the use of Shakespeare in American schools at the turn of the twentieth century, see Roberta E. Pearson and William Uricchio, *Reframing Culture: The Case of the Vitagraph Quality Films* (Princeton University Press, 1993), pp. 76–7.

private memory bank of the spectator. Thus it was that at least some of Shakespeare's words, for some picture-goers, would not so much have been absent from the presentation as simply displaced from the public space of exhibition to the private space of reception, from that of exterior declaration to that of interior resonance. Audiences for silent Shakespeare films were implicitly invited to do as the popular dramatic character Sylvester Daggerwood had himself done in George Colman's 1795 occasional piece *New Hay at the Old Market*, and allow snatches of Shakespearean quotation to accompany their dreams.[37]

Producers of Shakespeare films of the early cinema period understood the particularities of the reception context into which their films were being released. Accordingly, the films were typically composed of a sequence of the best known dramatic and iconic moments from the plays, whose familiar imagery was bonded to, and so quickly able to call to mind, well-known Shakespearean quotations. Thus it was that the *New York Dramatic Mirror* commended the production company Vitagraph on having omitted all but 'the vital scenes' from their one-reel (circa twelve-minute) 1908 film *Julius Caesar*, thereby keeping the story free from obscurity.[38] The action of such vigorously truncated versions of Shakespeare necessarily moved swiftly from one dramatic highlight to another, thereby implicitly establishing (or confirming) a 'best of', summary form in which the plays could circulate manageably and (more or less) intelligibly.[39]

CHAPTER ORGANISATION

Silent Shakespeare films, like all other films of the period, emerged from an industry subject to and driven by its own developments, trends and controversies. The nature of the films is, therefore, in part determined by that broader commercial history. In order to allow the story of the varied encounters between the silent film industry and Shakespeare to unfold more or less sequentially, chapters are organised in broadly chronological order in line with the more or less distinct developmental phases of the industry. For those more familiar with Shakespearean histories than

[37] See Jane Moody, '"Dictating to the Empire": Performance and Theatrical Geography in Eighteenth-century Britain', in Jane Moody and Daniel O'Quinn (eds.), *The Cambridge Companion to British Theatre, 1730–1830* (Cambridge University Press, 2007), pp. 21–42 (22).

[38] 'Review of New Films', *New York Dramatic Mirror* (12 December 1908), 6.

[39] On Shakespeare's contributions to consensus building through mimetic forms of cultural reproduction, see Pearson and Uricchio, *Reframing Culture*, pp. 66–7.

cinematic ones, a brief sketch of those phases is interleaved with the chapter descriptions that follow.

The principal interests of Chapter 1 pre-date the invention of cinema. This chapter contextualises the arrival of Shakespearean cinema by looking backwards to a range of nineteenth-century Shakespearean cultural forms whose dominant interests or forms of expression would, in time, percolate into the production and reception of Shakespearean cinema. It examines the performance conventions and aspirations that film inherited from the nineteenth-century stage: the celebration of spectacle over poetry, the painterly framing of the stage, the exacting quest for realism, the taste for pantomime. The area in which it particularly claims to break new ground, however, is in considering the role of the magic lantern as a means of suggesting Shakespeare a suitable subject for projection.

Chapter 2 offers a detailed case study of the first Shakespeare film – a short made in 1899, featuring a few brief scenes from Herbert Beerbohm Tree's contemporaneous London stage production of *King John*. In the context of the colourful and salacious reputation of the film industry in the pioneering years (1895–c.1906), the appeal not only of Shakespeare but also of the Bible, Dickens, Racine, Pushkin, Thackeray and other literary figures of comparable cultural 'weight' is self-evident. These reputable literary sources proved invaluable players in the campaign to transform the industry's reputation into something more morally edifying and culturally admirable: the *King John* film formed part of this bid for respectability.

In the pioneering years, the film industry offered what Tom Gunning has influentially described as 'a cinema of attractions', a medium whose primary mode of address was a vigorous appeal to the admiration of the eye.[40] In line with this tendency, films of this period made from literary sources tended not so much to narrate the plots of their cited source texts as to 'pictorialise' brief excerpts from them, making few story-telling concessions to the spectator not already familiar with the source text. They may therefore be thought of as *alluding to* or even *quoting visualised extracts from* known literary works (including Shakespeare) rather than making any concerted effort to *adapt* them. The *King John* pioneering Shakespeare film works in line with this tendency.

By 1907, however, a cinema of 'monstration', of the conspicuous display of projected visual delights, was no longer the industry's dominant mode of address: this had ceded to a cinema whose narrative aspirations now took

---

[40] Tom Gunning, 'The Cinema of Attractions: Early Film, Its Spectator and the Avant-Garde', *Wide Angle* v.8, n.3–4 (1986), 63–70.

precedence. Across the years 1907–13, known as the 'transitional period',[41] a conventionalised syntax for cinematic story-telling was established and refined. And it is in this same period that the film industries of Europe and America pursued a systematic and conscious campaign to reach out beyond the masses to a more culturally discriminating (and, significantly, a higher paying) audience as part of the industry's 'uplift movement'.[42] Turning to sources whose artistic and literary merit was already securely established formed part of this drive to boost the cultural credentials of the industry and to appeal thereby to a 'better class' of patron. Unsurprisingly in such a market, Shakespeare became a well-plundered resource for those production companies keen to assert their artistic ambition and thereby enhance their market placement.

Chapter 3 focuses centrally on the early transitional years 1908–9. From 1908 onwards whole Shakespearean plots were regularly being compressed – with varying degrees of wit and imagination – to be shoe-horned into the one- or two-reel format then the industry norm. The nimbleness with which a story was told (through mise-en-scène, performance, cinematography, editing style) now mattered keenly in securing the reputation of a particular moving picture and of the production company that had produced it. This chapter takes two striking one-reelers as case study: the 1908 Clarendon *Tempest* and the 1909 Film d'Arte Italiana *Othello* (*Otello*). These two films illustrate with particular clarity a tension widely present within Shakespeare films of the period as a resolute attempt at cinematic story-telling and visual ambition came into conflict with a counter-impulse to temper or even arrest cinematographic aspirations for the production of Shakespeare pictures.

Whereas Chapter 3 attends to the formal, aesthetic properties of the films themselves, Chapter 4 concentrates on market imperatives and institutional identity through a study of the Vitagraph Company of America. Vitagraph was a big-business, prolific and powerful industry Trust

---

[41] There is no definitive consensus amongst film historians about how precisely to identify the industry's early developmental phases. On the ways in which early cinema history has been categorised, and some of the problems inherent in doing so, see Tom Gunning, 'The Intertextuality of Early Cinema: A Prologue to *Fantômas*', in Robert Stam and Alessandra Raengo (eds.), *A Companion to Literature and Film* (Oxford: Blackwell, 2004), pp. 127–43. In identifying 1907–13 as the transitional period, I follow Charlie Keil, *Early American Cinema in Transition: Story, Style and Filmmaking, 1907–1913* (University of Wisconsin Press, 2001).

[42] Eileen Bowser, *The Transformation of Cinema 1907–1915* (NY: Scribner, 1990), p. 43. On the relationship of the use of literary sources to the industry's bid to move up market, see also Andrew Higson, 'Heritage Discourse and British Cinema Before 1920' in John Fullerton (ed.), *Celebrating the Centenary of Cinema, 1895* (Sydney and London: John Libbey, 1998), pp. 182–9 (partic. 186).

company that released twelve Shakespeare and Shakespeare-related films in the transitional period. Since their films were vigorously marketed and enthusiastically received in their moment of first release specifically *as* company products, this chapter takes them on their own terms by considering them as such. As part of this institutional study, the individual Vitagraph films – *Macbeth* (1908), *Julius Caesar* (1908), *King Lear* (1909), *A Midsummer Night's Dream* (1909) and *Twelfth Night* (1910) – are considered both as purveyors of the company brand and as interpretive readings of Shakespeare. Thanhouser's *A Winter's Tale* (1910) and Cines' *Brutus* (1910) are put alongside these for comparative purposes. By centrally considering the working practices of one particular production stable and the detail of the films that emerged from that stable, I show how a recognisable, even branded, set of interpretive priorities and cinematographic codes came to be associated with a company.

The pioneering days and transitional period taken together (1895–1913) are called the 'early cinema' period. These are the years pre-dating the arrival of the feature film (a single story film of four or more reels). Chapter 5 leaves behind the early cinema period, taking the account into the feature film era through its examination of two *Hamlets*. Both Cecil Hepworth and Hay Plumb's 1913 English film starring Sir Johnston Forbes-Robertson and Eleuterio Rodolfi's 1917 Italian film starring Ruggero Ruggeri were transmediated reworkings of high-profile stage productions of *Hamlet*. Both stage Hamlets had acquired an international reputation and both films were given an international distribution. In response to Forbes-Robertson's stage *Hamlet* from 1897, George Bernard Shaw had claimed: 'Nothing so charming has been seen by this generation. It will bear seeing again and again.'[43] The moving picture that Gaumont was to release sixteen years later made it possible to do just that. Film provided the technology to make both Forbes-Robertson's and Ruggeri's stage Hamlets available for repeat viewings, iconising in lasting form two performances of distinction. The comparison between films is illuminating about the different registers referenced by variant styles of acting and about the relative resistance and kinship of the two central actors to established European pantomimic performance codes.

Chapter 6 takes the Shakespeare tercentenary year, 1916, as an exemplary moment in which to take stock of Shakespearean film-making. The narrative for James Barrie's British all-star riotous burlesque, *The Real Thing*

---

[43] Shaw, *The Saturday Review* (2 October 1897). Quoted in John A. Mills, *Hamlet on Stage: The Great Tradition* (Westport, Connecticut and London: Greenwood, 1985), p. 176.

At Last, was based upon an entertaining juxtaposition of two hypothetical productions of *Macbeth*, one an underplayed British version, the other a more colourful American one. The film traded explicitly upon comically stereotyped contrasts about national interpretive priorities and confidently referenced other film productions of *Macbeth* already, or soon to be, in the public domain. This chapter's focus on the Triangle-Reliance *Macbeth* starring Herbert Beerbohm Tree, the American big-budget Fox *Romeo and Juliet* starring screen vamp Theda Bara and the rival Metro *Romeo and Juliet* starring screen idols Francis X. Bushman and Beverly Bayne allows Barrie's satirical hypotheses about American approaches to Shakespearean film-making to be tested in practice.

In Chapter 7, the account reaches the 1920s. By then, the silent era was at its height: the conventions of what was subsequently to become known as classical narrative cinema were firmly established[44] and cinema had become a dominant force in the way in which mass urban populations in the West spent their leisure time and their money. Moreover, its influence extended well beyond the masses: the phenomenon of the cinematograph and its forms of narration and reception were of interest to artists and intellectuals too.[45]

Chapter 7 focuses on two individual stars of the Weimar film industry of the 1920s, Asta Nielsen and Emil Jannings, both of whom were lauded for their artistic gravitas and actorly intellectualism and whose appeal crossed the usual demographic boundaries. The Hamlet that Nielsen plays in the 1920 film was famously conceived in radically re-gendered terms – a female Hamlet who, since birth, has been obliged to disguise her sexual identity in order to safeguard the throne of Denmark. There is arguably something appealingly subversive in any era about the perform-ance of an assumed masculinity, as Shakespeare's own festive comedies celebrate. In 1920, however, that appeal takes on a particular force in its topical examination of androgyny as a fashionable sexual aesthetic. At the moment of the film's release across Europe and the US, modish manifes-tations of womanhood were sufficiently in flux to complicate the gender landscape and perhaps even give a broader application to this Hamlet's

---

[44] For an account of the emergence and features of classical Hollywood cinema, see David Bordwell, Janet Staiger and Kristin Thompson, *The Classical Hollywood Cinema: Film Style and Mode of Production to 1960* (NY: Columbia University Press, 1985).

[45] On how artists and thinkers such as Maxim Gorky, Virginia Woolf, Ezra Pound, Vsevelod Pudovkin, Max Reinhardt, Berthold Brecht, Walter Benjamin, Salvador Dalí and Arnold Schoenberg allowed the phenomenology and mechanisms of cinema to inform their work, see Bordwell, *On the History of Film Style*, p. 12.

private agonies about the ambivalence of her gender constructions and the *in between-ness* of her resulting appearance. Nor was Nielsen herself new to *travestie* roles, having already played many breeches parts in earlier films. This chapter explores how the 1920 film prompts reflection on the power and frisson of Nielsen's transfixing on-screen presence with its inbuilt references to other movie roles, the nature of the Hamlet who emerges from that performance, and the role of the film's expressionist sets in constructing and commenting on character.

Dmitri Buchowetzki's grandly visualised but less interpretively radical six-reel German *Othello* (1922) uses the well-known stage and screen presences of Emil Jannings as a blacked-up Othello and Werner Krauss as a maniacal Iago to revealing effect. It was not the first time Jannings and Krauss had appeared together on screen and they both had known screen presences which inflect the particularity of their high-key performances in this film. The film telegraphs its interest in Iago's distaste for racial difference and as such it provides a chilling aperitif to some of Krauss's later film work for the Third Reich – in particular in the 1940 propaganda film *Jud Süß* in which an avaricious and lascivious Jew is exposed as heinous in every way before finally being punished for his presumption, greed and lust. In this chapter I bring alongside the German *Othello* an earlier Italian *Othello* of 1914 (from production company Ambrosio), and the almost contemporary Anson Dyer animated short which pastiched contemporary performance practices related to *Othello*.

The book's Afterword brings the consideration of wordless Shakespeare performances up-to-date through a focus on the work of the highly successful contemporary mime-based physical theatre company Synetic Theater. Synetic's three recent Washington DC silent Shakespeare productions have had sell-out audiences and correspondingly euphoric reviews. In relation to the long-standing, and now revivified tradition of rendering Shakespeare wordlessly, and drawing on an interview with Synetic's director and lead actor, in the Afterword I ask what cultural prejudices wordless performances of Shakespeare have to combat, what dramatic impulses they bring to the fore and what aspirations and cravings they might satisfy.

Synetic Theater has helped to make wordless Shakespeare performance into a theatrical form for the cognoscenti. From an audience's point of view, it is Shakespeare not so much without the words as beyond the words – an exquisitely finely worked theatrical experience, the detail of whose eloquence often emerges from a playful and knowing engagement with the words not spoken. This draws upon a different cultural register from that which typically drove the nineteenth century's engagements with word-less Shakespeare. Then, mute Shakespearean performances were not the stuff of the Kennedy Arts Center and the discerning theatre-going tastes of East Coast audiences. More commonly, they formed part of the staple fare of the lower-life music halls and illegitimate theatres (see Chapter 1). These less elevated productions were, as one contemporary observer entic-ingly described them, 'the burlesques and pantomimes' which displayed 'a strange prodigality of power – but power all run to seed'.[46] The cry of this particular commentator in response to such anarchically wordless fare was that there should be 'no more Shakespearean imitations'.[47] The rest of the book examines the variety of ways in which the silent film industry has played its part in disregarding that cry.

[46] E. S. Dallas, 'The Drama', *Blackwood's Magazine* 79 (February 1856), 227–31 (229).
[47] Dallas, 'The Drama', 231.

CHAPTER I

Shakespeare without words:
the nineteenth-century legacy

There is always something arbitrary about the beginnings of stories. Few things arrive with arresting suddenness upon the scene. It is more usual for ideas or inventions to have an incremental lead-in time in which stages of progression move its development towards a point which only subsequently will be labelled a watershed moment. Histories thrive on the retrospective identification of such moments – in part because it makes a story neatly narratable.

The history of silent Shakespeare films has such a moment. The classical stage actor-manager Herbert Beerbohm Tree has scooped the pioneering honours in this respect. In September 1899 – less than four years after the Lumière brothers' first cinematograph exhibition in Paris – Tree licensed the entrepreneurial film-maker William Kennedy-Laurie Dickson to film scenes from his London stage production of *King John* for the British Mutoscope and Biograph Company (BMBC). It has, therefore, become habitual to tell the history of Shakespeare in moving pictures from that point onwards, iconising the departure point and so investing the story with both impetus and tidy narrative shape.[1] But this story, like all others, has a pre-history that contributes to the cumulative anticipation of its official beginning. In acknowledgement of this, this chapter will cast its eye backwards to the time before the emergence of the first Shakespeare film.

It is not my project here to log the technological developments in the many Victorian optical toys that contributed to the emergence of modern cinema as we now know it: that story has been ably told elsewhere.[2]

---

[1] John Collick is the exception in this respect. See Collick, *Shakespeare, Cinema and Society* (Manchester University Press, 1989), pp. 12–32.

[2] For accounts of the precursors to cinema, see, for example, Michael Chanan, *The Dream that Kicks: the Pre-History and Early Years of Cinema in Britain* (London and NY: Routledge, 1996); Franz Paul Leisegang, *Dates and Sources: A Contribution to the History of the Art of Projection and Cinematography* (London: MLS, 1988); Virgilio Tosi, *Cinema before Cinema: The Origins*

23

Nor is it my aim to discuss how theatrical practices of the stage or the musical hall influenced cinematic practice in general: those broad debts of one medium to another have also been well documented.[3] Rather, the emergence specifically of Shakespearean cinema is to be the focus. In pursuit of some of the antecedents that influenced the ways it was both produced and, importantly, understood, in this chapter I offer a summary of Shakespeare's presence in a sample range of other nineteenth-century cultural forms. This will involve attending to different aspects of Shakespearean endeavour and expression, the influence of which would in time percolate into the production and reception of Shakespearean cinema.

I do not seek to be comprehensive in this, but rather illustrative. I therefore chart five elements of nineteenth-century cultural life as these relate to Shakespeare: the magic lantern, the pantomimic and spectacular stage traditions, the quest for theatrical realism, the desire to frame performance and the taste for narrative. To my knowledge, no detailed work has been done before on Shakespeare in the magic lantern: I therefore devote proportionally more weight to these little known pre-cinematic projected Shakespearean tales than to other sections. The section on wordless and spectacular Shakespearean performances is also grounded in some concentrated primary research. Other sections, however, draw gratefully upon primary research on the spectacular, realist, archaeological, pictorial, illegitimate and burlesque stages of the nineteenth century already conducted by others.

It is the contention of this chapter that the diverse body of Shakespearean forms to which the Victorian age was privy helped to make the emergence of silent Shakespeare films less of an oddity and more organically part of a broader landscape in their moment of first release than they might now seem in ours. The projection, performance, pictorial and narrative histories studied in this chapter therefore provide a backdrop against which the films themselves, of interest in future chapters, can then stand out in sharper relief as a more intelligible product of their moment.

---

of Scientific Cinematography (London: BUFVC, 2005). For an account of the optical toys and projection machinery of the 1890s, see Charles Musser, *High-Class Moving Pictures* (Princeton University Press, 1991), partic. p. 50.

[3] See A. Nicholas Vardac, *Stage to Screen: Theatrical Method from Garrick to Griffith* (Cambridge, Mass.: Harvard University Press, 1949); Ben Brewster and Lea Jacobs, *Theatre to Cinema* (Oxford University Press, 1997).

SHAKESPEARE AND THE MAGIC LANTERN

In 1895, four years before William Kennedy-Laurie Dickson was to shoot his pioneering Shakespeare film in London, he was working on kineto-graph moving pictures for Thomas Edison in New Jersey.[4] During this work, he co-authored with his sister a lengthy pamphlet both extolling the virtues of moving pictures and placing them, momentarily at least, in context. The kinetograph, he wrote:

stands foremost among the creations of modern inventive genius. It is the crown and flower of nineteenth-century magic, the crystallization of Eons of groping enchantments.[5]

The vested interests of his own employment made it apt for Dickson to celebrate contemporary advances partly at the expense of past achieve-ments: such a position was also, however, a symptom of the spirit of his age more generally. Dickson was not just a proselytising enthusiast for technical development, but also, in effect, a practical modernist, *his* alle-giance to a model of progress emerging not just from the study, but also from the workshop and studio. Dickson was, in fact, himself involved in ushering in the technology that would prove both one of the most effec-tive engines of the modernist agenda and also, perhaps, its most potent symbol.

In its paean of praise for the present and enthusiastic absorption in the possibilities of the future, Dickson's expression of an emergent modern-ism, like many more fully articulated subsequent versions, risked under-valuing the significance of past endeavours.[6] These past endeavours had to suffer the courteous but clear put-down of being labelled merely part of a primitive anticipation of some later form that would succeed in fulfill-ing their unknowing aspirations. Some of the 'nineteenth-century magic' and 'enchantments' upon whose technical, industrial and socio-cultural

---

[4] On Dickson's pioneering and controversial work, see Stephen Herbert and Luke McKernan (eds.), *Who's Who of Victorian Cinema* (London: BFI, 1996), pp. 41–2. For an account of his work, see Paul C. Spehr, 'Throwing Pictures on a Screen: The Work of W.K-L. Dickson, Filmmaker', in McKernan and Mark van den Tempel (eds.), *The Wonders of the Biograph*, special issue *Griffithiana* (2000), 66–70.

[5] W. K.-L. Dickson and Antonia Dickson, *History of the Kinetograph, Kinetoscope and Kineto-phonograph* (NY: Albert Bunn, 1895), p.52. Facsimile edition (NY: Museum of Modern Art, 2000).

[6] For an influential modernist dismissal of the 'eternal and useless admiration of the past' and rejection of the notion that 'we are the summation and continuation of our ancestors', see F. T. Marinetti, 'The Founding and the Manifesto of Futurism', *Le Figaro* (20 February, 1909). Reproduced in Lawrence Rainey (ed.), *Modernism: An Anthology* (Oxford: Blackwells, 2005), pp.3–6 (5, 6).

achievements the motion pictures were able to build, however, were far from 'groping'. These need rescuing both from an artificially imposed teleology and from perfunctory judgement.

Prime among these was the magic (or optical) lantern. The lantern had a history, profile and range of effects that removed it decisively from the realm of the rudimentary. It was an invention, an institution even, with considerable reach and influence in its own right. Since it has been neglected in accounts of early Shakespearean film, its history and uses bear rehearsal.

The lantern had been a well-established part of European education and socially diverse entertainment since the latter half of the seventeenth century. By the nineteenth century its influence in America was considerable too, with between 75,000 and 150,000 lantern shows on offer each year, of significantly varying styles.[7] Lanterns formed part of ghostly exhibitions, church meetings, travelling shows, variety divertissements and special lectures.[8] Nor were they solely the domain of the professional lanternist and the public arena: at a price, they could form part of domestic entertainments too.[9]

The lantern worked by projecting onto a wall or screen images drawn, painted or eventually printed onto glass slides. These slides were inserted in turn into a slot in the side of a box (lantern) illuminated from behind first by a candle and then, as the technology developed, by a paraffin flame, a carbon arc and in time an electric bulb. The projection could be in vivid colour and the projected image sharp and clear. Using more than one lantern or a lantern that contained multiple slide-loading points (a diunial or triunial) could enable slides to replace each other in rapid succession. Some slides also included adjustable mechanical sections that could be

---

[7] For a history of lantern shows in America, see Charles Joseph Pecor, *The Magician and the American Stage* (Washington D.C.: Emerson and West, 1977) and Xenophon Theodore Barber, *Evenings of Wonders: A History of the Magic Lantern Show in America*, unpublished PhD dissertation, New York University (1993). I take the estimated number of annual lantern shows in America at the end of the nineteenth century from Terry Borton, *Cinema before Film: Victorian Magic Lantern Shows and America's First Great Screen Artist, Joseph Boggs Beale* (forthcoming). Excerpts posted at: www.magiclanternshows.com/filmhistory.htm.

[8] For an iconographic history of lantern shows and audiences, see David Robinson (ed.), *The Lantern Image* (London: MLS, 1993).

[9] For Samuel Pepys' account of the lantern show he hosted in his home, see Robert Latham and William Matthews (eds.), *The Diary of Samuel Pepys*, vol. VII '1666' (London: G. Bell and Sons, 1972), p. 254. For Charles Dickens' account of a lantern show he was planning in his home, see letter to Cornelius Felton of 31 December 1842, reproduced in M. House, G. Storey, K. Tillotson, *et al.* (eds.), *The British Academy Pilgrim Edition of the Letters of Charles Dickens*, vols. 1–12 (Oxford: Clarendon Press, 1965–2002), vol. III (1974), p. 416.

moved or removed mid-projection and/or a pulley system that enabled a section of the slide to circulate repeatedly. In this way a fountain could be seen spouting water continuously, a sleeping man could accidentally swallow a rat each time he opened his mouth to snore or bathing beauties could be seen alternately dipping into and emerging from the water. The manipulation of the effects levers on the slides and the changing of the slides themselves, therefore, could effect a sudden or gradual animation of a person or the transformation of a scene. A single effects slide could even combine lateral movement (for example, of a boat) with vertical movement (for example, of waves) to create a stunning effect of dramatic dynamism when projected onto a large screen.[10] Equally, however, simply generating an unexpected eye movement in a figure previously thought to be inert could, with minimal effort, create a comically arresting effect of lifelikeness. Olive Cook comments on the memorable humour of one such example when, as part of a perkily inventive biblical slide sequence, the whale rolls its eyes at the audience after vomiting Jonah upon dry land.[11] And finally, the lanterns themselves could be moved (shaken, tilted or even moved around in changing relationship to the screen strapped to the lanternist's body).[12] These greater or lesser adjustments in projection position used in combination with slide levers, swift changes, kaleidoscopic chromatropes and dissolves could generate interestingly composite effects of movement on the screen.

As early as 1713, Jonathan Swift had reported that 'I went afterwards to see a famous *moving* picture, and I never saw anything so pretty' (my emphasis)[13] and by the mid-nineteenth century, the lantern's range of possible effects simulating movement was impressive. The experience of viewing projected moving images communally in the dark that the cinematograph was in due course to offer, was, therefore, a development of, not a complete departure from, experiences that had also been on offer to previous generations. And it was not only the basic conditions of public exhibition and communal reception that cinema appropriated from the

---

[10] I am grateful to Richard Manwaring Baines for generously showing me his collection of effects slides, including an exquisitely painted 'wreck and rescue' lifeboat slide from the 1840s.

[11] Olive Cook, *Movement in Two Dimensions* (London: Hutchinson, 1963), p. 84.

[12] For a mid-nineteenth-century description of the ways in which on-screen movement could be simulated in lantern shows, see Benjamin Pike Jr., *Catalogue of Optical Goods* (1848). Quoted in George Kleine, 'Progress in Optical Projection in the Last Fifty Years', *Film Index* (28 May 1910), 10.

[13] Jonathan Swift, *The Journal to Stella*, (ed.) George A. Aitken (London: Methuen, 1901), Letter 62 (March 1713), p. 530. Quoted in Laurent Mannoni, *The Great Art of Light and Shadow: Archaeology of the Cinema* (University of Exeter Press, 2000), p. 121.

lantern tradition: it also adopted some of the lantern's exhibition conventions, and even its subjects. The musical accompaniment at all early cinema exhibitions was, for example, reminiscent of lantern shows, and the tradition of the live lecturer offering scripted or extemporised comment on the screened images was also directly inherited from established lantern practice.[14]

By the latter half of the nineteenth century, popular slide sequences were being mass-produced and internationally distributed.[15] Supplying the market with a mass-produced product inevitably ushered in a degree of predictability in the types of sequences that could be exhibited, even in geographically diverse locations. The stock-in-trade lantern sequences tended to fit the following broad types: phantasmagoria (based on ghosts and phantoms), morality tales (warning against the dangers of drink),[16] Bible stories (mostly told through painted biblical scenes), travel narratives/geography lessons/missionary reports, tales for children (*Cinderella*, *Dick Whittington* and *Aesop's Fables* were all popular), adventure stories (notably *Robinson Crusoe*, *Robin Hood* and *Don Quixote*), sentimental melodramas (tales of penury, bereavement, unemployment, illness, personal sacrifice, misadventure and cold weather), comic sketches (with titles such as 'Man swallowing rats', 'Lady on kicking donkey', 'Punch with growing nose'), grand historical subjects (Wellington's battles, the death of Nelson, kings and queens of England), and pictorial accompaniment to well-known stories or songs (in addition to the ever-popular Defoe, authors such as Bunyan, Milton, Swift, Dickens, Longfellow and Tennyson were also regularly plundered as a source for slide sequences).

Though not central to the stock repertoire, Shakespeare did appear regularly in the magic lantern and, reciprocally, enlisted the lantern's help in theatrical productions on occasion also. As early as 1821, for example, Edmund Kean included lantern slides in his stage *King Lear* at Drury Lane to augment the visual effects of the production.[17] The memorialising of celebrated theatrical performances could also be aided by projecting images of famous stage actors in Shakespearean roles as part of touring, culturally

---

[14] Moving picture lecturers are discussed in the Introduction, pp. 10–13.

[15] Major slide manufacturers included Bamforth, Lancaster, Theobald and Co., Carpenter and Westley, Newton, Riley Brothers, Briggs, Keystone, Eastman Kodak Co., Lumière, Unger und Hoffmann. For an account of the industrialisation of the lantern business, see Mannoni, *Great Art of Light and Shadow*, p. 289.

[16] Morality tale slide sequences had titles such as 'The Drunkard's Children', 'Shadowed by Sin', 'From Workhouse to Mansion: or, the Reward of the Righteous', 'The Two Roads'.

[17] See Terence Rees, *Theatre Lighting in the Age of Gas* (London: Society for Theatre Research, 1978), pp. 81–3.

edifying lantern lectures. Images such as 'Mr. Kean in the Character of Richard the 3rd', 'Mrs Siddons in the Character of Queen Catherine' or 'Ellen Terry as Lady Macbeth' contributed to the cult of celebrity by bringing the image of famous Shakespearean players to larger and more diverse audiences than could have attended the performance of place-specific and time-bounded theatre productions.[18] In addition, a Shakespearean image was occasionally used as an economical point of collective recognition to illustrate a lecture or a lantern show about something else entirely: Lady Macbeth in night-gown bearing dagger and drugged posset could contribute to phantasmagoria horror shows; Lear and Poor Tom could illustrate 'delusional insanity' and 'feigned insanity', respectively, in a lecture on mental illness.[19] A surviving scripted commentary for a mid-nineteenth-century lantern show reveals that in the midst of slide sequences such as 'A very clever trick of clowns', 'Miss Lucy swinging from a Walnut tree', 'Punch and Judy' and 'Mr Pickwick running after his hat', the lanternist-showman (calling himself Timothy Toddle) dropped in two separate cameo lantern sequences from *Macbeth*: 'The Combat between McDuff & Mackbeth' (sic) in which Macduff's castle is surprised, and the later revenge duel ending with the slaying of Macbeth.[20] In *c*.1870, a later lanternist who inherited Toddle's lantern script made some modifications to it in a discernibly different hand. His additions included two further Shakespearean sequences: a 'Scene from Hamlet' which featured the ghost and so allowed for the fun of hammed ghost vocals in the accompanying commentary; and 'King Richard' and 'The Death of Richard' from *Richard III*, showing the horseless King Richard fighting on and dying, again with dramatic quotation to accompany.[21] The tenor of the scripted commentary from both Toddle and his successor suggests that such lanternist-showmen were adept at extracting maximum excitement and drama from their slides.[22]

---

[18] Mr. Kean and Mrs Siddons appear in Timothy Toddle, 'A Magical Lantern Entertainment', in Dennis Crompton, David Henry and Stephen Herbert (eds.), *Magic Images: The Art of Hand-Painted and Photographic Lantern Slides* (London: The Magic Lantern Society (MLS) 1990), pp. 47–53 (53). The Ellen Terry slide is from the author's private collection.

[19] The hand-coloured slide of 'Lady Macbeth' is reproduced in Mervyn Heard, *Phantasmagoria: The Secret Life of the Magic Lantern* (Hastings: The Projection Box, 2006), p. 290. The line-drawn slides of Lear and Poor Tom, drawn by 'A.J.C.', are held in the Archive of the Bethlem Royal Hospital, Box A07/1, inventory nos. LSC-090 and LSC-091, respectively.

[20] Toddle, 'A Magical Lantern Entertainment', p. 51.

[21] The surviving 24-page manuscript, complete with later additions, is now held by the Magic Lantern Society of Great Britain. A helpful transcription of it is reproduced in Crompton, Henry and Herbert, *Magic Images*, pp. 47–53. I take the *c*.1870 date of the later handwritten modifications from there. These Shakespearean sequences appear on p. 51.

[22] The detail of Toddle's lantern manuscript is discussed in Judith Buchanan, 'Shakespeare and the Magic Lantern', *Shakespeare Survey* 62 (2009, forthcoming).

From 1850 onwards, several different English versions of slide sequences based on 'The Seven Ages of Man' would additionally have been available for inclusion in a divertingly cultural rag-bag of lantern offerings of the sort Toddle was peddling. 'The Seven Ages of Man' slide-sets were each structured as seven-slide sequences, with accompanying light animation effects to enliven some of the ages and a scripted reading from *As You Like It* produced by the slide producer to be read alongside the projection with as much declamatory enthusiasm as an individual lantern lecturer might choose to muster.[23]

Other slide sequences, however, offered a more sustained Shakespearean narrative. Later in the century (post-1878), for example, Theobald and Company of London produced a twelve-slide hand-painted sequence depicting a compressed version of the whole of *Romeo and Juliet*, with an accompanying scripted reading.[24] *Macbeth* was also considered both sufficiently dramatic and sufficiently well known to be amenable to distilling for lantern treatment of various sorts. In one skittish English lantern version from *c.*1880 entitled, as its opening slide colourfully announces, 'Ye Fearful Tragedie of Macbeth', an effect slide shows the three hand-drawn, hand-painted witches seen in profile and pointing in a chirpy parody of Fuseli's well-known painting. In a later slide from the same sequence, a duelling Macduff cuts off Macbeth's head by means of a moving mechanical effects lever. The appeal of this sequence could always then be comically enhanced by moving the lever forwards and backwards in quick succession causing Macbeth's head to be alternately severed from and returned to his neck.[25]

It was, however, an American family firm of slide manufacturers and slide painters, Casper W. Briggs and Company of Philadelphia, that showed the most applied commercial interest in telling Shakespearean tales

---

[23] Multiple versions of a *Seven Ages of Man* seven-slide sequence were issued, each with a published one-page version of the speech from *As You Like It* II.vii, to be read in conjunction with the exhibition of the slides. The Magic Lantern Society's Slide Readings Library holds three lantern scripts for *The Seven Ages of Man*: Millikin and Lawley of London's pre-1872 script (serial no. 91903); York and Sons of London's pre-1887 script (serial no. 90802); and Alfred Pumphrey of Birmingham's post-1875 script (serial no. 91677). The active trading years of the issuing company in each case helps delimit the possible range of dates for the slide readings.

[24] MLS Slide Readings Library holds a script for the Theobald twelve-slide *Romeo and Juliet* lantern sequence. Serial no. 90478.

[25] I am grateful to lanternist and lantern historian 'Professor' Mervyn Heard for providing details about, and showing me some of his collection of remarkable nineteenth-century slides on Shakespearean subjects. It is difficult to date these sequences precisely although the weight of the glass in the slide, style of the illustrations and nature of the slide surround (type of wood or tape, with or without a manufacturer's mark) helps produce an approximate date.

through the lantern. Briggs released two separate series of Shakespearean painted-slide sequences, the first in the early 1890s, the second in 1908. The earlier of these went under the series title 'Shakespeare Illustrated'. Each Shakespeare play included in the series was represented by a set of eight to fourteen slides that, when projected in sequence with suitable narration and atmospheric piano accompaniment, depicted a succinct pictorial version of the plot. The plays thus 'lanternised' by Briggs as part of the 'Shakespeare Illustrated' series included *Romeo and Juliet*, *A Midsummer Night's Dream*, *The Taming of the Shrew*, *The Merchant of Venice*, *As You Like It*, *Timon of Athens*, *The Merry Wives of Windsor*, *Twelfth Night*, *Hamlet*, *Othello*, *King Lear*, *Macbeth*, *Cymbeline*, *A Winter's Tale* and *The Tempest*.[26] The slides were mass-produced line-drawn images, collodion on glass, which were then hand-coloured for those customers who could afford the premium edition. Although I have found no surviving trace of any published lectures or readings to accompany these, widespread precedent within the industry suggests that the company might well have issued such readings alongside the slide sequences, as a guide to the lanternist in preparing the show. Some lanternists would then have adhered to these published scripts rigorously. Those of a more independent bent, however, would no doubt have gone 'off-script' and improvised according to their own preferences.[27]

The surviving slides from the Briggs 'Shakespeare Illustrated' series are archived (though not yet catalogued) in George Eastman House, Rochester (NY). Lacking space to describe them all, I take one sequence, *Hamlet*, as a sample for analysis.

The *Hamlet* sequence comprises eleven line-drawn surviving slides, some of which are artistically coloured.[28] However, another Briggs series entitled 'English History: 1486–1603', released in parallel with 'Shakespeare Illustrated', included a slide entitled 'Shakespeare reading Hamlet to his Family'. Close in subject as this slide was to the *Hamlet* sequence, it must have formed an almost irresistibly neat introduction (and/or conclusion)

---

[26] The 1890s dating of the 'Shakespeare Illustrated' series is not definitive, but the mahogany of the wooden frame surrounds, the collodion used to coat the slides and the dates of the reproductions of the paintings from *The Art Journal* on which they draw, help to narrow the window.

[27] To sample the improvisatory verve with which some lanternists constructed their commentary, see the transcript of Toddle's manuscript.

[28] There has occasionally been an inferential discrimination made to place a particular slide as part of the 1890s as opposed to the 1908 Briggs sequence. Such discriminations are made based on style of illustration, character of slide mount and the placement of the image within a run. I cannot be certain my discriminations are right in all cases, but I offer them here as my best inference in the light of the available evidence.

to the *Hamlet* sequence for any lanternist who owned both runs, as, presumably, many of Briggs' customers did. Lanternists, after all, had the
freedom and opportunity to plunder their own slide holdings and com-
pile their running order from any combination of slides that pleased
them. Since lanternists were frequently improvisatory showmen, it seems
reasonable to assume that a lanternist who found himself in possession
of a single slide trailing its evident kinship with another sequence from
his collection, would naturally have sought to create a linked narrative
across the two. 'Shakespeare Reading Hamlet to his Family' is a simply
executed line-drawn image in which, a poised, confident and recognisably
'Droeshoutian' Shakespeare (with trimmed beard, high forehead, doublet
and ruff) sits at a table beneath a portrait of Elizabeth I. Although a scroll
is on the table before him and he holds a piece of paper in his left hand,
he refers to neither as he tells his story with right arm raised expressively.
Despite the slide's title ('Shakespeare *reading* ...' – my emphasis), he is
clearly speaking *ex tempore* and enjoying doing so. His family leans in
attentively around him. His wife (in right of foreground) pauses in her
sewing to listen to the tale; his elder daughter (in left of foreground) sits
on the floor leaning on his knees; his younger daughter sits beside him,
resting her head against his shoulder; his son (who unlike Shakespeare's
son by the time *Hamlet* was written, is visibly still alive) stands quietly in
attendance; a domestic servant peers in around a corner in depth of field
to catch the story; a dog lies contentedly on the tiled floor at Shakespeare's
feet. It is an image of unalloyed domestic contentment and of rapt collective attention to a gripping tale. As an appealing possible preface to Briggs'
Hamlet slide sequence, it would then have been followed by images from
the Shakespearean drama itself. In such a case it would have been down to
the dexterity of the lanternist and the fluency of his accompanying commentary to negotiate the transition from the prefatory meta-narrative to
the substance of the tale itself.

   Once the cinema came into being and made its comparable claim on
Shakespearean material, it happened upon (or perhaps even mimicked)
just such a device to ease an audience in to the tale told via a prefatory
image of its telling. Milano's 1913 film *Una tragedia alla Corte di Sicilia*
(*A Winter's Tale*), for example, begins with a scene of a stereotypically
recognisable Shakespeare figure sitting at a table reading *A Winter's Tale*
to assembled family and friends. From there, the film then segues into a
dramatisation of the action being read. And in 1916, the American company Thanhouser employed a related story-telling device by opening its

film of *King Lear* on an image of the distinguished actor Frederick Warde sitting in a wing-backed arm-chair reading *King Lear* in the privacy of his own study. As he reads the words, he imagines himself into the central role. Through a dissolve, Warde transmutes into the white-bearded Lear shown on the front cover of this volume, and the action of the drama is then played out before our eyes, apparently conjured by the power of Warde's own literary imagination as a reader.[29] With self-subverting irony, both these silent films then unspool as wordless cinematic tributes to the power of Shakespearean language to conjure a performance in the mind of the reader or listener.

Briggs' pictorial lantern account of the dramatic action of *Hamlet* to which the image of Shakespearean story-telling (when thus appropriated) would have ceded is offered in simple, stylised form. The remaining eleven slides carry titles, written onto the (unprojected) edge of each slide to help the lanternist retain their sequencing. There follows a summary description of each slide, prefaced in each case by its given title.

1. 'Hamlet – Ghost Scene'. A line-drawn image which fulfils the function of an establishing shot. A night-time scene of an imposing castle, troubled seascape, impressive plinthed statue of a mounted king, armoured ghost of the same king, Hamlet facing the ghost and two further watchers (Horatio and Marcellus?) in Elizabethan dress. In its detail and clarity, the style reflects that of a Victorian children's storybook illustration.

2. 'Hamlet – A Platform Before the Castle' [artistically coloured]. On the ramparts in moonlight, Hamlet, dressed in showy black Elizabethan mourning garb with plumed hat, cape and sword, is restrained by Horatio and Marcellus holding pikes as the ghost appears in full armour in depth of field. The whole has a night-time blue sheen cast across it, but the slide-painter has picked out the ghost from the rest in translucent gold.

3. 'Hamlet's Soliloquy'. Hamlet's downcast figure, now with hat removed, has dark hair and a Victorian moustache. He walks towards us in a columned, vaulted room in the castle, observed by Ophelia who sits with a book by a window in frame left and overheard by the eavesdropping King and Polonius behind a draped curtain in frame right.

---

[29] This introductory device is present on the *King Lear* print held at the Folger, but not in the GEH print from which the DVD version (*Thanhouser Collection*, Vol. 7) has been taken.

4. 'Hamlet's Advice to the Players'. Hamlet stands frame right speaking with gestural emphasis to three players, right arm forward. Whereas he has reassumed his plumed hat, the players hold their more modest ones respectfully in their hands. Drapes, statuettes, a gothic window and a chandelier are visible behind. The setting is palatial.

5. 'Hamlet Surprises the King at Prayer'. In a small, largely unadorned chapel with stone-vaulted ceiling, a bearded Claudius in ermine-trimmed kingly robe kneels in centre frame, elbows resting on his *prie-dieu*, hands together in supplication, face upturned towards the crucifix on the altar before him in the left of the image. Hamlet, having entered the chapel through a door in the right, pulls away in quasi-repulsion from the figure he sees kneeling at prayer before him, right hand poised over the hilt of his sword. The effect generated is, appropriately for the dramatic moment, one of both consternation and unresolved dilemma about how to respond to the figure of the king at prayer.

6. 'Hamlet's Interview with his Mother'. Though the image does not appear visually cluttered, the slide is inventively packed with narrative information. Hamlet, bare-headed again, stands in the middle of his mother's room beneath the two gilt-framed portraits of King Hamlet and King Claudius respectively, which hang, square-on to our gaze, on the wall above the door. Hamlet is pointing towards an arched alcove at the back right corner of the room where stands the translucent ghost of his father. The ghost is in armour with an ermine-trimmed kingly robe draped about his shoulders – the same robe that appears in both portraits and that Claudius himself wore in the previous slide. Despite being set back, the ghost seems larger than Hamlet – a colossus of a man (take him for all in all). His ghost, in Hamlet's vision and ours, is perspective-defyingly imposing, even from afar. Gertrude sits before Hamlet in right of frame, her hands clutched together and raised towards him pleading, presumably, for his sanity and her life. She ignores his imperiously gestured suggestion that she should look upon the ghost. At Hamlet's feet in the left of the image lies Polonius' body, which has evidently recently fallen through the arras that hangs there. In sum, therefore, it is an economically organised pictorial account of the entire closet scene, telescoped into one encapsulating moment, which the lanternist-narrator could embellish at will.

7. 'Ophelia Scattering Flowers' (Figure 1.1a). Ophelia with hair loose, flowing dress and floral coronet has entered through a door in the

middle of the back wall and is starting to distribute her flowers across the (conventionally) black and white diagonal tiled floor. Laertes stands with head bowed to the right. Another courtly onlooker stands at the back watching while Claudius and Gertrude look on, caught between horror and sympathy at Ophelia's grief, while leaning against a side table in the left of the image. Two royal guards peep in through the door in the back.

8. 'Ophelia' (Figure 1.1b). Uniquely in this *Hamlet* lantern tale, the image of a gamine Ophelia sitting on a low bough by the edge of the brook was not drawn by a slide artist specifically to fit the sequence. Rather, this one image is lifted directly from English painter Arthur Hughes' 1852 painting 'Ophelia'. This was reproducible onto glass directly from the photographic plate taken of *The Art Journal*'s printed lithograph.[30] Unsurprisingly, given its provenance, the image is decisively different in style and treatment from all others in the sequence. *They* are largely determined by the amount of narrative information that can be contained in a single image. Aesthetics, that is, never take primacy over plot, and the aesthetics, if not crude, certainly lack nuance. Even details of perspective, for example, can be compromised to heighten narrative clarity. This Hughes painting, by contrast, is conspicuously spare on narrative detail but rich in unexpected associations, technical acumen and significant whimsical charm. Elaine Showalter has described the painting as showing:

a tiny waiflike creature – a sort of Tinker Bell Ophelia – in a filmy white gown, perched on a tree trunk by the stream. The overall effect is softened, sexless, and hazy, although the straw in her hair resembles a crown of thorns.

Showalter further argues that Ophelia is on offer here as a 'juxtaposition of childlike femininity and Christian martyrdom'.[31] There is certainly a spiritual quality to the painting. Ophelia's face is serene, abstracted, even Madonna-like, and her waiflike fragility is emphasised by her delicately outstretched arm and by her isolation in a landscape

---

[30] I am grateful to lantern historians Stephen Herbert and Mo Heard for discussing this process with me. There may have been a copyright arrangement made between Briggs and *The Art Journal* for reproduction rights. Equally, however, Briggs may simply have taken copies of the images from the *Journal* without paying. There was precedent for both approaches. I can find no surviving evidence to suggest one way or the other in this case.

[31] Elaine Showalter, *The Female Malady: Women, Madness, and English Culture, 1830–1980* (London: Virago, 1987), pp. 84–5.

so much bigger than herself. The straw in her hair is indeed evocative of a crown of thorns, but also, perhaps, of a halo. She is victim and saint, child and sprite, Ophelia and Madonna, and a complex anomaly as part of this pictorial sequence.

9. 'Hamlet – a Church Yard' [artistically coloured]. This slide returns the style of pictorial story-telling to the line-drawn illustrations of the majority of the sequence. Two cloaked figures of Hamlet and Horatio stand in the moonlit churchyard the far side of an open grave in which the gravedigger stands, leaning on his spade. Hamlet holds the skull and talks of Yorick to Horatio. A collection of ribs and skulls are scattered about at their feet where they have been exhumed.

10. 'Duel between Hamlet and Laertes'. Hamlet in the left of the image and Laertes in the right face each other in the foreground of the picture, each seen in profile. Each clutches a rapier and, in addition, has a regular sword slung from his belt. Beyond them, the king and queen look on from their thrones with assembled courtiers standing to either side and behind them. The queen is raising a small tray towards Hamlet on which sits a cup. Duellists and courtiers alike have put their hats 'to their proper use' (on the head). A weighty stone pillar sits partially in view on the right, the floor is wooden boards and the ceiling is again vaulted stone supported by massy pillars.

11. 'Hamlet Kills the King'. The setting is unchanged but its decorous symmetry has now been disrupted. The queen lies in a poisoned faint to the right. Laertes lies dying in left foreground, his sword and hat scattered in front of him. He just manages to raise himself on his elbow to point accusingly at Claudius with his left hand. Hamlet is lunging with his rapier at the king and the assembled courtiers have been thrown into disarray, arms in the air in horror, condemnation, exaltation and, perhaps, self-protection. The image is bursting with energy – the more striking after some of the rather cautious and static images that have preceded it. This is evidently the moment when the drama bursts into active life.

In addition to these extant slides, the numbering on the slides suggests there may also have been a couple more that have not survived: perhaps one of the play-within-the-play and/or one of Hamlet's body being borne aloft as a suitable closing image for the story. Whatever the missing slides depicted, sufficient numbers survive to demonstrate clearly the manner in which the story was compressed for lantern projection – a distillation of a succession of iconic moments creating 'action images' (as American lanternist and lantern historian Terry Borton calls them). In this, these

Shakespearean slide sequences were working precisely in the spirit of edition illustrations of the period, which were often similarly dependent on the accompanying text to make sense. The lantern sequence joined with edition illustrations in confirming a truncated version of the drama composed exclusively of the most heightened and well-known moments from the drama, enabling the play to circulate in accessibly simplified and consensually recognisable summary form.

Of the surviving *Hamlet* slides, the painterly 'Ophelia' slide (number 8 in the descriptive list above) is clearly an oddity. However, the anomalous inclusion of such images is characteristic of Briggs' work. The company regularly appropriated existing works of art for their slide sequences, embedding them, as here, in broader narratives as an unexpected visual treat to be happened upon amid more ordinary artistic fare – Darley's India ink-wash

Figure 1.1a *Hamlet* Slide 7: 'Ophelia scattering flowers'.
Courtesy of George Eastman House, Rochester, NY.

Figure 1.1b *Hamlet* Slide 8: 'Ophelia-Hughes' Briggs' 'Shakespeare Illustrated'
lantern slide series, 1890s. Transparency, collodion on glass. Full slide: 3.25 × 4 inch.
Courtesy of George Eastman House, Rochester, NY.

drawing 'King Lear in the Storm', Becker's engraving 'Othello before the
Doge', Hans Makart's sensually intense painting of the balcony scene from
Romeo and Juliet.[32] The effect of projecting these artistic inserts in the context of the show as a whole must have been strikingly odd. Hughes renders
Ophelia, for example, in a pre-Raphaelite style which inevitably differs
markedly from the more pared down, naïve style in which she appeared in the
previous slide 'scattering flowers'. Her extended right arm in the earlier slide
might perhaps be seen as an anticipation of the yet more delicately extended
right arm of Hughes's Ophelia, so constituting a suggestive bridge into the
succeeding slide (Figures 1.1a and b). In practice, however, that single echoed gesture across slides serves if anything, simply to draw attention to the

[32] Felix Octavius Carr Darley's ink wash of Lear was one of thirty Darley drawings produced as
photogravures in a deluxe edition entitled *The Darley Gallery of Shakespearean Illustrations* (New
York, Philadelphia: J. M. Stoddart, 1884). Carl Ludwig Friedrich (Becker)'s 1892 steel engraving
helps to date the Othello sequence as one of the last produced of the 'Shakespeare Illustrated'
series. At the time of writing, a photographic image of the Becker engraving may be viewed
online at: www.thelostleaf.com/detail.asp?artID=119 and of the Makart painting at: www.pho-
tographersdirect.com/buyers/stockphoto.asp?imageid=657464. On the use of Makart's 1860s
painting within Briggs' *Romeo and Juliet* sequence, see Buchanan, 'Shakespeare and the Magic
Lantern'.

markedly different character of the two images as a whole, and of the two versions of Ophelia on offer within them. The daring disruption of stylistic consistency robs the sequence of a sense of artistic unity, and even of character stability. The inclusion in these Shakespearean sequences of a known work of art may, of course, have served as a gratifying nod to the artistic cognoscenti who, having recognised the work, might murmur modestly to their neighbour of their familiarity with it.[33] Even unrecognised, however, such inclusions provided some aesthetic variety to the telling of the tale and, in doing so, confirmed the iconic status of the character whose role in the narrative transcends any single manifestation, or even style of presentation. Ophelia, that is, can look like this or she can look like that. She can inhabit this or that sort of landscape. She can be eroticised, infantilised or idealised. Throughout all such variations in interpretive emphasis, however, the mythic dimensions of the story she occupies enable her to remain incontrovertibly 'Ophelia', possessed of a range of accumulated dramatic and artistic meanings. The progress of the story can, therefore, accommodate the stylistic adjustments without dislocating.

The appropriation of this painting into a progressive lantern sequence has one further effect also. Like all fine art interpretations of dramatic material, the Hughes painting freezes an evolving moment from the drama of the play, converting it into a stand-alone work of art, arrestingly stripped of context and temporality. Thus the drama is deliberately caught in a state of permanent suspension from which both causation and consequence are kept absent. In contradistinction to the dynamic theatrical provenance from which it derives, therefore, Shakespearean painting is always partly defined by its resolute stasis – by, in effect, its simultaneous allusion and resistance to dramatic imperative. Reinserting that image of temporal arrest back into an unfolding narrative (if of one composed of a succession of still images), as the Briggs lantern slide sequence does with its painterly inserts, therefore, has the interesting effect of re-injecting into a painterly moment some of the evolving dramatic force which its gallery life had necessarily denied it. The moment of exquisite anacrucis just before her death in which Hughes's Ophelia is eternally poised is thus reanimated. When viewed as part of the slide sequence, Ophelia is now allowed a life before this point, and, indeed, a death after it.

Precedent suggests that more Shakespearean slide sequences will have been made and exhibited at the time than there is now surviving evidence

---

[33] As such, it would have fulfilled a similar function to the *tableaux vivants* or stage pictures on the nineteenth-century stage, which made recognisable artistic allusions for the gratification of those whose range of cultural reference allowed them to recognise the visual quotation.

of. (Being turned into 'yesterday's thing' by the arrival of cinema did not serve the lantern well in terms of the archiving and preservation of its materials.) Nevertheless, even those that have survived and that have thus far proved traceable are sufficient to attest that Shakespeare had a lantern presence that has so far been largely overlooked. The surviving Shakespearean lantern sequences are, of course, of interest in their own right as part of the magic lantern's rich and varied history. They also bear pertinently on the history of the publication, dissemination and reception of Shakespearean illustration and painting in the period. Significantly for present purposes, however, they confirm the relevance of a back story to any historicised account of Shakespeare's appearances on screen.

Magic lantern slide sequences continued to be produced and exhibited well into the twentieth century, and often even alongside the increasingly dominant rival medium of the cinematograph. Such was the lantern's longevity, ubiquity and associated confidence that many in the lantern community initially thought it could not only survive, but might even benefit from, the new craze for motion pictures. Writing in the *Optical Magic Lantern Journal Almanac* in 1897, for example, Edmund H. Wilkie of the Royal Polytechnic addressed the question of possible competition directly. Of the motion picture industry he wrote that:

far from superceding [sic] general lantern work, it will most likely act in the contrary manner, and by directing the public attention to optical exhibitions give a powerful impetus to dissolving view entertainments generally.[34]

The lantern's confidence at this stage was not entirely fanciful. In the early days of the cinematograph, the lantern could still, after all, boast capacities that lay beyond the brief of the new medium as it had thus far developed. These most particularly concerned its ability to tell a story. In relation to Shakespeare, for example, it was not until 1907, eight years after the pioneering BMBC film of *King John*, that the cinema first aspired to tell a 'complete' Shakespearean story in moving pictures. Before that point, there had been no attempt at narrative cohesion in the Shakespeare films made. The very early Shakespeare films presented individual scenes, or a collection of unconnected theatrical 'moments', acted out for the camera and exhibited as part of the mixed genre programmes on variety bills. Despite their value as a recorded slice of extra-cinematic life, as a brief memorial account of a particular performance and sometimes also as an

---

[34] Quoted in David Robinson, 'Magic Lantern Shows', in Richard Abel (ed.), *Encyclopedia of Early Cinema* (Abingdon and NY: Routledge, 2005), pp. 407–8.

advertisement for a live theatre show that could be enjoyed elsewhere, their value as an autonomous story-telling vehicle was yet to be established. The earliest Shakespeare films were, in fact, narratively less ambitious and so less satisfying than the Shakespearean lantern slide sequences of the 1880s with their abridged but coherent pictorial story-telling and their accompanying scripted readings supplying the gaps.

The two media did co-exist for some years. *The Optical Magic Lantern Journal* of London expanded its brief and re-launched itself as the more inclusive *Kinematograph and Lantern Weekly*, the world's first regular film journal. Equally, the pioneer American cinema trade paper *The Moving Picture World* in its early years served both the film industry and the stereopticon trade. Magic lanterns often supplied the aperitif to the film show and the filler during reel changes in moving picture houses (and continued to be used to project advertising slides in cinemas even after the Second World War). In the early days, many travelling lanternists equipped themselves as able film projectionists, enabling them to provide multi-media shows for their established audiences who were anxious to sample the new technological wonders but without necessarily having to stoop to the perceived cultural taint of entering the music halls, vaudeville theatres, penny gaffs or, post-1906 in the US, the nickelodeons.[35] However, by the start of the First World War, the lantern was a form in terminal decline: the moving picture industry had appropriated and expanded its territory and left it with only a dwindling constituency and marginalised role.

In its inventive and decorative dalliances with Shakespearean dramatic narratives, the magic lantern had offered bright, beautiful, and sometimes partially animated, projected images of Shakespeare to Victorian audiences. The presence of these Shakespeare projections on lantern screens of the nineteenth century necessarily adjusts the way in which we think about early Shakespeare films. The 1899 Tree *King John* film and its 1900 *Hamlet* successor starring Sarah Bernhardt cannot, that is, precisely be called the beginning of the story of 'Shakespeare on screen', nor even entirely of 'Shakespeare in projected moving pictures'. These first Shakespeare films would, of course, have been startlingly different in the effect they had upon an audience from the earlier slide sequences. After all, they replaced the pretty but largely slightly saccharine Victorian artistry of painted slides with the weight and interest of real, and famous, Shakespearean actors enacting grand passion and dramatic moment. And

[35] For an account of travelling shows in America that combined short moving pictures with projected lantern slides and a lecture, see Musser, *High-Class Moving Pictures*, pp. 61, 79–84, 87.

they replaced striking, but occasional, choreographed single movements implemented by the practised expertise of the lanternist with the persuasive appearance of natural and continuous movement 'caught' on film. It was precisely these things about the cinematograph (in particular the fascinating magic of continuous movement) that seized the popular imagination and stole the lantern's market. As W. Stephen Bush reported in 1908:

If lectures on Shakespearean plays … with the limping aid of the slide attract thousands, why should not the moving pictures attract tens of thousands? Recently the chairman of the entertainment committee of a great institution told me of a conversation he overheard between two boys coming out of a lantern slide entertainment. "How did you like it?" asked one of the other. "All right," was the reply, "but I would have liked them better if they had moved."[36]

They were to move, and indeed, by then already had. Even in helping to point up the profundity of the tonal shift that the introduction of live actors and continuous movement brought to a show, however, Shakespearean lantern sequences had already made their modest contribution to the viewing culture into which these first Shakespeare films were received.

WORDLESS SHAKESPEARES AND
SPECTACULAR SHAKESPEARES

In understanding the charge that the wordless, or largely wordless, performance of Shakespeare could carry, and how it might have struck early twentieth-century audiences viewing the earliest Shakespeare films, the nineteenth century once again provides instructive precedents. In this section I review a range of nineteenth-century theatrical productions in which the status of Shakespearean words was significantly compromised, and some of the debates that emerged as a result. To contextualise these, however, we need to go further back yet.

In the Restoration, the spoken word on stage, unlike musical entertainment or pantomime, was considered potentially seditious and so in need of monitoring. Regulation of theatrical entertainment from 1660 onwards was by means of royal patents, and these were initially granted only to two theatres: Drury Lane and Covent Garden. In 1766 a further patent was bestowed upon the Haymarket (although of a slightly less secure variety than the initial patents had provided). The effect of these patents was to license speech in the designated (and therefore regulatable) 'major'

---

[36] Bush, 'Shakespeare in Moving Pictures', 446–7 (447).

theatres, and by implication to ban it in all other 'minor' theatres. The Licensing Act of 1737 (and the additions to it of 1751 and 1755) consolidated the effect of this speech ban by making its breach an offence in law. Patents were later divided and sold, thus complicating the picture. Nevertheless, the distinction between the major (speeched) and the minor (speechless) theatres remained in force in principle until the repeal of the Licensing Act in 1843.

What impact did the speech ban have on Shakespeare productions? A colourful illustration is provided by Robert William Elliston's version of *Macbeth* (titled *The History, Murders, Life and Death of Macbeth*), produced in September 1809 for the Royal Circus, one of London's unpatented theatres. Unpatented theatres became adept at developing inventive manoeuvres to minimise the constraints upon their productions that the ban necessarily imposed. One response was to produce 'ballets of action': Elliston's production, improbably from a modern perspective, was one such.[37] In these 'ballets', recitatives (musically accompanied sung speeches) became a standard means of delivering dialogue without the need for it to be officially labelled as such. The musical accompaniment was often of the most sparsely token sort in order to keep the production, if only just, on the right side of the law. As one contemporary observer remarked, the minor theatres offered performances 'in doggerel rhyme, played to the accompaniment of a tinkling Piano-Forte'.[38] So Elliston's *Macbeth*, performed in mime, without spoken dialogue but with recitative, was proclaimed in the extended title of its published version 'a matchless Piece of Pantomimic and Choral Performance'.[39] The near-exclusion of speech from this production, as from so many others of the time, was a necessary act of deference to the laws that applied to all the unpatented theatres.

---

[37] Elliston's *Macbeth* was advertised as a 'Grand Ballet of Action'. See Watson Nicholson, *The Struggle for a Free Stage in London* (Boston and NY: Houghton, Mifflin, 1906), p. 289; Joseph Donohue, *Theatre in the Age of Kean* (Oxford; Blackwell, 1975), p. 49. And for an illuminating account of this production and its implications, see Jane Moody, *Illegitimate Theatre in London, 1770–1840* (Cambridge University Press, 2000), pp. 130–3. The term continued to be used well into the century. See, for example, Percy H. Fitzgerald, *Principles of Comedy and Dramatic Effect* (London: Tinsley Brothers, 1870), p.337.

[38] William Thomas Moncrieff, 'Remarks' on *Rochester; or King Charles the Second's Merry Days. A Musical Comedy*. p.v. Dated June, 1828. (BL 643 a.14.) See also Joseph Donohue, 'Burletta and the Early Nineteenth-Century English Theatre', *Nineteenth-Century Theatre Research* 1 (1973), 29–51.

[39] *The History, Murders, Life, and Death of Macbeth: and a full description of the scenery, action, choruses, and characters of the Ballet of Action, of that name ... with the Occasional Address, spoken by Mr. Elliston; And every Information, to simplify the Plot; and enable the Visitors of the Circus, to comprehend this matchless Piece of Pantomimic and Choral Performance* (London, 1809). See George Raymond, *Memoirs of Robert William Elliston, Comedian* (London, 1857), pp. 156–71.

In the 'Occasional Address' for his 1809 *Macbeth*, Elliston highlighted both the trammelling constraints upon his actors and the height of their dramatic aspirations, constraints notwithstanding:

> Though not indulged with fullest pow'rs of speech,
> The poet's object we aspire to reach;
> The emphatic gesture, eloquence of eye,
> Scenes, music every energy we try
> To make your hearts for murder'd Banquo melt;
> And feel for Duncan as brave Malcom felt;
> To prove we keep our duties full in view,
> And what we must not *say*, resolve to *do*;
> Convinc'd that you will deem our zeal sincere,
> Since more by *deeds* than *words* it will appear.[40]

In appropriating Shakespearean material for the unpatented stage, the Royal Circus was in part mounting a challenge to the traditional hierarchies which had attempted to impose a direct correlation between the dignity of the material and the propriety of the theatrical venue in which it was played. Taking Shakespeare into the relatively frivolous playing space of the Royal Circus may have smacked of the brazen, but keeping the actors bereft of 'fullest pow'rs of speech' judiciously kept the production just short of the actionable. As Jane Moody has shown, the cultural and legal brinksmanship in which the production indulged not only kept the theatre out of trouble but also proved significantly profitable.[41]

Elliston's popular *Macbeth* production was mounted during an inventive period in the life of the minor theatres. At this time, some of those theatres without a patent to perform speech enacted their observance of the letter of the law but defiance of its spirit by holding up linen 'scrolls' or 'banners' in view of the audience, upon which was written the dialogue that they were not permitted to vocalise. The Royal Circus's *Macbeth* was one that experimented with banners in this way. Although, therefore, its drama did, as advertised, appear more 'by *deeds* than *words*', words were not entirely absent from the production: they were simply displaced from an acoustic to a visual plane, finding expression in material form as stage properties. The banners held aloft by actors at key moments carried slogans such as 'Macbeth ordains a solemn Banquet' or 'Destruction to the

---

[40] The 'Occasional Address' was written for Elliston by Dr Thomas Busby and published alongside *The History, Murders, Life and Death of Macbeth* (London, 1809). On Busby's own skirmishes with the speech ban, see Rowland E. Prothero's anecdotal footnote to Byron's 'Letter to John Murray' (18 October 1812), in Prothero (ed.), *The Works of Lord Byron: Letters and Journals* Vol. II (London: John Murray, 1898), p. 176n.
[41] See Moody, *Illegitimate Theatre in London*, pp. 130–2.

Tyrant' (this last carried by Macduff as Birnam Wood begins to move, as if a realistic part of the action rather than a necessary explanation of it).[42] Thus it was that, in ways that would be echoed in the title cards of the cinematograph nearly a century later, Shakespeare's dramatic language was replaced by pared-down plot summaries and snatches of dialogue offered to the audience as part of the visual design of the production.

In other contemporary productions, the phenomenon of exhibiting scrolls or banners extended to longer sections of dialogue as well. In each case, actors would exit, fetch the dialogue scrolls from the wings and re-enter to display them to the audience. In 1828, the musical playwright William Moncrieff reminisced disparagingly about how two minor theatre plays, *Black Castle* and *Blood-Red Knight*, sought to circumvent the speech ban:

[A]ll that could not be rendered clear by action, was told by means of what were called 'scrolls:' – pieces of linen, on which whatever the Dramatis Personæ wished to communicate to each other, for the better understanding of the audience, was expressed in writing, painted on the cloth, and which the Performers alternately fetched from the different sides of the stage, and presented to the full view of the Public, who might then literally have been called the *reading*, and not unfrequently [sic] the *spelling* Public! ... It was no unusual circumstance, for as many as from ten to twelve pieces of the best Irish linen to be cut up, in furnishing these scrolls, on the production of every new piece; this it was the business of the decorator or property-man of the Theatre to attend to; and he not being generally much of a scholar, used often to commit some curious mistakes in orthography, to the infinite amusement of the savans [sic], and mistification [sic] of the illiterate.[43]

Like the 'generous' interpretation of the conventions of recitative, the use of scrolls was an ingenious, if short-lived (and evidently idiosyncratically implemented) challenge to the logic of the speech ban. The *effect* of the scrolls, however, anticipates the later effect of the intertitles of silent films. In both instances, words were stripped of vocal inflection and performance emphasis, and became instead part of the visual scheme of the piece. Like the earlier stage scrolls, intertitles were similarly to impose a temporary interruption of the performed action in order to supply dialogue, plot summary or location report in written form. The alternate suspension of action and dialogue that the intertitles of silent film brought in was not,

---

[42] See Jane Moody, 'Writing for the Metropolis: Illegitimate Performances of Shakespeare in Early Nineteenth-Century London', *Shakespeare Survey* 47 (1994), 61–9 (63). For a discussion of later illegitimate Shakespearean productions, see Moody, *Illegitimate Theatre in London*, 133–47.

[43] Moncrieff, 'Remarks to the Second Edition', in *Tom and Jerry; or Life in London*, 2nd edn. (London: Richardson, 1828), pp. v–vi. Dated July 1828. In *Richardson's New Minor Drama, with Remarks, Biographical and Critical, by W.T. Moncrieff.* Vol I, part II. (BL 643 a.14).

therefore, a process of word/image desynchronisation entirely foreign to the nineteenth-century stage, nor even to Shakespearean performance. And in both media, the alternate concentration on mimed action and exhibited language offered word and image as proximate rather than collaborative communicators.

The repeal of the Licensing Act assisted the minor theatres but left the speech ban in place for the theatrical interludes of the music halls. In 1870, the theatrical commentator, Percy Fitzgerald, commented on the anomaly:

> How can it be explained to a foreigner visiting a place like the Alhambra, and lost in admiration at its wonderful scenery, stage effects, and ballet, that the place dare not go one step further and have dramatic dialogue?[44]

Anomalous as it was, the prohibition still proved the spur to creativity and legal circumvention in the late nineteenth-century music halls, as it had done in the minor theatres earlier in the century. The sustained denial of the right to speak both consolidated the profile, and promoted the practice, of wordless, pantomimic performance in popular theatrical life. The codes for acting in mime were passed on actor to actor and were well understood by audiences. They were also formalised in published acting manuals that offered detailed notes, and accompanying line drawings, stipulating precisely how to arrange the face, and what gesture or stance to adopt in order to communicate the gamut of emotional states.[45] So when the moving picture industry later, inevitably, adopted pantomimic acting codes into its range of communicative strategies, there was already a lively culture of pantomimic performance practice on which film actors could draw and with which audiences were already to some extent familiar.

In the latter half of the nineteenth century, however, it was not only in those performance spaces in which words were expressly prohibited that words and images were held in a counterpoint relationship, as was subsequently to be the case in silent films. Even when, after 1843, dialogue was permitted on stage, an integration of dialogue and action was not always persuasively achieved. It was perhaps by then in the theatrical culture that these things should operate as separate communicative systems. The major theatres were not immune to this: there too, where the presence of words had never been controversial, the relationship between language and spectacle could sometimes feel more like a civil encounter than a wholesome collaboration. The pre-eminence of visual effect was not to be unduly

---

[44] Fitzgerald, *Principles of Comedy*, p. 325.
[45] Acting manuals are discussed in Chapter 5.

compromised by integrating speech too intimately into its world. The eminent actor, William Charles Macready, for example, complained that, in Charles Kean's Shakespearean revivals at the Princess's Theatre in the 1850s, 'the text [was] allowed to be spoken ... like a running commentary upon the spectacles exhibited'.[46] Language was thought to be functioning as an appendage – a supplementary, and near-superfluous, addition to the visual impact of a production. And comments similar to Macready's on Kean's failure to integrate the text into the heart of his productions, continued to be made about Shakespearean productions throughout the century.

By 1870, Fitzgerald was even sardonically wondering whether it was worth making a distinction between the legitimate theatre and the music hall in this respect:

For many [theatrical managers] ... have been all but turning their theatres into music halls ... by exhibiting shows that appeal chiefly to the eye, and in which, if the dialogue be missed, the loss is small.[47]

Fitzgerald was dismayed at the erosion of language in productions across the spectrum of theatrical registers – including in the old patented theatres. Elements of populist pantomime had insinuated themselves, as he saw it, even into officially 'worded' productions. In 1893, another commentator suggested that the same tendencies had displaced words, even Shakespearean words, completely for some scenes, while relegating them to merely a 'species of incidental music' for others.[48]

In Macready's opening storm scene for *The Tempest* back in 1838, the dialogue had been drowned out by other effects. For the equivalent scene of Charles Kean's 1857 lavish production at the Princess's Theatre, more honestly perhaps, the words were completely removed, as Kean's own acting edition testifies.[49] During the cacophony of sound effects, the deck flamed and the ship (constructed to simulate a thirteenth-century vessel) seemed to founder with all on board into an illusory sea of turbulent 'water'. The scope of Kean's vision may be gauged from an introductory note to his souvenir edition of *The Tempest*:

The indulgence of the public is requested should any lengthened delay take place between the acts, during the first representations of *The Tempest*. This appeal

---

[46] William Charles Macready, *Reminiscences and Selections from his Diary and Letters*, edited by F. Pollock (London, 1875), vol. II, p. 446.

[47] Fitzgerald, *Principles of Comedy*, p. 340.

[48] Joseph Knight, *Theatrical Notes* (London: Lawrence and Bullen, 1893), p.148.

[49] See Charles Kean, *Shakespeare's Play of The Tempest, Arranged for Representation at the Princess's Theatre ... by Charles Kean, F.S.A. ...* (London, 1857).

is made with greater confidence, when it is stated that the scenic appliances of the play are of a more extensive and complicated nature than have ever yet been attempted in any theatre in Europe; requiring the aid of above one hundred and forty operatives nightly, who (unseen by the audience) are engaged in working the machinery, and in carrying out the various effects.[50]

The labours of this battalion of unseen stage-hands did not go unnoticed, and one impressed reviewer hailed it the 'most elaborate specimen of stage appliances ever witnessed in this country'.[51] The delays seem to have been deemed the necessary price to pay for the commitment to spectacle and, in the years that followed, such delays became habitual. In 1882, for example, the wedding scene in Irving's *Much Ado About Nothing* at the Lyceum was praised for the spectacular, breath-taking beauty of its scenery. The cost to the audience for such delights was, on this occasion, a fifteen-minute preparatory delay as the scenic artists and stage hands did their work.[52] In practice, of course, even audiences for moving pictures would, in time, be kept waiting for their visual pleasures while reels were changed. However, the formal properties of filmic construction, unlike those of stage representation, could allow for a fluidity and speed of scene changes, and even for a simultaneity of action in different locations through cross-cutting, that makes the clunkingly material business of scene changes on the spectacular stage – with its sounds of hammering off, printed requests for indulgence and fifteen-minute waits – look significantly strained in retrospective comparison.

The tendency to edit dialogue, enhance visual effects and insert long dialogue-free processional, dance or mime sequences in stage productions of Shakespeare throughout the century was not limited to the English stage: the American and European nineteenth-century stage similarly felt the draw of a spectacular pictorialism that had a commensurate impact on the attention given to the words.[53] Where the dramatic language risked detracting from a scene's visual impact, the spectacular theatrical tradition had no compunction in either subordinating it to other stage business or simply excising it. As late as 1900, a satirical article by John Hankin that appeared in *Punch* unsparingly lampooned the appeal of the popular stage. Hankin wrote in a verse style loosely imitative of that in *The Tempest*, dryly predicting how a production of *The Tempest* might appear as mounted by

[50] *Shakespeare's Play of The Tempest ... by Charles Kean ...*, p. ix.
[51] *The Athenaeum* (4 July 1857). Quoted in Frederick J. Marker, 'The First Night of Charles Kean's *The Tempest*, from the Notebook of Hans Christian Andersen', *Theatre Notebook* v.25, n.1 (1970), 20–3.
[52] See Dennis Kennedy, *Looking at Shakespeare: A Visual History of Twentieth Century Performance* (Cambridge University Press, 1993), p. 30.
[53] See Kennedy, *Looking at Shakespeare*, pp. 32–4.

Tree, the spectacular actor-manager of Her Majesty's Theatre. The premise of this spurious drama was that Tree's productions were lavishly overblown in style. The central character is a composite of Prospero and Tree himself as the voice explaining the appeal of scenic display, as opposed to subtlety of acting or poetic appreciation, on the Victorian stage.

> These our actors
> As I foretold you, are a bore at best.
> The things the British Public really like
> Are cloud-capp'd towers and gorgeous palaces
> And solemn temples, triumphs of the art
> Of that egregious wight, the scene painter.
> Poor SHAKESPEARE'S insubstantial puppets fade.
> Only the *scenes* remain ...
> I'll play *Macbeth, Othello*, and *The Dane*
> In such attractive guise you'll never know them;
> And deeper than did ever plummet sound
> I'll drown the "Book"![54]

In mocking the taste for 'cloud-capp'd towers and gorgeous palaces', Hankin broadens the target of his satirical attack. His broadside lands not only on Tree's own scenic excess but also on the public taste that implicitly licenses the subordination of character and language to the eye-catching trappings of the pictorial settings, pageantry, interpolated dance and mime sequences and elaborately choreographed mass *tableaux* of the *scenes*.

Thus it was that when the new medium of cinema necessarily excised spoken language completely from its Shakespearean productions, it not only tapped into a non-verbal Shakespearean performance tradition in the pantomimic conventions of the minor theatres (and of nineteenth-century ballet):[55] it also traded upon and extended the legitimate stage's tendency to erode the significance of language in preference to other forms of scenic display. Shakespeare on silent film institutionalised that erosion by evicting

[54] John Hankin, '*The Tempest* in a Teacup', *Punch* (9 May 1900), 330.

[55] Shakespeare first appeared in ballet in Noverre's *Antoine et Cléopâtre* (Stuttgart or Ludwigsberg, 1761). This was followed by Eusebio Luzzi and Luigi Marescalchi's *Giulietta e Romeo* (Venice, 1785). Other early productions of note include Vincenzo Galeotti's *Romeo og Giulietta* (Copenhagen, 1811). *A Midsummer Night's Dream, Hamlet, Othello, Macbeth* and *The Tempest* also all became ballet subjects for late eighteenth- and nineteenth-century audiences. Limits on space prohibit attentive consideration of Shakespearean ballet here, but see, for example, Arthur Graham, *Shakespeare in Opera, Ballet, Orchestral Music and Song: An Introduction to Music Inspired by the Bard* (Lampeter: Edwin Mellen Press, 1997) and Camille Cole Howard, *The Staging of Shakespeare's 'Romeo and Juliet' as a Ballet* (Lampeter: Edwin Mellen Press, 1992).

spoken language from the performance frame entirely. Nonetheless, its privileging of other forms of performance communication over language had clear points of kinship with some of the Shakespearean instantiations that had preceded it. Given such a background, it is reasonable to assume that early twentieth-century audiences would have been more predisposed to understand silent Shakespeare films as emerging from a rich and varied tradition of non-verbal, or minimally verbal, expressions of Shakespeare than are early twenty-first-century audiences. In such usefully diverse cultural company, there was certainly space for silent Shakespeare films to be appreciated primarily for what they were rather than sniped at for what they were not.

SHAKESPEARE AND THE REALIST ASPIRATION

Alongside the taste for spectacle on the commercial stage went an ever more exacting view of realism. In the early nineteenth century, experiments were made with increasingly ambitious realistic sets (including a ninety-foot-long water tank staging naval battles for the 1804 season at Sadler's Wells). With Charles Kemble's famous archeologically authentic production of *King John* at Covent Garden in 1824, designed by antiquarian James Robinson Planché, theatrical realism on the English stage had decisively arrived. Theatrical managers throughout the century thereafter paid minute attention both to the historical accuracy of costumes, properties and settings and to the perceived veracity of its account of the world beyond its doors, upon which the theatre was increasingly, and expensively, trading.

Theatre designers went to extraordinary lengths: boats were depicted sinking in real water, real trees bearing real fruit were imported onto the stage, a stage butcher's shop displayed real beef carcasses, real horses ran on treadmills, and an entirely accurate, fully to scale, reconstruction of the Sala della Bussola in Venice was constructed for the trial scene in *The Merchant of Venice*.[56] Such effects strained the resources of the theatres to their limit. As theatres bid each other up in terms of the exactitude of their recreations of dramatic locales, scenic artists were despatched to Venice, Rome and Verona to ensure that the detail of the set would be an accurate, scale representation of the original place. Audiences' expectations naturally shifted in line with the sets to which they had become accustomed.

Moving out of the theatre to real, extra-theatrical locations rather than trying to replicate those locations within the theatre was the obvious next

---

[56] See Donohue, *Theatre in the Age of Kean*, p. 35; Vardac, *Stage to Screen*, pp. xxiv, 75; Michael Booth, *Victorian Spectacular Theatre 1850–1910* (London: Routledge, 1981), p. 40.

step. In 1885, T.F.T. Dyer's review of E.W. Godwin's *As You Like It*, performed in the woods of Coombe House, praised the production for its setting. Its primary virtue seems to have been that it went one better than being realistic – it was real:

> when the opportunity is afforded of replacing artificial scenery by a natural stage ... there can be no doubt as to the advantage of change, especially as the object of all histrionic art is to represent as faithfully as possible, even to the smallest detail, whatever subject may be introduced.[57]

The desire for performances given in the appropriate setting had significant financial consequences for the Victorian theatres as they strove to create sets copied in minute detail from the outside world, and occasionally took other productions, like Godwin's, out of the theatres into that world.

This was not, however, a practical solution. Real locations, such as a wood in which dizzy mortals could become lost and fall in love with each other, or a sea out of which Ferdinand could emerge with garments miraculously unspoiled, or a Veronese square in which Montagues and Capulets could bite their thumbs provocatively at each other, needed to be presented in ways which did not actually require an audience to huddle in damp woods, shiver on windy beaches or journey to Italy. Victorian theatre laboured under the considerable strain of its own exacting aspiration towards a realism which – theatre being ultimately about pretence, about *not* being the thing itself – it could never satisfy completely. There was, therefore, an ambitious striving towards a form of presentation which could accommodate a convincing realism without actually displacing its audience to Verona or a castle at Inverness or a Mediterranean beach. Such a form was not, as history was to show, an impossibility. It was, however, yet to be invented.

Proponents of elaborate staging argued that they only offered those things that Shakespeare would himself have employed, had he not been so cruelly fettered by the paucity of the material resources then available to him. Tree was one of the most prominent voices that seemed to have privileged access to Shakespeare's mind on this subject. In 1901, about the vision scene in *Henry VIII* he wrote:

> Surely no one reading the vision of Katharine of Aragon can come to any conclusion than that Shakespeare intended to leave as little to the imagination as possible, and to put upon the stage as gorgeous and complete a picture as the resources of the theatre could supply.[58]

[57] T. F. T. Dyer, 'Foresters at Home', *Art Journal* (October 1885), 301.
[58] Herbert Beerbohm Tree, 'The Living Shakespeare: a Defence of Modern Taste' (1901). Reproduced in *Thoughts and Afterthoughts*, 3rd edn. (London: Cassell, 1915), pp. 60–1.

From such assured and imaginative reconstructions of a Shakespeare who had yearned for the very theatrical resources that the Victorian theatre now enjoyed came scenically congested stages, enormous crowds of supers, exorbitant property bills and habitual delays to accommodate elaborate scene changes.[59]

Into the midst of the theatrical expense and scenic congestion came film with its portable cameras and its location shoots. Unsurprisingly, the use of 'real scenery' proved a popular attraction of the new medium. Silent Shakespeare films, while sometimes torn by a counter-impulse to claim theatrical descent by parading stage sets and backdrops, were also to delight in their capacity to show real woods, trees, fields and beaches. The Tyler Film Company, for example, advertised the 1912 Éclair film production of *The Tempest* in England (now lost) as 'presented in popular style, with magician feats, sumptuous staging, *fine natural scenery*, perfect acting ...' (my italics).[60] The 'fine natural scenery' was evidently considered a sure-fire selling point – and specifically, of course, a selling point *over theatre*. In the presentation of the real, film could offer what theatre could only effortfully, and expensively, gesture towards. In a review of the 1913 Frederick Warde film of *Richard III*, the *New York Times* was clear about the advantages of the screen in this respect:

As a picture of conditions as they existed in England ... it is far and away ahead of any possible stage presentation ... the scenic effects are incomparably better through the moving pictures than they ever are in real life.[61]

With the arrival of cinema, 'real' locations, rather than elaborate and expensive mock-ups, could finally be represented (if only in two dimensions) within a theatrical auditorium. If a kingdom for a stage was what was required, film was able to provide.

SHAKESPEARE PERFORMANCE AS FRAMED PICTURE

If film was driven by visual spectacle, and able to deliver the 'real', it was also a framed presentation from whose contained world an audience was decisively excluded. Here too the Victorian stage had inadvertently adumbrated the new medium's arrival by aspiring to present itself as a framed

[59] See Booth, *Victorian Spectacular Theatre*, p. 59.
[60] *KLW* (28 November 1912). Quoted in Ball, *Shakespeare on Silent Film*, p.151.
[61] *NYT* review. Quoted in the programme for *Richard III* as shown at the Olympic Theatre, Broadway of 107th Street, 22 March 1914. Held in the *Richard III* copyright file at LOC. (CIL 1299: 9 September 1913).

and distant work of art. From about 1830 onwards, theatrical productions started to court the effect of a still painting. Stage compositions of actors and scenery would be carefully arranged to mimic known works of art, often encapsulated in a stylised held tableau at the end of a scene – referred to in stage directions as 'pictures'.[62] The delight in such moments for the audience lay in recognising a work of art across contexts; it was the identified resemblance that evoked the applause. And this, in turn, flattered the audience for having recognised the allusion.

On a more material level, the very construction of the playing space on the Victorian stage itself offered a visual experience not unlike that of viewing a picture. As Russell Jackson writes:

> The play's action was 'realized' as fully as possible, framed behind a proscenium arch which corresponded to a picture-frame in its effect, and moved typically from one grand tableau to another. Within the picture was a world which the spectators could contemplate but with which they could not communicate directly. The Victorian theatre's conventions for serious drama excluded any open acknowledgement of the audience's presence by the characters.[63]

The introduction of gas lighting in theatres from 1815 onwards had illuminated the stage more effectively. This, in turn, encouraged the use of greater stage depth because actors could now be seen even when at a significant remove from the audience and the foot lamps. As the century progressed and the lighting of stage recesses became more effective, the action retreated upstage and the sense of going to the theatre in order to peer in at a world apart, a world behind the proscenium arch, was enhanced.[64]

The tendency to regard Shakespeare's plays as pictorial subjects on the stage as in the artist's studio was taken to its natural conclusion in 1880, when Squire Bancroft famously encased the Haymarket Theatre's proscenium in a two-foot wide gilt picture frame. Fitting a moulded frame around the three sides of the proscenium arch, and then completing the effect by adding a fourth side along the front edge of the stage, made explicit the residual function of the proscenium as an architecture of enclosure and symbolic separation.[65] Spectators and players were demonstrably divided, with a literal and symbolical barrier between them. But theatre was here stepping beyond the established character of its own medium.

---

[62] For examples of stage pictures, see Booth, *Victorian Spectacular Theatre*, pp. 9–10.

[63] Jackson, 'Actor-Managers and the Spectacular', in Jonathan Bate and Russell Jackson (eds.), *Shakespeare: An Illustrated Stage History* (Oxford University Press, 1996), pp. 112–27 (114).

[64] Kennedy, *Looking at Shakespeare*, p. 29.

[65] See Richard Southern, 'The Picture-Frame Proscenium of 1880', *Theatre Notebook* v.5, n.3 (1951), 59–61. Southern also challenges Bancroft's claim to originality in his fully framed proscenium arch.

Performance was being reified as a thing apart, holding its audience decisively outside a fully encasing frame. About Victorian theatre-going, Fitzgerald wrote, with characteristic despondency:

We go not so much to hear as to look. It is like a gigantic peep-show, and we pay the showman, and put our eyes to the glass and stare.[66]

Fitzgerald used 'peep-show' metaphorically to convey a sense of the detached voyeurism to which, in his opinion, the theatre-going experience had been reduced. From our perspective, however, it is tempting to interpret the framing of stage presentation, and, yet more obviously, Fitzgerald's peep-show simile, as part of the cumulative anticipation of *the* 'gigantic peep-show' that would appear in the form of early cinema by the turn of the century. Certainly, the film frame performs a similar function to a fully encasing proscenium: it encloses its subject while emitting seemingly contradictory signals about the relationship that an audience can adopt to that subject. That is, it decisively excludes the audience from its enclosed world of light and shadow while simultaneously inviting them into an imaginative absorption with the characters who inhabit its privileged space apart.

SHAKESPEARE AS NARRATIVE

In addition to the theatrical legacies, there was a non-theatrical factor that contributed to Victorian conceptions of Shakespeare upon which silent Shakespeare films were eventually to draw. In 1807 Charles and Mary Lamb had published *Tales from Shakespeare* in which they recast Shakespeare's plays as stories accessible to children. Lambs' *Tales* were extremely popular and occupied an important place in the education of many Victorians. Further simplified retellings followed, such as Mary Macleod's popular *The Shakespeare Story-book* (1902).[67] It is understandable, therefore, that, in the popular imagination, Shakespeare should frequently have existed as much as narrative as poetry. It is telling, for example, that for the descriptive programme of his 1904 stage production of *The Tempest*, Tree did not write his own plot synopsis, but simply quoted generously from Lamb. And the Lambs' *Romeo and Juliet* was reprinted in two instalments in the American *Motion Picture Classic* magazine of September and October 1916 to familiarise audiences with the story ahead of the Metro *Romeo and*

---

[66] Fitzgerald, *Principles of Comedy*, p.15.
[67] Mary Macleod, *The Shakespeare Story-book* (London: Wells, Gardner, Darton & Co., 1902).

Juliet release in late October.[68] It was, after all, in the Lambs' phrasing that many people knew what happened in Shakespeare's plays: the simplest and quickest way to communicate plot to an audience was, therefore, to cite their telling of it. This interest in narrative in due course offered fruitful ground for film adaptation. Although silent film could not convey the subtleties of Shakespearean language, it could tell a story, and its confidence in doing so developed fast once the initial fascination simply of seeing projected pictures move in lifelike ways was no longer sufficient to satisfy audiences. Since it was specifically as story that Shakespeare existed for sections of the community, film would in due course step into a role for which it was naturally suited, appropriating narratives and offering remade encounters with them in newly animated form.

*

In the course of the century preceding the arrival of film, the stage, and more particularly the Shakespearean stage (in both its legitimate and unruly manifestations), had already experimented with many of the component elements that were later to find unified expression in silent film. In many ways silent Shakespeare films constituted a natural continuation, and stylised exaggeration, of some of the directions in which stage productions had in any case been moving. Where theatre had been diluting its concentration on language – replacing large sections of poetry with interpolated dialogue-free sequences of pantomimic action – film dispensed with spoken language altogether. Where the minor theatres had experimented with dialogue scrolls to circumvent the speech ban, film was able to provide title cards to supplement action without needing to despatch characters to the wings to fetch them. Where variety theatres and vaudeville houses had traded in truncated, simplified versions of Shakespeare presented in skittish vein, film inherited and exaggerated that tradition. Where theatre had demonstrated a hunger for increasingly elaborate and visually arresting effects, film was able to offer them in new and frequently less laboured ways. Where theatre had desired realistic, or even real, settings, film was able to supply them effortlessly. Where theatre had pretended to be an artistically framed and distanced presentation, film was in its very nature exactly that. Where theatre generated a celebrity culture, film enshrined that celebrity in lasting form and disseminated

---

[68] *Motion Picture Classic*, v.3, n.1 (September 1916), 49–52 and v.3, n.2 (October 1916), 29–33. The Metro *Romeo and Juliet* is discussed in Chapter 6.

it to a mass market internationally. The new medium of film was thus able to pursue with ease many of the formal effects and socio-cultural functions that theatre had been straining to fulfil. Moreover, nineteenth-century Shakespearean lantern slide sequences had already taken strides towards normalising the idea of projecting onto a screen Shakespearean stories told in pictures with accompanying speech; and the prevalence of Shakespearean paintings, ballets and tales retold in simplified form by Lamb and others had already educated audiences in accepting versions of and allusions to Shakespeare in pictorial and narrative terms without chafing against the linguistic losses thereby incurred.

None of this, of course, made the emergence of silent Shakespeare films inevitable, and we should be wary of retrospectively imposing an artificial teleology upon the nineteenth century's engagements with Shakespeare. Nicholas Vardac seems to fall victim to such a pattern of mind when he maintains that: '[t]he motion picture finally made its appearance in response to the insistence of social pressure for a greater pictorial realism in the theatre'.[69] Such a claim needs qualification. The motion picture did not come into existence in response to the desire for a greater pictorial realism in the theatre. Once it existed, it did appropriate and release some of the accumulated tension that the intensity of this desire had created. Moreover, it proved popular in part because it could cater to some of the same realist aspirations that had been driving the commercial theatre. It was not, however, summoned into being by a single transferred aspiration from another medium. Rather, a series of real industrial, technological, economic and broader social forces came together in the work of several entrepreneurs (Eadweard Muybridge, Thomas Edison, William Kennedy-Laurie Dickson, the Lumière brothers, Robert W. Paul) to nudge the technologies and the commercial structures towards a marketable outcome.

By the 1890s, all the predispositions, precedents and aspirations may have been in place to provide an environment conducive to the emergence of Shakespearean film-making, but these things in themselves were not sufficient. The nascent film industry needed a clear incentive to appropriate Shakespearean material. In the next chapter, therefore, attention is turned to a set of commercial and cultural imperatives that drove the industry's production decisions in the early cinema period.

[69] Vardac, *Stage to Screen*, p. xxv.

CHAPTER 2

Biograph's pioneering film of King John (1899)

King John (BMBC: W. K.-L. Dickson and Walter Pfeffer Dando, 1899)

In December 1895, the Lumière brothers gave their pioneer screening of a series of projected one-minute films on their 'cinématographe' in a basement café in Paris. In February 1896, the English pioneer Robert W. Paul followed suit with the first exhibition of his broadly equivalent 'theatrograph' and the British film industry of the Victorian period was born.

A range of other optical amusements had come and gone in the preceding years. It was not, therefore, immediately obvious that the new medium's popularity would be sustainable once the initial intense burst of enthusiasm for its novelty value had subsided. However, systems of production, distribution and exhibition expanded at a dizzying rate over the next two years, requiring quick decisions and considerable business acumen from those hoping to exploit the appetite for moving pictures. By the late 1890s, the still embryonic British film industry was proving to have staying power. It was, however, in many respects a bruising business to be in. The industry was already being called to account about the respectability and suitability of the material it chose to shoot. The savvy and lucrative exploitation of a burgeoning new market in search of amusement and titillation, therefore, constantly needed to be balanced against the damage that could be done by allowing too much adverse publicity. At the very least, the film industry needed to secure the good will of those opinion-formers and law makers who had it in their power to close down the penny gaffs and shop-front theatres in which they touted their wares.

The bruising character of the business came into sharp focus over a British Mutoscope and Biograph Company (BMBC) 'giddy' (animated picture with a risqué subject) made in late 1898 or very early 1899.[1] The

---

[1] The BMBC was the daughter organisation of the American Mutoscope and Biograph Company (Biograph).

'giddy' in question was variously entitled *Studio Troubles* and *Wicked Willie* (in reference to the name of the boy who appeared in it) and in its short life it sparked a furore of significant proportions. *Studio Troubles* came to epitomise the corrupting salaciousness from which it was thought the industry urgently needed redeeming. Later in 1899, the same production company would release a short film taken from a stage production of Shakespeare's *King John*. This film was the pioneer in the context of a Shakespearean film history and its production, character, exhibition and reception are the subject of this chapter. First, however, I discuss two separate factors whose combined influences come together in the film: the BMBC's damaged reputation in 1899 and the 1899 Tree stage production of *King John*.

STUDIO TROUBLES ABOUT *STUDIO TROUBLES*

Although *Studio Troubles* itself has not survived, much about this controversial picture is recoverable from the paper trail left in its wake.[2] An outraged letter that appeared in *The Southport Visiter* (sic) (from a correspondent identified only as 'A. F.') on 5 January 1899 helpfully narrates the action of the lost picture:

An artist is seen seated in his studio at work upon a canvas, with a nude female model posed near by him. Upon hearing approaching footsteps, he rises and adjusts a folding screen so as to hide the model from [the] sight of anyone who may enter. No sooner has he done this than a lady and a boy about fifteen (evidently intended for her son) come into the studio. While the artist is engaged in conversation with the lady, the boy has discovered the nude model, and is tickling her. The mother and [the] artist discover this, and of course at once bring the boy away, the model throwing kisses whilst this is being done.[3]

Studio Troubles was controversial on two immediate levels. Most obviously it presented saucy action featuring an inflammatory combination of an adolescent boy and a naked female model. Secondly, in the person of the mother (shown in the single surviving still to be a redoubtable figure of telegraphed respectability, hat tied firmly under chin),[4] the film implicitly

---

[2] The film's details, including a reproduced still, are minutely well documented in Richard Brown and Barry Anthony, *A Victorian Film Enterprise: The History of the British Mutoscope and Biograph Company, 1897–1915* (Trowbridge: Flicks Books, 1999), pp. 102–7.

[3] The letter, headed 'Animated Photographs A Protest', is quoted in Brown and Anthony, *A Victorian Film Enterprise*, p. 102.

[4] The still was published in Jack Wiggins, 'Peepshow', *The Cine-Technician* v.4, n.17 (Sept.–Oct. 1938), 76.

parodied a prudish disapproval of saucy fun and of the insistence that an end should be put to it. For an animated picture to succeed in indulging a voyeuristic taste for erotic titillation while simultaneously parodying the opposition to it was clearly provocative. It is, perhaps, unsurprising that the very voices of respectability implicitly lampooned in the film, whose action in removing the boy swiftly from the scene brings the film to its hasty conclusion, were provoked into speaking out.

Once they did so, the film's off-screen fortunes soon rivalled its on-screen action for colour and controversy. The row started in January 1899 with a local campaign in Southport to suppress the film. As opposition gathered momentum across other British towns through the spring and summer of 1899, *Studio Troubles* started to assume a considerable symbolic weight, coming to represent everything that was degenerate and should be resisted in contemporary society. Newspapers were censorious, the clergy were worried and eventually concerns about it were even voiced in Parliament.[5] In August 1899, Samuel Smith, Liberal MP for Flintshire, followed up a parliamentary question on the subject with a letter to *The Times* in which he claimed that if such 'vicious and de-moralizing pictures' were not suppressed, 'we shall see a rapid decay of English morals to the level of Paris, with the same deadly results on the life of the nation.'[6] For the beleaguered British Mutoscope and Biograph Company, *Studio Troubles* was proving to be remarkably aptly named.

The nation evidently needed rescuing. Its standards, Smith had declared, were in danger of sinking to deplorable Parisian levels. Letters from MPs had appeared in *The Times* in early August 1899. The following month, the BMBC once again achieved some celebrity. This time, however, it was for a very different sort of production. Their scenes from Shakespeare's *King John* constituted the first film ever made on a Shakespearean subject. The nation's predicted decline was temporarily stopped in its tracks, and, as King John fends off the French at the last moment in Shakespeare's play, so too the fact of his filming seemed to push back the encroaching threat of Parisian ways from the nation's moral borders.

It would be wrong-headed to suggest that *King John* might have been made as a direct result of the bad publicity generated by *Studio Troubles*. The BMBC were churning out far too many other films in this period – several a week in the summer months – to justify drawing a direct causal link between any two. However, it was certainly hoped that the mere fact of a Shakespeare film would function as a sanitising and legitimising influence on the questionable reputation of the industry as a whole and of the BMBC in particular. Interviewed for *The Westminster Gazette* on 21 September 1899, William Thomas Smedley, the company's chairman, expressed his now much-quoted hope that 'such classical reproductions of Shakespeare on the mutoscope would remove the stigma, which, justly or unjustly, at present is apt to be cast on moving pictures'.[7] Having been himself thoroughly immersed in 'the stigma (...) apt to be cast on moving pictures' through the misfortunes of *Studio Troubles* in August 1899, Smedley must have particularly enjoyed having the chance to come off the defensive the following month and claim the moral high ground freshly armed, as he was, with the company's pioneering and culturally edifying film of Shakespeare's *King John*. As distractions from bad publicity went, aligning oneself with Shakespeare was undoubtedly a good one.

TREE'S STAGE PRODUCTION

If the industrial motivation for the BMBC to reach for Shakespeare came from bad publicity about scurrilous pictures, the direct theatrical spur for the project lay with Herbert Beerbohm Tree, the spectacular actor-manager of Her Majesty's Theatre, London. Tree's stage production of Shakespeare's *King John* opened at Her Majesty's on 20 September 1899 and ran, with a ten-day interruption in mid-December, until 6 January 1900. Tree's Shakespeare productions were known for their lavishness, visual splendour and the liberties they took with their source material. For *King John*, Tree cut and reordered the scenes from the Shakespeare text, so that the 'real story' of the piece could, as he explained in an accompanying pamphlet to the programme, be told 'in quick, coherent and logical manner'.[8] As with all his Shakespeare productions, *King John* proved extremely popular and in its three-month run was seen by more than 170,000 people.[9]

In 1895, Tree's production of *Trilby* (in which he played Svengali to enthusiastic reviews) had also been an enormous commercial and critical

---

[7] ' "King John" in the Mutoscope. A Glimpse at Mr. Tree for a Penny', *The Westminster Gazette* (21 September 1899), 4.

[8] Held in the Tree *King John* production file, Theatre Museum.

[9] Collick, *Shakespeare, Cinema and Society*, p. 35. The production's popularity can be gauged from a satirical engraving about it that appeared in *Punch* (18 October 1899). Reproduced in Judith Buchanan, *Shakespeare on Film* (Harlow: Longman-Pearson, 2005), p. 23.

success on the London stage. An 1896 American Biograph short entitled 'The Kissing Scene Between Trilby and Little Billee', drawing upon the same source material, was exhibited in London in 1897, its profile inevitably boosted by Tree's recent, acclaimed stage production. Given their interests in common, it seems likely that Tree would have been aware of the film, and, if so, it must have grated with his well-tuned commercial instincts that others were receiving enhanced publicity (and returns) partly on the back of his successful stage production. Having incidentally been beaten to it in 1897 in relation to *Trilby*, in 1899 he was no doubt anxious to stamp his own authority on the cinematic tie-in that could accompany his own stage production.[10] Tree's collaboration with the BMBC in 1899 made such a tie-in possible. And so it was with scenes from his stage production of *King John* that Shakespearean material and the film medium first joined forces to participate in that exchange of cultural authority – aesthetic validity for mass appeal – that has animated so many film-makers, and so many films, since.

THE *KING JOHN* FILM

The *King John* film was shot in the BMBC's open-air studio on the Embankment in early or mid September 1899, during the final rehearsal period for the stage production. Ball enlivened his account of these events by conjuring an imaginary 'casual itinerant' who happened upon the excitement down by the Embankment.[11] Though Ball's observer was merely a fictional device, as it happens a real 'casual itinerant', H. Chance Newton, *did* have a curious encounter with Tree and his company that September, and wrote it up for an article which appeared in *The Sketch* on 20 September 1899. Newton describes how he called upon Mr Tree at Her Majesty's to 'elicit the very latest particulars regarding the above named production' only to find:

that popular actor-manager and his numerous adherents just passing through a most trying ordeal. In other words, Mr. Tree and the whole strength of his company were being 'biographed' wholesale, retail and certainly for exportation ... It was truly a very quaint experience to see this extensive company of players, who will tonight (Wednesday) essay to present, in most realistic fashion, *King John* to the earnest playgoers of London, hurrying off clothed in more or less 'complete

---

[10] James Ellison makes this point in 'Beerbohm Tree's *King John* (1899): A *fin-de-siècle* Fragment and its Cultural Context', *Shakespeare* v.3, n.3 (December 2007), 293–314 (309).
[11] Ball, *Shakespeare on Silent Film*, p. 23.

steel' and in perfect make-up … to be snap-shotted, as it were, for pictures to be presently shown in all sorts of places in Europe, but especially at the Palace Theatre, London. For the going and coming and the to-ing and fro-ing of the latest King John and his vast retinue a new and picturesque awning had been prepared outside Her Majesty's Theatre, and several 'Black Marias' had been chartered for the carrying of the company, from the stalwart King (Mr. Tree) to the little fair-haired Prince Arthur (Master Charles Sefton) … There was also something of humour in the sight of [the actors] hurrying back with the dark-blue-armoured King John Tree at their head, newly escaped from the clutches (and the 'kodaks') of the Animated Photographers.[12]

Having gone to the theatre expecting to attend a final rehearsal, Newton found instead the company scurrying about town 'clothed in more or less "complete steel"', having already been, as he graphically expresses it, ' "biographed" wholesale' – an 'unlooked-for (…) expedition!', to quote Shakespeare's King Philip, if ever there was one (*King John* II.i.79).[13] The camera operatives for this 'biographing', from whose 'clutches' the company would in due course 'escape', were the film entrepreneur William Kennedy-Laurie Dickson (who had previously worked for Edison) and his associate Walter Pfeffer Dando. The *King John* film they shot 'wholesale, retail and certainly for exportation' lasted three or four minutes.

Although for many years this resulting film was thought lost, just under a minute's worth of it survives (now available on the BFI *Silent Shakespeare* DVD). The surviving scene depicts the death by poison of King John (Tree) in the gardens of Swinstead Abbey. The action is blocked on a flat plane, played vigorously and with relish upon a shallow stage, against a theatrical backdrop. Those present in the scene are, from left to right, the Earl of Salisbury (S. A. Cookson), Prince Henry (Dora Senior), King John (Tree) and the Earl of Pembroke (James Fisher White).[14] Shot square-on from a

---

[12] H. Chance Newton, 'About Town: "King John" at Her Majesty's', *The Sketch* (20 September 1899), 388. Newton (known by his pen name 'Carados' for his theatrical chat in *The Referee*) included a chapter of reminiscences about Tree ('Tales of Tree') in *Cues and Curtain Calls, Being the Theatrical Reminiscences of H. Chance Newton* (London: John Lane, 1927), pp. 112–54.

[13] The precise site of the BMBC's open-air London studio is not known, but it was somewhere at the rear of the Tivoli Theatre, probably on a roof-top garden (in imitation of the company's earlier New York studio), overlooking the Embankment Gardens. An open-air studio was desirable because natural lighting (enhanced by additional lamps) was more conducive to producing a visible film image on the cameras of the time than the artificial lighting available for indoor filming. For details about the Embankment studio, see Brown and Anthony, *A Victorian Film Enterprise*, p. 64.

[14] These credits do not precisely accord with those given on the BFI DVD. I have made my identifications aided by a collection of signed photographs held in a souvenir programme for the stage production (author's private collection) which detail costumes clearly. In *The Sketch* (27 September 1899), Salisbury is wrongly labelled as Falconbridge, and Pembroke as Salisbury. Salisbury (Cookson) is also incorrectly credited in the BFI DVD as Robert Bigot (F. M. Paget). (Identifying the characters was not made easier for *The Sketch* by the fact that White receives two separate credits in the theatre programme: as 'Mr. James Fisher' for the part of Pembroke and

static camera, a lightly bearded, poison-racked King John, seated in a garden chair and wearing a loose white robe, writhes in pain, earnestly mouths
inaudible words, grips his chair, frantically wipes his hand apparently to
rid himself of Prince Henry's solicitous attentions, shrinks from contact,
clutches at his chest, stretches out his arms in despair, appeals directly to the
camera and, with histrionic ceremony, collapses back on the point of death.

In technical and artistic terms, the BMBC's film of Tree's *King John* is
unremarkable. Nevertheless its claim to critical attention is assured by its
pioneering status. Later, in 1916, Tree was to say these very early Shakespeare
films could only possibly be meaningful to whose who were perfectly familiar
with the play, and could recall the lines appropriate to the action.[15] For those
who *were* thus well versed, the Shakespearean lines that would be brought to
mind by the *King John* surviving footage would be those from Act V, scene
vii in which John graphically describes the poison working on him:

KING JOHN: There is so hot a summer in my bosom,
                 That all my bowels crumble up to dust:
                 I am a scribbled form, drawn with a pen
                 Upon a parchment, and against this fire
                 Do I shrink up ...
                 ...
PRINCE HENRY: O, that there were some virtue in my tears
                 That might relieve you!
KING JOHN: The salt in them is hot.
                 Within me is a hell, and there the poison
                 Is, as a fiend, confined to tyrannize
                 On unreprievable, condemned blood.

                                                      (V.vii.30–33, 44–48)

The progress of this interchange is precisely detectable in the surviving
film, and Tree graphically expresses, through gesture, the various stages of
burning, shrinking up, urgent desire for cool relief and rejection of Prince
Henry's tears. At some points in the film, he is even discernible mouthing the words, in a practice that was later to become known as 'mugging'
(discussed in Chapter 5). It is not known precisely what adjustments, if
any, Tree may have made to his performance of King John as played for
the camera. This scene might, for example, have been both accelerated and
gesturally enhanced for the new medium. The performance we glimpse in

    as 'Mr. J. Fisher White' for the part of Falconbridge in a conventionalised attempt to play down
    doubling in the casting.)
[15] Helen Duey, 'Shakespeare in the Films: An Interview with Sir Herbert Beerbohm Tree', *Woman's
    Home Companion* (June 1916), 91.

the surviving film clip is certainly not one characterised by restraint. In response to the stage production, a reviewer for the *Illustrated London News* suggested Tree's performance was 'a little over emphatic in detail and at one point needlessly hysterical'.[16] Inevitably, not all agreed.[17] Nonetheless, since Tree was known for the expressiveness and uninhibited dimensions of his acting, it is possible that the extravagance of his screen performance might not drastically misrepresent the tenor of his stage performance.

We know that the surviving death scene was only part of the film of *King John* as originally made, since the Biograph Chairman referred to the *King John* film as 10,000 frames in length (a length which would equate to three or a maximum of four scenes) and *The Daily Chronicle* of 22 September 1899 referred to '*Three* scenes from Mr. Beerbohm Tree's production "King John"' (my emphasis). Furthermore, a series of four stills depicting three separate scenes from the film was published in *The Sketch* on 27 September 1899 (Figure 2.1).[18]

The first, labelled 'The Battlefield Near Angiers', shows King John urging Hubert to murder Arthur against a woodland backdrop. The second, 'The French King's Tent', shows Lady Constance (Julia Neilson) on her knees against a draped background. With arms raised to Heaven, she is emoting to the French King (William Mollison) and the Dauphin (Gerald Lawrence) about her son Arthur's imprisonment, in the presence of Pandulph (Louis Calvert).[19] The third is from the surviving death scene, set against a stage backcloth of the orchard of Swinstead Abbey and featuring the Earl of Salisbury (Cookson), Prince Henry (Senior), King John (Tree) and the Earl of Pembroke (White). The fourth, also set in the orchard, follows on immediately from its predecessor and depicts Pembroke, now in left of frame, standing behind the dead king and crowning Prince Henry; Salisbury, still in the far left of frame but now kneeling; and Falconbridge the Bastard (Lewis Waller) kneeling to the right of Salisbury, next to the newly crowned Prince Henry.[20] These four stills, therefore, represent three scenes.[21]

---

[16] 'The Playhouses', *ILN* (30 September 1899), 451.

[17] Mrs George Cran (an enthusiastic champion of Tree), for example, claimed King John was played 'with unusual simplicity and directness'. *Herbert Beerbohm Tree* (London: John Lane, The Bodley Head, 1907), p. 54.

[18] *The Sketch* (27 September 1899), 413. These stills were first brought to public attention by McKernan.

[19] This scene corresponds to III.iv in the play (II.i in Tree's reorganised version of it).

[20] Waller is identifiable from details of his costume – particularly the visible paw of a lion couchant on the front of his tunic. The paw is easier to see in the still deposited in the PRO (now The National Archives) for copyright purposes than in the still from *The Sketch*. I am grateful to Luke McKernan for showing me this still.

[21] The last two scenes – the death of King John and the crowning of Prince Henry – were probably filmed as separate shots (since reels would not then have been long enough to incorporate both),

Hubert   King John   Arthur
(Mr. McLeay).   (Mr. Tree).   (Master Sefton).
THE BATTLEFIELD NEAR ANGIERS (ACT I., SCENE 4).

King John instigates Robert de Burgh to murder young Arthur of Brittany, the rightful heir to the throne.

The Dauphin   Lady Constance   The French King   Pandulph
(Mr. Gerald Lawrence). (Miss Julia Neilson). (Mr. William Mollison). (Mr. Louis Calvert).
THE FRENCH KING'S TENT (ACT II., SCENE 1).

The Lady Constance, mother of Arthur, bearing that her boy is a prisoner in King John's hands, passionately denounces those who have deserted him.

Faulconbridge.

Faulconbridge   Prince Henry   King John.   Lord Salisbury
(Mr. Lewis Waller). (Miss Dora Senior).   (Mr. S.A. Cookson).
THE ORCHARD OF SWINSTEAD ABBEY (ACT III., SCENE 5).

The last moments of King John. The dying King is brought into the Orchard of Swinstead Abbey.

Lord Pembroke   Salisbury.   Prince Henry.   King John.
(Mr. James Fisher).
THE ORCHARD OF SWINSTEAD ABBEY (ACT III., SCENE 3).

The little Prince Henry (afterwards Henry III. is accepted by the Barons as John's successor.

Figure 2.1 Stills from the BMBC *King John* published in *The Sketch* (27 September, 1899), p. 413.
a. 'The Battlefield Near Angiers' b. 'The French King's Tent'
c. 'The Orchard of Swinstead Abbey' d. 'The Orchard of Swinstead Abbey'

EXHIBITION

Some or all of the three *King John* scenes shot were first exhibited at the Palace Theatre of Varieties on Shaftesbury Avenue, London on 20 September 1899. The *King John* film therefore shared its opening night with that of the stage production from which it derived.[22] Whereas at Her Majesty's, however, the play itself constituted a full evening's entertainment, at the Palace, the *King John* film was just one tiny contribution to a far more varied evening of entertainments. The Biograph programme itself was full of contrast, including not only the filmed *King John* and a shot of Queen Victoria in her carriage inspecting the Honorary Artillery Company but also a number of films with a clear sporting bias: the Henley regatta, polo at Hurlingham, an international hurdles race at the Queen's Club, the Cambridge May bumps (rowing races). It was, as ever, left to the accompanying musicians to make sense of the transitions of pace and tone between actualities and brief sketches, the light-hearted and the serious, that constituted the standard fare on cinematograph programmes of the period.[23] For all its variety, however, the Biograph programme was itself only part of what one got for one's ticket price at the Palace in Autumn 1899.[24] The projected Biographs were sandwiched between a varied line-up of live performers – comedians, 'Kokin' the Japanese juggler, acrobats, a violinist, a singer, 'Whirlwind dancers' and actors performing brief dramatic sketches.[25] The Palace, that is, lived out its music hall credentials with some verve.

Taking a little piece of Shakespeare from Her Majesty's to the Palace in commodified form was, on the face of it, offering high culture to the masses in easy to digest, bite-sized chunks. In practice, however, the masses that frequented the Palace were not as starkly removed from the audiences

but since the action followed on directly, and in the same location, they were considered part of the same scene. See Brown and Anthony, *A Victorian Film Enterprise*, p. 271.

[22] The Palace doors opened at 7.45 pm and the programme began at 7.50 pm. Curtain-up for the stage production was at 8 pm. The *King John* film, like other Biograph titles of its moment, was also released as a series of mutoscope cards. The habit of releasing titles in both formats ceased soon afterwards as the mutoscope market declined.

[23] Biograph films at the Palace were normally accompanied by Alfred Plumpton's small orchestra. Brown and Anthony, *A Victorian Film Enterprise*, p. 195.

[24] Ticket prices at the Palace in September 1899 ranged from a shilling for an amphitheatre seat to two and a half guineas for the best private box.

[25] The Palace Theatre of Varieties Programme (25 September 1899) (hereafter 'Palace Programme'). Held in the Palace Theatre Archive, Palace Theatre, London. (Catalogued under 'Theatre Programmes: American Biograph 1897–1902'.)

at Her Majesty's as might be supposed. As one commentator remarked in 1898:

The Palace is certainly the most refined music hall in London. It wears an air of respectability over it from end to end, and you could introduce it to your wife's relatives without the slightest hesitation. I don't think we have sat in an atmosphere so intensely respectable for months. Mr. Morton (the Palace's elderly manager) seems to have taken an ordinary music hall show and veneered it up carefully for family consumption, with the result that he has produced a Moral Aggregation of Attractions which are amusing without being low.[26]

Given the Palace's claims to respectability and Her Majesty's to popularity, the two venues might even have assumed some potential cross-over of clientele. That this was possible must have made the deal Tree made with the BMBC (to shoot scenes from his stage production) appeal to his commercial instincts as well as to his self-regard. It was not, that is, impossible that audiences at the Palace might have their appetite whetted sufficiently by the Biograph's short taster experience of *King John* to wish then to see the whole show live at Her Majesty's up the road. Ticket sales for the theatre production could in this way be directly boosted through the exhibition of the film.

Advertisements for the Palace programme that ran in *The Times* throughout October, November and December 1899 reveal that the *King John* film remained on the Biograph programme throughout the autumn and early winter of 1899. From 6 November onwards, top of the bill amongst the live performers was, additionally, Tree's own wife, Mrs Herbert Beerbohm Tree. Thus a member of the Palace audience in November 1899 would have been treated both to a live version of Mrs Beerbohm Tree in three dimensions and to a flickering cinematic memory of her husband in two. The succession of Trees on offer during the course of the evening must have served to remind spectators (as if they needed reminding) of the differences in status between a live performance and a celluloid record of such a thing. The difference had, of course, already been clearly and efficiently established by the film's title as listed on the Palace Theatre programme – 'A Scene – "King John," now playing at Her Majesty's Theatre.'[27] The players on the screen were, that is, pre-billed as concurrently being elsewhere – 'at

---

[26] 'Jingle' writing in *Pick-Me-Up* (23 April 1898). Quoted in Barry Anthony, *The Kinora: Motion Pictures for the Home, 1896–1914* (Hastings: The Projection Box, 1996), p. 7.

[27] 'A Scene' was evidently used as an imprecise marker meaning simply 'an excerpt' rather than literally meaning only one scene. Evidence for this comes from a reviewer's account that '*several* short scenes' from the stage production (my emphasis) were included in the Palace Programme. Ellison, 'Beerbohm Tree's *King John*', p. 310.

Her Majesty's Theatre' in fact. Part of the baffling magic of their cinematic presence was, therefore, as always, derived from the physical dislocation of their substantial selves from their projected image.

The film seems to have been given an immediate international promotion, and, as *The Daily News* reported on 19 September 1899, there were plans, even before it received its first London exhibition, that it should also be shown 'in Glasgow, New York, Paris, Berlin, Vienna, Milan, Brussels, Amsterdam, Ostend, and in other large cities where the Biograph is showing'.[28] The film was far too short to have been intended as a presentation whose meaning was autonomously self-contained: its purpose was not so much to *tell* a story as to allude to one and thus advertise where it *was* being told. As part of the era of the 'cinema of attractions', it captured visual delights from the world beyond the theatre and projected them as pleasure-giving spectacle within it.[29] Its value resided in the simple, transfixing magic of recorded movement, and in its referentiality: and in this case the extra-cinematic world referred to (a stage production) was itself a packaged presentation, itself a text.

A cautious article that appeared in *The Photographic News* on 22 September 1899 speculated that the film of *King John* as exhibited 'at the Palace Theatre and elsewhere ... is to be worked as a kind of advertisement for 'King John' [the stage production]. It will be interesting to note whether it has that effect or not.' In the article's closing lines, the writer's scepticism about this new marketing gimmick momentarily cedes to a prescient suggestion that the animated two-dimensional show might ultimately be so successful as to supplant the live production to which it was originally designed merely to allude: 'But if these pictures are made common, will the public be so anxious, as now, to witness the original performances? That remains to be seen.'[30]

It was in line with the Biograph's worldwide policy, and more specifically with W. K-L. Dickson's own practice from his time in the US, to offer local views to theatre managers in order to enhance the appeal of their bills for a specifically targeted local spectatorship. As exhibited at the Poli Wonderland Theater in New Haven in 1896, for example, the Biograph programme, at Dickson's instigation, had included some particularly

[28] *Daily News* (19 September 1899). Quoted in Kemp R. Niver (ed.), *Biograph Bulletins 1896–1908* (Los Angeles: Locare Research Group, 1971), p. 40.
[29] Gunning, 'The Cinema of Attractions', 63–70.
[30] *Photographic News* (22 September 1899). Quoted in Brown and Anthony, *A Victorian Film Enterprise*, pp. 63–4.

popular views of a Yale football team training session.[31] As exhibited at the Palace Theatre, London, scenes from Tree's theatre production at Her Majesty's must have fulfilled a similar pleasure-giving function to that which scenes of the Yale football team fulfilled as exhibited in New Haven. Both presented the topical and the familiar, generating a sense of pride by association in local, celebrated achievement. It is not known whose initial idea the *King John* film was. Tree and the BMBC might separately have had reason to approach each other to make common cause. Though history does not record who made the first move, as an idea for a subject to appeal to Londoners, it certainly smacks of Dickson's strategy employed elsewhere.

The *King John* scenes were also, however, exhibited abroad, through the extensive Biograph network. Beyond London, the film's principal interest would have been different. No longer could it have functioned as an advertisement for the stage production, or even, more simply, as an 'actuality' celebration of the local. Elsewhere it presumably played best as a rare record of and insight into a celebrated English actor and production. In the US, the film's altered function was appropriately reflected in an altered title: 'Beerbohm Tree, the Great English Actor taken with all the scenery and effects of the original production'.[32] The film was thus marketed as being able to offer all that the stage production had done. In fêting Tree, the film's title also claimed some of the accumulated theatrical glory of the actor and production for itself.

AFTER-LIFE

Until 1990, it seemed that no print of the *King John* film had survived its early exhibition round. In the apparent absence both of the film and of the helpful stills from *The Sketch* (yet to be unearthed), film historians could only speculate which scene or scenes the 1899 *King John* might actually have depicted. The fact of the location of the filming – on the London Embankment where the BMBC had its open-air studio – provided the prompt for Ball's speculation. Although Shakespeare does not include the Magna Carta in his *King John* play, Tree had interpolated into his stage production a stunning Magna Carta *tableau*, designed by Walter

[31] For details of the Poli Theater Biograph programmes of 1896, see Charles Musser, *The Emergence of Cinema: The American Screen to 1907* (NY: Simon Schuster and Prentice-Hall, 1990), pp. 155–6.
[32] See Brown and Anthony, *A Victorian Film Enterprise*, p. 228.

Hann[33] and held for a full minute, in order to plug what was perceived as the Shakespearean gap.[34] Photographs of this theatrical *coup* survive in all accounts of the production (in reviews, archive files and in the commemorative programme). Having seen some of these, Ball was persuaded that the film scene shot was likely to have been the granting of the Magna Carta, the choice of location by the Thames clearly indicating an attempt to reproduce Runnymede:

Evidently there was material here which could be caught by a motion picture camera. ... [T]he site on the Embankment gives the clue. Here was greenery and the Thames, an approximation to Runnymede. The tableau of the granting of the Magna Charta needed no words, only pantomime for its effect.[35]

The irony about the assumption underpinning Ball's speculation about the scene shot is that, as is now evident both from the surviving film clip and from the stills published in *The Sketch*, the actors' performance was given on a studio stage in front of a series of scenic backdrops (the battlefield at Angiers, the French King's tent, the orchard at Swinstead Abbey).[36] Although the BMBC's studio may have been by the Thames, therefore, and even surrounded by natural greenery plausibly evocative of Runnymede, the immediate real-world environment of the shoot upon

---

[33] Hann (sic) – not Hamm, as Ball gives it in *Shakespeare on Silent Film*, (p. 22).

[34] Two non-Shakespearean pictorial *tableaux* were interpolated into Tree's production, the other being of the Battle of Angiers. The Tree archive (University of Bristol Theatre Collection) includes the fly plot for Tree's *King John* which details both *tableaux*. Photographs of both are also included in the production's commemorative programme (author's private collection). Shakespeare's omission of the Magna Carta from the play was strategic: the charter did not, after all, accord easily with Elizabethan political philosophy which regarded it less as a triumph for popular liberty, than as a weak and regrettable concession made by the monarch. The nineteenth century, however, thought otherwise, and Tree was not the first to revive interest in it. In 1823, it was included in Henry Milner's play *Magna Charta; or, The Eventful Reign of King John* at London's Coburg Theatre. In 1852, Charles Kean reminded his audience (for Shakespeare's *King John*) that it was 'the instrument by which the liberty of England was founded'. Playbill (9 February 1852), Princess's Theatre file, Theatre Museum. For accounts of the political implications of the production, see B.A. Kachur, 'Shakespeare Politicized: Beerbohm Tree's *King John* and the Boer War', *Theatre History Studies* 12 (1992), 25–44; Ellison 'Beerbohm Tree's *King John*', 293–314.

[35] Ball, *Shakespeare on Silent Film*, pp. 22–3.

[36] Given the vastly altered dimensions of the playing space (a loss of width and depth from the stage at Her Majesty's), it is unlikely that backdrops imported from Her Majesty's would have fitted the Biograph stage. These backdrops were therefore probably painted specifically for the Biograph shoot, in close emulation of those in use at Her Majesty's. The fact that the same background woody scene from the first of *The Sketch*'s *King John* stills is visible as the scenic backdrop in a later publicity photograph of the Biograph indoor studio in Regent Street supports this theory: Biograph kept and reused these scenic cloths because they were Biograph property. Photograph reproduced in Brown and Anthony, *A Victorian Film Enterprise*, p. 134. I am grateful to Richard Brown for an interesting correspondence about this backcloth.

which Ball's initial speculation was based had no bearing on the subject of the film.

With typical conscientiousness, Ball continued to test his hypotheses even after his book was published. Having subsequently corresponded with an aging Charles Sefton (Tree's Prince Arthur),[37] he therefore learnt of the filming of the scene in which the boy Arthur plays unsuspectingly with John's crown on the grass behind a conspiratorial John and Hubert. (This, presumably, was the one filmed scene Sefton was able to remember seventy years on, since he had himself taken part in it.) On the basis of his discussion with Sefton, in autumn 1973 Ball then published a follow-up article in which he specifically revoked his earlier suggestion that a Magna Carta scene might have formed part of the *King John* film.[38]

This emended version did not, however, achieve the critical penetration of Ball's earlier speculation. Cruelly, it was the Runnymede speculation – which Ball himself had recanted – that claimed the imagination, received the exposure and so passed into critical circulation. And as it made its presence felt in the ensuing history of Shakespeare films, it acquired an increasing ring of authority as repeated by a succession of critics.[39]

It was Luke McKernan who was able to arrest the self-confirming literature on this subject and set the record straight by documenting how the surviving scene was discovered in an attic in the Netherlands and depicted not the non-Shakespearean granting of the Magna Carta (as received wisdom had it for more than twenty years), but rather – as one part of the longer film originally made – the wholly Shakespearean death of King John.[40]

I have dwelt upon the contested history of this early film clip of a Shakespeare theatre production because in its subsequent reputation,

---

[37] Sefton was his stage name, Lt. Col. C. C. S. O'Mahony his real name.

[38] Ball, 'Tree's *King John* Film: An Addendum', *SQ* v.24 (1973), 454–59. In replacing the supposed Magna Carta scene with the John/Hubert conspiracy scene, the revised account was correct as far as it went, but still incomplete.

[39] Manvell *Shakespeare and the Film*, p. 17; Richard Foulkes, *Shakespeare and the Victorian Stage* (Cambridge University Press, 1986), pp.12–13; Collick, *Shakespeare, Cinema and Society*, p. 36.

[40] Luke McKernan, 'Beerbohm Tree's *King John* rediscovered', *SB* v.11, n.1 (Winter 1993), 35–6; McKernan, 'Further News on Beerbohm Tree's *King John*', *SB* v.11, n.2 (Spring 1993), 49–50; McKernan, 'A Scene – *King John* – Now Playing at Her Majesty's Theatre', in Linda Fitzsimmons and Sarah Street (eds.), *Moving Performance: British Stage and Screen, 1890s–1920s* (Trowbridge: Flicks Books, 2000), pp. 56–68. Though the collection of films including *King John* was found in 1948, the films (as happens in busy archives) lay unviewed in the Nederlands Filmmuseum for years. It was not until 1990 that the films were finally transferred from their unperforated 70mm format onto 35mm copies. Once in preservation and access format, they were then catalogued and the significance of the 1899 footage was revealed. *King John* received its first public exhibition for ninety-five years at the National Film Theatre, London on 17 June 1994, and in its centenary year, 1999, was made commercially available by the BFI.

arising out of its assumed loss, it brings to the fore the question of how demonstrably 'Shakespearean' material has to be in order to be considered Shakespearean at all. For many years the scene shot was thought to be an interpolation by Tree and not from the Shakespeare play at all. Tree's granting of the Magna Carta *tableau* had elicited some hostile comment when played upon the stage.[41] By contrast, in its subsequent life as a (supposed) scene on film, its Shakespearean-ness was not questioned and the lost film retained unchallenged its status as the first Shakespeare film ever made. Its claim to be such was undeniably slim, for in itself, as imaginatively reconfigured in the critical literature, it would have merely depicted actors wordlessly acting out (or 'pictorialising') a moment conspicuously omitted from the Shakespeare play. Evidently, a greater degree of latitude from some sense of a source can be allowed in relation to a film than to a stage production before the valorising 'Shakespeare' label need be forfeit. The simple fact of having been transmediated, as we will see in relation to later films also, seems additionally to license other forms of divergence and adaptive experiment.

Tree narrowly pipped Sarah Bernhardt to the post in scooping the honours for the first Shakespearean film: her duel scene from *Hamlet* was released the following year.[42] Having acquired pioneer status in this respect, Tree went on to become a proselytising enthusiast for the possibilities the medium brought to Shakespeare. In 1905, he arranged to have the storm scene from his stage production of *The Tempest* shot on film; in 1911 he collaborated with William G. Barker in adapting his *Henry VIII* stage production for the cinema; and in 1916 he was himself wooed to go to Hollywood to star in a feature-length *Macbeth*.[43] These multiple forays into Shakespearean film-making, and the enhanced celebrity it brought for Tree, suggest that the 'very quaint experience' of being 'biographed' in 1899 was one that had proved appealing. After one day on set for *Macbeth*, his pleasure in the project, as reported to *Pictures and the Picturegoer*, is fully apparent:

It is quite wonderful ... how many things can be done in pictures for the Shakespeare tales that cannot be done on the stage ... [I]t is possible to illuminate

[41] See, for example, the review in *The Morning Leader* (21 September 1899), 4.
[42] See Ball, *Shakespeare on Silent Film*, pp. 23–8.
[43] On the storm scene, see Ball, *Shakespeare on Silent Film*, pp. 30–2; on *Henry VIII*, see Jon Burrows, *Legitimate Cinema: Theatre Stars in Silent British Films 1908–1918* (University of Exeter Press, 2003), pp. 62–76; on *Macbeth*, see Roberta E. Pearson and William Urrichio, '"Shrieking from Below the Grating": Sir Herbert Beerbohm Tree's *Macbeth* and his Critics', in A. J. Hoenselaars (ed.), *Reclamations of Shakespeare* (Amsterdam and Atlanta: Rodopi, 1994), pp. 249–71.

and accentuate many details so as to produce a marvellously truth-telling commentary on the text and at the same time heighten the dramatic values ...

... The pictorial possibilities grow, as one studies [the scenario] in the light of this strange new art, into something very beautiful and wonderful – not precisely a play in the Shakespearean sense, perhaps, but a dramatic narrative of great power.[44]

But to track Tree's career in this express fashion is to allow the account to race on. Films of 1916 belong to a different world – a world of commercially ambitious, technically proficient, interpretively attentive, market-canny, star-driven, multi-reel production: it is not until Chapter 6 that the present account will catch up with such material. In the next chapter, therefore, I make a more moderate leap – from 1899 to the years 1908 and 1909 and the charming, but as yet only inconsistently implemented, ways in which the movies began to turn Shakespearean 'pictorial possibilities', as Tree saw them, 'into something very beautiful and wonderful'.

[44] *Pictures and the Picturegoer* v.9, n.105 (19 February 1916), 483–4.

CHAPTER 3

Conflicted allegiances in Shakespeare films of the transitional era

The Tempest (Clarendon: Percy Stow, 1908)
Otello (FAI: Gerolamo Lo Savio, 1909)

LITERARY ADAPTATION IN THE FILM INDUSTRY'S PIONEERING AND TRANSITIONAL ERAS

The pioneering years of cinema (1895–*c.*1906) saw the release of a handful of films offering brief, cinematically animated, visual quotations from Shakespeare plays. This approach was in tune with the era's film-making impulses in relation to adaptation more generally, which typically privileged brief cameo references to literary works over a consistent narrative drive. For Shakespearean moving pictures, this 'peak moment' approach to a source, as Tom Gunning terms it,[1] formed part of an exhibitionist cinema initially more interested in showcasing its visual wares than in telling a shaped story. Literary subjects cinematically exhibited in this period, therefore, typically made little attempt at autonomous, internal coherence. Instead they were 'read' partly through the processes of recognition and supplementation, deriving their narrative character, in as much as they did so at all, from extra-cinematic data (principally knowledge of the source) imported by spectators into the moving picture theatre. This text-allusive/audience-collusive approach produced a clutch of short Shakespeare-related films in cinema's first decade, typically of two or three minutes screening time each.[2]

---

[1] Gunning, 'The Intertextuality of Early Cinema', p. 128.
[2] Brief films of a Shakespearean cast from the early days included: the 1899 *King John* film; Sarah Bernhardt's 1900 *Hamlet* duel scene featuring synchronised sound; Georges Méliès' 1901 largely unShakespearean *Le Diable et la Statue* featuring Venetian lovers Roméo and Juliette and a balcony scene; a 1902 *Burlesque on Romeo and Juliet*, distributed by Edison, with another Shakespeare-imitative balcony scene; Edison's 1905 *Seven Ages of Man* which, in the Lantern tradition, provided an illustrated gloss on Jacques' speech; the AMBC's 1905 Macbeth–Macduff fight scene (kilted warriors on a stage); Méliès' probably only mildly Shakespearean 1905 *Le Miroir de Venise (Une*

In the transitional era (*c.*1907–1913),[3] however, this cherry-picking approach to a literary or theatrical source ceded to more sustained engagements with story-telling and to a desire to tell autonomous narratives cinematically. A parallel, related, development in the film industry during this period was the increase in the length of films. One-reelers (constituting between ten and fifteen minutes screening time each)[4] were still being released in the years 1908–10 but as the industry's first decade was left behind, increasing numbers of two- and then three-reelers (of *c.*20–45 minutes screening time) also began to appear on the varied moving picture programmes of the period. This, of course, aided story-telling possibilities considerably by providing more space in which plot complexities and character detail could be explored.

In this period, the number of Shakespearean films being made also increased dramatically as companies competed for status, impelled by the industry's concerted drive to assert its reputable character and artistic aspirations. The year 1907, for example, saw just three focused Shakespearean releases: *Hamlet* and *Shakespeare Writing Julius Caesar* both by Méliès, and an *Othello* from Italian production company Cines. All three were a new departure for Shakespeare films in that they told a shaped and self-contained story. Released by the story-telling possibilities thereby opened up, and keen to optimise the appeal to culturally aspiring audiences, in 1908 there was then an explosive flurry of Shakespearean releases on both sides of the Atlantic. In America, this included Lubin's *Julius Caesar*, Kalem's *As You Like It*, Biograph's *The Taming of the Shrew* and, from Vitagraph, *Antony and Cleopatra*, *Julius Caesar*, *Macbeth*, *The Merchant of Venice*, *Othello*, *Richard III* and *Romeo and Juliet*. In Europe, the year's Shakespearean releases included two *Othello*s (a comic adaptation from Nordisk and a version experimentally including integrated sound from Pathé), two *Hamlet*s (Cines and Milano) and two *Romeo and Juliet*s (Cines

---

Mésadventure de Shylock); the 1905 storm scene from Tree's stage production of *The Tempest*; and Messter's 1907 *Death of Othello* from the Verdi opera (also with synchronised sound). For details, see Ball, *Shakespeare on Silent Film*, pp. 22–34.

[3] On the industry's developmental phases, see the Introduction, pp. 16–20.

[4] A debate about correct running speeds was current at the time. 'There is no hard and fast rule that can be laid down governing speed. It may, however, be said that 70 feet per minute is about as fast as a film should be run under any circumstances, with 45 as the limit the other way ... In general, the film should be run at the speed that will produce a minimum of flicker, combined with the lifelike, natural motion of the figures. It is as likely as not that the speed should be changed several times in different portions of the same film.' *MPW* (9 May 1908), 413. On variable film speeds, see also Brownlow, 'Silent Films – What Was the Right Speed?' in Thomas Elsaesser (ed.), *Early Cinema: Space, Frame, Narrative* (London: BFI, 1990), pp. 282–92.

and Gaumont). 1909 saw a further fifteen Shakespearean releases, and 1910 twenty-two more (some of which were parodies). 1908–10 remains, in fact, the three-year period in which more individual Shakespeare films were released than in any equivalent period before or since.[5]

As story-telling settled into being the film industry's dominant aim across this period, a strict adherence to theatrical forms of representation or to a courted theatrical-style attention in that story-telling also started to look conservative. Between 1908 and 1911, film-makers varied in how resolutely they strove to break free from theatrical-style shoots; by 1912, however, various conservative presentational forms were looking decidedly retrograde. The static, frontally placed camera directed at a shallow set and recording theatrical-style entrances and exits in and out of left and right of frame in scene-length, uninterrupted takes was certainly still a part, even a significant part, of the film industry's narrative repertoire. Nevertheless, its status had been relegated to being only the most unadventurous way to shoot a scene and tell a story. Cut-ins that gave privileging attention to a character or an event by varying the focal length (through mid-shots or close-ups), entrances and exits that alluded to off-screen playing space behind the camera (disrupting the theatrical notion of the fourth wall), cross-cut sequences that juxtaposed related planes of action, location-shooting, trick photography, moving cameras and even adjustments in focus made while shooting – all were being used in varying degrees to give new dynamism to the theatrical tradition.[6]

At the same time, however, film-makers – and, in particular, those adapting material from theatrical sources – were rarely single-minded in resisting the mise en scène and filming conventions of a more timid, 'theatrical' cinema. Certainly they explored cinema's distinctive story-telling possibilities, but they were often also caught by a counter-impulse to signal a sustained allegiance to the material's medium of derivation. The resulting adherence to a set of conventions more usually associated with theatre practice was more than an unthinkingly atavistic approach to medium-appropriate codes. Rather, in relation to Shakespeare moving pictures at least, it seems to have been partly strategic. Though many films of the early cinema period are less than entirely settled in their performance and cinematographic style, Shakespeare films seem systemically torn

---

[5] It will, however, be remembered that the films produced were only one- and two-reelers: the greatest number of titles does not, therefore, represent a vast amount of overall film footage.

[6] On the use of close-up and of racking focus in *The Musketeers of Pig Alley* (1912), for example, see Gunning, *D. W. Griffith and the Origins of American Narrative Film* (Urbana and Chicago: University of Illinois Press, 1991), p. 275.

in this respect as they attempt to reconcile their various vested interests. Grounding their own culturally equivocal status as 'films of plays' in the more secure standing of theatrical practice may, in Vachel Lindsay's terms of 1915, have been a regrettable and stultifying denial of cinema's own particular genius:[7] what it constituted, however, was an intuitive bid to be taken seriously by association with a medium that had already achieved that distinction.

The two case study films of this chapter are the English 1908 *Tempest* from the Clarendon Film Company and the 1909 Italian *Othello* from Film d'Arte Italiana (FAI).[8] Neither film has as yet received much critical attention. Ball had seen neither and so was only able to comment on them in relation to the secondary literature. The FAI *Othello*'s lack of commercial availability has debarred it from mainstream consideration. The 1908 *Tempest*, though commercially available, has proved difficult to assimilate into the obvious sub-categories of the unfolding account of Shakespeare in the silent era.[9] It does not emerge directly from a Tree stage production (as did the 1899 *King John*, the 1905 *Tempest* and the 1911 *Henry VIII*), nor does it star Tree (as the 1916 *Macbeth* did). It is not a studio product from one of the major American Shakespearean picture-makers (Vitagraph, Thanhouser, Biograph), nor from one of the major Italian Shakespearean producers (Cines, FAI). It is not a star vehicle (as, for example, were the 1900 Sarah Bernhardt duel scene from *Hamlet*, the various Frank Benson Shakespeare films for the Co-operative Cinematograph Company, the 1913 Forbes-Robertson *Hamlet*, the 1912 Frederick Warde *Richard III* and the 1922 Emil Jannings *Othello*), nor a memorably radical intervention into an interpretive understanding of the play (as the 1920 Asta Nielsen *Hamlet* was). It is not part of the rash of Shakespeare films made in 1916 to coincide with the Shakespeare tercentenary (unlike J. M. Barrie's *The Real Thing at Last*, Broadwest's *Merchant of Venice*, Thanhouser's *King Lear* and the three other American films discussed in Chapter 6), nor a daring update of or offshoot from a Shakespearean drama (like the 1911 Nordisk *Desdemona*, the 1911 Gaumont *Le Roi Lear au Village* (*A Village King Lear*) or the 1912 Vitagraph *Indian Romeo and Juliet*). Lacking an immediate broader context in which to sit, this film has proved difficult

[7] Lindsay, *The Art of the Moving Picture*, p. 194. Quoted in the Introduction, p. 6.
[8] *The Tempest* is available on the BFI's DVD *Silent Shakespeare*. The 1909 *Othello* may be viewed on a 35mm print (with Russian intertitles) in the LOC. Call no. FEA 4253.
[9] Though *The Tempest* has not attracted much attention, it has attracted some. See, for example, Neil Forsyth, 'Shakespeare and *Méliès*: Magic, Dream and the Supernatural', *Études Anglaises* v.55, n.2 (April/May/June 2002), 167–80.

to accommodate within accounts of the era's Shakespearean cinematic endeavours. Ball (having not seen it) declared that, were it not for a specific reference to its Shakespearean character in one of the cinema trade papers, given its production provenance with Clarendon, he 'would doubt if this *Tempest* were Shakespeare at all';[10] and, although Kenneth Rothwell opens his *History of Shakespeare on Screen* with a substantial and wide-ranging chapter on silent Shakespeare films, neither the Clarendon *Tempest* nor the FAI *Othello* receives a mention in that account.

Though both case study films defy easy categorising, I have selected them as representative films for this chapter for the clarity with which they display the inner tussles embedded to varying degrees in all such films from the period. By no means irrelevantly, they are both also a pleasure to view.

THE TEMPEST (CLARENDON: PERCY STOW, 1908)

As acutely as any play, at the turn of the twentieth century *The Tempest* was dividing opinion about what might constitute an appropriate style of staging. Herbert Beerbohm Tree, for example, had asserted that this play more than any other 'demanded the aids of modern stage-craft'.[11] George Bernard Shaw, on the other hand, approving the minimalist theatrical experiments of William Poel (who had attempted to channel the dissatisfaction with large-scale late Victorian spectacular theatricals into a constructive and stageable non-scenic alternative)[12] saw a direct correlation between 'multiplying the expenditure' and 'spoiling the illusion'. Shaw claimed that '[t]he poetry of *The Tempest* is so magical that it would make the scenery of a modern theatre ridiculous'.[13] Most suited to the effects available in a modern theatre, or most requiring the poetry to be allowed the space to breathe, to play upon the imagination unhampered by sets and scenery? There was considerable investment (emotional and material) on both sides of the debate. Since film potentially enabled dramatic presentation to be taken so much further in the direction of satisfying 'the external senses', the hitherto theatre-based debate about the value of suggestion versus demonstration proved far from irrelevant in relation to the new medium. Indeed, if anything, that discussion came into yet sharper

---

[10] Ball, *Shakespeare on Silent Film*, p. 77.
[11] Tree, 'A Personal Explanation', *The Tempest: As Arranged for the Stage by Herbert Beerbohm Tree* (London, 1904), p. v.
[12] On Elizabethanism, see Dennis Kennedy, *Looking at Shakespeare*, pp. 35–7.
[13] Reproduced in Edwin Wilson (ed.), *Shaw on Shakespeare* (London: Cassell, 1962), p. 183.

focus once the cinematograph started making its claims on Shakespearean material.

Clarendon's 1908 film of *The Tempest* was directed by Percy Stow and features a cast whose names have (thus far) proved unrecoverable.[14] In keeping with the standard approach to literary or dramatic adaptation of its moment, the film attempts to shoe-horn a simplified version of the action of *The Tempest* (minus the Stephano–Trinculo comic subplot and the attempted murder of Alonso) into the standard one-reel format. This inevitably creates a fairly breathless romp through the action of the play.

Cinematic impulses

Unlike many other British silent Shakespeare films, the Clarendon *Tempest* was not a cinematic memorialising of a celebrated stage production. Rather, it was conceived as a stand-alone moving picture, without direct inspiration from a prior stage production. Its cinematic autonomy is felt in many aspects of the film's construction and presentation.

In pursuit of the sort of narrative clarity deliverable in the new medium, for example, the film reorders the action of the Shakespeare play. It plucks events from the reported narrative of the drama's pre-history (the arrival on the island, the release of Ariel from the tree, Caliban's advances on Miranda) and absorbs them into the chronologically organised unfolding of the action. This re-sequencing effectively neutralises the disruptive power of the drama's past to inflect and infect the present. Whereas, therefore, the processes and effects of *remembering* are one of the driving impetuses of the Shakespeare play, the film removes the disquieting function of memory from the drama by ironing out the play's eloquent a-chronologies, so ensuring that wrongs done at one point in time occupy the same presentational status as wrongs remembered, avenged and/or forgiven at another. In constructing a single linear narrative from the play, the drama

---

[14] I am grateful to Fred Lake for his generous attempts to help me identify this cast from his own extensive collection of early star cards. The film was listed in *The Bioscope* weekly throughout December 1908, and in the first edition of January 1909, as one of the 'Latest Productions' and as 780 feet long. See, for example, *The Bioscope* (10 December 1908), 14. The BFI National Archive print from which the DVD version derives is 708 feet long, lacking the first section in which Prospero and Miranda are cast out to sea in a boat and a small amount of footage from the end also. Luke McKernan and Olwen Terris, *Walking Shadows: Shakespeare in the National Film and Television Archive* (London: BFI, 1994), list the print as lasting eight minutes if run at sound speed (24 fps). Run at a more usual silent era speed of 16 fps, however, this would constitute about eleven minutes viewing time. The film seems to have generated little interest on release and was not reviewed in any of the popular trade papers.

thereby loses the force generated by the intermittent eruption of powerful and disturbing recollections from the past into the flux of present-time action. The compensation for this loss is narrative clarity.

The tendency to eliminate a-chronologies from the dramatic account was commonly adhered to in the early cinema period as films re-spun their source material into a sequence that would aid intelligibility even as presented in largely languageless form. Nevertheless, there were exceptions to this. The ghost of Hamlet senior in the Italian Cines production of *Hamlet* (*Amleto*) in 1908, for example, leads young Hamlet into a rocky cavern where he stands in depth of field and, with the dramatic panache of a theatrical impresario, shows his son a brief but inflammatory film, projected onto the back wall, featuring the historical account of his own self sleeping in the orchard and then falling poisoned from his garden bench.[15] It was a narrative strategy Cines was to employ again in their 1909 *Macbeth* (*Macbett*) in which Dante Capelli as Macbeth tells Lady Macbeth (Maria Caserini Gasperini) of the witches' appearance and prophecy with the help of a superimposed vision that appears above his head as he 'speaks'.[16] And in the 1912 *Tempest* film (now lost) released by French company Éclair, at Prospero's behest Ariel summons an enacted vision (back projection?) of Milan in his island cave to illustrate to Miranda his tale about Antonio's treachery.[17] Given Cines' willingness to experiment with retrospective explanations by means of a vision and Éclair's adventurously daring choice to retain the Shakespearean explanatory flashback in their dramatisation of *The Tempest*, Clarendon's decision to narrate the play's back story sequentially in order to avoid potentially confusing temporal disruptions cannot, therefore, be taken as inevitable,

---

[15] The Cines *Amleto*, directed by Caserini, was reissued in 1910. I have seen two German-language prints of it: at the BFI National Archive and Il Centro Sperimentale di Cinematographia (CSC) in Rome. Neither print is complete but considerably more footage survives in the print on deposit in Rome. The BFI National Archive print is short but sensibly sequenced. The material history of the Rome print is unknown, but the film has evidently been spliced together at some point from individual surviving filmstrips to keep these together. This has been done with some cursory attempt to put related sections together, but apparently without knowledge of the characters or the narrative sequence of the original drama that might help make sense of it. The result is an almost unintelligible pickle of a film, in which scenes tumble into each other dramatically out of sequence, some individual scenes have been disruptively split up and other scenes are duplicated and appear twice. As currently sequenced, therefore, Ophelia oscillates between extravagant madness and demure sanity, a title card introducing Ophelia's madness serves as preface to Gertrude's closet scene, and the play-within-the play's strategic re-enactment of the murder of Hamlet Senior precedes the ghost's inventive filmic account of that death. Restoring this film to a version that corresponds to its original release will form the basis of a future project.

[16] *Macbeth* (Cines: dir. Mario Caserini, 1909). Russian titles on surviving print. 16mm, 2 reels. Copies held at the Folger (call number MP 24 (1–2)) and at the LOC (call number FEA 4251–4252).

[17] The action of the film is reported in *The Bioscope* 17 (21 November 1912), 319.

even for a transition era film. It was, however, in tune with Clarendon's clarifying agenda throughout.

Having no known ancestry in a stage production[18] also freed the film from the tug towards a textual authenticity experienced by some other Shakespeare films. The intertitles for *The Tempest* carry no direct Shakespearean quotations; instead they simply provide an economical introduction to the succeeding scene in each case.[19] As further testimony to its confident assumption of its own medium identity, it breezily embraces a scenic realism of the sort the theatrical purists had feared would spoil the illusionism of this drama. Thus the film's visual delights include a real cleft tree from which Ariel can be magically liberated by Prospero, a real sea in which the Neapolitan ship can seem to founder, a real beach upon which Ferdinand can be washed up, and real logs for him to shift in a real woodland setting.

It is not, however, only in its capacity to reorganise the action and present real locations that the 1908 *Tempest* enjoys its own visual reach and cinematic potential: its special effects too suggest a gleeful engagement with the technical resources on offer. The film's most cinematically flamboyant sequence is, appropriately, the tempest and shipwreck scene (which occurs half way through the film in the story's re-chronologised form). In a decisive rejection of theatrical practice with its necessarily horizontal (and earth-bound) axis of attention, the camera is here pointed directly at the sky to record a foreboding, if impressionistic, view of dark scudding storm clouds. Wonderfully savage vertical and jagged lacerations made directly onto the film print energise the stormy skies with sudden, suggestive streaks of lightning. And then the sequence moves from this atmospheric evocation of a storm to a shot of Prospero and Miranda inside Prospero's cell and looking out through a jagged rocky scenery arch to a shot of real sea beyond. On this sea a (toy) boat is seen to break up and sink (Figure 3.1a). The cave entrance creates a mini proscenium-style arch through which Prospero and Miranda, like playgoers themselves, can watch the unfolding action of the vessel's sinking. It is an intricately layered shot that uses effects of superimposition created by rewinding the film in the camera and re-shooting over the same strip of film with areas of

[18] Luke McKernan rightly reminds me that we cannot be sure there was not a local amateur production whose influence may be felt in this film. If there *is* a stage production in the film's prehistory, however, the film leaves it well behind in an extremely committed piece of cinematic adaptation that rethinks the play from first principles and entirely without Shakespearean language.

[19] In the film's surviving form, some intertitles serve to baffle rather than clarify. 'Friends once more', for example, makes no sense without some prior explanation about the earlier impediments to friendship. The footage missing from the start of the film may have supplied the necessary background to explain this.

the lens masked. The sequence as a whole, from lightning scratches on the print to the superimposed view of a real sea, creates a bravura impression of technical wizardry (by 1908 already a signature of Percy Stow's innovative film-making).[20] Rather than merely functioning as an advertisement for its own entrepreneurial accomplishment, however, this sequence serves as the perfect backdrop and dramatic showcase for the fairytale-esque Miranda's increasingly distressed and decorously frantic pleading for the lives of those she believes she is seeing shipwrecked. Distraught at the capsizing of the ship and the attendant loss of life, she appeals across the mouth of the cave from frame right to her father in frame left. Like a study in perspective, the sinking ship is seen at the vanishing point in centre distance, with Miranda and Prospero flanking the cave mouth in the foreground as visually symmetrical but emotionally starkly differentiated counter-weights to that central drama. The effect is almost that of a balanced triptych, in which the imagery of the side panels is angled towards and comments upon the scene on the centre panel. Performance is not, therefore, eclipsed by the cinematography here, but intensified through it. And the illusionism of the shot construction maps onto the play's action at this point in ways expressive of the comparably illusory character of the shipwreck that Shakespeare's Prospero choreographs.

The film's medium-savvy delight at its capacity to evoke a magical and dramatic kingdom through its own simple but effective arsenal of special effects is further in evidence in its use of stop motion shooting. This effect is most interestingly and purposefully deployed in the teasing chase game that Ariel (a child actress) plays with Ferdinand. As part of this game, she repeatedly appears and disappears in order alternately to entice and frustrate him as he attempts to catch her. Innovatively, the film shows us the scene from two contrasting perspectives – first from that of Ferdinand, for whom Ariel is tantalisingly alternately visible and invisible, and then from that of Miranda, for whom Ariel is consistently invisible. For Miranda, Ferdinand's intermittent lunging gestures, apparently at thin air, inevitably look inexplicable and idiotic. By subjectivising the spectator's perspective differently in alignment with two successive characters and revealing the action as a decisively different event depending on whose perspective is being privileged, the film courts a relativist view of the island's action. Events in this territory, it seems, do not have a definitive character, only a variety of ways of being understood by different perceivers. As an adaptation of a Shakespeare play that presents an island territory made and

---

[20] See McKernan's 'Percy Stow' entry in Richard Abel (ed.), *Encyclopedia of Early Cinema* (Abingdon and NY: Routledge, 2005), p. 613.

Figure 3.1 Cinematic experimentation and conservatism in
The Tempest (Clarendon, 1908)

a. Cinematic adventurousness: a multi-layered shot shows Miranda pleading for
the lives of those on board the storm-tossed ship.

b. Cinematic timidity: a cluttered frame composition squanders the potential
impact of each piece of action shown.

unmade according to the subjective impressions of individual perceivers (being, for example, green to one and tawny to another, lush to one and meagrely resourced to another), challenging the objective given-ness of any event through such perspective-varying means seems attuned both to the spirit of its source and the medium of its adaptation.

Cinematic resistances

For all its joyous, atmospheric, and interpretively purposeful uses of location shooting, effects of superimposition, varying of perspective, scratches made directly onto the print and stop-motion shooting, the surviving Clarendon *Tempest* was clearly divided in its allegiances, and in its will to assert its distinction from theatre. Thus it oscillates between enjoying its cinematic fluidity on the one hand and, for scenes such as the arrival on the island or the conjuring of the tempest, scuttling back more nervously into theatrical sets, stagy landscapes, and unadventurous theatrical blocking of entrances and exits on the other. In fact, every expression of cinematic adventurousness in this film is counter-balanced by one of cinematic suppression. Other shots, for example, refuse to select aspects of the scene for the audience's focused attention from an array of possibilities and, as a consequence, emerge over-cluttered and confusingly blocked. One notable instance is the reunion scene near the end, which attempts to combine multiple sites of action within one panoptic shot. It includes a series of first-time encounters (between Miranda and the king's party) and reunions (including that between Ferdinand and Alonso) and it also simultaneously features Ariel's request for freedom and consequent release by Prospero in far right of the frame (Figure 3.1b). Given the quantities of action simultaneously absorbed into the one shot, the potential impact of any one aspect of it is lost amidst the over-busy frame organisation of baffled and gladdened courtiers, wondering lovers, paternalistic magus and skipping Ariel. It is, in fact, a scene crying out for a change of shot and an adjusted camera placement. Such an intervention could have excluded some of the other distracting character clutter that detracts from the potential dramatic charge of, for example, Miranda's first encounter with a brave new world or Ariel's first taste of freedom. Other films of a similar date were able to be more nimble than this in experimenting with more selective frame composition and an occasional cut-in to a tighter focal length to pick out a key detail of a scene. The retained theatrical-style breadth of attention and also the theatrical style of the blocking of the characters' movements in this film once again signals, if in stereotypically short-hand form, the film's reluctance to break away from a medium, theatre, whose established legacy it feels timidly obliged to court in order to legitimise its own presumption in adapting Shakespeare for film at all.

The theatrical debt to Tree

While some scenes in the Clarendon *Tempest*, such as the tempest-conjuring scene, gesture towards theatrical conventions of a general character, other aspects of the production engage with specific theatrical legacies. In particular, Stow's film remembers in several particulars Tree's vision as made manifest in his lavish stage production of *The Tempest* at His Majesty's Theatre London in the 1904/05 season. The missing-link-evocative appearance of Stow's Caliban in ragged skins, with unkempt, shaggy hair and an apish gait, for example, invokes Tree's Caliban as iconised in Buchel's illustrations. Whereas most giants of the nineteenth-century stage – including Macready, Kean and Ryder – had chosen to play Prospero, Tree had taken the innovative step of casting himself as Caliban.[21] In this simple act, he nudged the play's balance of imaginative sympathy in a direction that would in due course decisively influence readings of the play as a whole. Tree chose to draw out the pathos and humanity in his Caliban in ways that partially redeemed him from the ungrateful savage monster that had been his dominant identity as played on the nineteenth-century stage.[22] Nevertheless, his rendering of Caliban was still colourfully stomach-turning at intervals, including for his memorable first entrance in which he appeared munching on raw fish. The entrance of Stow's Caliban – in which he lollops across a field, squats down centre-foreground, uproots grass and eats it – therefore works as a tame imitation of Tree's post-Darwinian wild man and infamous, fish-eating entrance. The identity of the little girl who plays Ariel in the 1908 film is, like that of the other players, not known. Nevertheless, the fact that the part is played by a young tripsy girl who takes on the role with hoppity-skippity energy was also fully in accord not only with Tree's production (in which Ariel was played by his own daughter Viola Tree), but with casting trends of the previous fifty years more generally. This was a period which loved balletic, delicate,

---

[21] On Tree's 'extraordinary [casting] choice', see Cran, *Herbert Beerbohm Tree*, p. 67.
[22] A.T. Vaughan and V.M. Vaughan, *Shakespeare's Caliban: A Cultural History* (Cambridge University Press, 1991), pp. 180–88.

feminine spirits just as the age more generally fetishised fairies in artistic and theatrical representation.[23]

Most significantly, however, the final scene of the Stow film is a pale, and slightly rushed, imitation of Tree's carefully constructed final *tableau* from the stage production. The closing 'picture' of Tree's production was given the following tonally charged stage direction in the published script:

> *we see the ship sailing away, carrying* Prospero *and the lovers, and all their train.* Caliban *creeps from his cave, and watches the departing ship bearing away the freight of humanity which for a brief spell has gladdened and saddened his island home, and taught him to "seek for grace." For the last time* Ariel *appears, singing the song of the bee. Taking flight at the words "Merrily, merrily shall I live now," the voice of the sprite rises higher and higher until it is merged into the note of the lark –* Ariel *is now free as a bird.* Caliban *listens for the last time to the sweet air, then turns sadly in the direction of the departing ship. The play is ended. As the curtain rises again, the ship is seen on the horizon,* Caliban *stretching out his arms towards it in mute despair. The night falls, and* Caliban *is left on the lonely rock. He is a King once more.*[24]

In this inventive and designedly pathos-laden *tableau*, Tree allowed himself, as Caliban, the poignancy of observing not one but two significant departures from his world – first that of Prospero (played by William Haviland) and companions setting sail for home without him, followed by that of Ariel (Viola Tree) delightedly taking possession of her newly acquired freedom. Caliban's pained sadness at achieving the thing he had apparently desired – to be 'King once more' – is thereby rendered the more acute by the comparison with Ariel's unconflicted and joyous assumption of the liberty that had also been her articulated yearning.

The broader implications of this final *tableau* in which Caliban holds out his arms 'in mute despair' at being left alone on the island are difficult to miss: the ill-educated native craves the company, civilising influence and, presumably, continued subjugation of the European colonisers. He is retrospectively grateful for the expansion and enrichment of his world and, therefore, cannot help but rue the departure of those who had bestowed these things upon him. An empire, it transpires here, is a welcome good for the colonised as well as an asset for the colonials. The final tableau which serves as the affecting post-curtain coda to the production leaves night falling on the despairing Caliban '*left on the lonely rock ... a King once more*'. The

---

[23] See Russell Jackson 'Shakespeare's Fairies in Victorian Criticism and Performance', in Jane Martineau (ed.), *Victorian Fairy Painting* (London: Royal Academy of Arts, 1997), pp. 38–45. The casting tendency continued. Thanhouser's 1911 film *Ariel* was also, for example, played by a 'young lady', commended for her 'sprightliness and mystery' in performance. *MPW* v.10, n.10 (9 December 1911), 818.

[24] Tree, *The Tempest: As Arranged for the Stage by Herbert Beerbohm Tree* (1904), Tree's III.iii. p. 63.

bleakness associated with having his kingdom thus restored to him unsparingly invests his earlier aspiration to be his 'own king' with a hollow ring.

The Stow film, made three years after Tree's stage production closed, was indebted to it in several respects, as its closing moment illustrates. The ornate bow of the Neapolitan ship heaves into view to moor between the set's back flats so that the courtiers may embark for home. As they troop along the shallow set to board, Caliban approaches them with raised arms of supplication, as in the Tree production, pleading to be taken too. He appeals first to Antonio, who brutally casts him aside. In response, he cowers briefly on a rock, but, desperate to be taken along, then resummons his energy to approach Miranda, who runs to her father, and Ferdinand, who ignores him and boards the boat. With irresistible finality, Prospero himself seals Caliban's exclusion from the party, raising his hand imperiously and ordering him to step back from the landing stage. Two mariners on the boat repeat the gesture, and a third shrinks away fearfully to avoid contact both with Caliban's alterity and, perhaps, with his frighteningly telegraphed neediness. The final surviving shot has Caliban, back to camera, arms outstretched ('in mute despair'?), clearly grateful, despite himself, for having been exposed to civilising influences. It seems likely that in the footage missing from the end of this film (see note 14 above) the boat would have departed leaving Caliban's lonely dejection on the shore the exclusive focus of the film's pathos-laden final image.

Caliban's evident regret at losing the civilised courtiers from his island world in the Clarendon film is reminiscent of the Tree production both in the specific choreography of its action and in the imperialist value system implied by such action. In both stage production and film, Caliban is still the native privileged by his proximity to the benefits of empire and so reduced to a sense of desolation at being deprived of its representatives. He is not yet, therefore, the eloquent emblem of the wrongly dispossessed native that he was often to become later in the twentieth century. In this early twentieth-century moment, still buoyed as it was by imperial confidence, the play is yet to undergo the decisive interpretive adjustment that would subsequently require the re-reading of the play, and in particular of the Prospero–Caliban relationship, in the light of a retrospective colonial angst.

In drawing on the choreography of the final scene of the Tree production, and on the political assumptions underlying it, the 1908 *Tempest* is a film that not only alludes to some general theatrical conventions but aligns itself with the detail, reputation and implicit value system of one stage production in particular. In comparison with the Tree production, however, the film's imitative aspects lack both poise and clarity as delivered in rather hasty and muddled fashion on screen. Once invoked, therefore, the comparison leaves the film looking anaemic in comparison with Tree's uncompromising commitment to the interpretive project: in emulating stage business from Tree, the Clarendon film is, therefore, far from its best.

A divided film

What are we to make of the Clarendon film's oscillating stylistic practices? As a moving picture that allows itself to explode out of studio space into real locations and innovative film-making with a charm and an energy that can enchant, the fact that it also succumbs intermittently to a contrary pull back into studio space, conspicuously stagy sets, timid, cluttered blocking and the pallid imitation of celebrated theatrical moments feels like a self-conscious move not to stray too far, or too consistently, from a theatrical heritage respectfully considered appropriate for a Shakespeare production. Playing host, as the film does, to a series of internal encounters between presentational styles of a more or less realistic, and more or less theatrical character, the film constitutes a site on which the contemporary extra-cinematic debates about how to 'perform' the delicacy of *The Tempest* play out forcibly. Indeed, it is a film that parades its divergent allegiances and internal antagonisms, alternating between stagy, shallow sets on the one hand and pleasingly expansive shore-line and woodland location shoots on the other; between clear references to a stage illusionism on the one hand and cinematic effects of superimposition, the varying of perspectives and direct interference with the film print on the other. Little wonder, perhaps, that the Clarendon *Tempest* has proved too thorny a candidate for inclusion in a selectively narratable history of silent Shakespearean film-making: interesting as they are, its internal abrasions problematise the placement of this film as a contributor to a broader history.

The Clarendon *Tempest* is, however, far from alone amongst Shakespeare films of the period in entertaining such stylistic divisions. The 1909 FAI *Othello*, for example, offers a differently modulated illustration of a similarly equivocal approach to medium allegiance.

OTHELLO (FAI: GEROLAMO LO SAVIO, 1909)

Film d'Arte Italiana was founded in Rome in 1909 by Charles Pathé as the Italian equivalent to the Film d'Art commercial movement he had previously founded in France.[25] FAI shared Film d'Art's aim of nurturing a

---

[25] See Georges Sadoul, *Le Cinéma Devient un Art: L'Avant-Guerre* (Paris: Denoël, 1951), vol. III, p. 95.

literary and theatrical cinema as a prestigious alternative to a more populist film industry agenda and the Italian company benefited from having
its international distribution handled by the well-established, international
operation of its parent company Pathé. The plundering of works by classical authors was, as ever, a useful tool in fulfilling FAI's charter to distance
itself from more down-market moving picture entertainments. In its early
years of production, FAI even made films of some Verdi operas (including a 1909 *Il Trovatore* and a 1911 *Aida*). But it was Shakespeare who featured most frequently in FAI's campaign to produce a cinematic record of
weighty cultural landmarks. Between 1909 and 1911, therefore, FAI made

Figure 3.2 'All the masterworks, the best authors, the biggest
stars at the cinematograph.' A 1910 Pathé advertising poster
depicting the faces of authors whose work the cinematograph
had appropriated. The cameos include Hugo, Goethe,
Dumas, Dante, Dickens and Schakespeare (sic).
Author's private collection.

four Shakespeare films: *Otello* (*Othello*, 1909), *Re Lear* (*King Lear*, 1910), *Il Mercante di Venezia* (*The Merchant of Venice*, 1910) and *Giulietta e Romeo* (*Romeo and Juliet*, 1911).

Alongside FAI's desire to tap a prestigious artistic heritage for the film industry was an analogue commitment to showcasing beautiful Italian locations. For some Shakespearean plays, of course, Italian locations could carry a particularly apposite charge. In 1908, international audiences had seen an American Vitagraph film of *Othello* that had placed a gondola on wheels in a wooden trough against painted backdrops in an attempt to simulate the impression of canals.[26] In comparison with such clunking efforts to evoke Venice, the Italian film industry had reason to feel smug in the quality and realism of the sights it could offer. So it was that in 1909 FAI despatched cast and crew to Venice to shoot the opening scenes of their *Othello* against the narratively 'authentic' (and scenically beautiful) backdrop of the Grand Canal, the Doge's Palace and Venetian back waterways. Understandably, they sought to extract maximum cultural and financial returns from the investment. The distributor's advertisement in *MPW* for the American release of the FAI *Othello*, for example, boasted:

Many have seen *Othello* but never in such a setting. The stage has been noted for wonders of scenic fidelity but to enact this marvelous tragedy along the very waters and in the very gardens and palaces as the immortal Shakespeare pictures them with his versatile pen is to add an interest which could not be obtained in any other way ... Imposing facades, beautiful colonnades, magnificent porticos and marvelously wrought gateways, all come under our view as we pass from one scene to another of this great play.[27]

It was a marketing strategy that evidently worked since FAI repeated the formula for their subsequent 1910 *Merchant of Venice* (shot in Venice) and 1911 *Romeo and Juliet* (shot in Verona), both of which starred the beguiling emerging film star Francesca Bertini. Moreover, other Italian production companies followed suit. In 1914, for example, the Turin-based Ambrosio company produced an exquisitely beautiful four-reel *Othello*[28] which, for the film's marketing 'puff' in the New World, promoted its Old World charm, and, specifically, its Venetian beauties:

MADE AT VENICE, ITALY! That's a Tremendous Advertising Feature in itself! ... The waterways of Historic Venice with its tales ten centuries old, of Passionate Loves and Fierce Vendettas ... In *Othello*, we offer a real masterpiece.

---

[26] See Plate 8, Ball, *Shakespeare on Silent Film*, p. 96.
[27] *MPW* (19 March 1910). Quoted in Ball, *Shakespeare on Silent Film*, p. 104.
[28] A print is held at the Cineteca in Bologna. The film's scene of Desdemona's murder is discussed in Chapter 7, p. 248.

It is the first of Shakespeare's stories filmed in its proper environment, as the Master would have wished.[29]

Whether or not filming Italian stories in Italy might have been precisely what 'the Master would have wished', it certainly, in Ambrosio's case, made for an attractive film. FAI's earlier one-reel *Othello* (1909), however, undermines Ambrosio's claim to be the first Shakespeare film shot 'in its proper environment'.

The FAI *Othello* was directed by the company's leading director Gerolamo Lo Savio, who also directed *The Merchant of Venice* and *King Lear*.[30] Othello was played by Ferruccio Garavaglia (who later played Tebaldo/Tybalt in the 1911 FAI *Romeo and Juliet*), Iago by Cesare Dondini (illicitly moonlighting on this production in breach of contract with The Dramatic Company of Rome),[31] Desdemona by Vittoria Lepanto (a leading player for FAI and favourite of Lo Savio),[32] Cassio by Alberto Nepoti (in his first film role) and Roderigo by Ugo Falena (who also helped direct). As FAI's first Shakespeare film and one of its very early films on any subject, its release acted as the company's calling card and marker of its cultural aspirations. Its Venetian exteriors therefore constituted a stylish introduction both to this particular film and to the company's work in general.

Exteriors in Venice

Filming the Venetian sections of the film predominantly as exteriors optimises the architectural beauties of the location shoot. In particular, Lo Savio's innovative decision to mount the camera on the back of a gondola for an edited three-shot sequence generates a pleasing sense of fluidity, space and

---

[29] *MPW* v.21, n.1 (4 July 1914), 21.

[30] Like most Pathé and FAI titles, *Othello* was initially released in a colour-stencilled print. The surviving safety viewing copy at the LOC, however, has neither colour-tinting nor colour-stencilling. The aniline dyes originally used to colour *Othello* may have faded beyond the point at which they are now discernible in the surviving nitrate print (held at the Russian State Film Archive – Gosfilmofond). The dyes used in both mono-tinting and in colour-stencilling were highly mutable and prone to fade – even under exposure to the intense electric arc tones of the projector on its early exhibition run. The preservation of colour has not always been the archiving priority it has more recently become: many colour-stencilled or mono-tinted films from the era therefore only now survive in black and white form. The boldness of the colour palette in other surviving FAI prints – including the two FAI Shakespearean films included on the BFI *Silent Shakespeare* DVD – adds significantly to the aesthetic intensity of the piece in each case, so its absence in this case is to be lamented. FAI's mechanisms for colour stencilling are described in Daan Hertogs and Nico de Klerk (eds.), *Disorderly Order: Colours in Silent Film* (Amsterdam: Stichting Nederlands Filmmuseum, 1996), pp. 12–13.

[31] Dondini was sued and required to pay a 10,000 franc fine plus 7,000 francs expenses and to return all money he had been advanced as salary for The Dramatic Company of Rome. *KLW* (28 January 1909), 759.

[32] She also played Carmen (1909), Rigoletto's daughter (1910) and Lucrezia Borgia (1910) for Lo Savio.

movement. The camera sits behind Iago (Dondini) and Roderigo (Falena) as they are taxied around the Venetian waterways. The gondolier, back to camera, maintains a steady rhythmic stroke from the front of the boat. Iago and Roderigo are seen in profile, leaning in conspiratorially towards each other, as they plot how to expose Othello's marriage to Brabantio. Meanwhile the background scenery is both gorgeous and ever changing as the boat moves. A single shot would have been sufficient to convey the idea of conspiracy and travel towards Brabantio's house. The edited sequence of three shots is an unusually otiose indulgence for a one-reeler: Lo Savio was evidently pleased with the effects achieved. In the first gondola shot, we glide across the Grand Canal towards St. Mark's Square while, within the boat, the frantic whispering and hearty conspiratorial laughter act as counterpoint to the measured punting. The second shot shows a narrow back waterway, while the boat passes under an attractive footbridge (Figure 3.3a). And the third shot shows the gondola approaching the landing stage at Brabantio's house (Figure 3.3b). As it turns in to moor, Brabantio's heavily bearded

Figure 3.3 Exteriors in Venice. *Othello* (FAI, 1909).

3.3a. The gondola-mounted camera creates a touristic travelling shot of the Venetian waterways. Here, Othello and Desdemona are just visible in top right of frame, standing on the bridge under which the gondola will pass.

3.3b. Iago and Roderigo in the gondola and Brabantio on the
mooring stage communicate and respond to the news of Desdemona's flight
through a series of parallel gestures.
All stills from the 1909 *Othello* are reproduced courtesy of the Motion Picture,
Broadcasting and Recorded Sound Division of the LOC.

figure comes into view on the landing stage, gesticulating fiercely in reciprocal engagement with the conspirators' gesticulations to him: the parallelism
of their gestures is suggestive of an elaborately mimed aria performed by
antiphonal, mimetic figures in heightened pantomime.

This three-shot sequence is bursting with visual energy. Like a brief touristic guide, it evokes the bustle and the romance of the city, introducing a
world in which people must necessarily encounter each other constantly,
but which also provides occluded spaces and shadows in which plots may
be hatched, secrets generated and confidences disclosed. Its fluidity further suggests a world in which things change and which might well favour
those who know how to read and direct its changes, rather than those
who remain fixed in one place. And, additionally, it testifies to a production whose aesthetic aspirations to invest energy and interest in its frame
composition are matched by its thoughtfulness about how to make visual
effect engage purposefully with the interpretive agenda.

Each of the gondola-mounted shots absorbs two planes of action simultaneously: the developing relationship within the boat as Iago draws an unsuspecting Roderigo into his confidence on the one hand and the changing architecture and social scenery of the Venetian settings they pass on the other. In the second shot of the sequence, for example, there is a natural, dynamic play of light and shade in the visuals as the boat, and those in it, are plunged into the bridge's shadow and then emerge back into sunlight beyond. And the specifics of the setting simultaneously move the plot forward with impressive economy. For upon the bridge, below which the gondola-mounted camera passes, Othello and Desdemona are clearly, if briefly, seen, arms entwined, stopping to admire the scenery during an evening stroll.[33] The inflammatory sight of the amorous couple on the bridge fuels Iago's efforts to gain Roderigo's trust and purse. And so the world viewed in passing does more than provide the scenic backdrop to the action within the boat: instead, it actively intensifies it.

Later film productions of *Othello* (including, in the silent era, the Ambrosio film of 1914 and the Buchowetzi/Jannings German version of 1922) make a feature of putting either Othello or Desdemona in a gondola as an economical means of denoting 'Venice'. But bestowing a constantly shifting, water-borne perspective not upon either of these but upon Iago – as Lo Savio does here – makes for a more organic alliance of character and setting, and one intuitively appreciable within the symbolic visual scheme of a silent film. Pitting Iago's capacity for movement and variable perspective directly against Othello's and Desdemona's comparative stasis and fixed perspective from their observed stationary position on dry land plays evocatively to a reading of the character of all three: Iago as an improvisatory opportunist; Othello as a man and soldier who depends on psychological certainty and singularity of vision; Desdemona as a character dangerously wedded to an *idée fixe* even as circumstances are transformed around her.

Interiors in Cyprus

Inevitably, however, the film does not sustain this level of visual innovation and ambition for its duration. Like the Clarendon *Tempest* of the previous year, it also exemplifies the pattern for literary pictures of the

[33] During the filming of this scene, Garavaglia (playing Othello) and A. Pezzaglia (the Doge) threw a local Venetian youth into the canal for taking saucy liberties with Vittoria Lepanto (Desdemona) while she was leaning over the bridge. Ball, *Shakespeare on Silent Film*, p. 103.

transitional era by finding itself torn between modes of presentation. However, whereas in *The Tempest* the codes almost alternate, but without any obvious rationale in relation to setting or action, in the FAI *Othello* the distribution of theatrically bounded moments on the one hand and of more adventurously cinematographic ones on the other adheres to a more systematic pattern. Thus, in *Othello*, it is almost always the exteriors that are shot with a greater degree of imaginative freedom and the interiors that are stagily blocked and statically shot in long takes. And since the film's exteriors are largely Venetian (optimising the use of stunning real-world backdrops in the first half of the film) whereas its scenes in Cyprus are more frequently interiors, shot in patently cramped studio space, the film's presentational differences correspond exactly to its geographical division, creating a film whose overall structure seems schematic.

Soon after the arrival in Cyprus, therefore, the film effectively tames its urge to roam, reeling itself back into studio space and restricting itself to a fixed camera position (Figures 3.4a and b). Furthermore, the action is now consistently blocked – by artificial compulsion at times – to occupy the centre foreground of the shot in clear range of the fixed camera position. This deployment often generates visibly effortful character movements to and from the designated optimum position on set. Other compromises in terms of the fluency or plausibility of the action are sometimes required in order to facilitate these movements.

The performance implications of this come into focus by charting the progress of an individual scene – in this case, a long pivotal scene from the second half of the film. Desdemona (Lepanto) sits reading in a public room in the Cyprus camp, her chair positioned in the foreground of the shot, just right of centre (leaving a clear line of vision through to the Pathé rooster sign propped incongruously against the back wall of the set).[34] Emilia ushers in Cassio (Nepoti) from the set door 'upstage' (theatrical terms are apposite here) frame left. Cassio enters, comes downstage and crosses to Desdemona's chair where, through gesture and title card, he enlists her help in his suit to the general. As he then exits through the same door through which he entered, Othello and Iago enter through another door in the back of the set. The simultaneous timing of this allows Iago to catch sight of Cassio's disappearing figure and check his stride to express surprise and suspicion. Othello (Garavaglia) and Iago come downstage and Desdemona and Othello have an impassioned exchange about Cassio in

[34] For a discussion of the strategically visible placement of company logos in films of this period, see Chapter 4.

the centre foreground, observed by Iago from frame left. In this exchange, Garavaglia gives an effective if exaggerated performance that alternates between impassioned suspicion of Desdemona on the one hand and relenting tenderness towards her on the other. The vehement and concessionary gestures and expressions that he employs in this performance correspond closely to those stipulated for just such emotions in the pantomimic acting manuals referred to by European silent film actors of the period (discussed in Chapter 5). During this volatile exchange, Desdemona gets out her handkerchief to soothe Othello's brow. Apparently reconciled to her, Othello embraces her and they exit together through the door in the back of the set, Desdemona accidentally dropping her handkerchief in centre foreground on the way. Once they have gone, Iago steps eagerly into the centre foreground to retrieve the dropped handkerchief but, before playing with his find with predictably wicked glee, he returns swiftly to his position in left of frame. Iago's resulting peripheral position both clears the line of sight to the Pathé rooster once again, and, importantly, leaves space for Othello to re-occupy the centre-ground, as on his subsequent re-entry he then does. Character placement on the set is, therefore, partly anticipatory, strategically leaving room for the next entrant each time and thereby trailing a heavy-handed sense of expectation. As Othello re-enters (into the space strategically left for him), Iago tucks away the handkerchief. A physical tussle then ensues between general and ensign in the privileged centre-ground as Othello commissions Iago, via both gesture and intertitle, now to *prove* Desdemona unfaithful rather than to leave him thus on the rack.

This blow-by-blow account of the action illustrates the duration of the shot: all the stage business described, from Desdemona reading onwards, takes place in one unbroken take, shot from a viewing position imitative of a mid-stalls seat in a standard proscenium arch theatre. As the camera points at the small set awaiting the next character or piece of business, characters line up in sequence to come downstage and perform, in effect, on the apron – optimally placed for full visibility and clarity of focus. It is, therefore, a scene whose cinematography, blocking and lack of editing telegraph a sense of compressed and, in this cinematic context, stultifyingly inhibited theatricality. Such artificial composition was roundly mocked when discernible in later productions. In an uncharacteristically damning piece on the 1916 Thanhouser *King Lear*, for example, one trade reviewer wrote:

Time after time, we found characters walking or running down to the foreground, to stop and then go ahead in the approved "movie" manner of many years ago. This should be very funny to those of your fans who know something

Figure 3.4 Interiors in Cyprus. *Othello* (FAI, 1909).

a. Characters are stagily arranged on a cluttered set before a static,
frontally placed camera. In this shot Othello strikes Desdemona in the
centre of the foreground.

b. Desdemona is smothered on the bed in right of shot but slips to the floor
to die in the foreground. Emilia holds the cross above the prie-dieu
as she testifies passionately to Desdemona's innocence. Both Emilia's open-stance
gesture of uninhibited protestation and Othello's defensive gesture of consternation
and guilty horror adhere to the pantomimic acting codes discussed in Chapter 5.
Stills courtesy of the LOC.

of Shakespeare and realize what can be done in the films by intelligent handling.
... The director evidently had little knowledge of the value of different camera
angles, and the photography was all straight, hard, old-school camera work.[35]

In mixing more fluid camera work and imaginative blocking with this
'straight, hard, old-school' approach, *Othello*, like *The Tempest* before it, is
a film of uneven daring and quality. In *Othello*, the beautiful, cinematically fluid Venetian world on the one hand is pitted against the theatrical,
cramped, studio-shot, Cypriot world on the other. There were clearly practical reasons for this, Venice being available to FAI for a location shoot
in the way that a fortified Cypriot camp was not. Unlike in *The Tempest*,
however, the very unevenness of this film incidentally works with the
emotional trajectory of the play. Thus it is that Othello's free and open
countenance and Desdemona's right to speak find apt visual expression in
the spacious Venetian settings of the first section of the film, showcasing
to good advantage the central characters and their own liberality towards
the world while also giving Iago the opportunistic run of the city. By
contrast, the sets in Cyprus start containing Othello and Desdemona in
apparently ever more circumscribed spaces, while Iago's malignant glee in
such spaces seems equally apt as he watches the incremental imprisonment
of Othello. As walls and other characters now contain and cramp the central characters, the emotional pitch is correspondingly intensified. While,
therefore, I do not impute interpretive design to the film's schematised
division in presentational codes, nonetheless, in making the playing space,
and related psychological space, feel tightly claustrophobic for the play's
Cyprus action, the studio sets of the second half of the film do incidentally
contribute in interpretively apposite ways to the insularity and emotional
intensity of this dramatic world.

The presentation of Othello

Part of the theatrical 'feel' of the Cyprus scenes derives from the film's
refusal to break up a static long-shot with any alteration in perspective or
focal length. This is particularly noticeable in the encavement scene (in
which Iago prods Cassio to discuss his mistress Bianca that the secretly
observing Othello may think they are discussing Desdemona). The careful stage-management of this scene seems to crave the camera's selective highlighting of its internal detail. However, no such concessionary

---

[35] 'Ordinary Movie Presentation of Famous Old Tragedy', *Wid's Film Daily* v.2, n.50 (14 December
1916), 1170. Other reviews, and my own viewing of this film, suggest this is a harsh judgement.

moves are made: Iago talks to Cassio in the foreground with Othello semi-hidden in depth of field, all seen in an unedited long-shot filmed from the standard, frontally placed camera. Othello, surreptitiously beckoned by Iago to creep forward from his hiding position to verify the identity of the handkerchief, is visibly horrified by what he sees and retreats again.

At the heart of the dramatic action of this Shakespearean scene is a piece of business readable in two radically different ways: the objective version in which Cassio is laughing about 'the bauble' Bianca, and the subjective one, as strategically arranged for Othello's eyes, in which Cassio is apparently bragging about Desdemona's sexual attachment to him. Film is potentially well placed to play these crucially conflicting versions against each other. Reading this film scene with post-transitional era eyes makes us long for the camera to be turned around and for our perspective to be occasionally aligned with Othello's, as it habitually is in subsequent film adaptations. This would allow us to see the 'guilty' Cassio that Othello sees (rather than just the frivolous one that we see), and the incriminating handkerchief of Othello's perception (rather than just the planted prop in a giddy tale of amorous skirmishing that we see). But the scene has no cut-in, no change of perspective, no variation in focal length, no edit, no playing with audience alignment and, therefore, no enlisting of audience sympathy. And, given the lack of words, without sympathetic variation in perspective, it is impossible for Othello to appear other than an over-trusting dupe, undignified in his willingness to collude in the scene as Iago's pawn, and simple-minded in failing to identify the trickery being practised on him, the crudeness of which the unsparing cinematography makes plain to us.

A largely wordless production of *Othello* may perhaps always be inclined to render Othello vulnerable to ridicule. While all Shakespearean characters are reduced in dimensions by being rendered silently, Othello is subject to a more pronounced adjustment in scale than might be the case for Oberon, Antony or even Lear. Shakespeare's Othello is, after all, a raconteur, a rhetorician, a story-teller. He woos Desdemona with lyrically spun tales of romantic adventure and then, with breath-taking and ironic panache, announces himself '[r]ude' in his speech (I.iii.81) as a way of exposing and disposing of the prejudiced assumptions of his Venetian audience. From this early moment in the drama, in which he unmans his detractors by wielding language with deadly modesty, the play then charts the systematic unstitching of Othello's language to a point where he is bereft of both syntax and obvious sense: 'Pish! Noses, ears, and lips! Is't possible? Confess? Handkerchief? O devil!' (IV.i.40–2). From this point of linguistic collapse, however, his power to narrate, to self-console and to propagandise through language is then restored to him with a vengeance by the end of the play and he choreographs his own death as the highly performative climax to a colourfully narrated tale he himself tells about a Venetian killing a Turk. Indeed, he scripts his death directly into the story in a suicide act which symbolically allows him to be both protagonist and antagonist from his own tale (the Turk who must be slain *and* the Venetian who must slay him). Language and action, narration and enactment become one in the exquisite choreography of Othello's suicide. His death – ('I took by th' throat the circumcisèd dog/ And smote him thus' *He stabs himself* (V.ii.364–5)) – both illustrates and concludes his own story. Othello's narration of infamy and of death transmutes seamlessly into the exculpation of his own infamy and the performance of his own death, so emblematising the intimacy of the verbal and the visual in this drama. Without that encounter between the verbal and the visual, between stories told and their enactment, Othello himself loses much of his dramatic force.

In November 1909, *The Bioscope* expressed a similar nervousness about what silent cinema might do to Shakespeare in general and to Othello in particular. In the context of a broader appreciation for the FAI production's scenic effects (for which 'there can be nothing but praise'), the reviewer expressed scepticism about how possible it was to render the weight of a tragic character through mime alone:

it seems to be rather a hopeless business to attempt a wordless Shakespearian performance. It is very hard for any actor to invest Othello with due dignity and greatness by gesture alone ... M. Garavaglia ... acts well, and laughter is as far from us as tears; but he is simply unconvincing, and an unconvincing Othello is as bad as a gentlemanly Hamlet.[36]

Garavaglia may have been unconvincing from *The Bioscope*'s point of view partly because he was restricted to 'gesture alone'. It was, however, also true that the production did not intervene through camera angle, point of view, or editing – as it might have done, even at this transitional moment – to lend plausibility or sympathetic engagement to Othello's passions and anxieties. Viewed consistently from a dispassionate distance, and frequently in a shared frame with Iago, Othello cannot but tend towards a cartooned caricature of an idiotic gull.

---

[36] *Bioscope* (11 November 1909), 45.

Exhibition and reception

For the film's US release, the *MPW*, by contrast, found the acting 'competent' and a welcome aid in appreciating the play's 'marvelous delineation of human passion'. However, this review concentrated mostly on the picture's ambassadorial role in helping Shakespeare reach a wider audience and promote the cultural and educational value of the film industry in general:

That a play of this character can be so satisfactorily placed on the screen is strong evidence of the progress of the motion picture. It enables thousands to become acquainted with great dramatic masterpieces who would never otherwise know about them ... To have successfully performed that is sufficient honor; and it has been done in this instance.[37]

The praise for the film itself is self-evidently tame. It is credited with performing its cultural and institutional work successfully rather than lauded for its individual merits as a beautiful picture, technical or performance triumph or imaginative interpretation of the Shakespearean drama. Nevertheless, many critical things could have been said that were not. On neither side of the Atlantic, for example, did the stilted blocking of the interiors, the conspicuously cramped nature of the sets or the length and unvarying character of the Cyprus scenes provoke comment (though reviewers did criticise similar traits in other films). In fact, the trade papers typically chose to concentrate on the film's noteworthy scenic beauties. In doing so, they were, in effect, reviewing only half the film. For American reviewers in 1909, there was, perhaps, still too much cultural capital invested in the perceived classiness of both Italian cinema and Shakespearean cinema for a film that represented a liaison of the two to be subjected to serious criticism. It may, therefore, be partly for reasons of critical habit and contemporary cinematic modishness that the film escaped its critical deserts.

This respectful tendency in review serves as a reminder that Shakespeare films from non-anglophone countries were at no disadvantage on the international market in this period. Indeed before *c.*1913 when the American domestic market started aggressively favouring its own films and its own stars specifically to the detriment of foreign imports, Shakespeare films from continental Europe may even have had certain market advantages in terms of perceived artistic quality, authenticity and style. The films could

[37] *MPW* v.6, n.17 (30 April 1910), 690.

compete on more or less even terms because the international distribution of films in different language prints lacked the complexities of dubbing and sub-titling subsequently to be ushered in by the sound era. Indeed, throughout the silent era, the international distribution of film prints was relatively simple. Since import duties were paid per foot of film, films would typically be exported without their title cards. Upon arrival in the country of exhibition, a new set of translated title cards in the appropriate language would be shot and spliced in, in accordance with the instructions about content and placement sent by the production company or distributor.[38] Calculating the total footage without intertitles in this way could represent a considerable saving. Slight discrepancies in prints might occasionally result – and some are still detectable where prints in more than one language survive[39] – but the ease of multi-lingual distribution encouraged not only Italian, but also French, German and Danish film-makers to produce Shakespearean material in this period for an international market.

Ease of distribution did not of itself, however, guarantee an easy viewing experience at the point of exhibition. Indeed, despite all that filmed Shakespeare, unlike theatrical Shakespeare, seemed to promise in terms of a predetermined, predictably stable performance not dependent on actorly whim or audience mood for its particular character on any given night, film shows in this period nevertheless remained alarmingly vulnerable to individual waywardness. An anecdote recounted in the July 1911 issue of *MPW*, for example, reveals that, for all the worthy hopes expressed that the FAI *Othello* (still being shown in the US in 1911) would prove educative, the actual encounter that some picture-goers had with it in their local moving picture house was far from educative – or, at least, not educative in quite the ways intended. Taking as his title 'The Murder of Othello', the article's author, H.F. Hoffman, took mischievous pleasure in reporting the problems by which this particular screening of *Othello* was beset:

let us proceed with the Murder of Othello. He was murdered by an operator last Friday night … The big laugh … came with the first scene when the title and sub-titles came through reading backwards … But the fun didn't end there. Instead of clipping his film at once and reversing the upper reel, the operator let

[38] See Paolo Cherchi Usai, *Burning Passions: An Introduction to the Study of Silent Cinema* (London: BFI, 1994), p. 57.

[39] Where producers' instructions lacked precision, or were insufficiently attended to by the distribution agent in the country of import, there was always the possibility that the title cards could be reinserted in slightly different places. Where this happened, it generated a film not only in a different language but one also differently punctuated by its moments of action-suspending dialogue or plot summary.

the whole thing go through the way it was. We are all aware that Othello is not the easiest subject in the world to follow, even under the best of circumstances. The title and all the sub-titles are extremely necessary, even to those who know it, and a good lecture should go with it for those who do not ... [In] his dilemma [the projectionist] ... hit upon the idea of hiding his mistake by speeding up his machine when the sub-titles appeared, so as to get over them more quickly. But the racket of it only made matters worse by drawing [the audience's] attention to him. All thought of how the audience was enjoying the picture was far from his mind, but they were enjoying it just the same ... When [the titles] appeared and he put on the high speed the audience would howl with delight. He was greeted with mock applause, laughter, cat-calls and other noises. Nobody felt bad when Othello breathed his last. The program was short on comedy anyhow, and this filled the bill very nicely.[40]

In the transitional era, the exhibition of prints remained, in fact, plagued by material contingency and human error, as this salutary tale attests. Exhibition practice had its highs and its lows, as did also the formal aesthetics of the exhibited films. While there were moments of magical effects and stirring performances, there was also the clatter of the projector to contend with and the opportunity for some projectionists (and some projectors) to spoil the show. Moreover, as Hoffman makes clear, it was a time in which an accompanying lecturer speaking words from the play, or providing a clarifying synopsis of the action, could play a key role in the better resourced exhibition venues (while being sorely missed at others).[41]

The formal character of the Clarendon *Tempest* and FAI *Othello* illustrate forcibly how in this transitional period the presentational codes of films adapted from theatrical sources were caught between the adventurous and the static, between the desire for invention and the will for conservatism. The industry had not yet quite dared to break from some cinematised theatrical conventions to which it felt a cultural allegiance. In their attempts to inhibit their use of the specifically cinematic resources available, Shakespeare films from the transitional period might even at times be accused, in Charlie Keil's formulation, of a deliberate 'stylistic retardation'.[42] Such self-denying tendencies partly revealed an innate lack of confidence on the part of film-makers in the specificity of their

---

[40] H. F. Hoffman, 'The Murder of Othello', *MPW* v.9, n.2 (22 July 1911), 110.

[41] The use of accompanying lecturers is discussed in the Introduction, pp. 10–13 – including a risible commentary on a filmed *Othello* (not FAI) given in Berlin in 1912.

[42] Charles Keil, '*From the Manger to the Cross*: The New Testament Narrative and the Question of Stylistic Retardation', in R. Cosandey, A. Gaudreault, T. Gunning (eds.), *Une Invention du Diable? Cinéma des Premiers Temps et Religion* (Sainte-Foy: Les Presses de l'Université Laval, 1992), pp. 112–20 (112).

medium as an entirely suitable vehicle of transmission for such elevated dramatic material. Nevertheless, the industry in this period was simultaneously feeling the temptation to range and narrate according to its own medium proclivities and capabilities. These contradictory impulses bump up against each other in exposing proximity in silent Shakespeare films of this period.

Being the point of encounter for seemingly incompatible elements makes a transitional era Shakespeare film a site of contest. The minor tussles, willed suppressions and tonal clashes at play create lines of friction within the films themselves – and these are clearly visible in both the 1908 *Tempest* and the 1909 *Othello*. The uneven viewing experience these stylistic vacillations generate, however, makes of these films eloquent cultural expressions of the broader ontological dilemma the film industry was experiencing in this transitional moment. By 1908/9, the medium was no longer a novelty that could simply rejoice in its capacity to capture movement persuasively on screen. Nor, however, was it yet entirely confident of its own cultural status, beleaguered as it so frequently was by slurs about its moral tenor. In these few short years it sat poised on the cusp of daring to believe in itself as a valid medium of interpretation for the heady cultural fare of a Shakespeare play and not quite yet able to discard the conventions that paid deference, if of a token and distorted sort, to the material's theatrical pedigree. The delightfully layered and inventive shots of *The Tempest* set against its palely theatre-imitative scenes and the visually fluid gondola shots of *Othello* set against the stultifying stagy blocking of the studio shots in Cyprus created films of verve and tedium, of invention and regression. It would be for a non-European production company to sit more lightly to the notion of heritage and so dare to embrace cinematic inventive possibility, and indeed self-parody, in its rendering of Shakespeare. It is this company that is the subject of the next chapter.

CHAPTER 4

Corporate authorship: the Shakespeare films of the Vitagraph Company of America

Vitagraph's *Julius Caesar* (1908), *Macbeth* (1908), *Romeo and Juliet* (1908), *Othello* (1908), *The Merchant of Venice* (1908), *A Midsummer Night's Dream* (1909), *King Lear* (1909), *Twelfth Night* (1910); Méliès' *La Mort de Jules César* (1907); Cines' *Brutus* (1910), *Julius Caesar* (1914); Thanhouser's *A Winter's Tale* (1910); Film d'Arte Italiana's *Re Lear* (1910)

In the early cinema period, it was a production company that was recognised as the maker of a film, and by production company that pictures were clearly branded at each stage in the cycle of marketing, distribution, exhibition and reception. The clearest understanding of the 'authoring' of films in this period was, therefore, corporate. Rarely did a named individual – be it director, scenarist, actor or camera operative – emerge from anonymity to disrupt the corporate branding of, for example, an early 'Biograph', 'Edison', 'Vitagraph' or 'Lubin' picture. The consistency of this commercial imprimatur may be gauged from the fact that the first ever film star should have been promoted unnamed. She was launched in 1908 as 'the Vitagraph Girl' – a company asset whose market label identified her as part of the corporate product. By 1912, actors were becoming 'stars', a few directors were becoming known for an identifiable body of work and Edison took the lead in publishing the names of their scenarists.[1] Before this point, however, individual creative and technical contributions were subsumed within the broader identity of the company.

This chapter examines the Shakespeare films produced by one company, the Vitagraph Company of America. Between 1908 and 1912, Vitagraph produced twelve Shakespeare and Shakespeare-related films. These were vigorously marketed and enthusiastically received upon first release specifically as company products: it is, therefore, in such terms that they are

---

[1] See Robinson, *From Peepshow to Palace*, p. 155.

studied here. Vitagraph's reputation and output are considered through illustrative case studies in which I examine the humour of the frame composition on *Julius Caesar* (1908), the interpolation of a non-Shakespearean fairy spirit in *A Midsummer Night's Dream* (1909) and the purposeful use of a repertory company in *Twelfth Night* (1910). Additional reference is made to Vitagraph's *Macbeth* (1908), *Romeo and Juliet* (1908), *Othello* (1908), *The Merchant of Venice* (1908) and *King Lear* (1909), to Georges Méliès' *La Mort de Jules César* (*Shakespeare Writing Julius Caesar*) (1907), Cines' *Brutus* (1910) and *Julius Caesar* (1914), Film d'Arte Italiana's *Re Lear* (1910) and Thanhouser's *A Winter's Tale* (1910).[2] Understanding the market imperatives that governed the production of these films brings them into sharper relief. A brief description of how company brand recognition worked in general within the American film industry of the early period therefore precedes a consideration of the particular uses to which Vitagraph put its own company image.

THE VITAGRAPH COMPANY OF AMERICA

'It's a Vitagraph!': production company brand recognition

Spectators in cinema's pioneering days were accustomed to going to see the 'Biograph' at one exhibition hall or the 'Vitascope' at another, the 'Cinematographe' in one theatre or the 'Vitagraph' in another. Moving picture programmes were exclusively composed of film titles from a single manufacturing supplier. Although in the transitional era some exhibitors and theatre managers began buying in films from more than one manufacturer, many still counted it advantageous to remain within a network of affiliated exhibitors exclusively supplied by the distribution wing of a single production company.[3] Whether sourced from one production stable or from several, the programmes themselves would typically unspool before their audiences as a sequence of cinematic surprises as different genres and styles of film (actualities, sporting highlights, short pictorial sketches, enacted reconstructions of significant events, animated shorts and commercial

---

[2] The Vitagraph *Dream* and *Twelfth Night* are on the BFI *Silent Shakespeare* DVD, *A Winter's Tale* on the *Thanhouser Presents Shakespeare* DVD. Prints of the Vitagraph *Julius Caesar* and *King Lear* and of the Cines *Brutus* and *Julius Caesar* are held at the BFI National Archive. A print of *Romeo and Juliet* is at the Folger. No print of the Vitagraph *Macbeth*, *Merchant of Venice*, *Othello* or of Méliès' *La Mort de Jules César* survives.

[3] Exhibitors who de-coupled themselves from the monopolising relationship with a single production company then rented films from a selection of distributors through the federated film markets ('film exchanges').

advertisements) bumped up against each another in abrasive, arresting and unprepared-for ways.[4] Even when – as occasionally happened – an individual film title was favoured with a particular advertising push at the point of exhibition (through billboards outside the theatre, early forms of lobby card inside it or promotional postcards), it was still the film's production company that chiefly determined that film's identity in the marketplace, and so dictated the terms in which it was promoted and viewed.

Post-1905, Vitagraph was the largest American production company of the early cinema period. In 1908 it helped to found the influential Motion Picture Patents Company that attempted to regulate the industry by curbing the activities of the independents and protecting the interests of its member companies, the 'big ten' (Edison, Vitagraph, Kalem, Lubin, Essanay, Kleine, Selig, Pathé, Méliès and Biograph). Of these, Vitagraph remained the most prolific and efficient exporter of films in the pre-war years. In 1908, the year in which it produced its first Shakespeare film, its net annual profit was an impressive $279,814 (equivalent to $6,703,100 in 2008). By 1913, the year that marked the end of its Shakespeare film cycle, its profits had quadrupled to $1,116,349 (equivalent to $24,311,600 in 2008).[5] It is difficult to overstate the company's profile or influence on the domestic and international market in the early years. It was, in sum, one of the most powerful industry players worldwide.

The company's primary goal was clear: to have its name convey an assurance of quality, cultural prestige and wholesome values that would be immediately recognisable by the market.[6] It wanted to be seen as a company of elevated ambitions realised through elevated subject matter and it promoted this image through its vast publicity machine. A promotional pamphlet from *c.*1911 carried one version of the mission statement:

The Vitagraph Company is noted for its elaborate feature films, sparing no amount of pains and expense in their production ... Some of these productions

---

[4] Nickelodeons dedicated to the exhibition of moving pictures began to appear *c.*1905/6. These often published programmes that included film titles as well as production company details. With the introduction of purpose-built moving picture houses, the practice of including moving pictures as part of a broader variety entertainment that had been prevalent in the pioneering years tended to recede.

[5] Figures from Vitagraph chairman Albert E. Smith's autobiography *Two Reels and a Crank: From Nickelodeon to Picture Palace* (Garden City, NY: Doubleday, 1952), pp. 251–2. 2008 equivalents are calculated from the conversion tables of the Federal Reserve Bank of Minneapolis, a member of 'the Fed': http://woodrow.mpls.frb.fed.us/research/data/us/calc/.

[6] For a rich critical history of Vitagraph and its public image, see Pearson and Uricchio, *Reframing Culture.* For more on Vitagraph, see also Anthony Slide, *The Big V: A History of the Vitagraph Company* (Metuchen, N.J.: The Scarecrow Press, 1976); Paolo Cherchi Usai, *Vitagraph Company of America: Il cinema prima di Hollywood* (Pordenone: Studio Tesi, 1987).

involved an expenditure of twenty thousand dollars and it was money well employed, when the amount of pleasure extended and the good accomplished is considered as compensation.[7]

The company's articulated project was both to extend pleasure and to accomplish good: their films were to be known not just as entertaining but as pictures simultaneously able to perform a socially edifying function – to inform, educate and inspire.

It was Vitagraph's production of prestigious 'deluxe' pictures that acted as a flagship for these cultural aspirations. The twelve films Vitagraph released with a Shakespearean subject were part of the larger tally of prestige pictures for which the company became widely known. In 1908, their most prolific year for Shakespearean productions, they released *Antony and Cleopatra*, *Julius Caesar*, *Macbeth*, *The Merchant of Venice*, *Othello*, *Richard III* and *Romeo and Juliet*; in 1909, *King Lear* and *A Midsummer Night's Dream*; in 1910, *Twelfth Night* and in 1912, *As You Like It* and *Cardinal Wolsey* (*Henry VIII*). Nor did Vitagraph restrict itself to Shakespearean adaptations to establish its literary credentials.[8] Other Vitagraph adaptations of reputable plays and novels of the period included *Salome* (1908), *Oliver Twist* (1909), *A Tale of Two Cities* (1911) and *Vanity Fair* (1911). A small collection of spin-offs, spoofs and updatings – including *A Midwinter Night's Dream; or Little Joe's Luck* (1906), *A Modern Oliver Twist* (1906), *The Wrong Flat; or A Comedy of Errors* (1907), *An Indian Romeo and Juliet* (1912) and, slightly later, one in a series of 'Freddy' adventure comedies, *Freddy Versus Hamlet* (1916) – suggested that the company's approach to adaptation could be playful as well as more earnest. Added to these engagements with a specifically English literary heritage were classical stories such as *Elektra* (1910) and Arthurian ones (via Tennyson) such as *Launcelot and Elaine* (1909). In the heady Vitagraph production years of 1909–12, biblical sources appeared alongside secular literary ones. Old Testament films included the multi-part serial *The Life of Moses* (1909), *Jephthah's Daughter: A Biblical Tragedy* (1909) and *Saul and David* (1909). New Testament films included the devotional picture *The Way of the Cross* (1909) and a more oblique take on the Gospel narrative as seen through the eyes of two non-apostolic witnesses, *The Illumination* (1912).

---

[7] *Vitagraph Life Portrayals: How and Where Living Pictures are Made* (NY: Vitagraph Company of America, n.d. [circa 1911]). Quoted in Pearson and Urrichio, *Reframing Culture*, p. 60.

[8] Given Vitagraph's aspirations to produce edifying pictures, it is ironic that police censors insisted the three goriest scenes of its 1908 *Macbeth* (the stabbing of Duncan, the brandishing of the bloody dagger and the fight between Macbeth and Macduff) be cut for the film's Chicago exhibition. *MPW* v.2, n.24 (13 June 1908), 511.

In addition to securing a literary, classical and biblical pedigree, Vitagraph also became patriotic narrators of American history, making a special feature of their historical films celebrating American character and glory. These included *The Life of George Washington* (1909) and *The Battle Hymn of the Republic* (1911), the latter ingeniously transmuting Julia Warde Howe's religious vision of God's justice into a historicised recruiting drive for President Lincoln's army. The company also kept a keen eye on royal news of topical interest. Their actuality film of King Edward's London funeral, therefore, received an intensive burst of publicity throughout June 1910 as exhibitors were urged to 'exhibit this film early while the interest is warm'.[9] Vitagraph's film of the royal funeral, like their subsequent film of President Taft inspecting the annual Brooklyn Sunday School parade in 1911,[10] extended their network of prestige associations from Shakespearean kings, emperors, dukes and generals to the real, contemporary world of monarchs and presidents. The cultural register of their high profile subjects was, therefore, crisply distinguished from the lower-life subjects (gangsters, cowboys, comedians, lovers, orphans and fetchingly impoverished heroines) that proved the staple earner for many of their competitors.

Audiences knew their film companies well. Just how well was made clear in an article entitled 'The Old Lady in the Audience: Mother Squeers Gossips About the Film Makers' that appeared in American trade paper *Motography* in 1911. The article conjured an imaginary picture-goer and lay commentator, 'Mother Squeers', who offered her home-spun impressions of the various studios and their output. Biograph, Edison, Vitagraph, Lubin, Gaumont Urban-Eclipse and Pathé each in turn became the object of her banter. Vitagraph, she declared, was

undoubtedly the most popular maker; and I've sometimes wondered why. I think it is because Vitagraph hits the taste of the average audience better than any of the others. The Vitagraph dramas have a very moral and respectable tone; the plots are just mental enough to make people think they are thinking ... [I]t releases these fancy films every now and then, biblical and classical subjects – you know the kind. Some of these have been of highest merit and some have not (at least I didn't like some of them), but they all showed ambition and went to swell the Vitagraph prestige. You may remember how well they were boosted in advance. Vitagraph knows how to advertise.[11]

[9] Price: 9 cents per foot. *New York Dramatic Mirror* (4 June 1910), 32 (back page advertisement).
[10] 'Vitagraph Notes', *MPW* v.8, n.28 (15 July 1911), 49.
[11] 'The Old Lady in the Audience: Mother Squeers Gossips About the Film Makers', *Motography* (May 1911), 77–8.

The characteristics of the Vitagraph product identified by Mother Squeers must have been broadly pleasing to the company. It was, after all, in almost exactly these terms that Vitagraph sought to brand itself – as producing prestige films with reputable sources and laudably artistic aspirations without alienating 'the average audience'. Their company image as the purveyors of cultural nourishment to a movie-going public eager to be thus fed was, in fact, one that they worked hard to perpetuate (as Mother Squeers' recognition of their high profile advertising also acknowledges).

The line-up of Vitagraph subjects thus far outlined makes sense of the company's appeal to a movie-going public happy, as Mother Squeers put it, 'to think they [were] thinking' and who had, at the least, some cultural ambition. As Roberta Pearson and William Uricchio have influentially demonstrated, in line with Mother Squeers' earlier testimony, the name 'Vitagraph' became inextricably associated with the idea of 'quality films'.[12]

The breadth of cinematic output emerging from Vitagraph's extensive Brooklyn production studios, however, reveals a greater tonal range than this strategically marketed reputation might suggest. In fact the 'quality films' on which the company based its distinctive corporate image constituted only a small proportion of their total releases. The 'quality films' certainly received the most high profile promotion – partly to recoup the enhanced outlay their more lavish sets and costumes typically entailed. But these market-leading prestige productions also served as the umbrella for, and in part the edifying distraction from, a host of more bread-and-butter cinematic fare that the company was simultaneously producing.

The majority of the Vitagraph pictures that might resist Mother Squeers' 'fancy films' label were a predictable line-up of popular comedies, romances, melodramas and Westerns. These were produced relatively cheaply, at considerable speed and featured members of the Vitagraph stock company in revolving cast combinations. In July 1911, for example, *MPW* revealed that Vitagraph was producing four films a week, with a concentration on comedies and Westerns.[13] By November 1912, however, the weekly output had increased to six.[14] Writing in 1916, the prestigious stage actor E.H. Sothern, who had made several films for Vitagraph as a side-line, remembered the conditions in which pictures were produced at

[12] Pearson and Uricchio, *Reframing Culture.*   [13] *MPW* v.8, n.26 (1 July 1911), 1506.
[14] *New York Dramatic Mirror* (6 November 1912), 36 (back page advertisement).

this dizzying rate, and the difficulties that such a hive of industry posed for actors trying to feel, or even to simulate, appropriate emotion on set:

You stand in the corner of an immense room where three or four other plays are going on. Probably you have only the illusion of scenery on two sides of you. At first you even hear the stage directions given to the other actors and lights are going up and down all about you and people are passing everywhere ... [I]f you let yourself become conscious of the people, sounds, light or shadow about you it will be impossible to present anything through the moving picture camera except surprise, horror, disappointment and despair.[15]

Out of this frenetic whirl of production, it was comedy that the company's Chairman, Albert E. Smith, remembers as being Vitagraph's dominant output from 1908 onwards: 'It was an age of laughter; comedy was king. The constant cry at Vitagraph was for humorous stories ... '[16] The comedies and other more or less formulaic genre films that rolled off the Vitagraph production line in the years 1907–17 included titles such as *The Washerwoman's Revenge* (1907), *Western Courtship: A Love Story of Arizona* (1908), *A Lunatic at Large* (1910), *Cupid and the Motor Boat* (1910), *The Subduing of Mrs Nag* (1911), *The Way of a Man with a Maid* (1912), *Sheriff Jim's Last Shot* (1912), *Too Much Wooing of Handsome Dan* (1912), *He Fell in Love with His Mother-in-Law* (1913), *Hilda of the Slums* (1915), *A Villainous Villain* (1916), *Bullies and Bullets* (1917), *Noisy Naggers and Nosy Neighbors* (1917). These lively Vitagraph films, and the hundreds of others like them, had little discernible cultural ambition and were far from courting the prestige associations of the 'qualities'. They were tucked in discreetly in the shadow of the 'films deluxe' as highly saleable but not particularly noteworthy programme fillers.

Though vital to Vitagraph's continued economic success, these were not the pictures the company used as its calling card. Vitagraph therefore skilfully managed the delicate business of keeping their staple earner (stock genre films) and their signature product (culturally edifying dramas) tonally quite distinct. Creating such a clear tonal division in one's wares constitutes an unusual market model. It is testimony to the company's unrivalled marketing machinery that the decidedly populist tenor of the one did not inadvertently compromise the elevated credentials of the other.

[15] E. H. Sothern, '"The New Art" as Discovered by E. H. Sothern', *The Craftsman* 30 (September 1916), 572–643 (642). Excerpted in Bert Cardullo, Ronald Gottesman, Leigh Woods (eds.), *Playing to the Camera: Film Actors Discuss Their Craft* (NY and London: Yale University Press, 1998), pp. 28–32.
[16] Albert Smith, *Two Reels and a Crank*, p. 205.

The marketing puff for its forthcoming *Lady Godiva* in 1911 testifies to the consistency with which Vitagraph was able to maintain its reputation as a company of impeccable moral and artistic credentials (even in the face of potentially suspect material). Of all the possible eye-catching attractions *Lady Godiva* might have been advertised as showcasing, it was, with conspicuous innocence, the 'quaint streets, manners, customs and costumes of the people of the eleventh century' to which the company drew its exhibitors' attention.[17] In Vitagraph's hands, even *Lady Godiva* could be sold, apparently without irony, as a costume drama. Bearing in mind the overall Vitagraph output, Mother Squeers's chatty account of the 'fancy' character of the Vitagraph product is, therefore, as striking for what it does *not* identify as for what it does. In taking their 'films deluxe' as the sole determinant of Vitagraph's corporate character, she was, apparently, wholeheartedly buying into the company's own selective promotional strategy.

It proved, however, to be a market model and promotional strategy with staying power. Vitagraph was not only the most profitable of the early film companies, but also the only one from the first wave to survive into the 1920s. Its carefully managed image endured too, as is evident from the front-page cartoon of the 1924 *Vitagraph Pictures Annual Studio Yearbook*. The drawing shows two smart middle-class children in a movie theatre lobby; their father is buying tickets from a smart booth; their elegantly dressed mother scans the board of forthcoming attractions. The caption reads 'Oh, Daddy, it's a Vitagraph!' These children are clearly discriminating moviegoers who, knowing what to expect from different production companies, enthusiastically trust the Vitagraph imprimatur as the mark of a good film. Vitagraph's confidence in the extent of its brand recognition and the breadth of its appeal was as well placed in 1924 when the idealised children of the *Studio Yearbook* were relishing a Vitagraph picture in prospect as it was in 1911 when Mother Squeers was delivering her appreciative judgement.

Vitagraph's Americanism

Vitagraph was a thoroughgoing American commercial success and gave a conspicuous profile to its American credentials. Not only did it name itself in flag-waving terms as the 'Vitagraph Company of America', but its ubiquitous emblem – an eagle whose raised wings formed the 'V' of

---

[17] *MPW* v.8, n.28 (15 July 1911), 49.

the company's name – patriotically alluded to the eagle with raised wings that, since 1782, had been the symbol of America itself.[18] This America-evocative eagle made its presence felt in every aspect of the company's life: on employees' lapel badges, stamped on the cans that carried the film prints to exhibitors worldwide, prominently displayed on every company advertisement and appearing conspicuously and repeatedly within the films themselves.[19]

Moreover, the company further telegraphed its Americanism in its choice of subjects. From their early short, the jingoistic *Tearing Down the Spanish Flag* (1898), to the patriotism of *Barbara Fritchie: The Story of a Patriotic American Woman* (1908), *For Her Country's Sake* (1909), *The Life of George Washington* (1909), *Saved by the Flag* (1910), *One Flag at Last* (1911), *Tested by the Flag* (1911), *The Battle Cry for Peace* (1915), and *Womanhood, the Glory of the Nation* (1917), the company showcased its fervent nation-alism. Vitagraph's well-promoted Americanism is perhaps the more strik-ing for having emerged from a company founded by two Englishmen – J. Stuart Blackton (an erstwhile cartoonist/journalist who ran production for Vitagraph), and Albert E. Smith (who became the company's business brains). In 1899, these two were joined by a third Englishman, William T. ('Pop') Rock. With a combination of the cultural other's observant eye and the entrepreneurial immigrant's zeal to assimilate, these Englishmen built their company partly through fêting American military history and national character. In fact, so vigorously did the company's name, ubiqui-tous logo, choice of subjects and accompanying publicity brand Vitagraph a national flag-carrier that not only titles with a specifically patriotic fla-vour but, by association, *all* its films were understood in the market place not just as 'Vitagraph' pictures but *thereby* as categorically 'American' ones as well.

Which brings us to Shakespeare. If any cultural subject matter was already firmly patriotically branded in the first twenty years of the cen-tury, it was surely Shakespeare, that most definitive of *English* national icons.[20] What effect could being 'Vitagraphed' have on dramatic material that was itself already so clearly nationally inscribed?

---

[18] See Richard S. Patterson and Richardson Dougall, *The Eagle and the Shield: A History of the Great Seal of the United States* (Honolulu, Hawaii: University Press of the Pacific, 2005).

[19] I am grateful to Richard Birtwhistle for showing me from his private collection an employee's Vitagraph lapel badge and a pre-1920 Vitagraph film can bearing the imprint of the company eagle.

[20] For a sample discussion of Shakespeare as England's and England as Shakespeare's in this period, see Coppélia Kahn, 'Remembering Shakespeare Imperially: The 1916 Tercentenary', *SQ* v.52, n.1 (2001), 456–78 (461).

Vitagraph's Shakespeare

In the nineteenth century, the St. Charles Theater in New Orleans was one of the most prestigious theatrical venues in the American South. High-profile American actors of the day appeared there on tour, including Jenny Lind and Edwin Booth. An evocative image adorned the stage curtain to absorb the attention of patrons before curtain-up. The design featured an image of Shakespeare who, deprived of any of his conventional literary, theatrical or personal associations, had been symbolically resituated. Here, bathed in a halo of light, Shakespeare was to be seen being borne aloft on the wings of the American eagle.[21] The idea of a universal Shakespeare, a Shakespeare of common ownership not bound by national affiliation or mindset, was already enjoying some currency by mid-century, but this was not that. It was a precise emblem of what Michael Bristol has called, in relation to Shakespeare in America more generally, the 'massive transfer of authority and cultural capital to American society'.[22] As an image, it managed to wrap bardic reverence into a piece of uncompromising nationalistic appropriation.

There is a rich and long-standing vein of thought that sees Shakespeare, 'properly understood', as a 'spokesman for republican values' and *therefore*, spiritually, as an American. He has been declared 'American in his optimism' and in his status as a 'true democrat'.[23] In the second half of the nineteenth century, writes Virginia Mason Vaughan, Shakespeare was 'as American as Uncle Sam himself – and so he remains'.[24] It was not from nowhere, therefore, that the St. Charles' American eagle swooped down to bear away Shakespeare on its back and claim the English national poet as its own. The symbolic act of abduction was supported by a weight of thinking in American intellectual and cultural life well beyond this particular theatre.

---

[21] See Levine, *Highbrow/Lowbrow*, p. 23. (It was the version of the St. Charles Theater that stood between 1842 and 1899 – between two separate fires – that was thus decorated.)

[22] Michael D. Bristol, *Shakespeare's America, America's Shakespeare* (London and NY: Routledge, 1990), p. 10.

[23] Gail Kern Paster, 'Foreword' to Virginia Mason Vaughan and Alden T. Vaughan (eds.), *Shakespeare in American Life* (Washington DC: Folger Shakespeare Library, 2007), pp. 7–9 (7) and Virginia Mason Vaughan, 'Making Shakespeare American: Shakespeare's Dissemination in Nineteenth-Century America', in Virginia Mason Vaughan and Alden T. Vaughan (eds.), *Shakespeare in American Life* (Washington DC: Folger Shakespeare Library, 2007), pp. 23–33 (30–1).

[24] Virginia Mason Vaughan, 'Making Shakespeare American', p. 32.

Vitagraph's Shakespeare films participate in the American will to appropriate the Shakespearean name and legacy. The ways in which the company part-advertises and part-obscures its appropriations of Shakespeare as a Vitagraph (and *ergo* American) product inform the broader discussion of individual Shakespeare films that follows.

JULIUS CAESAR (1908)

Julius Caesar was directed, under the supervision of J. Stuart Blackton, by the company's new actor-director, William (Billy) V. Ranous, who brought with him to Vitagraph some highly prized stage experience. The film compresses the action of the play into a single reel (approximately twelve minutes' viewing time), beginning with Caesar ignoring the warning about the Ides of March and ending with the honouring of Brutus' self-slaughter upon a battlefield funeral pyre.[25] As with most other Vitagraph Shakespeare films, its title cards (in German in the surviving print) do not quote directly from the play, but mostly offer spare plot summaries to help the spectator make sense of the frenetic and histrionic action. Unlike some films of a similar moment, most Vitagraph films rarely sought Shakespearean 'authenticity' through textual quotation.[26] The Shakespearean story and the reputation were gratefully appropriated in each case, but there was also a resolute attempt to give each film an autonomous life as a piece of cinematic story-telling.

Julius Caesar, like most Vitagraph Shakespeare films of 1908, depends heavily upon studio sets. It does, however, escape from the confines of stagy backdrops and cramped sets to Brooklyn's Prospect Park for the battle of Philippi. The film is not extravagantly lavish in the way that the 1914 Italian Cines production of *Julius Caesar* would be and lacks the thousands of extras that featured in the crowd scenes for that Italian feature version (made at the height of the Italian spectacular style). Nor was its release accompanied by a luxurious commemorative programme glossily illustrated with

---

[25] For Vitagraph's own summary of the film's action, see Pearson and Uricchio, *Reframing Culture*, pp. 88–9.

[26] The significant exception to Vitagraph's usual title card practice is the lost film *Richard III* (1908) which, according to the synopsis in *MPW* v. 3, n.13 (26 September 1908), 245, included plenty of direct quotation, as if unwilling to deny its audiences some pithy, well-known Shakespearean treats: 'Now is the winter of our discontent'; 'Down to hell and say I sent thee there'; 'These tears look well; sorrow's the mode. With all my heart I'll not be out of fashion'; 'I'm busy, thou troublest me. I'm not in the giving vein'; 'Off with his head: so much for Buckingham'; 'Hence, bubbling dreams,/You threaten here in vain;/Conscience avaunt!/Richard's himself again'.

beautiful stills from the film, as the Cines film would be. It is visually more modest than this – and more modest in style than some other Vitagraph Shakespeares also. In its own moderate way, however, in step with the norms of its moment, the Vitagraph one-reeler did attempt to catch the flavour of a Roman setting in its costumes and production design.

Vitagraph branding

The opening street scene is played on a shallow studio set against a painted Roman backdrop. As a prominent part of a procession of Roman senators and soldiery, two 'SPQR' banners are held high by soldiers, each one topped – appropriately for Rome – by an eagle with wings aloft. Then the title card appears, and it bears two strikingly similar eagles with wings aloft, these ones – appropriately for Vitagraph – forming the familiar 'V' shape of the company emblem.

It was conventional for production companies to brand title cards with their corporate logo. Just as Vitagraph placed their eagle on their title cards, so Pathé similarly posted their rooster, the American Biograph an entwined 'AB' and the Thanhouser Corporation the letters 'TCo'. All were anxious to protect their intellectual and commercial property against practices of film piracy from less respectable quarters.[27] They feared lest, in a fast moving and voracious market, unscrupulous operators might appropriate some or all of a film negative, print copies and sell it on to exhibitors as their own, thus saving themselves production costs. In 1909, *The Bioscope* referred to this 'pernicious practice' as '[i]llicit duplicating' carried out by film 'fakers'.[28] Displaying their own logo regularly throughout the films helped studios guard against such practices. At least as importantly, it gave the company a platform for advertising its own company label.

If no other company could rival Vitagraph for advertising efficiency, so no other Vitagraph film could rival *Julius Caesar* for ready-made advertising opportunities. For in relation to this film, Vitagraph could insert its logo prominently into the scene of the action without disrupting dramatic cohesion or aesthetic consistency. When the army of Octavius and Antony encounters that of Brutus and Cassius for a pre-battle parley near the end of the film, for example, the preceding intertitle reads: 'Die Streitkräfte des Marcus Antonius und Octavio Cäsar und von Brutus und Cassius! "Worte

---

[27] On the Vitagraph Chairman's own history in film piracy, see Herbert and McKernan, (eds.), *Who's Who of Victorian Cinema*, pp. 134–5.
[28] *Bioscope* (11 November 1909), 5.

vor Taten.'" ('The armies of Mark Antony and Octavius Caesar and of Brutus and Cassius: "Words before blows."') (Figure 4.1a). Once again, two Vitagraph eagles with wings raised in Vitagraph's characteristic 'V' sit to the right and left above these words, balancing the card symmetrically with their familiar corporate poise. As the title card cedes to the battlefield action, however, the eagles then prove an almost exact point of continuity between the two shots. There, in symmetrically balanced positions in upper left and right of the frame once again, are two eagles of comparable size with raised wings, this time held aloft by a soldier from each army (Figure 4.1b). The visual rhyme from one shot to the next is conspicuous, inviting an audience to reflect on the relationship between the two.

The presence of the eagles in the parley scene is, of course, locally purposeful within the terms of the drama, demonstrating how both sides – Octavius's and Brutus' – seek to signal symbolically that it is they who are fighting for Rome and Roman values. But the particular placement of the eagles in the scene's blocking ensures that they communicate more than this also. The apparent superimposition of the Vitagraph eagle upon the Roman scene suggested by the mimicked plastics between shots implicitly marks the territory of the story told as the inscribed property of the story's tellers. Though eagles borne aloft clearly form a natural part of the fabric of this dramatic world, yet, as inflected by the previous anticipatory shot, their organic relation to the scene of which they form part is slightly unsettled. Within this cinematic sequence, they both belong and do not belong to a Roman world, acting in bi-partisan fashion both

Figure 4.1a and b. The visual rhyme between Vitagraph and Roman eagles in successive shots in *Julius Caesar* (Vitagraph, 1909).

as the indigenous symbol of Roman power and as an imported signpost to another world. The scene we are viewing, these ambivalent eagles now intimate, is not only a cinematic window onto a Roman drama but also a piece of thoroughly Vitagraphed Shakespeare.

Drawing out the significance of their own company logo from the very stuff of the scene was a marketing stratagem brilliant in its appropriateness. In Vitagraph's hands, therefore, a Shakespearean drama about Roman power becomes in part a covert allusion both to Vitagraph's own imperial aspirations as a powerful industry player and, through Vitagraph's Americanism and America's own Rome-evocative symbolic eagle, to the might of America itself as the new Rome in a new world order with its own Senate, Capitol, internal power struggles, grand causes and significant self-regard. If, in writing *Julius Caesar* in 1599, Shakespeare had appropriated Rome as a partial metaphor for English power, politics and social conventions,[29] Vitagraph re-appropriated Shakespeare's Rome, to bring its disquisition on power, the exercise of power and the challenges to it closer to home for an American audience.

In 1908 when the film was released, America was still coming to terms with the recent assassination of *its* head of state. In response to the assassination of President McKinley at close range in September 1901, the indignant might of America had been exercised in punishing its own political insurgents. The story of the assassination, presidential funeral, trial and execution of the culprit had itself been presented on film (part actuality footage, part enacted reconstruction) as an Edison picture.[30] In 1908, this political assassination was still fresh enough, and significant enough, in the public memory to make the assassination of Caesar at close range in the Capitol itself a topically resonant act as played in the US. Thus the slaying and funeral of McKinley and the pursuit and death of the assassin Czolgosz provided a contemporary filter through which the slaying and funeral of Caesar and the pursuit and death of the assassin Brutus could be read. America, like Rome before it, would rise to protect its own interests and authority. In indicating the 'more than merely Roman-ness' of the eagles carried high by a cast of American extras marching across Brooklyn's Prospect Park (Vitagraph's version of Philippi) at the end of *Julius Caesar*, Vitagraph is equivocating eloquently about their provenance: this representative eagle, and therefore this telling of the tale, is

---

[29] See James Shapiro, *1599: A Year in the Life of William Shakespeare* (London: Faber, 2005), pp. 172–8.
[30] For an account of the McKinley film, see Ian Christie, *The Last Machine: Early Cinema and the Birth of the Modern World* (London: BBC/BFI, 1994), p. 89.

both Roman and American. And in its symbolic elision of the Roman and
the American eagle, it is resoundingly, of course, a self-promoting reference to Vitagraph's own power, patriotism and, the savvy emblem of both,
its company logo.

The previous year, the experimental French film-maker, Georges
Méliès, had engaged yet more directly with Shakespeare, and specifically
with *Julius Caesar*, on the question of nationhood. Whereas Vitagraph
implicitly subsumed Shakespearean material into a celebration of individual patriotism, Méliès had instead advertised Shakespeare as himself the means of overcoming such potential divisiveness and ushering
in international accord. Méliès' innovative film *La Mort de Jules César*
(*Shakespeare Writing Julius Caesar* in its English release) (1907) depicted
Shakespeare (played by Méliès) making several unsatisfying attempts to
write the assassination scene from *Julius Caesar*. As Méliès' Shakespeare
wonders how to proceed, suddenly his characters appear before him (and
the audience) and play out the Capitol scene in a full Roman setting. The
film concluded with a dissolve into a bust of Shakespeare 'around which
all the nations wave flags and garlands'.[31] The trick photography here bears
the Méliès signature. As a sentimental vision of universal, and universal-
ising Shakespeare, however, it represents a position that Vitagraph's *Julius
Caesar* was symbolically to resist the following year. Sustaining its own
corporate and nationalistic visibility before a watching world, Vitagraph
had more in common with the image of bardic appropriation from the
St. Charles Theater than with Méliès' sentimental tribute to a universal-
ising poet.

Not all Shakespearean dramas could similarly justify the display of
Vitagraph eagles as an organic part of the scene.[32] In films where it could
not be as surreptitious in its deployment, equivocal in its significations or
potentially subliminal in its effects as it was in *Julius Caesar*, the insertion
of a 'V' or V-shaped eagle amidst the action often, therefore, constituted
an intrusive disruption. Though they could distract from the narrative, as
a commercial strategy, such interpolations made perfect sense. The surviving one-frame paper-deposit stills from *Othello*, *The Merchant of Venice*
and *Macbeth* (all 1908) held at the Motion Picture and Recorded Sound

---

[31] From the scenario given in *Complete Catalogue of Genuine and Original 'Star' Films (Moving
Pictures) Manufactured by Geo. Méliès of Paris*, compiled 1908. Quoted in Ball, *Shakespeare on
Silent Film*, pp. 35–6.

[32] We can, however, assume that the Vitagraph *Antony and Cleopatra* – no print of which survives – also showcased the Vitagraph eagles as part of the scene since it will have drawn upon the
company's same pool of stock Roman properties.

Figure 4.2a. The Vitagraph eagle appears on the cave wall in Vitagraph's *Macbeth* (1908). Billy Ranous as Macbeth.

Figure 4.2b. The Vitagraph logo appears on the right-hand arch in Capulet's house in Vitagraph's *Romeo and Juliet* (1908). Charles Kent as Capulet, Florence Lawrence as Juliet. Both stills courtesy of the LOC's paper print collection.

Division, Library of Congress in Washington (LOC), for example, show the Vitagraph eagle and representative 'V' present above the window in an exterior of Brabantio's house, on an interior wall of Shylock's house and on the oddly ornate wall of the witches' cave in *Macbeth* (Figure 4.2a). Moreover, the logo is multiply present in the surviving film of *Romeo and Juliet* (1908), appearing on the canopy above Juliet's bed, fixed to an arch at the Capulet ball (Figure 4.2b), in centre frame above the church door arch at Friar Lawrence's cell and above Juliet's sepulchre. In each case, the logo's presence in the midst of the Shakespearean action shows plausibly realistic set dressing bowing to commercial promotional strategies: not even Shakespeare was safe from the insistent product placement practices of the period.

*The wordless performance of grand passion:
embarrassment and self-parody*

The assassination scene in *Julius Caesar*, to which I now turn, incorporates not only the ever-present Vitagraph logo (affixed above a grand arch) but, in addition, has a more subtle form of authorial signature inscribed within its dramatic action. Out of the comedically unpromising raw material of the scene, Vitagraph creates one of the funniest sequences to be found in any silent Shakespeare film. For the scene's design, Vitagraph directly copied the set, statuary and deployment of characters from the French neo-classicist Jean-Léon Gérôme's iconic painting 'The Death of Caesar' (1867),[33] and, moreover, this painterly quotation within the film was identified and commented upon in review at the time.[34] The close association with this prestigious work of art lent gravitas to Vitagraph's own cinematic representation of the scene and, as I shall discuss, simultaneously released the comic potential inherent within it.

In the Vitagraph depiction, Caesar is seated in left of frame, rows of senators in banked benches on the right, conspirators milling around on the floor in between. Having callously ignored the repeated suits of the conspirators to enfranchise Publius Cimber, Caesar is stabbed first from behind by Cassius and then, as he rises wounded and descends to the

---

[33] A lithograph of the painting is reproduced in Pearson and Uricchio, *Reframing Culture*, p. 91. At the time of writing, a print is available to view (and buy) online at www.zazzle.com/the_death_of_caesar_by_jean_leon_gerome_print-228564908681002278.

[34] W. Stephen Bush, 'Shakespeare in Moving Pictures', *MPW* v.3, n.23 (5 December 1908), 447.

Figure 4.3 Still from *Julius Caesar* (Vitagraph 1908). Vitagraph's Capitol scene
pays homage in set, statuary and blocking to Gérôme's painting 'The Death of
Caesar' (1867). As momentous events are enacted centre-frame, the sleeping senator
in frame right misses the entire drama. The Vitagraph logo is mounted above the
arched entrance. Still courtesy of the paper print collection of the Motion Picture,
Broadcasting and Recorded Sound Division of the LOC.

floor of the Capitol, subsequently from all sides by the other conspirators. He staggers from side to side with measured symmetry and dies a
rather decorously stylised (and pragmatically ungory) death in centre
frame (Figure 4.3). The senators unconnected with the conspiracy all rise
in horrified consternation (or revolutionary support), wave their arms in
the air and flee the chamber to spread the word abroad. All, that is, except
one. For there is one elderly senator who sleeps on his bench throughout.
As the petitions are presented to Caesar, the senator sleeps. As Caesar is
stabbed, he sleeps. As the conspirators rouse themselves to proclaim libera-
tion in the streets, he sleeps still. As Antony breaks through the crowd and
is then left alone with the body to appeal dramatically to the gods and,
arm thrust in the air, assert his allegiance to his dead emperor, the senator
snoozes happily on the benches now deserted by his colleagues. In fact,

Figure 4.4 Still from *Julius Caesar* (Cines, 1914). The film makes provision for moments of still eloquence as well as of grand spectacle. Here Brutus, knife still in hand, contemplates the thing that he has done as he gazes back at the dead body of Caesar. Still taken from the film's lavish commemorative programme. Author's private collection.

were it not for an occasional sleepy twitch to remind us of his incongruous presence at the edges of the frame, the senator's sleeping performance would be almost missable.

The inspiration for the sleeping senator came directly from Gérôme who had inserted a sleeping senator on the benches in the right of his painting.[35] The film scene may, therefore, be seen in part as a cinematic homage to Gérôme. Nonetheless, in animating the painting (while only minimally animating the senator), Vitagraph transformed a single incongruous peripheral detail into a skittishly sustained point of puncture for the dignity of the scene as a whole. The sleeping senator becomes comic in

---

[35] Gérôme had a taste for depicting individuals abstracted from the emotional import of a scene: another Gérôme painting, 'Door of the Mosque El Asseneyn', shows a sentinel unemotionally smoking a pipe beside a row of severed heads. See 'Jean-Leon Gérôme Dead; French Painter and Sculptor Found Lifeless in Bed', *NYT* (11 January 1904), 7.

Figure 4.5 A lyre-player accompanies the meeting of Cordelia (Swayne Gordon)
with Kent, continues to play once the curtain is drawn back to reveal Lear and is
still playing after all other characters have left the set. Courtesy of the LOC's
paper print collection.

the film in ways he does not in the painting, since now his immobility is
dramatically juxtaposed with the frenetic levels of animation by which he
is surrounded, thus emphasising both its incongruity and its persistence.
Vitagraph's gleeful appropriation of the sleeping senator from the painting
and decision to leave him in place throughout the action suggests they
were aware of the contrapuntal fun to be had by juxtaposing contrasting tones of action within a single shot. When, therefore, the cataclysmic,
history-making piece of action takes place in centre frame, its gravitas is
gently ironised by the figure of the incognisant, nodding senator at the
periphery of the image.

It was a daring decision to risk detracting from the emotional intensity
of this particular scene through the inclusion of the snoozing senator.[36] It
was not, however, entirely uncharacteristic of Vitagraph: the inclusion of

---

[36] The decorous choreography and comedic inflection of Vitagraph's assassination scene makes it
the more surprising that police censors demanded the scene be cut before they would license
Julius Caesar for Chicago exhibition. Pearson and Uricchio, *Reframing Culture*, p. 66.

a divertingly comic touch in the corner of a big scene was almost, in fact, a signature trait. A further example comes in the Lear–Cordelia reunion in *King Lear* (1909). In the 1910 FAI *Re Lear* (*King Lear*), the beguiling Francesca Bertini (Cordelia) and theatrical star Ermete Novelli (Lear) draw out the emotional charge of the scene, which is allowed time for the pathos to work its effects. The *Lear* Quarto stipulates 'soft music' for this scene; Vitagraph took the cue and inserted an exaggeratedly soppy-looking lyre-player in the foreground of the shot (Figure 4.5). This figure provides the visual prompt for the real-world picture-house accompanist to supply appropriate 'soft music' at this point, colluding in the illusion that it emanates from the pictured musician. However, the lyre-player does more than simply cue a designated musical effect since, by monopolising audience attention, he gently sabotages the scene for comic effect. In parody of an angelic harpist, he plucks at the loose strings of his lyre with insistent sentimentality, eyes alternately closed and rolling skywards. His camera-hogging performance, like the sleeping senator's before him, is even allowed a moment on set alone after the other characters have exited the shot. The potential emotional intensity of the central action is here significantly diffused. Unlike FAI, Vitagraph did not, it seems, trust its principal actors to sustain the requisite pathos unaided.

Allowing a skittish flippancy to vie for supremacy with a more weighty significance as the determining tone of these scenes suggests an uncertainty on Vitagraph's part about how best to pitch the performance register for the big moments. They may have doubted their ability in any case to withhold comic effect from some scenes which, as the one-reel format demanded, had to play out at a speed and with a gestural emphasis not easily compatible with a high seriousness of tone. The peripheral presences of the snoozing senator and the lacklustre lyre-player seem to represent a preference for including an element of satirical undercut in dramatically fraught or emotionally intense scenes. And why might Vitagraph have sought to poke fun at its own endeavours in this way? Presumably to remain in control of the comedy (their generic specialism in this period) rather than accidentally becoming the victim of it.

Unsurprisingly perhaps, Italian films about Julius Caesar made no such irreverent intrusions into the grandeur and significance of the assassination of Caesar: there the acting was allowed to tell the story without diversion or dilution. The Cines one-reel *Brutus* of 1910, for example, directed by Enrico Guazzoni and starring Amleto Novelli, provided a serious-minded performance of the Capitol scene. In an impressively detailed review for the picture's American release in 1912, *MPW* captured the specific chore-ography and emotional charge of the moment:

To the left of the picture, as viewed from the audience, stands Cassius, a few feet behind Caesar. We watch his lips curl in a cruel smile as a senator makes a motion, and a parchment scroll is handed [to] the First Consul. Caesar glances at it and throws it on the floor with imperious gesture. As he does so Cassius snatches the robe from his shoulders. Caesar springs up and faces Cassius. He immedi-ately receives several downward dagger thrusts from the senators behind him. As he turns toward them, Cassius drives another home, and so it is until that sacred body receives the knives of all. Brutus is the last to inflict a wound; but he does it from the front, and the look that Caesar gives him – of reproach and surprise – shows that no other bolt from Jove can hurt either body or soul. Then Caesar covers his face with his garment and sinks to the floor. Not one vestige of shrinking is shown by him throughout the ordeal, not a trace of fear, on face or in action. The actor who took the character of Caesar merits much praise for preserving so thoroughly the dignity of the part.[37]

In the equivalent Vitagraph scene, the aspiration to preserve the dig-nity of the dramatic moment lost out to a counter-impulse to entertain. Vitagraph's flippancy is yet more starkly delineated when compared with Cines' feature-length (only partly Shakespearean) 1914 spectacular biopic *Julius Caesar* which had the time and inclination to mine the weighty poise of the moment without haste or embarrassment as is evidenced in, for example, Brutus' prolonged contemplation of the thing that he has done as he gazes back at the dead body of Caesar on the floor of the Capitol (Figure 4.4).

It was, it seems, an American phenomenon to reach for a satirical inflec-tion to give dynamism to a Shakespearean scene in this period. Neither Cines, Ambrosio, FAI, Milano, Rodolfi-Film, Hepworth or Gaumont were tempted in this respect. Britain produced earnest Shakespearean productions and, separately, it produced Shakespearean parodies, but no films that attempted to be both. In the US, however, Vitagraph was not alone in producing Shakespeare adaptations that both courted a persua-sive seriousness *and* occasionally ironised the silently frantic gesticulations playing out in centre frame.

A Winter's Tale (1910) was one of the first releases from the newly founded, American, smaller independent Thanhouser Film Company

---

[37] James S. McQuade '"Brutus". Kleine's First Cines Release – Extraordinary One-Reel Picture Based on Shakespeare's "Julius Caesar"', *MPW* v.11, n.3 (20 January 1912), 193. (The '12 January 1912' issue date given in Ball for this is incorrect.)

and served as an early expression of the company's cultural ambition.[38] The film was hailed a 'master-piece' (sic) for its artistic and photographic quality and the magnificence of its mounting and costumes.[39] For key moments, this film also applied a lightly parodic touch to the action. Present throughout the Sicilian scenes is an unexpected court jester/ fool who seems to have been parachuted in from beyond the orbit of this play's action. If he has any Shakespearean provenance at all, it is surely in *King Lear*.[40] He even looks similar in costume and in chubbiness of face to the fool in the Vitagraph *Lear* from the previous year. Curiously, his anomalous presence in *A Winter's Tale* seems to have provoked no comment in review – and the film was much reviewed (though principally by cineastes not Shakespeareans who might have been more alive to such interpolations). In the reunion scenes near the end of the film, the fool sits in the bottom left corner of the shot, blatantly sending up the touching scenes of reconciliation taking place at its centre. Thus when Perdita appears in Leontes' court and her story is recounted by the old shepherd, the fool alternates between leaning forward with excessively intense interest to hear the tale, and turning straight to camera, arms thrown in the air in mock-consternation, with deliberately hammed amazement. When it transpires that Perdita is the daughter whom Leontes had banished to her death years earlier, the fool cradles and rocks his jester's stick as if a baby, and then again looks straight to camera, head now on one side, in an exaggerated appeal to the audience to participate in the story's pathos (Figures 4.6a and b). As a succession of events of escalating narrative and emotional significance unfold before him and us, he takes delight in his marginal position to claim an alliance with the audience by commenting satirically upon each event in turn. The excessive nature of his interest (concern, sentimentality, amazement and joy at reunion), combined with his position outside the immediate sphere of the story (both narratively

---

[38] Between 1910 and 1916, Thanhouser produced seven Shakespeare films: *A Winter's Tale* (1910), *Romeo and Juliet* (1911), *The Tempest* (1911), *The Merchant of Venice* (1912), *Cymbeline* (1913), *Two Little Dromios* (1914) and *King Lear* (1916) and one film drama about the authorship of Shakespeare's plays entitled *Master Shakespeare, Strolling Player* (1916). *A Winter's Tale* was directed by Barry O'Neil from a scenario by Lloyd Lonergan and Gertrude Thanhouser (wife of company founder Edwin Thanhouser). Thanhouser's Shakespeare films are discussed in Ball, *Shakespeare on Silent Film*, pp. 68–93, 146–7, 151–5, 241–4. *Cymbeline* (1913) and *King Lear* (1916) are discussed in Buchanan, *Shakespeare on Film*, pp. 43–6. *A Winter's Tale* is commercially available on *Thanhouser Presents Shakespeare 1910–1916* (Thanhouser DVD Vol. 7).

[39] 'The Thanhouser Triumph', *MPW* v.6, n.21 (28 May 1910), 876.

[40] The Thanhouser fool is clearly not Autolycus. Ned Thanhouser (Edwin Thanhouser's grandson and producer of the *Thanhouser Presents Shakespeare* DVD) tells me he too has been unable to discover anything about this interpolated fool.

Figure 4.6a and b. Stills from *A Winter's Tale* (Thanhouser, dir. Barry O'Neil, 1910). Florizel (Alfred Hanlon) and Perdita (Amelia Barleon) arrive at the court of Leontes (Martin Faust) where Perdita is reunited with Leontes. In left of shot, an interpolated fool displays his cartooned responses to the drama of recognition and reconciliation taking place at the centre. Stills courtesy of the Motion Picture, Broadcasting and Recorded Sound Division, LOC.

and spatially), gives him the perfect platform from which to become an ironic commentator upon it. The fool's project is uncompromising pastiche: no potentially touching effect is left unpunctured by his ironising intervention, no moment of potential anxiety undisturbed by his own heightened mock-anxiety that serves as lightning conductor and so partial diffuser of our own.[41] The meta-narrative he provides makes fun of the gesturally emphatic and emotionally charged nature of the climactic scenes, before, perhaps, an audience had the chance to do so.

Playing this reconciliation scene from *The Winter's Tale*'s Act Five wordlessly was undoubtedly a challenge. Shakespeare wrote the scene as reported action, as if himself hesitant to present such acutely raw emotion directly on stage. This theatrical coyness then makes a subject of comment not only the extremity of passion experienced in the off-stage reunions ('They seemed almost, with staring on one another, to tear the cases of their own eyes' V.ii.11–12) but also the inability of words adequately to describe that passion ('I never heard of such another encounter, which lames report to follow it' V.ii.56–7). Reported action was not, of course, a viable option on silent film and Thanhouser shrank from attempting to represent in earnest the required heights of emotional transport through wordless action alone. Lest their efforts should fall short, or even the attempt appear ludicrous, they instead inserted a distancing mechanism into the scene. The film's satirising of its own narrative and performance processes through the figure of the fool left little room for subsequent would-be critics: it had stolen a march on them through its own entertaining processes of self-parody.

While exploring the potential of the frame edges to adjust the force of the action taking place at its centre, both Vitagraph and Thanhouser apparently lacked the confidence to allow the portentously charged moments, deprived as they were of words, to play entirely sincerely. Each company seemed to think that the big scenes, as presented on silent film, needed rescuing from ridicule by the addition of a satirical inflection of their own.

---

[41] The scene works in the tradition of *The Countryman and the Cinematograph* (Robert W. Paul, 1901) and Edison's *Uncle Josh at the Moving Picture Show* (Edwin S. Porter, 1902) in which the figure in left of frame responds as intermediary to the action taking place centre frame (on a cinema screen in those cases). The excessive responses of those audience proxy figures, however, were exposed as naïve and ridiculous, whereas their descendant, the Thanhouser fool, inverts the power balance by ironising the excesses of the central action.

There may be a clue to the spring for this in what Smith, Vitagraph's President, was to say about silent Shakespeare films as he reflected on the phenomenon from a later moment:

I contend that 'Old Will' had the movies to thank for an appreciable segment of new Shakespearean followers. Even the Bard himself would at least concede that among his new fans are many who, irritated by film versions, decided to look into the original to see if his plays are really as bad as the movies made out, and then found themselves implacably drawn into a new world.[42]

Vitagraph's Shakespeare films may indeed, as Smith worthily supposed, have served as a conduit to the original (worded) Shakespeare plays for newcomers. Underlying Smith's comment, however, is the calm expectation that the films will have irritated audiences. If this is more than a mere self-deprecating pose on Smith's part and such a position represents Vitagraph's general thinking from the period, it may well have been the fear of irritating that initially led Vitagraph to ironise their own Shakespearean endeavours as a wittily conceived bulwark against just such a possibility.

A MIDSUMMER NIGHT'S DREAM (1909)

A Midsummer Night's Dream, directed by Charles Kent and J. Stuart Blackton, starred Billy Ranous as Bottom who, drawing on some of his stage experience of a less elevated character, evidently took pleasure in the physical comedy the role afforded.[43] Lysander was played by Vitagraph's leading man Maurice Costello, whose two small daughters also appear in the film as part of Titania's sweet fairy retinue composed of little girls in white tutus and gauzy wings. Costello had played Antony in the company's *Antony and Cleopatra* (1908) and, as well as himself directing for the company, also later starred in a host of other Vitagraph quality productions including *Elektra* (1910), *A Tale of Two Cities* (1911) and the three-reel *As You Like It* (1912). Helena was played by Vitagraph's leading lady, Julia Swayne Gordon, an engaging screen actress with considerable stature, balletic grace to her movements and an expressive face. 'Little' Florence Turner who would play Viola opposite Swayne Gordon again in

---

[42] Albert E. Smith, *Two Reels and a Crank*, p. 263.
[43] On Ranous' theatrical experience, see Ball, *Shakespeare on Silent Film*, p. 40.

Twelfth Night the following year here played Titania.[44] She later became the 'Vitagraph Girl', a star adored on both sides of the Atlantic for her perky screen presence. Thirteen-year-old Gladys Hulette played Puck, reprising her screen debut as a delightfully sprightly miniature fairy in Vitagraph's *Princess Nicotine* (or *The Smoke Fairy*) just a few months before. Kent himself was the tall, imposing Theseus who holds himself with such dignity.

The film was greeted on release as that rare thing, a Shakespeare production sufficiently intelligible to be able to delight not only '[s]tudents of the great dramatist's works' but also 'the spectator ... not familiar with the works of Shakespeare'.[45] Here was a Shakespeare film with its own stand-alone value dependent neither on its source nor on supplementary knowledge of that source to make sense or give pleasure. The extraordinary compression required to make the story fit the one-reel format had been done by scenarist Eugene Mullin, who also scripted Vitagraph's *King Lear* and *Twelfth Night*. Sadly, however, the clarity that the film's first audiences enjoyed is largely now denied us, as the only surviving print is missing nearly a third of its original footage. Omissions include a brief section from the opening, the whole final scene back in Athens (including the performance of *Pyramus and Thisbe*) and a significant section from the middle. In the surviving print there is a particularly abrupt shot change between the discovery that Puck has put the love-juice on the eyes of the wrong Athenian and the cat-fight between Hermia and Helena; this is the result of a pragmatic splice made subsequently to cover the missing footage from this central section. The action lost from here includes Puck's anointing of Demetrius' eyes, Lysander's suit to Helena, Demetrius' awakening and parallel suit of Helena, Hermia's horrified discovery of Lysander's wooing of Helena and the quarrel between the male lovers. Delightful as the film still is in its surviving, incomplete and slightly fragmented form, compression tips over into mild confusion at intervals. This misrepresents the film as first released.

Vitagraph's pleasure in cinematic possibilities

The first in the run of Vitagraph Shakespeare films had been *Macbeth* (1908). Vitagraph used this release as a way of advertising the company's

[44] I asserted elsewhere that I doubted Ball's speculation that this was Florence Turner. Having studied more stills and star cards since, I am now persuaded that Ball was right: it is Turner.

[45] *Bioscope* (3 March 1910). Quoted in Ball, *Shakespeare on Silent Film*, p. 53.

industry-savvy status as producers of autonomous works of cinema (as opposed to dully respectful recordings of stage productions). They made clear their independence from a slavish allegiance to theatrical forms through a series of specifically cinematic magical conjurations, including scenes of double exposure for both the air-drawn dagger and Banquo's ghost. In line with the showcasing of cinematic magic of this earlier production, *A Midsummer Night's Dream* too enjoyed its capacity to create specifically cinematic illusions. Thus, for example, a series of simple stop-motion sequences makes Gladys Hulette's skipping, tripsy Puck appear and disappear with impish suddenness – and bestows on Bottom his ass's head. When Puck is instructed to collect the magic flower, a flying wire, some double exposure and a piece of careful frame composition, show her flying over a spinning globe. Such forms of trick photography bolstered the company's bid to present the cinema as an art form distinct from, rather than merely a wordless imitator of, theatre.

The film's use of outdoor locations helped to reinforce this. Unlike the mostly studio-bound *Julius Caesar* and *King Lear* made within the previous year, *A Midsummer Night's Dream* was shot in the open-air, in Prospect Park within easy reach of Vitagraph's Flatbush studios. That a specific point of commendation for the picture in reviews should have been its attractive use of natural scenery is no surprise: it is a visually charming piece in which appealing, well-dressed characters stumble entertainingly in and out of picturesque, sunlit, cheery copses. The density of vegetation visible in the film suggests that the filming took place in the summer. However, the film did not open until 25 December 1909. Such a delay was unusual in a period in which films were typically moved through the cycle of production, distribution and exhibition with commercially minded speed to take full advantage of the voracious market for new moving picture subjects. The Christmas release of *A Midsummer Night's Dream* almost certainly, therefore, represented a strategic deferral on the part of the company, to increase the impact of a seasonally festive, prestige film by bringing it out at a seasonally festive, holiday moment. The amount of favourable critical attention the film received through late December 1909 and early January 1910 suggests this proved a successful strategy.[46]

In its sequencing, dramatic energy and use of characters, *A Midsummer Night's Dream* is mostly attentive to the detail of the Shakespeare play and

---

[46] See Ball, *Shakespeare on Silent Film*, pp. 52–3.

keeps the three intertwined communities (of lovers, fairies and mechanicals) nicely in balance. One significant departure from Shakespeare, however, merits comment: whereas Shakespeare's wood outside Athens is ruled by Oberon, king of the fairies, Vitagraph's is ruled by an interpolated female fairy called 'Penelope'.

Penelope

Despite her long floaty dress, Penelope orchestrates events in the wood with all the influence and authority of an Oberon. Since the jealous lovers' quarrel between the two principal fairies in the wood is maintained despite the exchanged gender of one of them, as is their warm, even passionate, reconciliation at the end, it is difficult to avoid the impression that a same-sex love between Titania and Penelope is being delicately suggested in Vitagraph's version of the story. As Oberon does in the play, so here Penelope punishes Titania for her part in their quarrel by a form of sexual humiliation, offering a monstrous substitute in the form of Bottom to share her bed. And as Shakespeare's Titania does, so too this Titania is subsequently delighted to abandon the sleeping ass to be reunited with the fairy consort (here Penelope) who first caused her torment. Penelope and Titania clasp each other in relief at the end of the woodland sequences, and take their final exit by walking out of frame still entwined, without removing their transported gaze from each other's eyes (Figures 4.7a and b).

Penelope's changeling persona is a puzzle. Vitagraph offered no explanatory word on the subject and reviewers also failed to mention it – not even to express surprise. In the absence of contemporary comment, we can only speculate on the reasons for it.

It may, of course, simply have been that Vitagraph had more suitable actresses than actors available for casting in Summer 1909 and, wanting to showcase as many of them as possible in the latest flagship venture, created an extra female role for one of them. It is not known who the round-faced, Rubenesque actress is who plays Penelope,[47] though she looks not unlike the celebrated stage actress Rose Coghlan (who was to play a substantial Rosalind in the 1912 Vitagraph *As You Like It*). If Coghlan, or a comparably famous actress, became available at late notice, it is little wonder that

---

[47] There was no actress called Penelope (which might otherwise have explained the name) working for Vitagraph or for any of the East Coast companies in this period.

Figure 4.7 Stills from *A Midsummer Night's Dream* (Vitagraph, 1909).
a. Titania (Florence Turner) and Penelope (actress unknown) tiff over possession
of the Indian boy. b. Titania and Penelope are later warmly reunited.

Vitagraph took steps to create a prominent role for her within the drama. They might even have moved someone else aside if necessary to create the opening. If a late-in-the-day exchange of this sort *was* made, it would make sense of the title cards for some of the early prints in Britain which, according to *The Bioscope*, featured only the conventional appearances of 'Oberon' (with no mention of 'Penelope').[48] If Penelope was inserted at the eleventh hour to capitalise on an appealing casting opportunity, then Vitagraph communiqués to foreign distributors may not initially have been sufficiently explicit about the need to change the title cards to reflect this.

There may, however, have been reasons beyond the pragmatics of casting that predisposed Vitagraph to re-gender Oberon. Fairyland in general, and Shakespearean fairyland in particular, had been understood in the nineteenth century as a female domain. Puck and Ariel were regularly cast as women (or girls), and from 1840 onwards, in a trend started by Madame Vestris, Oberon was too.[49] Imitators of this particular piece of gender cross-casting included Augustin Daly in his 1895 production at Daly's Theatre and Herbert Beerbohm Tree in his famous 1900 production at Her Majesty's Theatre. The Atlantic posed little obstacle to theatrical gossip and if the idea of a female Oberon had some currency in late Victorian England, as it did, talk of this would certainly have reached the US. Vitagraph may, therefore, simply have done for Oberon what Asta Nielsen was subsequently to do for Hamlet (discussed in Chapter 7), tipping the role over from one suitable to be played by a woman into one that *was* a woman. The succession of Oberon-women on the stage must at the least have normalised the idea that Titania's fairy consort could be female.[50] Viewed in this light, Oberon's intriguing transmutation into Penelope does not cease to be a puzzle, but is less of a dramatic leap from understandings of Oberon in the early years of the twentieth century than it might seem in the early years of the current one.

Spectators at the time may not have reflected closely upon the implications of the radical act of gender displacement that Vitagraph had perpetrated. Certainly the prevailing climate and dominant representational modes would not have sensitised audiences to all interpretive possibilities, particularly perhaps in the US (whose audiences were considered, in

---

48 See the synopsis in *The Bioscope* (3 March 1910), 47.
49 See Jackson, 'Shakespeare's Fairies in Victorian Criticism and Performance', pp. 38–45.
50 This convention finds expression again in the ribald 1925 German film production *Ein Sommernachtstraum* (*A Midsummer Night's Dream*) in which, amongst an otherwise conventionally gendered cast, Oberon is played by the female Russian dancer, Tamara.

England at least, more prudish than European ones).[51] Watching the film now, however, it is difficult to imagine that Vitagraph was not conscious of the daring suggestion of a same-sex love they were offering to their spectatorship. In effect, Vitagraph dramatised an idea that could itself have been lifted straight from one of Shakespeare's festive comedies – that patterns of sexual attraction do not always conform to society's dominant (heterosexual) organisational principles. The insertion of Penelope into this version of the drama therefore resonates with other Shakespearean comedies (some of which Vitagragh themselves went on to adapt), and is far from neutral in its effects upon the rest of the film. For in a drama of explicit balance and contrasts between the fairy and mortal worlds, how could identifying the ruler of the fairy world as female not then adjust our view of the contrasting patriarchy of Athens with its conservative social rules, concern to uphold male authority and unbending implementation of the law?

A Midsummer Night's Dream in 1909

Although Vitagraph producers were technologically and commercially progressive, they were not, typically, progressive in their interpretations of Shakespeare – which makes their interpolation of Penelope the more striking. That significant departure aside, however, their vision of *A Midsummer Night's Dream* – discernible even within the confines of a highly compressed silent one-reeler – essentially conforms to nineteenth-century views of the play. Five years later, in 1914, Harley Granville Barker was to make a decisive move away from balletic, ethereal fairy spirits in his stage production at London's Savoy Theatre. Gone were the little girls with gauze wings and gone were the flying wires that encouraged a sense of airy lightness: in their place a new breed of fairy – ponderous, earth-bound and, according to an outraged review in *The Daily Mail*, 'sinister-looking … unlovely, unrecognisable'.[52] The production was an early herald of a decisive interpretive shift that would in time adjust readings of the play: the exquisitely delicate ballet of tripping fairies and well-meaning but

---

[51] See, for example, E. S. Dallas's mid-nineteenth-century tongue-in-cheek claim that Americans would put trousers on the legs of their pianofortes in order to avoid offending onlookers. 'The Drama', *Blackwood's Magazine* 79 (February 1856), 227–31 (228). In the US in 1909, in relation to Shakespearean moving pictures, there was a comparably ironic suggestion that a corset should perhaps be put on the Venus di Milo in order to satisfy an American taste for sexual decorum. *The Nickelodeon* (September 1909), 71.

[52] 'Did Shakespeare Mean This?', *The Daily Mail* (7 February 1914). On file at the Theatre Museum.

misled lovers bathed in ethereal moonlight and entangled in entertaining amorous pickles was to cede to a more tonally mixed exploration of the power of the imagination to debase as well as enhance. But the 1909 Vitagraph *Dream* preceded that shift. Indeed in 1911, just two years after its release, Beerbohm Tree, while reviving his production of *A Midsummer Night's Dream* at His Majesty's Theatre, wrote that the play 'presents a picture of pure love unsullied by any grossness of sensual passion.'[53] This was the world to which Vitagraph's *Dream* belonged. It remains wedded to a picturesque view of both delicate, feminine fairies and momentarily wayward lovers frolicking in an Arcadian retreat. By putting down a marker by which to recall the different set of interpretive priorities that used to dominate readings of this play, the film helps us to map the culturally revealing adjustments in tone and emphasis that the play's critical and performance history has undergone since.[54]

TWELFTH NIGHT (1910)

Though some of its scenes are out of sequence in the surviving print and the ending appears rushed, the Vitagraph *Twelfth Night*, released on 3 February 1910, is, to my mind, the most carefully produced picture of any of the company's surviving Shakespeare films. Its visually attractive sets are unusually well designed, its action carefully blocked, its frame composition detailed, its individual performances full of pantomimic flair and its cinematography technically astute. Vitagraph's own marketing puff for every film released was, naturally, enthusiastic, but there is a sense of enhanced pride in relation to this film in particular. The *Vitagraph Bulletin* was unreserved in its pre-release promotional push, calling it 'the best of all' its Shakespeare films:

Most elaborate preparations are being made ... A Shakespearean player of country-wide fame is one of the Vitagraph producers and he has been given absolutely a free hand in the selection of special players. If the Vitagraph could announce the cast of characters on the sheet you would be most astonished at the display of familiar names.[55]

[53] Herbert Beerbohm Tree, *Some Notes on A Midsummer Night's Dream, produced at His Majesty's Theatre (for the second time) on Easter Monday, April 17th, 1911* ... (London, 1911).

[54] See Buchanan, *Shakespeare on Film*, pp. 129–31.

[55] *Vitagraph Bulletin* (16–39 November 1909). Quoted in Pearson and Uricchio, *Reframing Culture*, p. 58.

'A Shakespearean player of country-wide fame' was a slightly hyperbolised billing for Charles Kent, the director of *Twelfth Night*. Kent was lauded by Vitagraph in terms unrelated to the quality of his direction or the aesthetics of the performances: the cultural capital he embodied in both his Englishness and his legitimate theatrical experience was a valuable commodity as part of Vitagraph's self-promotion as purveyors of quality aiming for cross-over markets.

In terms of its cultural project, Vitagraph cannot have been disappointed with the publicity the release garnered. In February 1910, *MPW* commended it as '[a]nother of the ambitious releases by this house', and expended as many words on the film's educational and improving mission to humanity as on its particular aesthetic, technical and interpretive virtues:

It elevates and improves the literary taste and appreciation of the great mass of the people, performing in this way service [sic] which cannot be measured in material terms. Such work is in the nature of an educational service, which is deserving of the heartiest support of all who are working for the improvement of humanity.[56]

Whether or not *Twelfth Night* was actually able to 'improve[] ... humanity', it certainly peddled a wholesome – even sanitised[57] – version of Shakespeare and did so through the line-up of 'familiar names' to which the *Vitagraph Bulletin* had referred.

Charles Kent and the Vitagraph repertory company

It was, of course, standard Vitagraph practice to deploy their principal players in different casting combinations for successive pictures, as 'Mother Squeers', commenting in 1911 on the distinctive features of individual production companies, had recognised:

Another reason why Vitagraph is popular is their stock company. The same players month after month – good dependable faces whom you come to like from very familiarity.[58]

---

[56] *MPW* v.6, n.7 (19 February 1910), 257.

[57] The darker scenes of torment to which Shakespeare's Malvolio is subjected are excised: Vitagraph's Malvolio is, therefore, far *less* 'notoriously abused' (V.i.375) than his Shakespearean counterpart. And whereas in *Dream*, Vitagraph seems to have introduced a same-sex love, in omitting Antonio from this production – the character whose 'desire' for Sebastian, '[m]ore sharp than filèd steel' (III.iii.4–5) is expressive about his orientation – this rendering of *Twelfth Night* is considerably more anodyne than Shakespeare's.

[58] 'The Old Lady in the Audience', *Motography* (May 1911), 77–8.

In *Twelfth Night*, Tefft Johnson (who plays Orsino) was the exception to this, having only recently arrived in the company from Edison. The other players, however, were indeed already 'good dependable faces' from the 'Vitagraph family'. One such was Julia Swayne Gordon. She had played a dignified Cordelia in *King Lear*, a wounded but proud Helena in *A Midsummer Night's Dream* and a Desdemona and Portia of unknown character in the lost Vitagraph films of *Othello* and *The Merchant of Venice*. She appears here as an eye-catching and ebullient Olivia whose dancing eyes are visible even through the veil she assumes to welcome Orsino's embassy. 'Little' Florence Turner (as invariably known) plays a sprightly Viola and I return to the particularities of her career below.

It was, however, in casting himself as a deliciously haughty Malvolio that Kent was able to make most purposeful use of the ongoing familiarity of Vitagraph players to their regular audiences. When he made *Twelfth Night*, his distinguished-looking tall figure would already have been recognised by his audiences as, for example, King Duncan in *Macbeth* (1908), Capulet in *Romeo and Juliet*, Caesar in *Julius Caesar* (1908), King Arthur in *Launcelot and Elaine* (1909) and Duke Theseus in *A Midsummer Night's Dream* (1909). A slightly bombastic authoritarianism was the common factor across these roles and it is this that is incidentally referenced as a point of parody in his Malvolio. The exaggerated assumption of faux authority by Malvolio and the gentle mockery of him that ensues would, no doubt, have been the more enjoyable for audiences accustomed to seeing Kent play authority in earnest in the earlier films. A repertory company that recycled its players across productions made possible just such cumulative role associations and the retrospective referencing (and, in this case, humorous puncturing) of an accrued set of character attributes.

It is tempting to see Charles Kent as a director specifically privileging himself as an actor within *Twelfth Night*. He does, for example, inadvertently become an eye-draw as the most engaging of the noblemen extras in the background of Orsino's court and ensures the centrality to many set-ups of his own self-aggrandising Malvolio. Significantly, he gives himself, as Malvolio, that most rare thing in any of these films, a cut-in to a mid-shot, allowing us to enjoy his stiff pomposity, smug pedantry and self-deluding vanity from close quarters as he reads the forged letter. Kent, however, conceived of the film as more than simply a highly compressed plot romp and more than simply a vehicle for his own talents. Not only in his dwelling on his own character's performance, therefore, but in his direction of other players too, he ensures that the detail of actorly expression becomes part of the telling of the story. Actors are allowed sufficient screen time to register fluctuating feelings, even in apparently inconsequential

Figure 4.8 Malvolio (Kent) finds the planted letter, observed by a mischievous
Maria, Sir Toby and Sir Andrew in *Twelfth Night* (Vitagraph, 1910). Courtesy of the
paper print collection at the LOC.

moments, so that not just the unfolding plot but the characters' own emotional vacillations also can become part of the dramatic landscape.

Viola's feelings before going in to seek employment with Orsino (personal grief, fear of discovery, amorous heartache on seeing him, pleasure
in her own liberating disguise and empowering resolve to seek work in his
employ) are evidence of this;[59] so too are Olivia's mood shifts as she dismisses Andrew Aguecheek's exasperating suit, graciously agrees to receive
Orsino's messenger, coyly welcomes 'Cesario', feels the first sharp stab of
love, authoritatively dismisses her companions, lifts her veil with a flir-
tatious desire for approval, scorns the message while, with increasingly
unsubtle expressions of ardour, wooing the messenger and revels in the
transport of her own new-found feelings. Even the (unknown) actress who

---

[59] In the surviving print, released on the *Silent Shakespeare* DVD, this scene appears out of plot
sequence, just before Viola goes to see Olivia.

plays Maria is given sufficient exposure to communicate an energetic *joie de vivre* and natural inclination towards mischief, both of which work in pleasing counterpoint to Kent's ponderous high-handedness as Malvolio (Figure 4.8). If *A Midsummer Night's Dream* was an energetic and prettily managed gallop through the plot, *Twelfth Night* makes a more concerted effort to be an actors' piece: that it should have been an actor, with actorly priorities, directing it is, therefore, not surprising.

Set and cinematography

Not that *Twelfth Night* lacked scenic attributes. The 'elaborate preparations' to which Vitagraph had alluded in their pre-release puff involved, for the standards of its moment, some notably detailed set construction and thoughtful set dressing. The lush, gilt-edged painting that adorns the wall in Orsino's court, for example, acts as a pleasing commentary on the character of its owner – the languid, indulgent pose of its pampered, supine, exoticised subject being conveyed to shore reinforcing the decadence of Orsino's own amorous mood and confirming the draw towards stillness that is acting upon Orsino's court in its paralysing self-regard. As such, it also acts as foil to Olivia's household's wholesale resistance to painterly arrest or indeed to any other form of decorous stasis. And simultaneously, of course, in its specific depiction of an elegantly respectful way for a lady to be carried ashore from boat to waiting lover, it throws Viola's fate into greater relief by acting as an ironic foil to her own turbulent arrival on the shores of Illyria. Moreover, the design of the set at Olivia's court, complete with marble columns, ornamental pool and artistic backdrop of a grand estate's gardens, worked with the advanced receptivity of the cameras of 1910 (more light sensitive even than they had been in 1908) to make it possible for action to take place simultaneously in different planes of action at different focal lengths. Thus the detail of the shot in which Olivia's companions troop out to leave her alone with Viola holds simultaneously in visible focus Olivia and Viola in the foreground, departing ladies-in-waiting and others strolling along an attractive walkway in the middle distance and Feste (actor unknown) dancing backwards in depth of field along the far side of the ornamental pool (Figure 4.9). In terms of the progress of the dramatic narrative, the busy visuals in depth of field do briefly detract from the interestingly complex exchange happening between the two central characters in the foreground. In aesthetic and technical terms, however, it is clearly a bravura moment.

Figure 4.9   Olivia (Swayne Gordon) shows her unveiled face to Viola (Turner) in the foreground while other planes of action are visible in depth of field either side of an ornamental pool in *Twelfth Night* (Vitagraph, 1910).

There is some footage missing from the denouement scene (as also from the beginning) in the surviving print of *Twelfth Night*.[60] Nevertheless, just enough frames survive to reveal a final scene that Shakespeare teasingly denies us: Viola restored to her female self and so actually seen 'in other habits' as 'Orsino's mistress and his fancy's queen' (V.i.383–4). It was not only part of Vitagraph's customary plot-clarifying agenda that the femininity of Viola/Cesario should be reasserted in the closing moments of the film (though that no doubt was part of it); it also helped to put 'little' Florence Turner appealingly on display in a range of costumes. By 1910, Turner had become a valuable company commodity and it was in Vitagraph's interests to showcase their star property appropriately.

'The Vitagraph Girl'

Florence Turner's potential was not immediately realised when she entered the industry. Her progress towards becoming what amounted to the

---

[60]   The film was released as 970 feet. It survives in 743 feet.

industry's first marketable 'star' is, therefore, revealing about the workings of the studio and the industry. Having been taken on by Vitagraph in early 1907, she supplemented the acting wages received for the small parts she was initially given (including bit parts in *Macbeth, Romeo and Juliet* and *King Lear*)[61] by helping out in other capacities for the company – as seamstress, cashier or clerk – as the need arose.[62] By high summer of 1908, however, her appealing petite-ness and facial versatility were winning her leading roles and she no longer needed to diversify in order to earn a decent wage. She spent the next two years shuttling between working for Vitagraph on the one hand (playing, for example, Jessica in *The Merchant of Venice* (1908), Queen Elizabeth I in *Kenilworth* (1909), Elaine in *Launcelot and Elaine* (1909) and Titania in *A Midsummer Night's Dream* (1909)) and, on the other, appearing in a series of Edison pictures for Edwin S. Porter. By 1909, however, she was already being heartily promoted as 'The Vitagraph Girl' and in 1910 she stopped moonlighting for Edison to consolidate her corporate allegiance and remove any ambiguity about her branded identity. She was not only the first actress to have been put under contract by a film company,[63] but also the first actress to be known as a named company asset. (Biograph followed suit by naming Florence Lawrence – an actress appropriated from the Vitagraph company and sometimes confused with Turner – the 'Biograph Girl'.)

Even before her own name was known, therefore, Florence Turner's popularity was assured. As late as 1912, a writer for *The New York Dramatic Mirror* opened his article about the actress with: 'Florence Turner. Do you recognize the name? Yes? No? If not, glance at the accompanying picture.' Though he could equivocate about whether her name might or might not trigger instant recognition, he was in no doubt about the universal familiarity of her face. In his own travels, as he reported, he had marvelled at the warmth of the response elicited when that well-known face was 'thrown upon the screen' in Scotland, England and Germany. 'In fact,' he continued, 'the face almost continually followed me during my wanderings over the globe'.[64] The popularity

---

[61] Turner did not play one of the elder sisters in *King Lear* as she is sometimes credited. Neither actress bears any resemblance to her (though one of Goneril's ladies-in-waiting, a short actress who waits by the castle gate, may be her).

[62] See Turner's own report of her various roles for the company in Leonard Crocombe, 'The Girl of the Film: Florence Turner', *Pictures and the Picturegoer* (6 June 1914). Quoted in Slide, *The Big* V, p. 34.

[63] Slide, *The Big* V, p. 34.

[64] Harvey H. Gates, 'Florence Turner Talks About Acting', *The New York Dramatic Mirror* (30 October 1912), 28.

of Turner's face was not so much down to its beauty (for her looks were not as classically attractive as those of some of her contemporaries), but to the apparently transparent and endlessly mutable way in which it registered emotion and so encouraged identification. The subsequent screen star Norma Talmadge reported her own youthful picture-going experience in these terms:

Leaning forward in my hard chair, I was as much a part of Florence Turner as was her own reflection on the silver sheet. I laughed when she laughed, suffered when she suffered, wept when she wept. A veritable orgy of emotions for five copper pennies.[65]

Turner's versatility as an actress ensured she played across genres and social strata. She also had the poise to sustain a one-hander in the 1911 Vitagraph one-reeler *Jealousy*, which, as a study in the art of dramatic expression, was unrelieved either by title cards or the intervention of any other actor.[66] From April 1910 onwards, she pioneered making personal appearances at movie theatres around Brooklyn where she gave little speeches and was enthusiastically received.[67] The *MPW*'s assessment in 22 March 1913 was that Florence Turner's 'work increased the sale of Vitagraph pictures over those of all other makes.'[68]

In 1912, Turner was indirectly compensated for having missed out to Florence Lawrence on the part of Juliet in the 1908 *Romeo and Juliet* by now being cast in the lead for the more imaginative and ambitious Vitagraph Shakespearean spin-off, *An Indian Romeo and Juliet* (no print of which survives). In this she played Ethona, a Mohawk princess, opposite Costello who played the Huron brave with whom her character tragically falls in love against the wishes of both tribes.[69] The Shakespearean drama of the forbidden romance, secret marriage and tragic ending of young lovers from opposed families was, therefore, neatly transposed to a native American setting – a re-racinating approach to the Shakespearean drama that has been much emulated since.

By the point in 1913 when Florence Turner left Vitagraph to branch out on her own, she had become completely identified with the company. So much was this the case that she retained the Vitagraph sobriquet even when no longer employed there. Mother Squeers had commended

---

[65] Norma Talmadge quoted in Albert E. Smith, *Two Reels and a Crank*, p. 191.
[66] Slide, *The Big* V, p. 35.   [67] *Ibid.*, p. 36.
[68] *MPW* (22 March 1913). Quoted in Slide, *The Big* V, p. 36.
[69] The details of the story and setting are given in *MPW* v.11, n.7 (17 February 1912), 581.

Vitagraph for being one of the first production companies to release the names of their players:

And Vitagraph hasn't shown any foolish aversion to featuring their players. Maurice Costello and Florence Turner are the best known names among the actor folks today, simply because they have been known so long.[70]

The profitable irony was that the Vitagraph name and imprimatur became the more emphatically known through releasing the names of their players even than it had been when Vitagraph was the sole authoring agent associated with each picture. Corporate value could now, after all, be vested in these corporate ambassadors and they, as its glamorous and culturally edifying representatives, could carry the Vitagraph brand with them in their own person. When Florence Turner appeared on the Brooklyn Stage in April 1913, for example:

The little actress was much affected by the cordiality accorded her [at the Fifth Avenue Theater] ... They showered flowers upon her and wildly waved flags bearing the Vitagraph print as she made her appearance upon the stage.[71]

Branded asset that she was, Florence Turner seems to have inspired both an intensely personal and a completely corporate response. '[T]he Vitagraph print' that was enthusiastically waved at her was, of course, the Vitagraph eagle. Like the stars themselves now making personal appearances in the extra-cinematic world, it too had found its way out of the films.

*

Back in 1896, when Albert E. Smith and J. Stuart Blackton gave touring film exhibitions featuring Edison shorts, Blackton would give a lecture to accompany the show. As Smith subsequently recalled, they often chose to emphasise the wonder of moving images by initially projecting the first frame of their most popular film, *The Black Diamond Express*, as a frozen image. This still image showed a steam train heading apparently straight towards the camera. Blackton the impresario (or 'terroristic mood setter' as Smith colourfully remembered him) would work the audience's anticipation with the following commentary:

Ladies and Gentlemen, you are now gazing upon a photograph of the famous Black Diamond Express. In just a moment, a cataclysmic moment, my friends, a

70 'The Old Lady in the Audience', *Motography* (May 1911), 77–8.
71 'Observations by our Man About Town', *MPW* v.16, n.1 (5 April 1916), 51.

moment without equal in the history of our times, you will see this train take life in a marvelous and most astounding manner. It will rush toward you belching smoke and fire from its monstrous iron throat.[72]

Here were a couple of showmen with a consciously employed instinct for the saleability of making the still image move and for thereby generating the gasp.

Before the cinematograph made its claim on him, beyond his life on the stage and in the study, Shakespeare had also previously found selective expression in a series of still, visual forms – including paintings, edition illustrations and even as a series of representative projected images through the magic lantern (see Chapter 1). What Vitagraph did for Shakespeare, as also for the Diamond Express, in a 'marvelous and most astounding manner', was to turn such moments of suspended animation into moving action. As the very name of their company – Vita-graph – evocatively attested, their business was to make the still image live. Temporality and dramatic impulse were allowed to erupt from the stuff of the still photograph and develop into swiftly crafted cameo dramas. Vitagraph even referenced the processes by which this was happening through, for example, the visual quotation of Gérôme's 'Death of Caesar' animated by the action of *Julius Caesar*. The effect of bringing this painting to life in *Julius Caesar* may be pitted against the contrasting effect of Orsino's grand painting in *Twelfth Night* – a painting which remains a painting, serving as the still point of artistic languor against which the varying degrees of animation of the characters, and of the film itself, may be measured. There was no monstrous iron throat or belching smoke in Vitagraph's Shakespeare pictures, but there was an energy and verve that converted still image into a story and, in the process, both contributed to the commercial success of the Vitagraph empire and confirmed its cultural credentials as a maker of quality pictures. Through the unrivalled profile and global reach these films were then able to achieve, they also became the spur that inspired many others to make moving pictures from Shakespearean material.

---

[72] Albert E. Smith, *Two Reels and a Crank*, p. 39. Smith and Blackton were not to make their own films until 1897.

CHAPTER 5

Pedigree and performance codes in silent films of Hamlet

Hamlet (Gaumont-Hepworth: Hay Plumb, 1913)
Amleto (Rodolfi-Film: Eleuterio Rodolfi, 1917)

'Hamlet', as Shakespeare wrote it, is very ill suited for interpretation on the screen, being essentially a drama of the soul and not of the body.[1]

HAMLET AND SILENT FILM

To say that *Hamlet* depends intimately upon the aesthetic, psychological and social functions of words spoken aloud may be to say little more than that it is a play. In the case of *Hamlet*, however, spoken language is much more than just the engine of the play's articulation: it is also one of its key dramatic interests. The play concerns itself directly and repeatedly with the encounters and discrepancies between private thought and public utterance. It plays daringly with the conventions of the inaudibility of the soliloquy (III.i.182–3), places acts of listening and of overhearing at the heart of its court politics and explicitly counsels against letting a gestural performance take precedence over a verbal one (III.ii.16–24). Hamlet allows himself to sound studiedly off-hand about '[w]ords, words, words' (II.ii.195), but his own are much more than just sounds in the air: they are the delicate twists and turns of thinking process rendered audible, of a troubled soul consoling itself with linguistic flippancy and linguistic profundity (and sometimes both at once) and of a self encrypting itself for some audiences while laying itself bare for others. Moreover, the play enjoys the tautly tuned interplay between speaking and not speaking, between linguistic revelation and strategic silence or evasion. When Hamlet says, 'But break, my heart, for I must hold my tongue' (I.ii.159), his willed suppression of language and the resulting dramatic tension derives

---

[1] Review of the British Gaumont film of *Hamlet*, *The Bioscope* (25 September 1913), 982.

from the exquisite, sustained poise of the delay before he *ceases* to hold his tongue. Similarly, the players' presentation of their drama in dumb show in Act V scene ii is offered as the teasing aperitif to the worded version that follows it. As such, the two parts of the play-within-the-play serve as a charged distillation of the cadences of the play as a whole. The modulations between linguistic suppression and expression and between wordless and worded performances sit both structurally and thematically near the centre of the play.

One of the sacrifices incurred by removing the spoken word from the performance space of this play, therefore, is the loss of the contrapuntal, and designedly provocative, engagement between the dumb show and its worded sequel and between their various proxies at large in the play. When dumb show is not balanced by speech, the frisson of that particular interplay is necessarily lost. Moreover, Hamlet himself insists on the crucial difference between 'that within which passeth show' on the one hand and 'the trappings and the suits of woe' on the other (I.ii.85–6). Silencing the drama necessarily invests the external 'trappings' with greater prominence while placing 'that within which passeth show' by definition beyond reach. The silent movie glories in that which is amenable to being shown. Even an inner life must be given some form of visual expression, however subtly suggested or symbolically configured, to have any purchase in this medium. Shakespeare's *Hamlet*, by contrast, specifically alerts its audiences to the potentially suspect character of manifestation and to the value of occlusion. Rendering this dramatic material in this medium of expression might, therefore, seem to constitute a peculiarly heightened encounter of antagonistic interests: *the* play of words in a form which emphatically privileges quite other communicative systems. The risk, in *The Biograph*'s terms from 1913, is of turning it into a drama more of the body than the soul.

Given the extent of *Hamlet*'s self-reflexive interest in the power, purpose and contexts of its speech acts, it is a striking irony that this play should have proved immensely popular to the silent film industry. The seasoned American Shakespearean film producers Vitagraph and Thanhouser sensibly, perhaps, fought shy of it (despite a near skirmish in this respect on Vitagraph's part and some skittish borrowings from it by both companies).[2] Nevertheless, approximately fifteen other production companies in Europe and the US – from the 1900 duel scene starring Sarah Bernhardt to the

---

[2] For details about the unmade Vitagraph *Hamlet*, see Ball, *Shakespeare on Silent Film*, p. 200. The offshoots are: *When Hungry Hamlet Fled* (Thanhouser, 1915) and *Freddy Versus Hamlet* (Vitagraph, 1916). Each is only tangentially Shakespearean.

radically re-gendered 1920 feature film starring Asta Nielsen – did take on the challenge. These included Jean Mounet-Sully, the distinguished French stage Hamlet, playing bowls with Yorick's skull in *c*.1909,[3] and, from 1910, three separate productions: Nordisk's Danish version starring the celebrated German stage Hamlet Alwin Neuss which, with an explicit eye on the tourist market, was filmed at Elsinore; the Italian company Cines' version (a reissue of Cines' own earlier version of 1908) in which the ghost of Hamlet senior informs his son of his own murder by projecting a cinematic account of it onto the back wall of a cave;[4] and the efficiently executed English Barker film starring Charles Raymond. In addition to the catalogue of more or less earnest silent film 'adaptations' of *Hamlet*, the extensive catalogue of creative reworkings, parodic offshoots and zany borrowings exceeds easy reckoning. These include *When Hungry Hamlet Fled* (Thanhouser, 1915), *Pimple as Hamlet* (Piccadilly, 1916), *To Be or Not to Be* (Beauty, 1916), *Hamlet Made Over* (Lubin, 1916), *Freddy Versus Hamlet* (Vitagraph, 1916), *The Barnyard Hamlet* (Powers, 1917) and *Oh'Phelia* (Anson Dyer, 1919). In an impressive variety of guises, therefore, *Hamlet* popped up frequently on moving picture screens throughout the silent era.

*

Despite the play's innate resistance to the priorities and strengths of silent cinema, *Hamlet* did hold distinct compensatory appeals for the film industry. Prime among these was its unrivalled status in the theatrical canon. Not only is *Hamlet* the supreme actor's play, it is also totemically 'Shakespearean'. An actor who wished to immortalise his (or her) artistry on film would find in *Hamlet* the most resolutely actorly vehicle through which to do so. Equally, if a production company wished to signal its own cultural legitimacy or artistic aspirations, the most emphatic, short-hand way to do that was to make a film of *Hamlet*.

Both *Hamlet* films considered in this chapter are multi-reel features and both sought to take advantage of the iconicity of the play and the profile of their star to produce a moving picture of ambitious quality and reach. The first is the 1913 English Gaumont production, directed by Hay Plumb, produced by Cecil Hepworth and starring the eminent sixty-year-old classical stage actor Sir Johnston Forbes-Robertson (1853–1937).[5] The second is a

---

[3] Ball, *Shakespeare on Silent Film*, p.108.   [4] Buchanan, *Shakespeare on Film*, p. 51.
[5] The film opened at the New Gallery Kinema in Regent Street on 22 September 1913. It was 5,800 feet in length. I refer to the film as 'English' rather than 'British' since it was specifically through a

1917 Italian production directed by Eleuterio Rodolfi for Rodolfi-Film and starring the eminent forty-six-year-old Italian classical stage actor Ruggero Ruggeri (1871–1953).[6] Both films had their roots in high-profile stage productions: Forbes-Robertson had regularly played Hamlet to critical acclaim in England and the US and came to the film fresh from appearing in the role in his Farewell (retirement) Season at Drury Lane; Ruggeri had also attracted considerable attention for his Hamlet at the Teatro Lirico in Milan two years before making the film. He was to star again as Hamlet in international touring productions twice during the 1920s – including a memorable visit to London in 1926. As had also been the case for a clutch of earlier Hamlets, therefore, these two Hamlet film performances need to be understood in the context of the stage performances that first suggested them. Alongside an account of the films' theatrical debts, here I consider the formal properties of each film, the reputations of each on first release, and how these reputations have been consolidated since. At the time of writing, neither film has yet been made commercially available.

FORBES-ROBERTSON AND THE HEPWORTH/ PLUMB PRODUCTION

Though not yet commercially released, the 1913 film starring Forbes-Robertson is widely known of in critical communities in ways that the 1917 Ruggeri film is not. The production stable from which the 1913 *Hamlet* emerged may in part account for its enduring profile. This was difficult to rival both for its rare distinction in personnel and for its resoundingly English character. As a result it generated some significant expectant excitement in England in 1913, even ahead of its September release. In fact, as soon as the filming project had been announced in June of that year, it became the subject of an intense and enthusiastic publicity campaign. The English trade paper *The Bioscope*, for example, referred to the project as 'without doubt one of the most interesting events that has ever taken place in the cinematograph industry'. No expense, it was claimed, had

version of Englishness that it was marketed. I have viewed two prints of the 1913 *Hamlet*: at the BFI National Archive and the Folger respectively.

[6] The 1917 Italian film is available to view in a print with French intertitles at the BFI National Archive, the Cineteca di Bologna in Italy and the Cinématèque de Toulouse in France (where it is inexplicably catalogued as having been made in 1910). It cost an estimated £4,000 to make and opened at the Teatro Vittoria in Turin in late November 1917. The prints at the Cineteca di Bologna and at the BFI National Archive are each approximately 4,500 feet in length (which, run at 18fps, translates into *c.*50 minutes' worth of viewing). It is these two prints that I have viewed.

been spared in the filming (reported to have cost an impressive £10,000), or in the hiring of the recently ennobled Sir Johnston Forbes-Robertson to immortalise on screen his well-seasoned but still immensely popular Hamlet.[7] *The Bioscope* was irrepressibly confident about the film's prospects, particularly when bearing in mind the respectable Hepworth Company's 'achievements in the past with this class of work'.[8]

A raft of indisputably 'quality' elements came together in this film, enabling producers, distributors and previewers to eulogise about it with almost nationalistic fervour. In July 1913, still two months before the film's release, *The Bioscope* surpassed even its own enthusiasm of the previous month:

The filming of 'Hamlet,' the greatest English play, with Sir Johnston Forbes-Robertson, the greatest living exponent of the most famous part in the whole world's drama, in the title *rôle*, has been perhaps the most notable event up to the present in the history of British cinematography, and it was only natural that Mr. Cecil Hepworth, the greatest British producer of cinematograph plays, should have been approached by Messrs. Gaumont, the originators of the enterprise, as the man capable before all others of carrying through successfully this most difficult of undertaking [sic]. There can be no man in this country today who has a deeper knowledge of cinematography, nor a greater capacity for applying his knowledge to artistic ends than Mr. Hepworth, and, although one has not yet had an opportunity of inspecting the result of his latest and most ambitious production, one has the utmost confidence in its success.[9]

For all the apparent hyperbole of declaring Forbes-Robertson 'the greatest living exponent of the most famous part in the whole world's drama', it was certainly true that his reputation for playing Hamlet was unrivalled. When he played the role in 1897 at the Lyceum, he had struck B.W. Findon as 'the Hamlet of all time' and 'something approaching an ideal Hamlet'[10] and, by critical consensus, he had retained a quiet ownership over the role since. In his autobiography, Forbes-Robertson warmly acknowledged the special status that *Hamlet* had assumed in his life and work, and even recorded his gratitude for its contribution to his economic security, claiming that a judiciously timed *Hamlet* revival had 'saved my

[7] His Hamlet had been well received in both England and the United States for many years. His autobiography, *A Player Under Three Reigns* (Boston: Little, Brown and Company, 1925) provides details of his many performances.

[8] *The Bioscope* v.19, n.348 (12 June 1913), 773.

[9] 'The Filming of "Hamlet": Interview with Mr. Cecil Hepworth', *The Bioscope* v.20, n.354 (24 July 1913), 275.

[10] B. W. Findon, 'Farewell of Forbes-Robertson', *The Play Pictorial* v. 21, n.129 (June 1913), 111.

financial position on many occasions'.[11] The performance he gave, in various modulated versions across its many theatrical outings, was predominantly a measured and an intellectual one, marked by a dignity and introspection and critically celebrated for its rejection of the emotional histrionics preferred by some of his contemporaries. In October 1897, for example, George Bernard Shaw commended Forbes-Robertson's Hamlet for 'seizing delightedly on every opportunity for a bit of philosophic discussion'. *The Stage* saw in his 1913 Hamlet a man of 'moral and intellectual superiority', and *The Era* admired how he combined '[g]reat nervous activity' with 'perfect self-restraint'.[12] His Hamlet, moreover, made a lasting impression. In 1960 Alan Dent was to hail it 'the supreme Hamlet between Irving's and Gielgud's' and, in acknowledgement of his status as *the* classical actor of his moment, after his death, the *Hamlet* edition he had himself used became a symbolic gift passed from one 'great' Hamlet to the next across the generations as a sign of privileged distinction amongst actors.[13]

Forbes-Robertson's stage appearances as Hamlet at Drury Lane in May and June 1913 attracted a blaze of appreciative publicity, in the theatre world and beyond. This 'Farewell Season' served as a high-profile theatrical flourish to fête him and launch him into his 'retirement' in America. Photographs of his languid and intellectual Hamlet were widely reproduced in contemporary trade journals and as commercial postcards, and a reproduction of J. Glulick's 1907 charcoal drawing of Forbes-Robertson's Hamlet holding aloft Yorick's skull was not only included in Drury Lane's 'Farewell Season Souvenir Programme' in June, but was also itself put out in postcard form (Figure 5.1). In buying Forbes-Robertson's Hamlet for its forthcoming moving picture, therefore, Gaumont was acquiring a well-established brand with a very well developed market profile.

It is not surprising that, from *The Bioscope*'s point of view, the film in prospect seemed to ooze prestige from every (as yet unseen) frame. From its source material (Shakespeare) to its cast list (Sir Johnston Forbes-Robertson, his wife Lady Gertrude Elliott and the rest of their Drury Lane company); from its production team (Hay Plumb and Cecil Hepworth) to its locations

[11] See Forbes-Robertson, *A Player Under Three Reigns*, p. 287.
[12] Shaw in *The Saturday Review* (2 October, 1897). Quoted in Wilson (ed.), *Shaw on Shakespeare*, p. 87; *The Stage* (27 March 1913), p. 19; *The Era* (29 March 1913), p. 19.
[13] Alan Dent, 'The World of the Cinema: Speculations and Regrets', *ILN* (14 May 1960). Unpaginated clipping on file at the Theatre Museum. On the history of Forbes-Robertson's own copy of the play, see Buchanan, *Shakespeare on Film*, pp. 1–2.

Figure 5.1 J. Glulick's 1907 charcoal drawing of Forbes-Robertson as Hamlet in the Farewell Season Souvenir Programme, June 1913. Author's private collection.

(including an elaborate reconstruction of Elsinore Castle at Lulworth Cove, the gardens of Hartsbourne Manor, home of Lady Robertson's sister, a private garden at Halliford-on-Thames and a private lake at Walton-on-Thames): in every respect, the film's faultless, even aristocratic, pedigree made itself felt. Forbes-Robertson's own credentials were not, of course, incidental to this. Hepworth reported that while filming at Lulworth Cove, '[t]he whole place frothed with excitement and everybody wanted to know when the "Sir" was coming and where the "Sir" would stay and for how long'.[14]

---

[14] Cecil Hepworth, *Came the Dawn: Memories of a Film Pioneer* (London: Phoenix House, 1951), p. 117.

Figure 5.2 The front cover of the Forbes-Robertson
souvenir issue of *The Play Pictorial* (June 1913).
Author's private collection.

Social status and the film's popularity became yet more inextricably
linked after the film's release. Two years after its domestic release, and
despite the war, on 7 July 1915 it was additionally given a US distribution.[15]
An advertisement in the American trade paper *MPW* sold it thus: 'This
famous actor, knighted by the King of England, needs no introduction'.[16]
In the following week's edition, an extended article clarified what it considered one of the indisputable selling points of the film: 'Sir Johnston

---

[15] The film had previously been released in Germany and India.
[16] *MPW* v.25, n.1 (3 July 1915), 18.

Forbes Robertson ... is a man of splendid education and family.'[17] Moving picture patrons were, that is, being appealed to on the basis of the breeding of its star: or rather, they were asked to infer the quality of the performance partly from the impressive pedigree of the performer. Elisions of this sort between Forbes-Robertson's perceived elevated social profile and acting style worked in both directions. Bernard Shaw, for example, who wrote *Caesar and Cleopatra* as a Forbes-Robertson star vehicle, praised his acting for standing 'completely aloof in simplicity, dignity, grace and musical speech from the world of the motor car and the Carlton Hotel'.[18] It was a mark of his dignity and timeless distinction not to be tarnished by the modern, the material or the modish. The comment evidently reached beyond his stage presence in its resonances. Forbes-Robertson was repeatedly hailed as both an actor of rare intelligence on stage and a gentleman of rare taste off it – and the two often seemed linked in contemporary perceptions of him.

Of no work was his status as both 'the classic actor of our day' and as a dignitary of the theatre world more assured than in his *Hamlet* (both stage and screen). *The Stage*, for example, declared that Forbes-Robertson was universally acknowledged 'the most courtier-like and princely Hamlet of our time'.[19] Indeed, his *Hamlet* could scarcely be mentioned without the epithet 'noble', or a synonym, as applied to actor, role or, by extension, production as a whole being in close attendance.[20] Long after the film's first release, the specific connotations of social distinction that had clung to it in the early days were still striking reviewers: 'Haste, as we know, had no place in the aristocratic ideal and there is no haste here.'[21] Even the

---

[17] 'Sir J. Forbes Robertson in Knickerbocker Production', *MPW* v.25, n.2 (10 July 1915), 312. See also 317.

[18] George Bernard Shaw, 'Bernard Shaw and the Heroic Actor', *The Play Pictorial* v.21, n.129 (June 1913), 124.

[19] *The Stage* (27 March 1913), 19.

[20] See, for example, the *London News* and the *London Graffic*, both 29 March 1913. Both quoted in Bernice W. Kliman, *Hamlet: Film, Television and Audio Performance* (Rutherford: Farleigh Dickinson University Press, 1988), p.264. See also Judson's review: 'There is no actor to-day whose playing of this character reaches so noble a height as Forbes Robertson', Hanford C. Judson, 'Hamlet with Forbes Robertson: The Knickerbocker Film Company Offers in Three Reels a Great Play With a Great Star and a Great Cast Supporting Him', *MPW* v.25, n.2 (10 July 1915), 317–18. In particular, see Adolph Klauber's influential review about Forbes-Robertson's princely and 'exquisite refinement', quoted in Charles H. Shattuck, *Shakespeare on the American Stage: from Booth and Barrett to Sothern and Marlowe* vol. II (Washington: Folger Shakespeare Library 1987), pp. 203–4. 'This is an aristocratic Hamlet, one that is every inch a prince,' was Kliman's summative comment on his performance in 1988 (Kliman, *Hamlet*, p. 271).

[21] 'Silent Film of 1913 Brings Back a Great Hamlet', *ILN* (14 May 1960). Unpaginated clipping available to view on microfiche at the BFI.

finished film's lack of pace, which elsewhere might have been considered a fault, was, in this case, turned to critical advantage as reflecting not just the distinguished credentials of the star, but also of the film.

HAMLET (GAUMONT-HEPWORTH: HAY PLUMB, 1913)

The Gaumont-Hepworth *Hamlet* contains some very pleasing moments, the most celebrated of which is the sequence preceding Ophelia's (Gertrude Elliott) death. Ophelia's poetically distracted walk through the woods and along the river bank with her dress reflected in the water is set against the evolving conspiracy between Claudius (Walter Ringham) and Laertes (Alexander Scott-Gatty) in their garden location. The cross-cutting between these two scenes (known then as 'alternating views' or 'switch-backs')[22] nicely relates and contrasts male and female responses to the death of Polonius (J.H. Barnes): the men plot death for another while Ophelia heads for the brook in search of her own.

In Shakespeare, Ophelia's death is a piece of off-stage action, reported by Gertrude. Her watery death is potently evoked through Gertrude's lyrical description: it is not, however, shown. In Forbes-Robertson's 1897 stage production at the Lyceum, no superfluous on-stage action had been allowed to detract from the verbal power of Gertrude's elegy. However, the case for showing Ophelia at *some* point in this scene, for putting on display the aestheticised death of poetic report, proved theatrically compelling and so, as his souvenir acting edition reports, after Laertes' stricken response to the news, he closed Act IV with an interpolated stage direction for a tableau: '*Enter* Courtiers, *carrying* OPHELIA *on a bier. Curtain.*'[23]

If the temptation to show the exquisite, unbearable beauty of the drowned Ophelia newly fished from the brook proved irresistible in the theatre, it is no surprise that once the resources of cinema were made available, an additional and fuller version of the death scene should have seemed an appropriate use of the medium. So it is that an expanded version of this tableau is preserved in the film also. It was a moment whose visual potential had already been much mined by nineteenth-century artists:[24]

[22] Bordwell, *On the History of Film Style*, p. 13.
[23] Johnson Forbes-Robertson, *Hamlet by William Shakespeare: As Arranged for the Stage by Forbes-Robertson and Presented at the Lyceum Theatre on Saturday September 11, 1897* (London: Nassau Press, 1897), p. 79.
[24] See, for example, the Millais 'Ophelia' of 1851–2; the Hughes 'Ophelia' of the same date (discussed in Chapter 1); the William Drake watercolour from the 1857 American edition of the play; the Harold Copping illustration from the New Variorum edition (Philadelphia, 1877); A. Robida's

the film artists could align themselves with, and now animate, that distinguished pictorial tradition. The film, therefore, delights in retaining the poetic delicacy of the moment through Ophelia's floaty dress, ethereally abstracted walk, watery reflection and the gently unkempt beauty of the riverside location, all seen through a well-judged shot length that keeps Ophelia part of a broader landscape waiting to make its claim on her with terrible but touching finality. Moreover, the appearance on the title cards of lines from Gertrude's elegy as apparently simple location indicators for Ophelia's river-side walk – 'There with fantastic garlands did she come', and subsequently 'There is a willow grows aslant a brook/ That shows his hoar leaves in the glassy stream' – increases the pathos of the scene. The lines are taken (out of sequence) from the report of Ophelia's death. Thus the title cards seem poignantly to acknowledge, and gently to advertise, the inevitable destination of Ophelia's walk. Those who recognise the appropriation and displacement of the words cannot but feel that, even as they watch her tripping along the riverbank collecting her flowers, they are simultaneously hearing the prophetically whispered news of her impending death. The interpolated sequence is beautiful in its elegiac qualities.

The sequence's use of specifically cinematic narrative conventions is not, however, characteristic of the style of the film as a whole. Despite its expensive and expansive sets, pleasing natural locations and ghostly superimpositions, the film is less torn between advertising its distinction from its theatrical roots and asserting a clear allegiance to them than such occasional bursts of cinematic energy might suggest. At its core, the film insistently and proudly proclaims its theatrical heritage. It may be that it only felt the freedom to experiment with cinematic possibilities in the scene of Ophelia's death and Claudius' plot because this was the longest sequence from which its theatrical star was absent. In Forbes-Robertson's presence (and therefore for the majority of the film), the conventions of theatrical presentation hold sway.

The first indication of this is given at the film's opening, in the prefatory extra-diegetic introductions to Hamlet and Ophelia. Each is shown in turn in a gently animated cameo mid-shot with a banner quotation appropriate to the depicted moment in each case displayed as part of the mise en scène across the bottom of the frame. Thus Forbes-Robertson's

wood engraving in the Parisian edition (Edouard Cornely, 1900, trans. Jules Lermina); C. Faivre's nineteenth-century engraving; C. Hentschel's engraving for the Henry Irving-Marshall edition of *The Works* (New York, 1893); several late nineteenth- and early twentieth-century versions by John William Waterhouse; Gordon Browne's illustration in Mary Macleod's *The Shakespeare Story-book* (London, 1902).

Hamlet is shown looking skywards, remembering something and noting it down in a small book. The banner (written, unlike the succeeding intertitles, in capitals) reads: 'MY TABLES – MEET IT IS, I SET IT DOWN'. Next, Gertrude Elliott's Ophelia is seen distributing flowers, accompanied by the banner quotation: 'THERE'S ROSEMARY. THAT'S FOR REMEMBRANCE'.[25] These introductory cameos serve most obviously to introduce the 'stars'. The particularity of the lines chosen to accompany them, however, carry an only lightly veiled assertion of the priorities and purpose of the film as a whole. As obliquely suggested by the oddity and incompleteness of the first quotation (reinforced by Forbes-Robertson's mimed actions), the film itself is self-consciously a memorial document that 'sets down', as is 'meet', a remarkable *thing remembered* – in this case a stage performance of *Hamlet*. Then, lest the point of the allusion contained in the first quotation was missed, the second re-expresses it: this film, implies Elliott's Ophelia, offers a tangible 'remembrance' of something now gone. The film to which these cameo appearances serve as aperitif then unspools as the scrupulously archived account of the acclaimed production that it formally remembers.[26]

The 'setting down' of the stage production promised by this introductory sequence is done with almost touching conscientiousness. The intertitles indicate this with particular clarity. In the same year that saw the British release of *Hamlet*, in the US J. Berg Esenwein and Arthur Leeds published *Writing the Photoplay*, one in a series of books on literary technique. In this writers' manual, Esenwein and Leeds described the uses to which intertitles (or 'leaders' as they were still sometimes known) could legitimately be put:

Properly used, leaders can accomplish four results very satisfactorily: (a) mark the passage of time; (b) clear up a point of the action which could not otherwise be made to 'register'; (c) 'break' a scene; and (d) prepare the mind of the spectator to enter into the scene in the right spirit.[27]

[25] Forbes-Robertson, *Hamlet* (1897), pp. 29, 75. Re-punctuated versions of I.v.108 and IV.v.175, respectively.

[26] For a lovely account of the film as souvenir, and of its playful engagements with the presence and absence of its central player, see Emma Smith, '"Sir J. and Lady Forbes-Robertson Left for America on Saturday": Marketing the 1913 *Hamlet* for Stage and Screen', in Linda Fitzsimmons and Sarah Street (eds.), *Moving Performance*, pp. 44–55. For an illuminating discussion of the animated introductory portraits of Forbes-Robertson and Elliott, see Burrows, *Legitimate Cinema*, p. 119.

[27] J. Berg Esenwein and Arthur Leeds, *Writing the Photoplay* (Springfield, Mass., 1913). Quoted in Robinson, *From Peepshow to Palace*, p. 157.

Even these uses, however, were considered a concession to a supplementary communicative form that should, more properly, be *de trop*. Ideally, the action should be fully visualised, rendering the leaders redundant. Two years earlier, Epes Winthrop Sargent had declared: 'The ideal photoplay is told entirely in self-explanatory action, without recourse to letters or other inserts.'[28] In some Shakespeare films, intertitles were kept within decorous bounds, merely offering plot summary in bite-sized chunks. In this *Hamlet*, by contrast, they go far beyond Esenwein's and Leeds' second stipulated usage of 'clear[ing' up a point of the action'. They incidentally hit all four markers (a) to (d) above, but are so densely packed with respectfully long verbatim quotations from Shakespeare's text (taken from Forbes-Robertson's 1897 acting edition), that they appear centrally driven by a more pressing need yet – to assert the production's authentic *Shakespeareanness*. While symbolically and conspicuously proclaiming the film's allegiance to the Shakespearean text, these long quotations also become an almost burdensome distraction from the played action:

> I have heard
> That guilty creatures, sitting at a play,
> Have by the very cunning of the scene
> Been struck so to the soul, that presently
> They have proclaimed their malefactions!
> .... I'll have these players
> Play something like the murder of my father
> Before mine uncle.

Not only are intertitles of this sort longer than is necessary to clarify the action, they also punctiliously notate the points at which words or lines have been excised. The excisions are conventionally indicated by a series of dots. In some intertitles, so numerous are these editorial markers as to become almost as prominent as the sections of text retained.

> Alas, my lord I have been so affrighted!
> .... As I was sewing in my chamber,
> Lord Hamlet, ... with a look so piteous in purport,
> .... comes before me.

This clear advertisement of *things missing* is symptomatic of the priorities of the production as a whole, which is caught throughout between on the one hand celebrating what is there, and on the other ruing what

---

[28] Epes Winthrop Sargent, 'Technique of the Photoplay', *MPW* v.9, n.2 (22 July 1911), 108.

is not. Its self-consciousness as a memorial document, therefore, constantly remembers the fuller, theatrical, worded version of which the film is merely the partial and necessarily capped souvenir. As such, it is a film which seems to take a quiet and quasi-scholarly pride in parading its limitations.

The Standard's report of the film's opening at the prestigious New Gallery Kinema on Regent Street on 22 September 1913 even suggests that the audience at this première was assumed to be the same sort of audience – perhaps even in part the same audience – that had already seen the stage production:

> The conditions at a first night of 'Hamlet' at the New Gallery Kinema yesterday were similar to those reigning at a West-end theatre on a first production. There were the same number of people in evening dress endeavouring to get tickets at the last moment; there was the same enthusiasm, the same clapping when the popular actor was first recognised.[29]

The prestigious and culturally ambitious New Kinema was perhaps the natural home for the Gaumont *Hamlet*. It offered a constituency that would revel in the prestige associations of the picture, appreciate the referential qualities of the performance to which they were privy and perhaps not balk at the more demanding, less concessionary aspects of the production as a work of cinema.

But there were other audiences to consider as well if the picture was to recoup its significant outlay. Perhaps it was to appeal to these that a tie-in novelisation of the film was produced that clarified the plot in punchier, more populist terms than those suggested by the film. The novelisation carried the following descriptive title: *Shakespeare's Hamlet: The Story of the Play Concisely Told. Produced in Conjunction with the Cinematograph Film Showing Sir J. Forbes-Robertson and Miss Gertrude Elliott and their Full Company from Drury Lane Theatre with 55 Illustrations Taken from the Film.* It sold for a shilling, a price that reflected its luxury production, numerous reproduced stills and other promotional photographs.[30] Its populist tone may be gauged, for example, from Ophelia's response to Hamlet at the play-within-the-play: 'Ophelia flushed faintly as Hamlet raised his dark

---

[29] *The Standard* (23 September 1913), 8. Quoted in Burrows, *Legitimate Cinema*, p. 138.
[30] *Shakespeare's Hamlet: The Story of the Play* ... (London: Stanley Paul and Co, 1913). Copy consulted in the Bodleian. Although the cover specifically claims that the novelisation's illustrations are 'taken from the film', they are actually an assortment of stills from the film and promotional photographs from the stage production (Smith, ' "Sir J. and Lady Forbes-Robertson ..." ', p. 49). The novelisation thus attempted symbolically to obfuscate the distinctions between stage and film production by integrating the photographic souvenirs of both into the same analogue story.

eyes to smile up at her. Was it possible this cruel mania would pass and he be once again the lover of her dreams?'[31] Whereas in the film Forbes-Robertson gave an intellectualised account of the prince in a performance marked by delicacy and restraint, the novelisation drew repeatedly upon the same well-plundered word bank to tell the story of a different sort of prince. Above all, he was a resolute character, with 'iron resolve' and 'stern resolve', 'suddenly stern', 'stern, relentless, too suddenly a purposeful man'.[32] He was also given to the passionate outburst and heroic gesture ('clenching his fists', 'reel[ing] back', 'laugh[ing] at their fears', 'break[ing] away from their detaining hands', 'runn[ing] at full speed', 'silenc[ing] her accusations with an imperious gesture', 'striding towards the dais, his eyes bright, his cheeks flushed', 'barr[ing] the way', 'press[ing] his own convulsed features to the other's death-stricken ones').[33] And his rejection of introspection in favour of action was fully conscious: '. . . it was too late to look back upon the past. He must go blindly on to the task he had vowed to perform whate'er betided'.[34] In short, this was the Hamlet of populist heroics and decisive action – a bold and active Hamlet who stands, perhaps, in a comparable relationship to Forbes-Robertson's more reflective Hamlet as Q1's avenging Hamlet does to Q2's more reflective one. It was, in any case, the very reading of the role that Forbes-Robertson himself had eschewed both in the editorial choices made for his acting edition and in the particularities of his own performance.[35]

In this period it was not uncommon to read the story of a picture before seeing it. In the US, the *Motion Picture Story Magazine* had been offering film stories to picture-goers since 1911. By 1913, there were two broadly equivalent British magazines largely devoted to telling film stories – *The Pictures* and *Illustrated Films Monthly* (whose first issue in September 1913 offered seven lavishly illustrated pages on the Forbes-Robertson *Hamlet*, including a synopsis of the plot). These film story papers were intended to assist readers both in their choice of picture and in comprehending those they then saw. In 1911, the editor of *The Pictures* had made the following case for the value of reading the story ahead of seeing the film:

When . . . the reader of one of our stories sees it realised by the cinematograph, he will be able to follow every scene with vastly improved facility: he will readily

[31] *Shakespeare's Hamlet . . .* (1913), p. 32
[32] *Ibid.*, pp. 8, 34, 38, 28. See also Burrows, *Legitimate Cinema*, pp. 130–1.
[33] *Shakespeare's Hamlet . . .* (1913), pp. 9, 15, 39, 56, 60. [34] *Ibid.*, p. 43.
[35] For an account of the 'more direct', 'more single-minded', 'more impulsive' and 'less philosophical' populist Hamlet of Q1, see Kathleen O. Irace, *The First Quarto of Hamlet* (Cambridge University Press, 1998), pp. 15–16.

seize details that might otherwise have escaped him: he will recognise the actors as old friends; and he will enter into the drama enacted before his eyes with a thoroughness of sympathy and appreciation which he could not feel were he witnessing it without having read the story.[36]

One of the striking aspects of the separately published novelisation of *Hamlet* is that it did not encourage the reader to 'recognise the actors as old friends', since there was little kinship between its Hamlet and that of the film. Read alongside the picture, or even alongside its own illustrative photographs, the far pacier and less reflective narrative of the novelistic tie-in must, in fact, have produced a rather odd impression of disjuncture or even outright contradiction upon the reading and viewing public. The commercial alliance of the novel with the picture produced variant versions of *Hamlet* which perhaps testified to an equivocal marketing strategy in relation to a film which – given its production costs – could not be exclusively sustained by the more cultured audiences of the type who frequented the New Gallery. It needed to reach beyond a theatre-going audience and this racier, plot-clarifying, story-telling publication, peppered as it was with gripping action, heroic attitudes and appealing pictures, may have helped it do so. If the film offered a careful 'noting down' of the theatre production, the novelisation offered a more market-savvy, radical and popularising rewrite of it.

Picture-goers who appreciated the pace and punch of the novelisation, however, were likely to find the film itself a taxing viewing experience. Not only do the lengthy intertitles inhibit the potential momentum of the piece, but shots are far longer than is the norm for this date. The camera, fixed to the spot, offers an unwavering, frontally placed, point of view and, most striking of all, there is almost no attempt to edit a scene by breaking it up with cut-ins of differing focal lengths or shots taken from differing perspectives. Even, for example, when the dying Hamlet is helped to the throne and has the crown put in his hands – a scene in which a close-up on Hamlet's final moments would seem almost irresistible as the next shot – the camera retains its respectful distance and alters neither its angle nor focus from a sustained shot of the whole court room. The throne with its dying occupant therefore remains just one small element in left of frame. As in his various stages of pained deliberation throughout the drama, so also even in death, this Hamlet is always framed and contained within the broader scene.

---

[36] *The Pictures* (21 October 1911), 1.

The film's central interest clearly ought to be the poised and engagingly intelligent central performance of Hamlet himself, a performance that had drawn such enthusiastic plaudits as played on the stage. However, the camera's respectfully withdrawn style of attention and diligent dwelling upon that performance in the context (always) of the larger scene, eventually leave Forbes-Robertson looking adrift in a territory not quite attuned to his particular virtues. He bravely continues to deliver the role and to speak the lines, as though inhabiting the Elsinore he knows of old. But this Elsinore has changed – it is, apart from anything else, now a mute world. And in it, Forbes-Robertson increasingly looks a tragically earnest but displaced figure, stranded in a medium to which he cannot quite accommodate himself and which, in this production, refuses to make much accommodation to him.

Not all films of this period were so unbending in their approach to their actors. In an article entitled 'Acting for the films in 1912', the actor Charles Graham remembers the effect on an audience of seeing 'close ups of enormously magnified faces' on the screen which allowed

a change in mood to be grasped more clearly by the boy in the back of the cinema gallery than the actor can hope to achieve by his facial expression on the most impressionable young woman in the front row of the stalls in the theatre.[37]

Also by 1912, the use of close-up in D.W. Griffith's work was not just habitual but, according to film historian Jacques Aumont, was already exceeding 'the role of pure functional repetition of a detail supposedly not clearly seen in the shot as a whole' to become 'a full signifying unit in the narrative discourse'.[38] Though such intimate emotional exposure of an actor's face and thoughtful absorption of close-ups into the broader narrative were regular features of other works of cinema by 1912, however, this was not the approach of the 1913 *Hamlet*.

Inevitably, perhaps, American trade reviews cut the film less slack than English ones: Edward Weitzel found Forbes-Robertson a 'sorry figure … picking his way gingerly' through a 'woeful spectacle'.[39] The film is weighty in conception and delivery, but other narrative, performance and stylistic considerations are sacrificed in order to privilege the courted gravitas.

[37] Charles Graham, 'Acting for the Films in 1912', *Sight and Sound* v.4, n.15 (Autumn 1935), 118–19 (119).
[38] Jacques Aumont, 'Griffith: the Frame, the Figure', in Thomas Elsaesser (ed.), *Early Cinema*, pp. 348–59 (356).
[39] Edward Weitzel, 'Obituary for Herbert Beerbohm Tree', *MPW* v.33, n.3 (21 July 1917), 430. These remarks are made in the wider context of Weitzel's unflattering obituary for Tree.

Most significantly, it fetters its own showcasing of Forbes-Robertson's subtle artistry by frustratingly denying us any intimate access to it. Despite its one charming foray into imaginative cinematography and thoughtful editing in the scene of Ophelia's riverside walk, it is, in fact, a production whose ongoing instincts are to 'note down' a theatrical production while resisting too concessionary an approach to the translated medium of expression in which it now finds itself. As a moving picture that offered, in one American reviewer's words, 'an exact replica of the stage business', it was, in sum, a film not entirely reconciled to its filmic identity.[40] As such, it left plenty of market space for a more populist and cinematically celebratory version to succeed it.

HAMLET (RODOLFI-FILM: ELEUTERIO RODOLFI, 1917)

It was the eminent Italian actor Ruggero Ruggeri whose 1917 film of *Hamlet* would gratefully claim that populist terrain. In this he worked in collaboration with actor-turned-director Eleuterio Rodolfi who had recently left Ambrosio to found his own Turin-based company, Rodolfi Film. By 1917, Ruggeri had an unparalleled theatrical reputation in Italy, having inherited the mantle of classical actor of his generation from Ermete Novelli (opposite whom he had played Iago in his youth).[41] Ruggeri also had a significant profile in the rest of Europe and America – particularly for his stage Hamlet with which he toured internationally and for which he was to become well known in England.[42] The immediate inspiration for the 1917 film was Ruggeri's stage Hamlet of 1915 at the grand Teatro Lirico in Milan. However, since *Hamlet* was the most performed foreign play on the Italian stage in the first twenty years of the twentieth century, the general precipitating background was *Hamlet*'s deeply entrenched popularity in Italian culture.[43]

Ruggeri's Milanese stage Hamlet in 1915 had divided opinion sharply. The prominent contemporary theatre critic, Renato Simoni, found that Ruggeri had given 'a great interpretation, which comes near the great interpretations of the past, yet without directly imitating them'.[44] In a

---

[40] Judson, 'Hamlet with Forbes Robertson', 317.

[41] For an account of their collaboration, see Amerigo Manzini, *Gli uomini del giorno* n.35 'Ruggeri' (Milan: Casa Edittrice Italiana: 1920), p. 16.

[42] See Ernesto Grillo, *Shakespeare and Italy* (Glasgow University Press, 1949), p. 123.

[43] See, for example, Leonardo Bragaglia, *Ruggero Ruggeri in sessantacinque anni di storia del teatro rappresentato* (Roma: Trevi Editore, 1968), pp. 4–5.

[44] Renato Simoni, 'Hamlet', in *Corriere della Sera* (21 April 1915). Quoted in Anna Cavallone Anzi, *Shakespeare Nei Teatri Milanesi Del Novecento (1904–1978)* (Bari: Adriatica Editrice, 1980), p. 30. Translated from the Italian (here and below).

Figure 5.3 Manzini, *Ruggeri* (1920), front cover.
Author's private collection.

retrospective written five years later for the Ruggeri volume of a series
entitled *Gli uomini del giorno* (*Men of Our Time*) (Figure 5.3), Amerigo
Manzini reported that not only had rehearsals been conducted 'with
a rigour and discipline which had not been seen in Italian theatre for a
long time', but that even the other actors in rehearsal had been struck by
the high seriousness of the reading Ruggeri was offering.[45] Then, in 1926,
Simoni's enthusiasm for Ruggeri's Hamlet was revisited in response to
the London leg of a touring production. Simoni reported that Ruggeri's
performance was received as 'a rendition such as that Burbage must have

---

[45] Manzini, *Gli uomini del giorno*, pp. 36–7.

given' – and this despite being delivered exclusively in Italian.[46] To be aligned with Burbage was, of course, a significant statement about the perceived truth and authenticity of the performance.

Not all commentators on Ruggeri's stage Hamlet, however, were as complimentary. Manzini acknowledged that the 1915 Milan production had provoked the traditionalists of the theatre world to 'screw up their noses at the sheer force of this innovative interpretation'.[47] Contemporary criticism is, however, best epitomised by Antonio Gramsci (1891–1937), the left-wing political theorist and cultural critic. Gramsci was sufficiently exercised by Ruggeri's stage Hamlet and its potentially deleterious effects upon the public, to make one of his intermittent interventions into the realm of theatre criticism in the left-wing newspaper *Avanti*. Here he slammed Ruggeri in no uncertain terms for pretentious, over-stylised gestures, precious actorly business, ostentatious, lime-light grabbing virtuosity and, most serious of all, as evidenced by his tremendous popularity, for having perverted the public taste by his flashy artifice.[48] Even allowing for Gramsci's hyperbolic style, there is something incontrovertible about the charge of 'virtuosity' levelled at Ruggeri's acting: certainly the performance he gives in the 1917 film has no truck with understatement.

In the early cinema period, film narratives had been dependent upon extreme compression or a hurtling pace, or both, to fit the one- or two-reel format. By 1917, however, films of feature length had been the norm for some years, and more expansive possibilities of scene-setting, character development, narrative complexity and even interpretive asides were possible as a result. These possibilities were embraced with a will in the Rodolfi-Ruggeri film, which revels in its story, setting, characters and in its ability to comment on these things through its untrammelled deployment of a repertoire of cinematic devices.

As a result, through its considered cinematography and editing, the film consistently channels and makes purposeful what in the central performance might otherwise appear merely overblown. Near the beginning of the film, for example, a desperate and distracted Hamlet kneels on

[46] Renato Simoni, 'Amleto di Ruggeri', in *Corriere della Sera* (10 June 1926). Quoted in Anzi, *Shakespeare Nei Teatri Milanesi*, p. 51.

[47] Manzini, *Gli uomini del giorno*, p.37.

[48] 'Ruggeri does not know how to divest himself of his virtuosity ... Ruggeri is in no small measure the cause of the aesthetic perversion in the theatre-going public. He can give an imitation of beauty and greatness even when the beauty and greatness cede place to an artifice of style and technique.' Antonio Gramsci, 'Ruggero Ruggeri', in *Avanti* (25 November 1917). Quoted in Anzi, *Shakespeare Nei Teatri Milanesi*, p. 33.

the battlements, atmospherically under-lit by the flickering flames from a fire. From his position in right of frame he reaches out exaggeratedly with his right hand across the dark space of the frame in an anxiety to make contact with his father's ghost. Rather than concentrating exclusively on the hyperbole of Ruggeri's gesture, however, the scene then cross-cuts between Hamlet's marginalised, reaching figure, and the figure of the superimposed ghost, shown in another part of the battlements and shot from a respectfully low angle. The sense of Hamlet's desperation to occupy the same space as his ghostly father but inability ever quite to reach him is, therefore, in part communicated by the frame composition and edited style of the sequence. These keep them isolated in separate shots, despite their literal proximity. Indeed, so firmly established is the spatial separation between father and son that even when a master shot subsequently shows them in frame together at opposite ends of the same battlements, the space between them remains untraversible: the editing has established a clear, fixed spatial sundering that even appearing in the same shot together cannot now unfix. In this sequence, therefore, a truth about emotional relationship, and emotional separation derives as much from the style of the shooting and the nature of the editing as from the marked agitation of the acting.

Such a productive collaboration between technical style and interpretive agenda is characteristic of the Rodolfi film as a whole in which mise en scène (the arrangement of characters and set), choice of shot (focal length, composition, angle and duration), editing (graphic relations, pace and sequencing) and technical effects (such as double exposure) are frequently inflected by some broader thinking about the meaning of the dramatic material. Not only, for example, does Ruggeri's Hamlet's desperate reaching out from within the isolation of his own frame testify powerfully to his mindset when faced with his father's ghost, but the strategic choreography of the action also prefigures another key moment later in the film. When, therefore, Ruggeri's Hamlet reaches out resolutely with his right arm into frame left again, this time to make contact with the Yorick he remembers incarnating the skull he now holds, the gesture obliquely recalls (though now in less urgent vein) his earlier attempt to reach his ghostly father. The parallelism both of the gesture and of the frame's spatial organisation in the two scenes also creates a suggestive association between the two unattainable objects – father and Yorick – to which Hamlet's gaze, reach and memory tend in each case. The association *takes* all the more by the skull's temporary, magical transformation into the face of the living man through a moment of double exposure. By actually giving the skull the lips, the eyes of flashing merriment and the grin upon whose disturbing absence Hamlet usually comments, the film plucks Yorick from the realm of the purely skeletal and invites him temporarily instead into the realm of the spectral – a realm already occupied by one ghostly inhabitant. And as if to emphasise their related status and function in this film as parallel visitations from the grave, the ghost and Yorick even share a spatial relationship to the Hamlet who has to some extent conjured them in an attempt to reclaim them for the world of the living.

The incarnated face superimposed upon Yorick's skull is more than simply a piece of technical cinematic bravado, though it is certainly that. The reading of Hamlet in the Rodolfi-Ruggeri film as a whole is of a man energetically resisting the irrevocability of death. This Hamlet seeks to deny and even, when possible, reverse the processes of corporeal disintegration that so linguistically absorb his Shakespearean counterpart: he resists the tug towards actually allowing corpses to be dust, the quintessence of which he more usually considers not just them but also himself. It is not only his unwavering endeavour to detain the ghost and his eagerness to reincarnate the skull with a living face that illustrate this. The graveyard scene, for example, closes with Hamlet, left alone, gathering bundles of foliage and, in a series of grand gestures, strewing them upon Ophelia's grave in ways directly imitative of Ophelia's own distraction.[49] In this context, Hamlet's appropriation of her role as the urgent gatherer and distributor of flowers reads as a desperate attempt to restore her too symbolically to his world: if the only way to secure her ongoing presence in his world is himself to be her, then that he will do. There may be a limit to how many spectres can be summoned from the grave, but not to how much Hamlet can refuse to be reconciled to a future when there is still a past, and a cast of characters

---

[49] This piece of business had been lifted directly from Tree's 1895 stage production. See Tree's account of it in *Hamlet from an actor's prompt book: the substance of a lecture delivered by Herbert Beerbohm Tree … October 1895 …* (London: Nassau Press, 1897), p. 35. Diego Angeli, the Italian Shakespeare translator, felt that his work was being defiled by this non-Shakespearean dumb show interpolation as it was played upon the Milanese stage in 1915. He accused Ruggeri in print of having added 'a completely made up scene which, moreover, distorts the Shakespearean concept of *Hamlet!*' Diego Angeli, 'Per l'offerta a Roma di un monumento a Shakespeare', *Il Giornale d'Italia* (31 December 1918), quoted in Gianfranco Bartalotta, *Amleto in Italia Nel Novecento* (Bari: Adriatica Editrice, 1986), p. 38. Ruggeri pointed out there were highly respectable precedents for such interpolations on the *English* stage. (Ruggero Ruggeri, 'Palinodia amletica', *Il Giornale d'Italia*, 10 February 1918, quoted in Bartalotta, *Amleto*, p. 39.) Angeli countered with a sarcastic assertion that Shakespeare could probably be relied upon to know more about his own plays and what should and should not be included than any actor, however illustrious. The scene, however, stayed and is also present in the film as evidence of Ruggeri's imperviousness to such criticism.

from it, with which to try to reconnect. In line with this broader pattern of characterisation, the reappearance of Yorick, magically emerging from the stuff of his own bones, illustrates Hamlet's conviction that the dead can yet be reclaimed by the living. This special effect is no indulgent add-on, but rather organically part of the interpretive conception of the film's central character.

In the 1913 Gaumont-Hepworth *Hamlet*, by contrast, the technical construction of the film shows little evidence of having been influenced by an interpretive agenda. Characteristically, the ghost scene on the battlements, for example, employs a focal length that takes in the whole scene at a glance – ghost, Hamlet and companions in one shot (though a shot that unusually allows itself a modest, and slightly shaky, pan to follow the gliding movements of the superimposed ghost). It includes no shots that isolate individuals within the broader scene and so does not attempt to make any editorial comment on the relationships between them. Moreover, unlike the equivalent scene in the Italian film, it was shot in broad daylight and so lacks the atmospheric quality generated by the eerie up-lighting from the fire. The quiet intensity of the acting, therefore, works without the sort of imaginative support from Hay Plumb's direction that would showcase rather than squander its potential force as a performance.

The Plumb-Hepworth partnership did include occasional technical flourishes such as the superimposed ghost and the melodramatic close-up on both the envenoming of the point of the foil and the poisoning of the cup. These occasioned considerable pride amongst the film-makers, as Hepworth's account of the shooting of the ghost scene makes apparent:

[O]ur work included some of the most difficult trick-work known to cinematography ... For instance, where Forbes-Robertson sees the ghost of Hamlet's father on the ramparts ... he had to do all his work without any visible ghost at all. He had to learn by heart that the ghost was in such-and-such a position on such-and-such a count – for the only cues he got were the counting of the seconds as the film turned through the camera. Then later on, when all that was done with, the stage, with the castle, had to be transformed into a huge dark room – a cage lined entirely with black velvet – while the ghost walked over the same ground to the same dismal counting ... The result on the screen shows that the requirements of the case were carried out with absolute fidelity by everyone concerned. But it was not done the first time, or the second time.[50]

---

[50] 'The Filming of "Hamlet": Interview with Mr. Cecil Hepworth', *The Bioscope*, v.20 n.354 (24 July 1913), 275.

Superimposed ghosts had, in fact, been part of the standard, popular cinematic repertoire since the turn of the century.[51] Hepworth's ghost was evidently complex to choreograph relative to the other scenes in *Hamlet*. Relative to ghost scenes in other films of the period (and even earlier), however, it is neither particularly innovative nor particularly noteworthy in the extent of its ambition or the quality of its execution. Despite the pride Hepworth took in them, the film's technical effects were modest in their formal character. Moreover, they seem to emerge more from a contained desire for momentary visual embellishment than from any integrated thinking about the force of the play or the particularity of an interpretive reading sought.

The particular worth of the English film is, therefore, primarily drawn not from its occasional flirtations with specifically cinematic attributes, but rather, as one contemporary reviewer pointed out in 1915, from its 'valuable contribution to *stage* history' (my emphasis).[52] Its concern to 'set down' a record of an extraordinary central performance makes it, in effect, an animated archival account of that celebrated theatrical moment. The film frustrates through the close-ups it craves but never delivers and the looked-for pace that nearly always eludes it. Nonetheless, the film should not be castigated for what it is not, but valued for what it is: a memorial of the dignified containment and subtly intelligent force of the physical presence of Forbes-Robertson's Hamlet.

PERFORMANCE CODES IN BOTH FILMS

Part of the English film's act of preservation of that extraordinary stage performance necessarily involves conspicuously alluding to the communicative form now missing from the performance: speech. This gaping lacuna was a source of constant frustration to Forbes-Robertson himself

[51] Cinematic superimpositions had both secular and sacred manifestations. See, for example, George Albert Smith's *The Haunted Castle* (1897) and *Photographing a Ghost* (1898), Lubin's *The Haunted House* (1899), Georges Méliès' various *féerie* films employing double exposure, the miraculous Jesus walking on the water scene from the Pathé Passion Play film of 1900 (reused in the Pathé 1902–4 film), Edison's *The Dream of a Rarebit Fiend* (1906) and Vitagraph's *The Haunted Hotel* (1907). And in Shakespearean pictures, it had been a feature too. The ghost of Banquo appeared in double exposure in both the Vitagraph *Macbeth* (1908) and the Cines *Macbeth* (1908). See the still of Banquo's ghost from the Vitagraph film reproduced in *KLW* (13 May 1909), 12. The Cines film is available to view at the LOC. Such comparisons show only that there was nothing particularly technically reaching about Hepworth's superimposed ghost in 1913.

[52] Hanford C. Judson, 'Hamlet with Forbes Robertson', 317.

and he was not above giving voice to this during filming.[53] Like many classical actors who made the transfer to film, this Hamlet is clearly visible throughout the film earnestly mouthing entirely inaudible speeches. However, his lip work does more than signal to an audience the mere fact that a conversation is taking place, since the speeches can stretch to considerable length. It is as if he, like many other English actors also, was anxious to signal his unerring allegiance to the spoken word, even (perhaps especially) in a medium partly characterised by its absence. The determination of such actors visually to pay homage to Shakespeare's language in this way self-subvertingly advertises the very thing these films are not – a vehicle for spoken poetry. Just as the conspicuously frequent inclusion of lines of dots in the intertitles alerted audiences to the fact of text excised, so the extended sequences of lip work from the actors alerted them to the fact of sound unheard.

The sense that there is meaning being conspicuously transmitted at the moment of production that is unrecoverable at the moment of reception informs much of the 1913 film. The production's respectful holding of the shot for the duration of some of Forbes-Robertson's prolonged (but inaudible) speeches, make this an inevitable response on the part of the spectator. That the 'unparalleled music' of Forbes-Robertson's voice[54] has been silenced becomes, therefore, a defining feature of the film. Nor is this sense of exclusion one particular to today's sound era spectatorship. The *MPW* reviewer in 1915 felt similarly deprived, claiming that Forbes-Robertson's screen Hamlet delivered 'only a part of the whole.'[55] This impression of incompleteness was deliberately courted by the film. Insisting 'on using the technique of the dramatic stage when he played before the camera' in this way could hardly endear him to American moving picture audiences.[56] A resolute theatrical obstinacy, however culturally elevated, was not what American audiences wanted of their moving pictures. Nor did they like lip play. An article in *MPW* in November 1916, for example, asked:

When will our screen actors and actresses learn that violent motions of the lips, the mouth and the jaws have very little expressive force before the camera? Unless words are heard falling from the lips all these maxillary exercises mean nothing at all to the spectator ... It is the art of the screen artist to express ... emotions

[53] See anecdote recounted in Preface, p. xvii.
[54] Mills, *Hamlet on Stage*, p. 173.
[55] Judson, 'Hamlet with Forbes Robertson', 317.
[56] 'B. Nichols Talks', *MPW* v. 18, n.7 (15 November, 1913), 721.

without words ... A good director ought not to tolerate mouthing as a form of motion picture expression.[57]

In 1921 in England, Agnes Platt published a book of advice about screen acting entitled *Practical Hints on Acting for the Cinema*. In it she broadly concurred with the *MPW*'s journalist on the question of 'maxillary exercise':

Cinema actors speak as they rehearse, because it has been found that a little movement of the lips adds to the naturalness of the pictures; but it is better to limit oneself to as few words as possible, and to be careful that the lip play is as quiet as can conveniently be managed, or the mouth looks very ugly. In American, too much movement of the mouth is known as "mugging it," and Americans are apt to say that our English cinema actors "mug it."[58]

Forbes-Robertson is certainly guilty of 'mugging it' in telegraphed fashion for extended sequences throughout the *Hamlet* film and is specifically arraigned for this in some reviews. Ernest A. Dench writing in *Pictures and the Picturegoer* in January 1916, for example, found that '[t]he eminent actor and his talented wife seemed inclined to rely on "lines" to the detriment of their facial expressions and gestures'.[59] This reliance was, of course, no accidental slippage on Forbes-Robertson's part, but rather a clear statement of allegiance to the conventions of another medium. One of the functions Forbes-Robertson fulfils in this film is, therefore, as an obstinate point of decorous resistance to cinematic possibility.

Ruggeri, like Forbes-Robertson, would also have known Hamlet's lines, having recently played the part on the stage. Though he was not principally known for his discipline as an actor, and though he too can sometimes be seen mugging it, for large swathes of the film he has trained himself *out* of speaking the lines and *into* trying to communicate their sense as precisely as possible through non-verbal means. As a result, his performance does not, as Forbes-Robertson's does, appear indelibly marked by a performance aspect that is missing. Unlike Forbes-Robertson, whose screen Hamlet was deliberately 'only a part of the whole', a partial allusion to the real *theatrical* performance, Ruggeri's screen acting trails no such sense of incompleteness. His strategic, and striking, use of compensatory facial expression and gesture is illustrated with particular force in the

---

[57] *MPW* v.30, n.6 (11 November 1916), 825.

[58] Agnes Platt, *Practical Hints on Acting for the Cinema* (London: Stanley Paul, 1921), p. 24.

[59] Ernest A. Dench, 'Stage Stars on the Screen', *Pictures and the Picturegoer* v.9, n.102 (29 January, 1916), 400–2 (401).

sequence in the film that runs from the nunnery scene into the scene of the instruction of the players.

In the Rodolfi-Ruggeri nunnery scene, Ophelia (Polish actress Elena Makowska)[60] is 'loosed' to Hamlet by the adults in her world, with her little casket of treasures that she is under commission to return to him. He rejects her proffered gifts. She looks to Heaven. He relents in depth of field and advances as if to embrace her tenderly from behind, only to stop himself mid-advance, change his mind suddenly and instead brutally reassume his antic disposition. His acting throughout is characterised by gestural extravagance and his reassumed antic disposition by a grotesquely extreme close-up on his maniacal laugh.

The scene then cuts suddenly to Hamlet's instruction to the first player not to saw the air with his hands. Most other silent *Hamlet* films coyly cut this exchange[61] and it is not difficult to guess why. In this medium, the scene could so quickly boomerang upon its makers and expose the cartoon aspects not just of the first player's histrionic style, but more worryingly, of the gestural excesses of a silent Hamlet himself. In context, the scene could easily embarrass a production. Ruggeri, however, is happy to move seamlessly from his own gestural extravagance in the nunnery scene into a set of imperious instructions to the first player to moderate *his* gestural style. With striking aplomb, he even illustrates the point by imitating the player's gesticulations in order to expose their excess. In the surviving French language print, the film's intertitle at this point reads: 'Ne fendez pas l'air de vos gestes emphatiques. Soyez sobres, modérés.' ('Do not saw the air with your emphatic gestures. Be measured, moderate.') Since Hamlet has himself just appeared as air-sawer *par excellence* in the nunnery scene, his subsequent attempts to rein in the melodramatic expressiveness of the first player draws attention to the performance codes of the piece and the role of excess in it. The entertaining contradiction between Hamlet's articulated *theory* of acting and his own recently demonstrated *practice* invites us to consider how emotion and ideas are communicated, and best communicated, in the film as a whole. Other little indications of self-aware humour in the film suggest that Ruggeri and Rodolfi might even have been consciously trading upon the comedy of the

---

[60] Makowska, who had been working in Italy since 1910, drew plaudits for her screen performances in an impressive variety of roles, including knock-about comedies, graceful romances, classical drama and sentimental melodrama.

[61] Even Forbes-Robertson, who includes the extensive Priam/Hecuba speech, cuts the instructions about moderating gestural style.

juxtaposition of this scene with the gesturally extravagant encounter with Ophelia – itself, of course, very far from 'sobre' or 'modéré'.

In the US, in the years preceding the First World War, the dominant performance codes shifted in stages from an inherited taste for the histrionic to an established taste for the verisimilar.[62] As early as 1908, for example, a writer in *MPW* was objecting to films that were little more than 'orgies of gesticulation'.[63] In comparison with such American squeamishness – a squeamishness shared by some in the British film industry too – the European film industries clung without embarrassment to the pantomimic codes for far longer. As is evident from French and Italian film-making into the 1920s, the desire to bring performances 'down' for the benefit of the intimately exposing camera and to court a naturalistic style of acting, was slower to become the desirable norm in continental Europe than it was in the US, and to a lesser extent in Britain also.

The distinctive acting conventions associated with pantomime had originally evolved partly to accommodate the theatrical speech ban (discussed in Chapter 1) that attempted to regulate the drama on certain European stages from 1660 onwards.[64] European pantomime as a form had, therefore, had time to evolve its own tightly systematised structures of economical wordless communication. To guide newcomers to the profession, these were formalised in published manuals. The manuals were didactic in character, determining how specific meaning should be properly communicated. In 1801, for example, Aaron Hill's *The Art of Acting*[65] included detailed notes on how precisely an actor should physically manifest joy, grief, fear, anger, pity, scorn, hatred, jealousy, wonder and love. Later, in 1882, Gustave Garcia's *The Actors' Art*[66] offered detailed and graphically illustrated instruction in how to position the hand to communicate authority, gentleness, grace, an elevated mind, sensuality, pleading, energy, dignity. It illustrated the precisely appropriate bodily pose to

[62] See Roberta Pearson's detailed analysis of the American shift in performance codes in *Eloquent Gestures: The Transformation of Performance Style in the Griffith Biograph Films* (Berkeley, Los Angeles and Oxford: University of California Press, 1992).

[63] Rollin Summers, 'The Moving Picture Drama and the Acted Drama: Some Points of Comparison as to Technique', *MPW* v.3, n.12 (19 September 1908), 213.

[64] See, for example, Joseph Donohue, *Theatre in the Age of Kean* (Oxford: Blackwell, 1975).

[65] Aaron Hill, *The Art of Acting; in which the dramatic passions are properly defined and described . . .* (London: J. Smelton, 1801).

[66] Gustave Garcia, *The Actors' Art: A Practical Treatise on Stage Declamation, Public Speaking and Deportment . . .* (London: T. Pettitt & Co., 1882), illustrated by A. Forestier. Despite Garcia's own professional expertise in singing and musical declamation, many of the book's line-drawn illustrations are annotated with quotations from Shakespeare, suggesting that its precepts were fully intended to apply to classical as well as musical theatre.

suggest attentive listening, an appeal to Heaven, gratitude, desire, doubt, disgust, command mixed with contempt, passionate anger, terror, accusation, reproach. And it stipulated exactly how one should arrange one's face to demonstrate tranquillity, joy, esteem, astonishment, eagerness, laughter, the various stages of grief, extreme pain, hatred, jealousy, learning, perspicacity, shrewdness mixed with hypocrisy and a variety of other intricate mood combinations (Figures 5.4a and b).

Although Garcia addresses the language of gesture and posture in one chapter and the language of speech in another, he evidently understood them as complementary communicative systems. By contrast, Charles Aubert's 1901 French publication, *L'Art Mimique*, explicitly clarified the pantomimic codes for performance, determining how gesture and expression could and should properly communicate with precision when entirely divorced from accompanying words.[67] Such expressive moods as astonishment, stupefaction, disbelief, sarcasm, disparagement, impertinence, mockery, despair, coquetry and so on, could each be generated by a stipulated facial and body arrangement. The exact physical criteria for representing each mood – from a curl of the lip to the set of the hips, from a raised eyebrow to an angle of the hand – were once again shown on a series of line drawings offered for instruction and imitation (Figures 5.5a–c).

In the pervasive way of such things, the nineteenth-century interest in and emphasis upon codified physiognomic and bodily poses filtered into the acting conventions of the major theatres too. In England, for example, Edmund Kean had been both heartily praised and roundly criticised for the bodily 'electricity' of his performances. The intensity of his physicality as exhibited on the legitimate stage inevitably exposed him to the charge of a vulgar lack of decorum and caused William Hazlitt, for example, to object to the 'pantomimic exaggeration' of his acting.[68] The tendency to evoke the pantomimic codes through dramatic styles of physical acting persisted through the century. By 1877, even Henry Irving was satirically lampooned for striving for pictorial effect through stylised poses, or 'attitudes', thought by his detractors to be unnecessarily exaggerated.[69] Irving's

---

[67] See Charles Aubert, *L'Art Mimique Suivi d'un Traité de la Pantomime* (Paris: Meuriot, 1901), published in English by Henry Holt in 1927 as *The Art of Pantomime*, trans. Edith Sears. I am grateful to Jon Burrows for having drawn my attention to this book many years ago.

[68] See Moody, *Illegitimate Theatre in London*, pp. 230–1.

[69] See the satiric studies of Irving's dramatic attitudes ('Remorse', 'Picturesqueness', 'Dignity', 'Desperation', 'Suspicion', 'Picturesqueness Phase II,' 'Persuasiveness', 'Hypocrisy', 'Melodrama') included in William Archer and Robert Lowe's critical pamphlet, *The Fashionable Tragedian* (Edinburgh: Thomas Gray and Company, 1877). In an authorial handwritten dedication (to H. L. Broekstad/Brockstad?) in one of the two Bodleian Library copies of *The Fashionable Tragedian*

Figure 5.4a and b. Frontispiece and composite line-drawings from Gustave Garcia, *The Actors' Art* (1880). Here Garcia suggests precise pantomimic attitudes to communicate fear where it 'assumes the form of terror or despair'. The final figure denotes 'authority, command, accusation'. Each attitude is illustrated with a Shakespearean quotation.

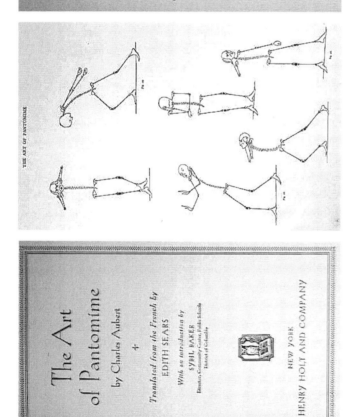

Figure 5.5a–c. Frontispiece and composite line-drawings from Charles Aubert, *The Art of Pantomime* (1901). Aubert gives detailed instructions about bodily and physiognomic poses to communicate exact states of mind and emotion.

perceived preference for dramatic 'attitudes', like Kean's before him, implicitly aligned him with conventions not historically the province of the more respectable stages on which he was performing. The mimetic acting codes subsequently to be enshrined in print by Garcia, Aubert and others had, after all, originally emerged from the practices of the illegitimate stage, sculpted and honed through burlettas, melodramas, pantomimes and other 'lower' forms of theatrical entertainment. They were, that is, associated with a set of conventions tonally beneath the legitimate stage.[70]

Like many other admired and reputable continental actors, however, Ruggeri was influenced by the sustained prevalence of the pantomimic acting codes and evidently felt no tonal slur upon his art as a consequence. The business of acting was not for him to reproduce naturalistic extra-theatrical behaviour, but to draw expertly upon a network of stylised and conventionalised signifying practices and to hone these to performed perfection. He opted to use the pantomimic codes with particular force in his screen acting where his performances needed to trade exclusively upon non-vocal communicative systems. In the encounter between Ophelia and Hamlet in the 1917 film, for example, Hamlet's quasi-relenting towards her and then pulling back obeys in each gestural and facial particular the stipulated pantomimic codes for tenderness, indecision, resolution and mad desperation. Ruggeri's heightened expressions and gestures can be matched almost picture for picture against Aubert's formalised line drawings illustrating how such emotions should be dramatically configured.

For Ruggeri, showman that he was, there even seems to have been something appealing about letting the words go and embracing the pantomimic codes with a will, as the camera seemed to demand.[71] Even in his stage work, Ruggeri had been commended and disparaged in roughly equal measure for his competence in playing what was not there ('*l'opera mancata*'), in expanding by action the gaps between the lines, in playing, that is, off the text.[72] Despite the much admired power and musicality of his voice, such comments about his stage work suggest that, at heart, he was always an actor for whom the silent cinema – so thoroughly dependent on the implied action between the lines – beckoned. Certainly the

---

(call no. M.adds.124 e.170(2)), Archer and Lowe impishly add the sobriquet 'the scurrilous pamphleteers' beneath their own signatures. It is also worth noting that it was to Irving that in 1882 Garcia had chosen to dedicate his acting manual stipulating a series of defined actorly poses.

[70] See also Moody, 'Writing for the Metropolis', pp. 61–9.

[71] Ruggeri had already made three films prior to *Hamlet*: *L'Istruttoria* (1914), *Il Sottomarino 27* (1915) and *Lulu* (1915).

[72] See Anzi, *Shakespeare Nei Teatri Milanesi*, p. 33.

Hamlet he plays on screen is cinematically compelling, even when played, as it so often is, in a blatantly high key.[73]

In the 1913 film, Forbes-Robertson had similarly made a tender advance towards Ophelia from behind her and then, apparently hearing something that indicated they were being overheard, had pulled himself up short.[74] As he did so, he withdrew his outstretched hand from her hair, lest warmth of feeling overwhelm his strategically feigned lack of concern for her welfare. This tender piece of interpolated business had been a trademark of his many stage productions of *Hamlet* and was commemorated in postcard form, a tribute to its emblematic status in representing the delicately feeling Hamlet for which Forbes-Robertson was known (Figure 5.6).

Ruggeri's approach to Ophelia almost directly replicates the choreography from the 1913 film – just one of several examples of imitative business between the two films. Though the action may be precisely recognisable across productions, however, the emotional tenor of the moment is vastly altered. Through the style of both acting and filming, the Italian film has dramatically heightened the moment. Ruggeri's Hamlet approaches and then rejects Ophelia with an enhanced, even a balletically expressive bodily force. In every arch of the eyebrow, fling of the arm, pronounced step towards or away from Ophelia, turn of the body and exaggeratedly derisive laugh, his performance gleefully embraces excess. But the excess of the performance is balanced by the energy in the cinematic delivery of the scene as a whole and so Ruggeri's uncompromising vigour does not entirely overwhelm the whole scene, as it might otherwise threaten to do. Rodolfi seems to have been aware that he was shooting a performance whose dimensions needed careful channelling in order not to create an embarrassing imbalance at key moments. With a characteristic eye on pace and balance, therefore, he employed a variety of shot lengths (from a wide angle on the whole scene to the extreme close-up of Hamlet's laughing mouth) and of possible points of spectatorial attention (Ophelia's wide-eyed, crestfallen face, Hamlet's expansive gestures of affection and then rejection, the King and Polonius listening anxiously behind a curtain) in the interests of distributing the energies of the scene more evenly. Here, as elsewhere in the film, Ruggeri's Hamlet lacks shading, being played in an unremittingly high key: but through sensitive and controlled

---

[73] Ruggeri and Irving were compared for their shared taste for the sustained dramatic gesture. See, for example, Grillo, *Shakespeare and Italy*, pp.123–4.

[74] Hamlet's awareness of the eavesdroppers had not been a feature of his stage productions (although reaching out to stroke Ophelia's hair and then pulling back from this tender temptation had been). See Mills, *Hamlet on Stage*, p. 181.

Figure 5.6 A commemorative postcard that accompanied the
Forbes-Robertson farewell season of *Hamlet* at Drury Lane (1913).
Author's private collection.

cinematic management, his performance – though neither tamed nor toned down – is rendered energetically compelling as a viewing experience, framed and contained within an expansive and engaging broader visual narrative.

Forbes-Robertson on the other hand was too subtle and elevated in style to reach readily for the uninhibited expressiveness of the pantomimic codes to facilitate clear communication. The association between excess and lack of refinement, or, conversely, between restraint and nobility was, and perhaps is, one deeply ingrained in the English consciousness. In the US, to suggest an actor was unsubtle, excessive or unrealistic in his/her acting was in no sense a neutral evaluation: it carried associations of forms of playing associated with melodrama and other 'lower' forms of theatrical entertainment.[75] However true this might have been in the US, in England the analysis of acting style had, in addition, long conveyed an explicitly defined class connotation. Thus in 1870 Percy Fitzgerald had maintained that *real* acting:

is not self-exhibition; it is an appeal to our intellect and our passions ... There is something noble in it, when followed on its true principles ... But the more it verges towards mere physical performance, the more the actor runs the risk of falling under ... contempt.[76]

This view, in which nobility of person and of performance were, in effect, elided, had a sustained influence on theatrical consciousness. In accordance with Fitzgerald's principles of dramatic acting, Forbes-Robertson's princely reserve as Hamlet was sublimated into the supreme exemplar not only of his art, but also *thereby* of his own nobility. Having interviewed Forbes-Robertson about his stage Hamlet in the US in 1904, John Corbin gave the following report:

Even sitting in a modern drawing room in a frock coat, and smoking the usual cigarette, he suggested more of the royal Dane than many an actor man ... gets into an entire performance ... [H]is large acquiline (sic) features have in repose a pale cast of melancholy that gives way when he talks to an animation restrained only by the inherent dignity of the man of the world and the scholar ... [H]is eyes [are] alight with meaning, his bearing erect and princely.[77]

---

[75] For an American analysis from the period of the difference between the 'subtle' and the 'blatant' actor, see Albert Goldie, 'Subtlety in Acting,' *The New York Dramatic Mirror* (13 November 1912), 4. Quoted in Pearson, *Eloquent Gestures*, p. 36.

[76] Fitzgerald, *Principles of Comedy and Dramatic Effect*, p. 260.

[77] Sunday issue of the *NYT* (13 March 1904). Quoted in Shattuck, *Shakespeare on the American Stage*, p. 203.

Figure 5.7a and b. Forbes-Robertson, painting and relaxing by a fire.
Commemorative postcards. Author's private collection.
Unusually for star cards of the moment, images of Forbes-
Robertson were not confined to his theatrical roles or framed
formal portraits. Several suggested the sort of lifestyle the actor led as a
gentleman of refined pursuits and gentlemanly leisure.

The image of Forbes-Robertson as a gentleman of breeding and distinction, aristocratic in style both on- and off-stage, was pervasive in reviews
of all his work. It was implicitly confirmed by a series of star postcards
that appeared on both sides of the Atlantic in the years 1910–13 showing
him engaged in leisured pursuits and adopting a series of studiedly leisured poses: reclining beneath a tree in extensive gardens, boater on head,

book in hand; caught (as it were) painting a portrait of his wife (Gertrude Elliott) at an easel in an elegant drawing room;[78] reading by an open fire in a smoking jacket with a dog curled asleep at his feet (Figures 5.7a and b). The pictures strategically sculpted, and supported, an image of Forbes-Robertson as a dignified gentleman *of a particular class*. His surroundings, dress and choice of activity or pose collaborate in confirming this impression. Forbes-Robertson's much vaunted 'nobility' of both person and stage practice was, undoubtedly, a widely acknowledged attribute in the man and his work. But, as his career advanced, it became also a discreetly executed piece of marketing to consolidate that professionally advantageous image. His official ennoblement in 1913 could even be said to have simply formalised the 'nobility' his public had detected in him for years, the royally sanctioned nomenclature finally catching up with his personal and professional reputation.

In the 1913 film, Forbes-Robertson gives a performance consistent with his stage performances – grave, unhurried and physically contained. His physical containment is clearly not unrelated in intent to his insistent mouthing of the words before the camera. Bearing in mind the 'contempt' that Fitzgerald said is liable to be incurred by the actor who 'verges towards mere physical performance', Forbes-Robertson's constant, if mute, allusion to vocal communication indicates more than simply his unerring allegiance to the indispensable value of Shakespeare's language (though it certainly indicates that). His tenacity in this respect also testifies to his self-conscious eschewing of the more obvious, more accessible and, by association, more plebeian *visual* communicative forms required for the medium in which he was now working. His conspicuous reluctance to privilege the visual over the verbal is, therefore, as much a statement about cultural register as it is about the relative merits of different systems of actorly communication. In declining an enhanced gestural and facial acting style, he was clarifying his rejection of 'meaner', 'contempt[ible]' performance forms and so implicitly confirming his distinction from the more physically demonstrative Hamlet of the film's tie-in novelisation.[79]

[78] Forbes-Robertson was happy for his aptitude for fine art to be publicised. It is, for example, partly through his painting of the wedding scene from Irving's 1882 Lyceum production of *Much Ado About Nothing* that we remember that piece of pictorial staging. See Richard W. Schoch, 'Pictorial Shakespeare', in Stanley Wells and Sarah Stanton (eds.), *The Cambridge Companion to Shakespeare on Stage* (Cambridge University Press, 2002), p. 66.

[79] See Fitzgerald, *Principles of Comedy and Dramatic Effect*, pp. 260, 326–7.

Forbes-Robertson's approach to acting for the camera may be instructively compared with that of the English classical stage actor Arthur Bourchier. Bourchier had appeared as Henry VIII in the Barker/Tree film production of 1911 and made a film of *Macbeth* for the German company Film Industrie Gesellschaft during the summer of 1913. The Forbes-Robertson *Hamlet* was released in September 1913, the Bourchier *Macbeth* less than a month later. Bourchier was specifically commended in the British trade press for adjusting his theatrical style of acting for the conditions of the new medium. The *KLW* commented that the 'quiet subtlety' that characterised his acting on stage 'would be impossible to efficiently translate through the medium of pictures', but that fortunately in the film *Macbeth*:

he has broadened his style, amplified his gesture, and developed increased facial expression, with the result that his success is far more pronounced than that which has attended several others of our eminent actors who have sought to act for pictures.[80]

Coming hard on the heels of the release of the Forbes-Robertson *Hamlet* as the Bourchier *Macbeth* did, it is impossible not to read the comparison with 'those of our eminent actors' who refused to moderate their style for the camera as an only lightly veiled reference to that most cinematically resistant of all film actors, Forbes-Robertson.

Forbes-Robertson makes no reference to his film of *Hamlet* in his autobiography.[81] It is a striking omission. His lack of interest in documenting his first foray into the medium perhaps suggests that it was only the chance to enshrine this particular dramatic material on film that had persuaded him thus to stoop at all. He made three films in total in his life: *Hamlet* (1913), *Masks and Faces* (1917) and *The Passing of the Third Floor Back* (1918). Each began life on the stage, and, even in their celluloid instantiations, each seems to have been reluctant to shed its theatrical associations. *Masks and Faces*, for example, was made to benefit the Academy of Dramatic Arts and was proudly reported by *The Bioscope* as 'a wonderful living record of our best dramatic art' and as a 'special type of typically English play':

It is a play that no other country in the world could have produced, and with native talent on native soil it can safely challenge the whole world as an English masterpiece of unexampled merit.[82]

---

[80] *KLW* (9 October 1913), 2555.

[81] Even the title of Forbes-Robertson's autobiography, *A Player Under Three Reigns*, suggests that his self-conception was peculiarly old-school British in being defined by a relation to monarchy.

[82] *The Bioscope* (8 March 1908), 993.

From his reception in this film, as also in *Hamlet*, Forbes-Robertson emerges as an actor epitomising a quality product of a specifically theatrical, and peculiarly English, character. It is a reputation whose appeal has proved lasting.

CRITICAL AFTERLIVES

The Gaumont-Hepworth *Hamlet* was given a selective international release in the years between 1913 and 1916. The Rodolfi-Ruggeri *Hamlet*, a film of comparable length, was given a European distribution in 1917–18, in a variety of language prints appropriate to the country of exhibition. Each film was in some degree intended to enshrine for posterity the performance of an internationally celebrated stage Hamlet. Given the proximity in time of their respective releases, and the obvious points of imitation and contrast in their productions, a contemporary comparison between both the individual Hamlet performances *and* the films as a whole would surely have been not only instructive but inevitable.

To my mind, these two comparisons yield different results. Ruggeri was later to become known as the '*mattatore*'[83] ('limelight grabber' or 'spotlight-chasing virtuoso' in approximate translation) in reference to his fundamentally populist and unsubtle approach. Forbes-Robertson undoubtedly offers a more nuanced Hamlet. But, as has been implicit in the argument throughout this chapter, a subtle Hamlet at the centre of a film which attempts to keep stately pace with its stately central performance does not necessarily rescue the production from being an exercise in celluloid taxidermy.

Mattatore-followers may well be sneeringly dubbed uncultivated or undiscriminating – a trend Gramsci initiated in relation to Ruggeri as early as 1915. However, the uncompromising energy of the performance given by this particular *mattatore* and the corresponding energy of the film that contains it offer pleasurable compensations for those on the receiving end of such a sneer. Rodolfi's film nicely balances Ruggeri's excesses as Hamlet with Elena Makowska's touchingly whimsical Ophelia and rescues the whole from absurdity by the imaginative agility of its formal construction. For all its energy and technical merits, however, relative to the Forbes-Robertson, the Ruggeri film has been critically neglected.[84] So what can account for the difference in their after-lives?

[83] Anzi, *Shakespeare Nei Teatri Milanesi*, p. 33.
[84] A glance at the relevant critical literature reveals the different levels of critical attention the two films have received. In *Hamlet in Film, Television and Audio Performances*, Kliman assigns an individual chapter to early silent *Hamlet* films in general and another exclusively to the 1913 Gaumont-Hepworth production. The Rodolfi-Ruggeri version is not discussed (although

The neglect of the 1917 *Hamlet* is dependent in part on the accident of its release date and the accompanying prosaic forces of circumstance which partly determined where prints are now to be found. Firstly, it was produced during the First World War, which impaired (although by no means eliminated) international film distribution.[85] More significantly, it came just too late to benefit from the intense interest that prestige Italian films had earlier generated in the US market. Between 1907 and 1914, Italian historical and literary subjects were (as discussed in Chapter 3) branded as everything that was Old World, artistic and therefore classily authentic. By 1916, despite the considerable success in the US of Italian spectacles such as *Cabiria* (1914) and *Il Leone di Venezia* (1914), George Kleine, the American distributor for Ambrosio, Cines and FAI pictures, had pulled the plug completely on the Italian imports. And by 1917, the American film industry was not just energetically exporting its own product across the world but had also emphatically signalled its lack of interest in importing foreign films – a pattern that would, of course, have a lasting impact on the fortunes of all other world cinemas.

An early casualty of the damming up of the important American market was the Rodolfi *Hamlet*, which was never copyright registered for US distribution. The resulting absence of a print in the US must, for pragmatic reasons, go some considerable way to explaining why the Forbes-Robertson film has been more critically in favour there – not necessarily actively preferred, simply available to critical communities in ways the other was not. Though true in the US, however, lack of an available print cannot account for the discrepancy in treatments in Britain as both

---

reference is made to the fragments from the Lux production mislabeled the 'Ruggeri version' at MOMA). In Kenneth Rothwell's engaging tour through silent Shakespeare films for his 2000 ISA occasional paper 'Early Shakespeare Movies: How the Spurned Spawned Art', the pragmatics of selection meant that the Rodolfi-Ruggeri *Hamlet* appears only in the filmography. Of the twenty-five papers under the collective heading 'Hamlet on Screen' in the 1997 *Shakespeare Yearbook*, one is on the Gaumont-Hepworth *Hamlet*, one on the Asta Nielsen/Svend Gade *Hamlet*. No Italian *Hamlet* is discussed. In the 'Shakespeare and Italy' *Shakespeare Yearbook* of 2001, none of the many Italian Shakespeare films from the silent era is discussed. In the Melzer-Rothwell *Shakespeare on Screen* filmography, under the heading 'Edition, History, Contents, & Evaluation', the Gaumont-Hepworth *Hamlet* is given sixty-five lines of descriptive analysis, the Rodolfi-Ruggeri *Hamlet*, eight. Ball did view an incomplete English language 16mm print of the film in Nebraska, courtesy of the 'Dudley Circuit Service'. Sadly, however, that surviving print was only a fraction of the film's actual length, being by his calculation 765 feet in total whereas the film's length on release was 7,448 feet. At best, the film had only minimum exposure in the US.

[85] The Forbes-Robertson *Hamlet* was not itself released in the US until 1915, after the War in Europe had started.

films are held in equally accessible prints at the BFI National Archive (formerly the NFTVA).[86]

Though unrelated to merit or even to the pragmatics of access, the disparity in where critical attention has been directed in Britain should nevertheless not surprise. A sense of cultural affinity with an English product, and cultural prejudice about an Italian one, remains largely unchallenged. Ball's judgement on Ruggeri's performance was that it was 'perhaps too Italianate' and few since have considered it.[87] Having emerged not only from England, but from the most distinguished of English actorly and cinematic stables imaginable has invested the Gaumont-Hepworth film with an automatic kudos. As has been evident from its initial marketing and throughout its reception history, its implicit and explicit allusions to a prestigious system of theatrical and cultural networks beyond itself have proved beguiling, amply compensating for other limitations. The Rodolfi-Ruggeri *Hamlet*, by contrast, lacks both the validation of a distinguished anglophone theatrical performance tradition *and* the market appeal of an association with English nobility (both literal indicator of endowed status and metaphorical allusion to actorly tenor). In the absence of these indisputable draws, it has failed to find its own alternative 'hooks' by which to secure an international and enduring profile. For reasons of both cultural preference and historical accident, therefore, it is a film that has slipped from critical view and needs recuperating.

*

One of the subjects of this chapter has been the differing cultural registers of variant styles of acting for the camera, from the expressively pantomimic to the gesturally abstemious, and the different strata of the picturegoing market to which these styles were assumed to appeal. It is striking in ways that accord with prevalent stereotypes that the British and American trade presses should have responded in markedly divergent ways to the attributions of national character that became associated with these performance styles. In 1909, for example, the British trade paper *KLW* compared English and Continental acting styles and predicted dourly what the comparison might mean for the future of the British film industry. In

---

[86] The films have been given equally helpful entries in McKernan and Terris, *Walking Shadows*, the BFI's catalogue of Shakespeare-related holdings.

[87] Ball, *Shakespeare on Silent Film*, p. 262.

summary, it feared that English film-makers would always be capped in their achievements:

> by the fact that English actors are, both by temperament and education, unable to equal the Continental performer in the graphic gestures which in films must take the place of dialogue. The typical English style of acting is quiet and restrained, and if an artist is unable to forget the traditions of his profession and throw himself into a piece with the abandon of a French or Italian actor, the manufacturer is hardly to be blamed.[88]

If Ruggeri's 'abandon' was thought to typify Italian acting, Forbes-Robertson's 'restraint' equally well fitted the *KLW*'s portrait of a 'typical' English actor. And he was certainly not tempted to '*forget* the traditions of his profession' (my emphasis) since the filming project itself was specifically conceived as an elaborately detailed act of formal remembrance of them. Nevertheless, it was not necessarily this that held back the 1913 film from greater cinematic success. In fact, in the case of the Gaumont-Hepworth *Hamlet*, *KLW*'s insistence that 'the manufacturer is hardly to be blamed' when faced with 'quiet and restrained' acting seems misleadingly to invest complete responsibility for a film's success in the actor. Had Hepworth and Plumb risked the wrath of the theatre purists and offered a variety of focal lengths on their subject, or some edited cut-ins on elements of a scene rather than reverentially restricting themselves to whole scene takes and an unflinchingly theatrical point of view, the film could have absorbed and channelled the impressive restraint of its central performance. But whereas the Italian production intervenes through cinematography and editing to render interpretively purposeful what Ruggeri had less subtly offered up as his pro-filmic performance for the camera, the English production respectfully refuses to intervene on the theatrical integrity of a scene and consequently fetters its own showcasing of Forbes-Robertson's artistry by frustratingly denying us access to it in medium-sensitive ways.

In 1911, however, the American trade paper *MPW* then made a similar analysis of differing acting styles to that proffered by the British *KLW* in 1909, but came to a tellingly different conclusion:

> The fact of the matter is, that it is the very infrequency and simplicity of the gesture that gives it effectiveness. When we see two Frenchmen or Italians gesticulate we take small notice, because we are accustomed to see the Latin races go through a perfect fury of gesticulation over nothing in particular. The gestures of Americans, or Englishmen for the matter of that, are, on the contrary, pregnant

---

[88] *KLW* (1 July 1909), 349.

with meaning, because the whole man has to be charged with the tensest emotion, before he seeks to give it utterance by gesture ... A wave of the hand, a turn of the body, a swinging of the arm means more than a hundred thousand excited gestures of a company of Frenchmen, Italians, or South Americans. There is a suggestion of the monumental about the gesturing of the Northern races.[89]

Whereas minimalism was cited as an excuse for self-flagellation in the British trade press and inspired prophecies of the failure of the national film industry, it was used as the cause for self-congratulation and assertions of national superiority in the American trade press. And it is tempting to see in this the embryonic signs of a more general journalistic habit of mind. The respective urge to castigate or promote one's indigenous film product would, that is, become a pronounced trend in British and American film journalism in later years, contributing, in time, to the fortunes of both national industries.[90]

It is to the British and American film industries, as viewed through the lens of Shakespeare films specifically of 1916, the tercentenary year, that the next chapter turns. It traces how the narrative, performance and tonal preferences in American Shakespearean movie-making diverged from British preferences and how early differing national market demands were sufficiently recognisable to become suitable material for satirical treatment.

---

[89] Louis Reeves Harrison, *MPW* v.10, n.5 (4 November 1911), 357. Quoted in Burrows, *Legitimate Cinema*, pp. 59–60.

[90] On the impact of negative film journalism on the British film industry, see James Park, *British Cinema: the Lights that Failed* (London: Batsford, 1990), Introduction.

CHAPTER 6

Shakespeare films of the 1916 tercentenary

The Real Thing at Last (Bushey Heath Co.: James Barrie, 1916)
Macbeth (Triangle-Reliance: John Emerson, 1916)
Romeo and Juliet (Fox: J. Gordon Edwards, 1916)
Romeo and Juliet (Metro: John W. Noble, 1916)

On Easter Sunday, 23 April 1916, a commemorative service was held at the Cathedral of St John the Divine in New York, to mark the tercentenary of Shakespeare's death. Two ennobled British actors, Herbert Beerbohm Tree and Johnston Forbes-Robertson, each gave an address and the eminent American actor Frederick Warde read the second lesson. The service closed with the singing of 'America'.[1] The congregation then repaired to Central Park where, despite the rain, a floral wreath was laid on Shakespeare's statue. As part of the tribute, Tree placed a 'British flag over the bust of the statue' and an American flag was placed beside it.[2]

The specific choreography of the event, complete with distinguished transatlantic casting and the ceremonial placing of the twin flags, suggested – as was presumably intended – a sense of shared ownership of the Shakespeare legacy. It was a more focused, bi-lateral British and American version of the 'universal homage' that the British Tercentenary Committee had said should be 'accorded to the genius of the greatest Englishman'.[3]

There were some, however, who saw difference, and entertaining difference at that, in the ways the British and Americans were taking possession of the Shakespeare legacy. Indeed, only a month earlier, in March 1916, the distinguished Scottish writer James (J.M.) Barrie (also recently knighted)

[1] 'Shakespeare's Name Rings Through St. John's Cathedral: Sir Johnston Forbes-Robertson and Sir Herbert Beerbohm Tree Principal Speakers at Tercentenary Celebration of the Actors' Alliance', *New York Herald* (24 April 1916), 6. The service was run jointly by the Actors' Church Alliance of America and the Civic Shakespeare Tercentenary Committee.
[2] '400 Stand in Rain to Pay Honor to Shakespeare', *New York Herald* (24 April 1916), 6.
[3] Israel Gollancz (ed.), *A Book of Homage to Shakespeare* (Oxford University Press, 1916), vii. The Gollancz tercentenary memorial volume is discussed in detail in Coppélia Kahn, 'Remembering Shakespeare Imperially: The 1916 Tercentenary', *SQ* v.52, n.1 (2001), 456–78 (456–7).

had mischievously produced a satirical film entitled *The Real Thing at Last* that specifically caricatured a set of perceived differences between British and American approaches to Shakespeare.

The Real Thing at Last, subtitled *The 'Macbeth' Murder Mystery*,[4] was, as Ball described it, 'a delightful spoof' on *Macbeth*, conceived as a response to the tercentenary preparations at that point in train in Britain.[6] To mark the anniversary, the British Tercentenary Committee had made elaborate preparations for a variety of theatrical productions, pageants, tribute concerts, recitations, publications, lectures, art exhibitions, tree-planting ceremonies, tours of Shakespearean sites of London and other commemorative events.[7] As a skittish way of pointing out the oversight in omitting moving pictures entirely from these plans, and perhaps also of puncturing the rather po-faced, reverential approach to Shakespeare of most official tercentenary events, the film that Barrie wrote (and co-directed with L.C. MacBean) was self-consciously silly. One of Barrie's biographers, J.A. Hammerton, described it as a piece of 'ineffectual trifling', another, Denis Mackail, as a 'bit of impudence'; *The Times* summed it up as 'a joyous piece of fooling'.[8] It certainly stood clearly distinct from the clutch of more earnestly engaged, feature-length Shakespeare films that the 1916 celebrations inspired in the American film industry.

The tercentenary year constitutes a useful exemplary moment to assess developments in the film industry and specifically in Shakespearean filmmaking. Under cover of the ostensibly fictional American and British Shakespeare film productions lampooned in *The Real Thing at Last*, the film succeeded both in alluding to real previous releases and in wittily anticipating the imminent release of the American feature-length *Macbeth* starring Tree. In fact, *The Real Thing at Last* identifies itself as, in part, a satirical trailer for the Tree *Macbeth*. In its more general gaze westward, however, it also incidentally provides a cultural filter through which two big-budget American *Romeo and Juliet* films released later that year may also be viewed. Sadly, none of these four films has survived. They each, however, leave

---

[4] Sheridan Morley, *Tales from the Hollywood Raj: The British, the Movies, and Tinseltown* (NY: Viking, 1983), p. 25.

[5] Ball, *Shakespeare on Silent Film*, p. 225.

[6] 'A Tragic "Movie": Sir J. M. Barrie's Cinema Burlesque', *The Times* (8 March 1916), 11.

[7] See *A Tribute to the Genius of William Shakespeare being the programme of a performance at Drury Lane Theatre on May 2, 1916, the tercentenary of his death* (London: Macmillan, 1916), xii; Kahn, 'Remembering Shakespeare Imperially', p. 459; *The Times* (24 April 1916), 6, 7.

[8] J. A. Hammerton, *Barrie: The Story of a Genius* (New York: Sampson Law, 1929), p. 286; Denis Mackail, *The Story of J. M. Barrie: A Biography* (London: Peter Davies, 1941), p. 490; 'A Tragic "Movie"', *The Times* (8 March 1916), 11.

behind a bank of accounts, reviews and debates that together tell an illuminating story. These gathered reports help reconstruct the detail and tonal
character of the films now lost to us. Simultaneously, they act as a gauge
of film industry confidence in its own suitability and efficacy as a medium
for interpreting Shakespeare, specifically in a year in which the conservative
weight of the Shakespearean establishment was at its most conspicuous.[9]

THE REAL THING AT LAST (JAMES BARRIE, 1916)
MACBETH (JOHN EMERSON, 1916)

Barrie's idea for *The Real Thing at Last* was, according to celebrated English
character actor A.E. Matthews, 'to show how Hollywood would make a
movie of Shakespeare's tragedy [*Macbeth*] by contrasting it with our own
humbler way'.[10] Like John Kendrick Bangs's 1909 theatrical farce *The Real
Thing* (from which Barrie probably derived the title of his film), Barrie's
film also evidently had farcical elements to it. The 'real thing' that was supposedly 'at last' being delivered here was a 'proper' version of Shakespeare
with which to celebrate the tercentenary. In this tongue-in-cheek version
of 'proper' Shakespeare, however, few proprieties are observed and much
absurdity let loose.

In the absence of the film itself, its various narrative twists must be
pieced together from the reports it has left behind. These do not add up
to a fully coherent account of the plot. Nevertheless, they all point to a
production that was evidently energetic, innovative, funny and, in some
respects, perspicacious. The *Cinema News and Property Gazette* (*CNPG*)
gave a report of the action that explained how the framework story specifically referenced the tercentenary as its point of departure:

The idea of the piece is that the cinema actors are furious at not having been asked
to help in the tercentenary celebrations, and the producer, named Thunder, with
a fat swan for a trade-mark, asks us only to wait and see how much Shakespeare
owes to them. Immediately you are plunged into a magnificent feast at King
Duncan's palace, where lovely ladies and shaggy thanes engage in the turkey-trot
and other delights of the kind. Then come the witches, lovely creatures, working

---

[9]   For other detailed discussions of America's tercentenary Shakespeare films, see Roberta E. Pearson
      and William Uricchio, ' "Shrieking From Below the Gratings": Sir Herbert Beerbohm Tree's
      Macbeth and His Critics', in A. J. Hoenselaars (ed.), *Reclamations of Shakespeare* (Amsterdam and
      Atlanta: Rodopi, 1994), pp. 249–71, and Luke McKernan, ' "A Complete and Fully Satisfying Art
      on its Own Account": Cinema and the Shakespeare Tercentenary of 1916', *Shakespeare* ('Silent
      Shakespeare' special issue), v.3, n.3 (December 2007), 337–51.
[10] A. E. Matthews, *Matty: An Autobiography* (London: Hutchinson, 1952), p. 155. Matthews's com-
      pany, the British Actors' Film Company, provided the cast for Barrie's film.

up Macbeth, who hesitates as if he had conscientious objections to murdering, and then the murder itself. Duncan seems to have grown cautious with the passage of centuries; he distrusts the climbing Macbeths, and spends the night under his bed, but in vain. Lady Macbeth gets a bucketful of blood to smear the pages and sleep-walks as she never did before. Then the screen warns Macbeth that General Macduff is after him. 'If you see a wood moving, it's a cinch!' The wood moves, and Macduff is after him indeed. He falls from the top of the keep after him, over bridges after him, over a whole landscape, till every weapon is left behind, and they run at each other like buffaloes.[11]

This account captures the zany flavour of the piece but omits to mention that its narrative was based upon the entertaining juxtaposition of two hypothetical productions of *Macbeth*, one an underplayed British period version, the other a brasher American updated one. The comparative structure enabled the film to trade upon comically stereotyped contrasts. Lady Macbeth rubbed at one 'very small spot of blood' in the British version but was 'covered in gore' in the American one.[12] In the British production, the cauldron was 'very small', the acting style contained and the plot recognisably Shakespearean; in the American one, the cauldron was an 'enormous glittering metal' property, the action exaggeratedly melodramatic and the potential for both goriness and sexuality enhanced.[13] Although most roles were doubled in the casting across British and American productions, for the witches, there were separate casts: three male actors in the British version sitting stirring their small cauldron, but 'three blondine cuties'[14] (one of whom was Gladys Cooper) in the American version, looking 'most glamorous' as they danced around their spectacular pot.[15] In the American version, the setting for the fight between Macduff and Macbeth was, with striking contemporaneity, the top of a sky-scraper where death-defying feats were enacted in breathtaking fashion (making even those watching its filming alarmed).[16] In the British version, by contrast, Macbeth and Macduff more modestly 'rolled about in a muddy ditch'.[17] The American sections of the film contained a string of joyous anachronisms appropriate to the contemporary setting but striking for a version of *Macbeth* – including telephones and telegrams. Title cards were pithily satirical: 'Macbeth receives a disquieting letter', 'Dear Macbeth, The King has gotten old and

[11] 'Editorial Chat', *CNPG* v.10 n.179 (16 March 1916), 3.   [12] *Ibid.*
[13] Matthews, *Matty*, p. 158.
[14] John T. McManus, 'Matthews of the Movies', *NYT* (17 January, 1937). Clipping on file at NYPL.
[15] Matthews, *Matty*, p. 158.
[16] Leslie Henson, *My Laugh Story* (London: Hodder and Stoughton, 1926?), p. 290.
[17] Matthews, *Matty*, p. 158.

silly: slay him. Yours sincerely, Lady M.', 'Those Macbeths – I don't trust them' and the 'telegram' report: 'If Birnham Wood moves it's a cinch.' The British version ended with predictably coy understatement: 'The elegant home of the Macbeths is no longer a happy one', while the American version blithely opted for closure of a kind deemed more appropriate for the predilections of the American market: 'The Macbeths repent and all ends happily'.[18] In sum, the British emerge from the film with a marked preference for the modestly performed, the materially spare and the appropriately historical; the Americans for the overblown, the sensationalised, the gory, the updated and, however improbable in plot terms, the happily resolved.

Godfrey Tearle played Macduff, Norman Forbes Duncan and Edmund Gwenn both Macbeth and 'Thunder' (the 'ultra-American' film producer whose rage at being overlooked precipitates the action).[19] Nelson Keys' principal role was as a cross-dressed Lady Macbeth (who 'stole the picture').[20] To add a whiff of adulterous possibility for the American version, he additionally played an interpolated character, '"the dramatic profession in a nutshell," who is always trying to take Lady Macbeth (also enacted by Mr Keys) out to supper'.[21] A.E. Matthews and Irene Vanbrugh both had bit parts. This was a distinguished line-up of actors who were, as Hammerton reports, 'accommodating enough to enter in [sic] the fun of the thing'[22] and indeed who did so for very little money.[23] Leslie Henson reports that he enjoyed playing a less than dignified Duncan on the day he had to stand in on set for an ill Forbes. Before settling down to sleep in his four-poster bed, Henson's Duncan hung his crown on a nail. When he subsequently heard footsteps approaching, he scuttled feebly under the bed to hide, only then to reappear in full view of his murderers to retrieve his forgotten crown from its nail before darting back to supposed safety under the bed, now clutching his prized crown.[24] The film seems to have thrived on such improvised fooling. Henson reports that, in a late-addition further framing narrative, he also played the part of Shakespeare.[25] I am, however, unclear how this authorial meta-drama fitted into the whole.

[18] Mackail, *Story of J. M. Barrie*, p. 451.   [19] 'A Tragic "Movie"', 11.
[20] Matthews, *Matty*, p. 158.   [21] 'A Tragic "Movie"', 11.
[22] Hammerton, *Barrie: The Story of a Genius*, p. 414.
[23] Their salary was ten shillings a day for a twelve-day shoot (as opposed to their customary £200 a week), and £1 a day each for Edmund Gwenn and Godfrey Tearle. Matthews, *Matty*, p. 156.
[24] Henson, *My Laugh Story*, p. 289.   [25] Matthews, *Matty*, p. 157.

The Real Thing at Last was first exhibited at the London Coliseum on 7 March 1916 as part of a benefit Royal Command Performance mounted to raise funds for the troops. As if the film did not contain meta-narratives enough (through the separate framing devices of both film producer Thunder and Shakespeare himself), for its première, Barrie choreographed a further preface to enliven the show by self-consciously demonstrating its distinction from theatre. A stage-set designed to 'represent[] in every detail the frontage of a picture-house, with box office, display posters and so on' was erected on the Coliseum stage. Before the lights went down and the projection began, the entire cast filed up onto stage from their front row seats, to be seen in their three-dimensional, substantive selves before then disappearing through a door in the set marked 'STAGE DOOR' as if themselves entering the picture-house ready to perform in the film to be exhibited. At this point Irene Vanbrugh, who remained on stage as 'the releaser' (a Barrie pun), touched a barrel with her magic wand, causing lots of tightly jammed-in film now to jump out of it. By this symbolic act of cinematic 'release', the film was loosed from the barrel and the real world of substantial actors to which the audience had just been exposed could cede to its shadowy projected counterpart. Accordingly, a screen descended in front of the picture house façade and the cast now made their reappearance on screen, transformed, as it were, into two-dimensional, cinematic versions of their former selves.[26] The film's high jinks ran for half an hour in total and were accompanied by composer Freddie Norton's live piano medley of popular songs, wittily adapted to suit the incidents on screen.[27] To sustain the effect of live and projected action working in dialogue with each other, Edmund Gwenn, 'distinctly overdressed and smoking a large cigar, acting as showman', supplied 'in an exaggerated American accent a running commentary on the scenes as they unfolded'.[28] The evening's entertainment, therefore, self-consciously enacted the lines of division and connection between the screen and the real world. While the impression was given that most of the cast had stepped *onto* the canvas from their previous position in seats in the stalls, Gwenn's on-screen character of the American film producer had apparently stepped *off* the screen onto the apron of the Coliseum in order to act as impresario and extra-cinematic commentator.

The introductory theatricals and Gwenn's live commentary were designed exclusively for the Royal Command Performance. The film itself, shorn of these particular accompaniments, was subsequently exhibited

[26] Matthews, *Matty*, pp. 157–8.   [27] 'A Tragic "Movie"', 11.
[28] Hammerton, *Barrie: The Story of a Genius*, p. 414.

around the country and reportedly did good business.[29] Its critical reception, however, was not consistently appreciative. After a lively description of its action, for example, the *CNPG* expressed consternation about the project *per se*:

And this is the kind of entertainment provided for royalty and society in wartime! Well! Well! I thought that the British Actors' Film Co. had intentions more serious than turning out sorry stuff of the above description.[30]

The film was not only considered injudiciously flippant, it was also interpreted in some quarters as an impolitic slight upon the US, as a reviewer in the same publication two weeks later made clear:

It is one of the most childish or primitive of errors to make sweeping generalizations on the foundation of a few particular cases, or, on the other hand, to particularize what are in reality general characteristics. In 'The Real Thing at Last' Barrie has achieved the distinction of making both mistakes at once. The type of photo-play which he satirizes in this boisterous burlesque of 'Macbeth', as being characteristic of, and peculiar to, the United States, is in truth peculiar to no country, and is anything but characteristic of screen dramatic art ...

It is not true that the dominant characteristic of American production is an irreverent modernization of the classics of the British stage. On the contrary, the American feeling for our classics ... errs, if it errs at all, on the side of fanatically reverent worship.[31]

The strength of feeling that Barrie's cinematic mischief-making provoked may have been as much related to the moment of the film's release as to its content. If it was thought provocative to be so skittish about Shakespeare in the name of the tercentenary, it was also, perhaps, considered politically inept to lampoon Americans – in particular for their taste for sensationalised fighting and happy endings – just when Britain was trying to persuade the US to enter the war.

Political diplomacy, however, was beyond Barrie's brief. His burlesque on the imperatives of the different film markets was humorously conceived and sympathetically executed. In its spirit and design, it was influenced not by the political needs of the moment but, more simply, by his observation of the American film industry's tendency to update stories, to play for sensationalised effects and to generate happy endings even, when necessary, by resolving tortured melodramas and impending tragedies into

[29] Matthews, *Matty*, p. 158.
[30] 'Editorial Chat', *CNPG* v.10, n.179 (16 March 1916), 3.
[31] Review by L. J. S. *CNPG* v.10, n.181 (30 March 1916), 13.

eleventh-hour rescues and sentimental reconciliations.[32] It is striking that, as early as 1916, a set of Hollywood narrative tendencies that we might still consider broadly characteristic should already have been sufficiently recognisable to be amenable to parody. (Given *The Real Thing at Last*'s treatment of its subject, however, it was – sensibly perhaps – deemed best not to seek an American distribution for this particular release.)[33]

A burlesque culture depends, of course, upon an output of serious work to which it can refer and from which it can draw its satiric energy, and there was no shortage of earnest *Macbeth* films available from either side of the Atlantic to serve as inspiration for Barrie's spoof. It seems likely, therefore, that the hypothetical *Macbeth* film productions satirised in *The Real Thing at Last* were responding, if in hyperbolised form, to real productions. The American Vitagraph 1908 *Macbeth* had, for example, already been officially censored for the goriness of its effects. Moments in that film such as that when 'you see the dagger enter and come out and see the blood flow and the wound that's left' reportedly made it 'worse than the bloodiest melodrama ever'.[34] By contrast, the murders in the British–German co-produced 1913 feature-length five-reel *Macbeth*, starring English actors Arthur Bourchier[35] and his wife Violet Vanbrugh, were specifically commended on having been enacted 'without anything that might be considered gruesome'. In addition, the Bourchier film included 'no obvious anachronisms', had been 'acted with rare discrimination' and conducted its fight scenes 'with fine fervour', though the whole was thought to lack some grand ceremonial touches.[36] That the 1913 Bourchier *Macbeth* was re-released in the US in March 1916 to capitalise on the wave of Shakespearean enthusiasm generated by the tercentenary only increased its relevance to the interpretive landscape with which Barrie was engaging. Here, then, were two instructive *Macbeth* production models – a gory American one and a more restrained (part-)British one – to provide fodder for Barrie's burlesque. In addition, reviews of the 1911 British Co-operative Cinematograph Company's *Macbeth* (starring Frank Benson) suggest that it, like the surviving 1911 *Richard III* from the same company, was

[32] Even *Romeo and Juliet* had been rewritten for the screen to provide a chirpier ending. See, for example, the parody *A Seashore Romeo* (Rex, 1915). The 1910 Pathé one-reeler, *Romeo Turns Bandit*, in which catastrophe is also averted and a happy ending secured, demonstrates that though such a tendency was most prevalent in, it was not exclusive to, the American film industry.

[33] Matthews, *Matty*, p. 158.

[34] '"Macbeth" Pruned in Chicago', *MPW* v. 2, n.24 (13 June 1908), p.511. See Chapter 4, n.8.

[35] Bourchier had played Macduff to Tree's Macbeth on the stage in 1911, and Henry VIII in Tree's 1911 stage and film productions of *Henry VIII*.

[36] *KLW* (9 October 1913), 2555.

specifically and consciously theatrical rather than cinematically ambitious in its style of representation.[37]

Most pertinently of all, however, *The Real Thing at Last* will have had Tree's forthcoming Hollywood film production of *Macbeth* in its satirical sights. Tree's *Macbeth* had been announced as 'about to be "filmed" for the cinematograph' at a reported fee of $20,000 as early as April 1912 – although it was at that point a British production that was anticipated.[38] It was, however, for the Hollywood-based Triangle-Reliance (Fine Arts) Corporation, under the general supervision of D.W. Griffith but directed by John Emerson, that Tree was finally persuaded to commit his performance of Macbeth to celluloid for a production that had, by then, enjoyed quite an expectant fanfare. The film was not released until early June 1916. It was, however, known to be in prospect the previous year and, as soon as filming started in February 1916, Tree appeared in the London-based periodical *Pictures and the Picturegoer* enthusing about the forthcoming release as 'a marvellously truth-telling commentary on the text' with wonderful 'pictorial possibilities' capable of producing 'a dramatic narrative of great power'.[39]

The role of this English classical stage actor in a feature-length Hollywood *Macbeth* points up some of the differences between English and American priorities in filming Shakespeare. For the making of the film, Tree imported to California with him a devotion to the Shakespearean text, presumably thinking it was for this that he had been signed. Accordingly, he presented himself on set self-consciously as 'a Shakespearean', and insisted on reciting large chunks of text for the camera, even though not a word he said would be audible in the film. His stubbornness in this respect posed a problem for the crew as they cranked through reels of expensive film stock paying silent (and, in this context, pointless) homage to the English star's vocal pedigree. While they did so, the film's action was stalled. The pace of the movie could not, however, finally be compromised and so, weighing courtesy against economics, the

---

[37] See *KLW* (16 March 1911), 1339. The Benson *Richard III* is on the BFI *Silent Shakespeare* DVD. No print of the Benson *Macbeth* survives. The 1909 Cines two-reeler *Macbeth* (starring Dante Capelli and Maria Caserini Gasperini, directed by Mario Caserini) and the French Éclair three-reel production of *Macbeth*, released in England in April 1916, might have added to the cosmopolitan mix as part of the cumulative iconography of screen *Macbeths* that informed Barrie's film. Titles and credits in Russian on the surviving print of the Cines film. Folger call no.: MP 24 (1–2), LOC call no.: FEA 4251–4252. The Éclair film is lost. Ball, *Shakespeare on Silent Film*, pp. 244–5.

[38] See Anonymous, 'London Letter', sub-headed 'Few Prominent Actors in Pictures', *MPW* v.12, n.2 (13 April 1912), 124.

[39] *Pictures and the Picturegoer* v.9, n.105 (19 February 1916), 483–4. Quoted at greater length in Chapter 2, pp. 72–3.

production team came up with a ruse to enable them to shoot sparingly, thus saving film stock, and yet without giving offence. Their solution was as condescending as it was simple: to pretend to their exalted guest, where necessary, that a dummy camera was rolling for the duration of his declamations.[40] A theatrically grounded, English respect for linguistic fidelity was even then, it seems, coming into conflict with an American concern to give pace and autonomy to the movie in line with the medium's own capabilities. Revealingly, in this particular encounter, the priorities of the moving pictures won out over those imported from another medium. Unlike the British film industry in 1913 for the making of the Forbes-Robertson *Hamlet* (see Chapter 5), Hollywood in 1916 had little interest in transcribing word-driven theatrical performances onto film.

Quite the contrary in fact: Emerson's plans for *Macbeth* reportedly diverged ambitiously from Shakespeare whenever an opportunity for spectacle or a racy action sequence presented itself:

[W]e can also add scenes merely described in the play, for instance the fight between Macbeth and Cawdor, and the Coronation, which will be one of the biggest scenes in the picture. In the film are also shown some wild dances of the highlanders, and at great rental expense we have secured some special large greyhounds.[41]

Despite the anticipated appeal of 'wild dances' and 'special large greyhounds', on release, the film was accused of a failure of nerve. The filmmakers had not, suggested *The Bioscope*, dared to break free sufficiently from prior forms and own the medium's autonomy: they instead undersold the medium's potential by conceiving of their film chiefly as an accessible taster experience for textual or theatrical Shakespeare. The reviewer issued the following rallying-call:

[T]he moving picture play is capable of serving some finer purpose than to be a mere *aperitif.* It is a complete and fully satisfying art on its own account.[42]

The Tree *Macbeth* did not, it seems, itself fulfil this commission, and was not, moreover, a commercial success. The rallying-call was, however, to be heeded by producers of other Shakespeare films later that same year.

For all its mixed reviews, ahead of its release, the Triangle-Reliance *Macbeth* had generated a considerable ripple of anticipatory excitement. Tree was not known for the restraint of his own Shakespeare productions or acting style: major Hollywood studios were not known either

---

[40] See Ball, *Shakespeare on Silent Film*, p.233; Morley, *Tales from the Hollywood Raj*, p. 30.
[41] Quoted in Morley, *Tales from the Hollywood Raj*, p. 25.
[42] 'Can Shakespeare be "Filmed"?' *The Bioscope* (29 June 1916), 1290.

for skimping on expenditure or for compromising on their own dramatic imperatives. Both film industry personnel and Shakespeareans must have wondered what sort of *Macbeth* film might emerge from this liaison of powerful but not entirely compatible forces. It was into precisely this anticipatory moment that *The Real Thing at Last* was released, impishly speculating about, among other things, what an American film production of *Macbeth* might look like. History does not record whether the Queen, who was present at the première, recognised the intended target of the film's caustic send-up, but looking back on events later that year, Tree himself was in no doubt about what Barrie's project had been:

There is [in England] a tendency to sneer at the serious work ... undertaken by striving artists such as Mr. Griffith – witness the brilliant ridicule by which the film of *Macbeth* was anticipated. I refer of course, to Sir James Barrie's recent remarkable contribution to Shakespeare's Tercentenary.[43]

Barrie's film had declared its up-to-the-minute topicality by satirically referencing a Hollywood film then in production, slated for release less than three months later, and, significantly, the allusion had been caught.[44] As with many burlesques, both the comic value and cultural punch of *The Real Thing at Last* were, therefore, partly dependent on the propitious timing of its release. By 1916, Shakespearean cinema was sufficiently established as a knowable entity for Barrie to embed in his picture cross-references to other Shakespeare films and justifiably assume these would be widely identifiable to audiences. And while evidently needling Tree, for others the allusions proved highly entertaining.

It was pointedly irreverent of Barrie to undertake the 'brilliant ridicule' of approaches to Shakespeare in a year of such widespread Shakespearean pomp. Equally, however, the outpouring of bardolatrous tributes inspired by the tercentenary was all but asking for a subversive foil. Barrie was not alone in finding the temptation irresistible, as evidenced by the unprecedented number of Shakespearean cinematic parodies released in 1916 (including Piccadilly's *Pimple as Hamlet*, Beauty's *To Be or Not to Be*, Lubin's *Hamlet Made Over*, Kalem's *Romeo of the Coal Wagon*, Keystone's *A Tugboat Romeo* and Vitagraph's *Freddy Versus Hamlet*). It was a medium

---

[43] Tree, 'Impressions of America Part I: "Not Bad for a Young Country"', sub-heading 'The Future of the Film', *The Times* (8 September 1916), 11.

[44] Sheridan Morley reported that, whereas his grandmother, Gladys Cooper (who played a witch in *Real Thing*), had thought their spoof entirely 'generalized', Morley himself was 'inclined ... to believe that [A.E. Matthews] at least well knew at whom [Barrie's film] was aimed.' Morley, *Tales from the Hollywood Raj*, p. 25.

that, though not yet accepted into the heart of the cultural establishment, had, in itself, come of age. Officially side-lined by those planning the Shakespearean tributes and yet sufficiently confident and proficient in itself to comment upon such an omission, the film industry was alarmingly well placed to lob small disruptive missiles over the wall.

However, the film industry did more than produce subversive Shakespearean trifles in 1916: it also contributed in non-parodic vein to the year's Shakespearean output. In Britain, Matheson Lang made a five-reel *The Merchant of Venice* for the Broadwest Film Company.[45] In America, the year ended with the release of the Thanhouser feature-length *King Lear* starring the eminent classical actor Frederick Warde as Lear and directed by his son Ernest Warde who also himself played an anxiously observing, fearful Fool.[46] Edmund was played, with considerable physical control and a few chillingly knowing straight-to-camera glances, by Hector Dion, reprising the Shakespearean villainy he had previously committed to screen as Iago in the 1908 Vitagraph *Othello* (and anticipating some later sound-era screen Iagos who would claim a similar intimacy with the camera). A prefatory sequence for the film shows an Edwardian gentleman (also played by Frederick Warde) sitting reading the Folio text of *King Lear* in a library chair. This gentleman's literary imagination proves so powerfully suggestive that his act of reading seemingly then conjures an enacted version of the drama into which he, and we with him, are swiftly transported. By means of a dissolve, the studious Edwardian gentleman morphs into the central character in the drama, complete with long flowing beard and irascible tendencies, and the story proper begins. In the course of the ensuing action, Warde's Lear is privileged by a series of strikingly effective iris-shots that emphasise his isolation and the action as a whole proceeds with some energy both in its cinematography and its central performance.[47]

The year's fullest realisation of *The Biograph*'s aspiration that cinema should adapt Shakespeare in ways that acknowledged the medium as 'a complete and fully satisfying art on its own account', however, came in the form of the two American *Romeo and Juliet* pictures. These two films

---

[45] On the Lang *Merchant*, see Ball, *Shakespeare on Silent Film*, pp. 245–52; Burrows, *Legitimate Cinema*, pp. 169–79; McKernan, 'A Complete and Fully Satisfying Art', 345–6.

[46] Father and son as Lear and the Fool are shown in the cover image.

[47] On the Thanhouser *Lear*, see Ball, *Shakespeare on Silent Film*, pp. 241–4 and Buchanan, *Shakespeare on Film*, pp. 44–6. A copy of the GEH print of the Thanhouser *Lear* is commercially available on the *Thanhouser Collection* DVD, Vol.7. This print lacks the opening framework device of the gentleman reading, and is also missing Dion's looks straight to camera. The print held at the Folger includes these.

served to demonstrate both the artistic legitimacy and market strength of cinema as an interpretive art form amongst others. Since the releases of these two films were intimately related, I examine them together as a dual case study through which to consider the assurance with which film production companies in 1916 were then able to take on both Shakespearean material, and each other, without derivative reference to other art forms either in their casting or manner of presentation. This case study also incidentally serves as a means of testing whether Barrie's satirical claims about the American film industry's characteristic approach to Shakespeare had any grounding in practice.

TWO 1916 *ROMEO AND JULIET* FILMS

In May 1916, the Metro Pictures Corporation announced that, as their lavish contribution to the Shakespeare tercentenary celebrations, they had a film of *Romeo and Juliet* in production.[48] It was to be shot in and around New York City, to be directed by John W. Noble and to star, as Shakespeare's star-crossed lovers, screen idols Francis X. Bushman and Beverly Bayne (promoted as 'the foremost stellar combination in motion pictures' of their day).[49] Through the spring, summer and early autumn Metro continued to drip-feed information, location reports, star, trivia and stills documenting the progress of the filming as part of the cumulative anticipation of the major production in prospect.[50] In May they had announced that the picture 'promises to be one of the most pretentious features ever offered on the Metro program'.[51] By October, with the film safely canned and printed, the scale of the claims, and the confidence with which they were being made, had increased. Now the production had become 'the most magnificent spectacle drama in the history of the screen' and one which could even 'eclipse[] the possibilities of the spoken drama'.[52]

[48] *MPW* v.28, n.6 (6 May 1916), 997; *MPW* v.28, n.8 (20 May 1916), 1342.

[49] *Metro Picture News* "Romeo and Juliet" Special Number (one-page free trade sheet). Deposited for copyright (19 October 1916). LOC call number LP 9354, Cols. 7–8. Hereafter, *Metro Picture News* Special. Industry rumours about a romantic liaison between the co-stars would have added an additional frisson of interest to their on-screen pairing. Their affair became fully public two years later, Bushman divorced and the co-stars married.

[50] For a still of the co-stars clasping each other as Romeo and Juliet, see *MPW* v.29, n.1 (1 July 1916), 19. For further reference to the film's impending release, see *MPW* v.29, n.2 (8 July 1916), 258; *MPW* v.29, n.7 (12 August 1916), 1086; *MPW* v. 29, n.11 (9 September 1916), 1711.

[51] *MPW* v.28, n.6 (6 May 1916), 997.

[52] *MPW* v.30, n.2 (14 October 1916), 178.

When launched as a 'special release' on 22 October 1916,[53] it unspooled in the Metro picture houses, and by special arrangement in some other venues, over an unprecedented eight reels. The early announcement back in May of the company's production plans, however, allowed some market-savvy competition to emerge in time for this release.

Thus it was that on 22 October 1916,[54] the same day as Metro's première, the Fox Film Corporation cheekily released a rival *Romeo and Juliet* feature film with a famously eye-catching heroine.[55] Dangerous screen vamp Theda Bara played a Juliet who, in her own words, was 'no Sunday-school girl' (Figure 6.1).[56] For the Metro production, not only is the film itself lost, but neither has a script or treatment survived. For an insight into the conception of this film, we are, therefore, dependent on the reminiscences from twenty years later of Metro's scenarist Rudolph de Cordova.[57] For the Fox production, by contrast, invaluable information about the way in which it was planned (if not how precisely realised in all particulars) can be gleaned from the surviving 77-page continuity script on deposit at the Library of Congress.[58] The detailed directions

[53] George Blaisdell's 'Review of the Metro *Romeo and Juliet*', *MPW* v.30, n.5 (4 November 1916), 685 gives the opening night ('initial presentation') for the Metro production as 19 October 1916 at the Broadway Theater, New York. Given the weight of other information pointing to a release date of 22 October, I think 19 October was a one-off preview for the trade. Metro unusually reluctant to announce their precise release date ahead of time – repeatedly given only as 'October', perhaps to discourage Fox from releasing simultaneously. However, both films were exhibited in New Orleans on 22 October, Metro bringing forward their opening night, originally booked for 29 October, to deny Fox a week of unchallenged publicity and trade. *MPW* v.30, n.6 (11 November 1916), 892.

[54] There is debate about the Fox release date. 23 October 1916 is given in *MPW* v.30, n.5 (4 November 1916), 766: 22 October 1916 given in *MPW* v.30, n.6 (11 November 1916), 837. It was copyright registered on 22 October 1916 and a review appears in *NYT* on 23 October. The AFI catalogue gives the release dates as 19 October (Metro) and 23 October (Fox). These dates refer to their New York first showing (for the trade in Metro's case). Their opening in other cities frequently coincided. Ball conscientiously documented the various release dates in his Card Catalogue. See '"Bara" Romeo and Juliet' cards 1–4.

[55] Fox had exploited the publicity generated by the Famous Players-Lasky's production of *Carmen* the previous year with their own copycat production, also starring Bara. 'Last winter the fans all het-up over the rival Carmens in the persons of Theda Bara and Geraldine Farrar. Now come the rival Juliets ...' 'Green Room Jottings', *Motion Picture Classic* v.3, n.4 (December 1916), 63.

[56] Theda Bara, 'How I Became a Film Vampire', *Forum* 62 (July 1919), 83–93 (92).

[57] Actor/writer de Cordova was brought in by Metro after several earlier scripts from other writers had proved unsatisfactory. For a one-page anecdotal account of the production, see Rudolph de Cordova, 'Twenty Years After', *The Picturegoer Weekly* (7 November 1936), 11. de Cordova's recollections include interesting details of scenes shot but not finally included in the film.

[58] Typed continuity script (77 loose pages): 'Romeo and Juliet. A Photoplay in Seven Parts. Adapted for the Screen by Adrian Johnson. Directed by J. Gordon Edwards for the Fox Film Corporation ...' LOC deposit (23 October 1916). Copyright registered LP 9376. (Hereafter, Fox continuity script.)

Figure 6.1 Theda Bara as Juliet. Publicity still. Author's private collection.

given in the script by Fox's scenarist, Adrian Johnson, suggest that he had something more chaste in mind for the picture's Juliet than the performance Bara was subsequently to commit to film.[59] Although one contemporary commentator thought it possible that the role of Juliet might just redeem Bara rather than Bara tarnishing Juliet,[60] the brazenness of the casting of an actress internationally celebrated, if not infamous, for

---

[59] The Fox continuity script is insistent about Juliet's modesty: 'Juliet's grace is exceeding' (shot 51, p. 16); 'Juliet casts down her eyes at his modest speech' (shot 53, p. 16); 'Juliet speaking title ['Good pilgrim …'] with modest ardor' (shot 55 p. 17), and their kiss on the bench at the Capulets' party is detailed as 'long and tender' (shot 57, p. 18) rather than anything more potentially pulse-racing. In the balcony scene, Johnson has her '… full of the delicacy of maidenhood' (shot 87, p. 25), and when she hears that Romeo is banished, he has her 'praying – eyes filled with rapt, devotional expression' (shot 183 (2), p. 50).

[60] 'At last Theda Bara yearns for an honorable love, even though a tragic one. "Romeo and Juliet" will satisfy her to her heart's content', *Motion Picture Magazine* (*MPM*) v.12, n.11 (December 1916), 123.

her on-screen seductive exoticism (in, for example, the 1915 films *Siren of Hell, A Fool There Was, Carmen, Sin* and *The Devil's Daughter*) was in tune with the headline-claiming tenor of the production as a whole.[61] The Juliet that the Fox film offered to the paying public was, as *Variety* euphemistically put it, 'far from orthodox' but was, for that very reason perhaps, 'likely to strike a popular note'.[62] The reviewer for the trade paper *Motography* was only marginally less coy: 'Somehow . . . we cannot help feeling that [Theda Bara's] type is just not that indicated in the work of the bard of Avon'.[63] Whether or not she was quite what Shakespeare had envisaged, Bara's comment-worthy presence in this picture drew plenty of attention, both critical and commercial, and certainly made for good box office both in the US and in the picture's subsequent international distribution. Indeed, everything about this *Romeo and Juliet* – from conception to the timing of its release – was marked by market opportunism on the part of the production company.

Fox also followed Metro in citing the Shakespeare tercentenary as the inspiration for their *Romeo and Juliet* film.[64] A more accurate account of their inspiration, however, would need to take account of their exploitative capitalising on the publicity that Metro was generating for their production. In a personal interview with Ball before she died, Beverly Bayne was in no doubt about the extent of Fox's commercial audacity. Fox, she reported, 'had spies among the extras' on the set of the Metro film, 'learned their intentions', and, in response to the three-month Metro shooting schedule, managed to film 'Bara's picture in six weeks' in order to rush it through post-production and still coincide precisely with the Metro release date.[65] Then as now, the market loved having alternatives to pit against, and compare with, each other. The Fox/Bara version, directed by J. Gordon Edwards and explicitly trading upon the publicity already generated by the Metro/Bayne one, went on general release in those picture

---

[61] For a succinct account of the actress's reputation and constructed screen persona, see Maria Wyke, *Projecting the Past: Ancient Rome, Cinema and History* (NY and London: Routledge, 1997), p. 89. See also Lucy Hughes-Hallett, *Cleopatra: History, Dreams and Distortions* (NY and London: Harper and Row, 1990), pp. 330–1, 340; Ball, *Shakespeare on Silent Film*, p. 239.

[62] 'Romeo and Juliet (Fox Corp.)', *Variety* 44 (27 October 1916), 28.

[63] George W. Graves, '"Romeo and Juliet". William Fox's Screen Interpretation Features Theda Bara', *Motography* v.16, n.19 (4 November 1916), 1042.

[64] It was advertised as Fox's 'offering toward the Shakespearian Tercentenary'. *MPW* v.30, n.3 (21 October 1916), 340–1.

[65] Ball's notes on his first interview with Bayne (30 October 1946). Ball's Card Catalogue, Card 4: 'Bayne *Romeo and Juliet*'. See also Ball, *Shakespeare on Silent Film*, p.363. The *Metro Picture News* Special reported that, 'The first picture was taken May 25, 1916; the last, August 23, 1916 – thirteen weeks to a day', Col. 3).

houses allied to the Fox distribution network in a five-reel format.[66] As five reels was the standard length for a feature film of its moment, it was able to fit exhibitors' regular feature slots. It could, therefore, be inserted into picture-house schedules, and so reach a wide audience, at relatively short notice.

The winning combination of star power, significant expenditure and cultural interest would in any case have assured each *Romeo and Juliet* picture its own mini-burst of publicity in its early exhibition run. The strategic coincidence of the timing of the double release, however, proved a profitable boost to both. As performance interpretations of Shakespeare, and ones released amidst a flurry of other Shakespearean tercentenary tributes, the two pictures were inevitably received as artistic rivals: in market terms, however, they became, in effect, mutually beneficial collaborators, as was acknowledged by exhibitors at the time.[67] Picture-goers who, for example, attended the Metro film at George Steiner's Playhouse on New York's Fourteenth Street in late October 1916 would also have wished to attend the Fox version playing simultaneously at The Academy Theater, 'less than a block away' up 'red-blooded' Fourteenth Street, that they might compare the two:[68]

Shakespeare on Fourteenth Street – playing to capacity in two big theaters within one block of each other – is a most interesting phenomenon. Shakespeare 'turning them away' on the lower East Side, where vast audiences sit spellbound by one of his greatest tragedies, is proof enough of the timely educational character of the screen ... Such pictures, be it emphasized once more, are of the greatest value and importance to the reputation and the prestige of the screen.[69]

There were other examples of striking proximity of exhibition venues and market rivalry throughout New York and in other cities across the US – including Philadelphia, Pittsburgh, New Orleans, Cincinnati, Boston, Louisville, Portland (Oregon).[70] In other parts of the world to which, despite the First World War, both companies succeeded in securing an international distribution during late 1916 and 1917, the exhibition of the two films

---

[66] The film was copyrighted as seven reels ('A Photoplay in Seven Parts', Fox continuity script) but re-cut as five to fit the standard exhibition schedules in the US.

[67] Exhibitors in Louisville, for example, admitted that 'the combined advertising [of the two pictures] attracts far more interest, and has its beneficial results.' 'Competition in Juliets Pays Managers', *MPW* v.30 n.7 (18 November 1916), 1047.

[68] See W. Stephen Bush, 'Classics and the Screen', *MPW* v.30, n.6 (11 November 1916), 863.

[69] *MPW* v.30 n.6 (11 November 1916), 825.

[70] On the simultaneity of screenings in these US locations, see Ball's Card Catalogue, 'Bayne "Romeo and Juliet" (9, 11)'.

was not always precisely concurrent but would still have generated comparison.[71] Through the autumn of 1916 in the US and the winter and spring of 1917 further afield, the post-flicks chat from either show would surely have seemed incomplete, and even perhaps ill-informed, without some comparative reference to the 'other' *Romeo and Juliet* then on the distribution circuit. Which Juliet was the better liked (Bara's allegedly 'vampire-Juliet' or Bayne's 'baby stare' and performance that, though tasteful, perhaps lacked 'fire and spirit')?[72] Which Romeo (Harry Hilliard's 'engaging personality' or Francis X. Bushman's differently engaging muscularity which appeared 'to unusual advantage in the scanted garb of the period')?[73] Whose sets and scenery were preferred (Fox's 'often glorious' including 'marble floors ... vine covered balcony ... heavy oaken door', or Metro's 'unusually elaborate' dressed sets including a set of '[e]ighteen buildings, reproducing the old market-place of mediaeval Verona')?[74] Which locations (Fox's attractively tree-lined walk and picturesque 'lake set' or the 'most lavish settings ever provided for a Shakespearian production' showcased by Metro)?[75] Which production's crowd scenes produced the better grand spectacles (Metro's '600 chosen players' or Fox's 'incomparable cast of more than 2500 persons')?[76] Which film used the text to better effect (Fox's 'economical, clear and able' scenario which 'departs from the Shakespearan [sic] ending' or Metro's 'fidelity to the text' which proved Shakespeare 'the greatest title builder [*ie writer of intertitles*] in the world of to-day')?[77] Which film was the

[71] In 'Australian Notes' (report dated '13 December 1916', *MPW* v.31, n.7 (17 February 1917), 994, Thos. S. Imrie reported that the Fox *Romeo and Juliet* was then playing at the Strand Theatre in Sydney 'and is doing big business at prices ranging up to two shillings'.

[72] Bara, 'How I Became a Film Vampire', 92; *Photoplay* 13 (May 1918), 23–4; 'Romeo and Juliet (Metro)', *Variety* 44 (27 October 1916), 28.

[73] *MPW* v.30, n.5 (4 November 1916), 840 and Blaisdell review, 685. For Bushman's own thoughts on his Romeo ahead of the picture's release, see Bushman, 'A Moving Picture Romeo and Juliet: The Restrictions and Latitudes of the Screen in Presenting the Greatest Lovers of All', *MPM* v.12, n.8 (September 1916), 111–15.

[74] *MPW* v.30, n.5 (4 November 1916), 840. Fox Continuity Script (Shot 25, p.8): 'JULIET'S CHAMBER – FULL SET'. *MPW* v.30, n.5 (4 November 1916), 685. *Metro Picture News* Special: 'Facts About Bushman-Bayne "Romeo and Juliet"', Col. 3.

[75] Juliet was pictured in the tree-lined walk (Continuity script, shot 118, p.34) where she is pictured again with Romeo immediately after their marriage. See *Metro Picture News* Special, Cols.1–2.

[76] *MPW* v.30, n.2 (14 October 1916), 178; Fox advertisement *MPW* v. 30, n.3 (21 October 1916), 341.

[77] *MPW* v.30, n.5 (4 November 1916), 840. Bara's Juliet is awoken by Romeo's kiss after he has taken the poison. See Continuity Script, Shot 279, p.75. And not only do the fathers shake hands over the dead bodies of their children, but the grief-stricken mothers with 'tear-dimmed eyes – go into each other's arms' (Shot 286, p.76). There are, however, plenty of titles that quote directly from Shakespeare throughout the film. See *MPW* v.30, n.5 (4 November 1916), 840. The *Metro Picture News* Special, Col 3 proudly announced that 'All the leading characters of the play really spoke Shakespeare's lines while going through the appropriate action. Whenever a player forgot a speech the camera was stopped, and he was obliged to begin over again.'

Figure 6.2 Bushman and Bayne in the balcony scene from the Metro *Romeo and Juliet* (1916). (This image is wrongly identified elsewhere as being from the Fox film.)[78]
Courtesy of Photofest, NY.

more exciting, the more dramatic, the more moving, the more beautiful, the more Shakespearean? (Figures 6.2 and 6.3.) Given the comparability in star appeal, profile, budget, and acclaim (both critical and popular) between the films, no self-respecting picture-goer could have felt satisfied knowing just one of these two releases.

Understanding this market predilection, exhibitors' publicity departments sensibly, and profitably, encouraged the comparisons. In an article entitled 'Competition in Juliets Pays Managers', a writer for *MPW* reported that the Metro film was playing at the Walnut Theater in Louisville while the Fox was playing at the Mary Anderson up the street, and that:

in many cases the public took a shot at both, largely for the purpose of drawing private conclusions and making comparisons … [I]n both cases the houses handled

---

[78] Photofest catalogue this image as the Fox film and it has been reproduced elsewhere as such. This needs correcting. Although there are some similarities with the Fox production – particularly in the set of Romeo's chin – this balcony image is definitely a publicity still showing Bushman and Bayne from the Metro production. This precise still is, for example, reproduced in the *Metro Picture News* Special as part of the promotion for the film.

Figure 6.3 Hilliard and a strategically demure-looking Bara in the Fox
Romeo and Juliet. Courtesy of Photofest, NY.

excellent businesses … A little feeling was to be seen in some of the newspaper
advertising, but those on the inside were of the opinion that this was designed to
attract interest, and also to make people see both shows in order to find out if one
show was so much superior to the other as was claimed in both cases.[79]

Metro was not above exposing a little corporate 'feeling' in the national
trade press either. Indignant at the late arrival of an interloping competitor
in the market place, they tried to place themselves above vulgar comparison. A fierce Metro advertisement in *MPW* on 28 October 1916 read:

Don't be misled. There is ONE, and only ONE Special Production de Luxe of
Shakespeare's Love Story of the Ages *Romeo and Juliet* WITH FRANCIS X.
BUSHMAN *The* Crowned King of Motion Picture AND BEVERLY BAYNE
Queen of the Screen … *DON'T BE MISLED by inferior imitations of a Masterpiece*
(italicisation and capitalisation retained).[80]

By contrast, such comparison was precisely what the brazen Fox Film
Corporation had been courting, as is feistily evinced by their own direct

---

[79] *MPW* v.30, n.7 (18 November 1916), 1047.
[80] *MPW* v.30, n.4 (28 October 1916), advertising supplement inserted between 490 and 491.

marketing appeals to potential audiences: 'What is Your Verdict? Comparison is *now* possible between the William Fox production … and that of another producer *who invited* the parallel'.[81] Buoyed by the eulogies their film was garnering, by the following week Metro had adjusted their marketing strategy, now coming off the defensive with a newly confident swagger:

Shakespeare at last a Box Office Triumph. Critics and Public declare Metro's special production de luxe … the greatest motion picture in the history of the art … [C]ompare and contrast this $250,000 production in Eight Acts with any other.[82]

New Yorkers may not have ripped up paving stones and besieged the premises in implicit support of one production and in angry defiance of the other as they had done in response to Edwin Forrest's and William Charles Macready's concurrent stage productions of *Macbeth* that had played in the city in 1849.[83] Nevertheless, a rivalry between two vibrant, eye-catching and much-discussed Shakespearean productions, and between their differing stars and performance styles, was once again generating a heightened buzz of critical evaluation and comparison in New York and beyond.

To catch the flavour of how contemporary audiences responded to the double dose of cinematic Shakespearean tragedy on offer in autumn 1916, we are dependent upon reviews such as that which appeared in the *New York Times* the day after the public openings of both films:

It would be difficult to say that one film excelled, for the two had points of excellence in common and each was better than the other in certain qualities. The Metro picture was a little more elaborate and longer and followed more closely the drama, while the Fox version, because it was more condensed, perhaps, took more liberties with the text.

Generally speaking, the interior or studio scenes of the Fox film were better than those of the Metro, while the outdoor scenes of the Metro were for the most part much finer than those of the Fox picture. In the Metro film the crowds were better handled and there was greater realism in the brawl scenes. On the other hand, the episode of the party at which Romeo first met Juliet was much better done in the Fox picture.[84]

The general tenor of the *New York Times* reviewer's comments is symptomatic. The Fox film seems to have carried more conviction in the domestic and intimate scenes, whereas Metro's achievements with the big spectacle and action sequences were generally found more impressive. In comparing

[81] Fox advertisement, *MPW* v.30, n.5 (4 November 1916), 952–3.
[82] *MPW* v.30, n.6 (11 November 1916). Quoted on Ball's Card Catalogue, 'Bayne Romeo and Juliet (3)'.
[83] For a useful summary of the events of 1849, see Levine, *Highbrow/Lowbrow*, pp. 63–6.
[84] 'Shakespeare Movie Way. Romeo and Juliet Make Love in the Tomb for Fox production', *NYT* (23 October 1916), 10.

the two, *Variety* found the Metro version to be in possession of 'finer art-istry' but the Fox version to offer 'more obvious theatrical "punch"'.[85] Perhaps a majority of the reviews preferred the Metro version for its deli-cacy, thoroughness, restrained dignity in performance, respect for the Shakespeare text, gorgeous costuming,[86] attention to detail in the crowd scenes and specially commissioned grand musical score based on themes from Gounod's 'Romeo and Juliet' and Tchaikovsky's 'Romeo and Juliet' symphony.[87] There were, however, some reviews that came out in favour of the Fox film. The reasons cited for this were that it was less burdened by intrusive and distracting title cards,[88] included some 'lavishly put on spec-tacles'[89] and, unlike the eight-reel Metro production, did not compromise the story 'in any attempt to obtain extra film footage'.[90]

However, the major draw that might have given the Fox film the edge for some audiences was, unsurprisingly, the indulgent attention it paid to its pleasing-on-the-eye Juliet. Her 'long dark curls' were reported as mak-ing 'many a beautiful picture'[91] and the script clarifies the film's strate-gic expertise at showing off its principal asset to fetching advantage in an appealing variety of arranged poses: snuggling little birds, picking flowers, burying her face in bunches of flowers, throwing flowers, pirouet-ting in front of a mirror, murmuring Romeo's name in her sleep, kissing the bottle of poison sensuously and extracting it later from her cleavage. Moreover, she was frequently seen doing each of these things, as repeat-edly stipulated in the script, in attentively gratifying close-up.[92] On four occasions, the script makes provision for her to be given the privilege of a look straight to camera (something not afforded to any other character in the film). After Romeo's departure on their wedding night she 'comes into

[85] 'Romeo and Juliet (Fox. Corp.)', *Variety* 44 (27 October 1916), 28.

[86] For details about the costumes (which alone cost $35,000), see the *Metro Picture News* Special, Col. 3.

[87] See *MPW* v.30, n.6 (11 November 1916), 829. The score, for full orchestra, was arranged by Irene Berg and Samuel Berg. See Ball, *Shakespeare on Silent Film*, p.237. The score could be adapted for a smaller ensemble, solo organ or piano for the more modestly resourced picture houses. It played with a 15-piece orchestra in Minneapolis and a 12-piece orchestra in Kansas City. See *MPW* v.30, n.7 (18 November 1916), 1040, 1041.

[88] See the *Film Daily* review from 26 October 1916 issue, included in *Film Daily Year Book* for 1924 (177). Partly referenced in Ball, *Shakespeare on Silent Film*, pp. 364 and 365.

[89] *MPW* v.30, n.6 (11 November 1916), 837.

[90] *MPW* v.30, n.3 (21 October 1916), 418.

[91] Hanford C. Judson's review in *MPW* v.30, n.5 (4 November 1916), 840.

[92] Both Juliets were able to benefit from the attentive close-ups that pictures systematically gave their stars in 1916. A revealing comparison from earlier in the industry's development is Florence Lawrence's 1908 Juliet for Vitagraph (discussed in Chapter 4), shot entirely in long-shot. Lawrence's Juliet remains remote throughout.

close foreground – looks to camera with ecstatic face – F A D E' (Shot 97, p. 28). When subsequently out picking flowers, she 'buries her face in the flowers – lifts her eyes to camera – ineffable happiness' (Shot 119, p. 34). As she collapses having swallowed the potion to induce a death-sleep: 'for one moment she looks to camera with glazing eyes – then she relaxes utterly and falls in a heap upon the floor – F A D E' (Shot 232, p. 64). And as she wakes from her death-sleep in the tomb to find Romeo dying beside her:

> – her eyes gradually open – she sits up – looks around – looks down – sees the body of Romeo – gets off Bier – with wild, dilated eyes kneels by it – She kisses him – Romeo's weak arms close around her – she makes inquiries – he speaks and explains briefly – Juliet suddenly looks to camera with wild terror – she speaks.

> SPOKEN TITLE: ——––– POISON! WHAT MEANS MY LORD? THY TREMBLING VOICE, PALE LIPS AND SWIMMING EYES – DEATH'S IN THY FACE. (Shot 277, p. 74)

Those occasions when Bara breaches the notional fourth wall by looking out, via the camera lens, to her audience in this way make a conscious claim to a direct intimacy with those looking on and looking in – an implied intimacy of engagement with the film's female star that no doubt added sparkle to the viewing experience for some sections of the audience. In sum, as the reviewer for *Variety* put it, the 'whole film is highly flavored with Miss Bara' and 'is put forward frankly to please' her 'enormous following among the picture fans'. It does this, said the discerning reviewer, by 'holding Juliet in the conspicuous position of the picture to centre attention upon her'.[93] In this enactment of the drama, other characters in the story and aspects of the production were, as *The Bioscope* put it following the film's British release, rendered 'merely accessory to the story of the ill-fated heroine'.[94]

The unembarrassed concentration on screen vamp Bara inadvertently remembers Barrie's satirical suppositions dramatised in *The Real Thing At Last*. In its treatment of Shakespeare, the Fox film played up both the glamorously sensual and the violent potential of its source material (the latter not only through the street fights but also in the vigorous ambushing of Friar John on his ride to Mantua). In *The Real Thing at Last*, the interpretive priorities that Barrie had ascribed to the American film industry were

[93] 'Romeo and Juliet (Fox Corp.)' *Variety* 44 (27 October 1916), 28. Also partially quoted in Pearson and Uricchio, 'Shrieking', p. 267.
[94] 'William Fox's Greatest Production: Theda Bara as "Juliet": An Artistic and Dramatic Triumph', *The Bioscope* (23 November 1916), 741.

ludicrously exaggerated. Nevertheless, the 1916 Triangle-Reliance *Macbeth* with its interpolated fight scenes, grand spectacles, 'wild dances' and 'special large greyhounds', and the two 1916 *Romeo and Juliet* productions with their glamour, eroticism, visual reach, uninhibited expenditure, uncompromising pace and ruthless commercialism as pitted against each other, incidentally suggest that, as a satirical portrait of a national film industry, Barrie's pastiche of the American industry's approach to Shakespeare may have been recognisable.

In 2003/4, a film of *The Merchant of Venice* then in production, directed by Michael Radford and starring Al Pacino as Shylock, found itself in an unseemly race to release with a rival version produced by and starring Patrick Stewart. Industry insiders predicted dourly that 'it will be difficult, if not impossible, to attract big audiences for two films screened close together', the market being unable to sustain, it was thought, two versions of the same dramatic material released simultaneously.[95] As it transpired, Radford's film came out first and, as a result, Stewart's film was shelved.

The two *Romeo and Juliet* versions of 1916, by contrast, ended up – despite Metro's initial misgivings – in a mutually beneficial commercial clinch. Though film preferences varied between critics, and there were occasional (company-sponsored?) side-swipes at one or other production in review, neither version was systematically asked to serve as critical punch-bag to showcase the brilliance of the other (as sometimes happens with related releases). In fact, both were repeatedly and enthusiastically praised for their overall achievements and for the educational and edifying benefits introduced to the industry as a whole by bringing culturally respectable fare to the screen, and so to the masses, with such commendable energy and delicacy. As the *MPW* proudly reported, even in the usually less culturally fertile stomping ground of New York's lower East Side, both Shakespeare productions were not only playing to houses full to capacity, but were even 'turning them away'.[96]

In adapting Shakespeare, however, the film industry of 1916 was also reaching out beyond its staple market in a conscious bid to appeal to the perceived aspirations of the more bourgeois sections of its audience base.[97]

---

[95] Chris Hastings and Catherine Milner, 'Hollywood rivals battle to bring *The Merchant of Venice* to screen', *Telegraph* (16 August 2003). Consulted online at: www.telegraph.co.uk/news/main.jhtml?xml=%2Fnews%2F2003%2F08%2F17%2Fwshakes17.xml.

[96] *MPW* v.30, no.6 (11 November 1916), 825.

[97] On the 'dual address' strategy, see Roberta E. Pearson and William Uricchio, 'The Bard in Brooklyn: Vitagraph's Shakespearean Productions', in McKernan and Terris (eds.) *Walking Shadows: Shakespeare in the National Film and Television Archive* (London: BFI, 1994), pp. 201–6 (202).

And exhibiting such 'classy' pictures in the new picture palaces – so different in tone from the penny gaffs, vaudeville halls, nickelodeons and morally suspect sink-hole exhibition venues that had attracted flak from the public decency lobby in the years before 1913 – proved a winning draw. Ahead of release, Metro had offered *Romeo and Juliet* to exhibitors as 'the supreme profit maker of the year'.[98] They were not wrong: it was a picture that broke exhibition records in movie theatres, and it did so across the spectrum of target markets, requiring exhibitors to buy in additional prints at short notice to cater to demand.[99] For a profitable period in autumn 1916, in fact, there was nothing short of a market storm in progress in the world of Shakespearean motion pictures.

*

The story of the two *Romeo and Juliet* film releases of 1916 enables us to take stock of the priorities and predispositions of Shakespearean cinema as manifest in two major American studios at a specific moment. It reveals an aspiration on the part of production companies, distributors and exhibitors to take a carefully packaged encounter with Shakespeare to audiences in a lucrative mix of edification and titillation. Both companies consciously and confidently used a healthy dose of film stardom as the sweetener for a measure of Shakespeare, and, reciprocally, added gravitas to the reputation of their stars through the association with Shakespeare. The volume and intensity of the critical debate these films generated illustrates the levels of investment felt by critics and audiences in individual Shakespeare plays, and even individual characters, and a shared concern that these should be sensitively rendered as played on the big screen. The fearlessness with which these high-profile films waded into these sensitivities is telling about how far the medium had come since the transitional era. Then, Shakespeare films had tended either to trail their indecision about medium allegiance or to temper their own embarrassment about rendering Shakespeare wordlessly at all by inserting parodic jokes into the film at otherwise emotionally intense moments. By 1916, Shakespeare films were no longer apologising for their differences from theatre, nor satirically undermining their own endeavours. Rather they were now happy to vaunt

[98] *MPW* v.30, n.2 (14 October 1916), 178.
[99] For reports on record runs and the requirement to buy in extra prints to cater to unprecedented demand, see *MPW* v.30, n.7 (18 November 1916), 1044; and *MPW* v.30, n.8 (25 November 1916), 1204.

their medium specificity and autonomy, and to play the action earnestly, confident in the cinematic modes of story-telling and screen performance they could bring to highly revered material imported from the very heart of theatrical culture.

The results met with approval from both camps. The Metro film was, for example, honoured by cineastes by being included in a composite production assembled by the National Association of the Motion Picture Industry for exhibition on 16 August 1917 to publicise to the trade the best of what was possible in motion picture production.[100] In a 1920 selective retrospective, a chronicler of the industry then declared the same film 'an unqualified classic' and 'one of the best sellers'.[101] And while the Metro film was being thus lionised by the film industry, the Fox film was given the stamp of approval by the Shakespeare establishment through being included on the programme for the 1917 annual Stratford-upon-Avon Shakespeare Festival. Since the film industry had been omitted from the official Shakespeare tercentenary preparations the previous year, this symbolic validation of a Shakespeare film represented a change in the institutional relationships between cinema and Shakespeare. In sum, 1916 was a watershed in the evolving recognition both of the film industry's ability to exhibit its own specifically cinematic strengths through the vehicle of a Shakespeare film, and, simultaneously, of cinema as a legitimate interpretive medium for an expressive, if necessarily partial, Shakespeare.[102]

By 1916, the film industry was star-driven. It had sophisticated networks of agents and company contracts for its stars, an appreciative global market to give them an international profile and a well-developed fan culture (with associated publications and commercial star-cards) to support the iconic screen figures of the age. Moreover, stars were not just figures on the screen, but celebrities in the real world also, whose in-person appearances, appropriately managed, could carry a significant (and profitable) charge. Bayne and Bushman's attendance at New York's Broadway Theater for the second night of the Metro *Romeo and Juliet* run, for example, was a carefully managed event. Their presence was intended to promote the film and specifically to give it a boost against the rival Fox film. Gratifyingly, it generated an additional burst of press interest and was

---

[100] 'Association's All-Star Picture a Winner', *MPW* v.33, n.9 (1 September 1917), 1351.
[101] Carolyn Lowrey, *The First One Hundred Noted Men and Women of the Screen* (NY: Moffat, Yard and Company, 1920), p.138.
[102] J. B. Sutcliffe, 'British Notes', *MPW* v.32, n.11 (16 June 1917), 1771.

written up for *MPW* the following week. Enthusiastic 'thousands' were
reported to have been inside the large capacity theatre to greet them, and,
in addition:

Outside hundreds were waiting bargain admittance. Perched on a ladder in
Broadway was an enterprising snap-shot man who came waiting to get a flash-
light of the stars as they entered the theater.

   Shortly after 9 o'clock the two stars appeared. It took half a dozen attachés
of the theatre to keep the admiring throngs away from them … [T]hey were
ushered to a box, where the spectators recognized them and applauded with such
vigour that Samuel H. Berg, who composed the magnificent musical setting for
the Metro production … dragged them on to the stage. Instantly there were cries
for a speech.

   Mr Bushman and Miss Bayne addressed the big house … Altogether it was a
big night.[103]

Both the presence of the entrepreneurial member of the paparazzi up a
ladder and the need for professional heavies to protect the stars from 'the
admiring throngs' were already, by 1916, part of the celebrity culture now
considered the industry norm.[104] The fact that being able to witness an
in-person appearance of the stars made for 'a big night' testifies to a level
of audience investment in the production that comfortably outstripped an
interest purely in the appeal of the picture or in the fates of the fictional
characters within it. When they watched the picture, these 1916 spectators
were clearly seeing and enjoying Bayne as well as Juliet, Bushman as well
as Romeo. In the next chapter, it is just such double vision – of character
and actor simultaneously – that comes under scrutiny in relation to two
Shakespeare films of Weimar Germany.

---

[103] 'Bushman and Bayne at Broadway: Stars of Metro's "Romeo and Juliet" Address Big House and
    Are Given Ovation', *MPW* v.30, n.6 (11 November 1916), 870. On the stars' promotional appear-
    ances elsewhere, see *MPW* v.30, n.8 (25 November 1916), 1198.

[104] An instructive comparison may be found, for example, in the crowds and related security for
    Leonardo di Caprio and Claire Danes at the November 1996 premiere of Luhrmann's *William
    Shakespeare's Romeo + Juliet*.

CHAPTER 7

Asta Nielsen and Emil Jannings: stars of German Shakespeare films of the early 1920s

Hamlet (Art-Film: Svend Gade/Heinz Schall, 1920)
Othello (Wörner-Filmgesellschaft: Dimitri Buchowetzki, 1922)

Despite the considerable critical and commercial success of Shakespeare films in the tercentenary year, neither the American nor British film industry then made another Shakespeare feature film until the sound era.[1] In the 1920s, therefore, the centre of Shakespeare film production shifted to the artistically ambitious German film industry. In this chapter I consider two major German productions of the early 1920s: Gade and Schall's 1920 *Hamlet* starring Asta Nielsen,[2] and Buchowetzki's 1922 *Othello* starring Emil Jannings and Werner Krauss.[3]

THE ASTA NIELSEN *HAMLET* (1920)

Background

In 1895, when Danish actress Asta Nielsen was fourteen years old, she went for her first stage acting audition in Copenhagen.[4] Informed that

---

[1] The next American Shakespearean feature made was Sam Taylor's 1929 *The Taming of the Shrew* starring Douglas Fairbanks and Mary Pickford; the next British one was Paul Czinner's 1936 *As You Like It* starring Laurence Olivier (from a treatment by J. M. Barrie). In between 1916 and 1929 in the US, Shakespearean excerpts appeared in other films. Between 1919 and 1924 in Britain, three different mini-series featuring Shakespeare were produced: Hepworth's Anson Dyer animated one-reel burlesques; a Masters Films series of one-reelers entitled 'Tense Moments from Great Plays' including Sybil Thorndike as Portia (1922); and Walterdaw's unremarkable 'Gems of Literature' two-reelers. None of these shorts attracted much notice. (See Ball, *Shakespeare on Silent Film*, pp. 264–5, 278, 284–5.)

[2] I have viewed prints at the BFI National Archive, the Folger and a German-language version that was intermittently commercially available on VHS in the 1990s. The Deutsches Institut für Film (DIF) in Frankfurt now has a restored colour print of the film: I am yet to see this.

[3] The 1922 *Othello* is available on Kino Video DVD.

[4] The audition was part of her preparation for the Theatre School of the Royal Theatre of Copenhagen, which she subsequently attended.

the candidate was to perform a speech of Agnes's from Ibsen's *Brand*, the acting tutor offered to read in for her. She declined: she had, she said, no intention of speaking and had not even learned the lines. In her autobiography, she reflects on this not as a display of eccentricity, but simply as an understandable performance preference: she remembers that she 'wanted to play the scene as an expression of emotions – silently therefore. The words seemed superfluous.'[5] Both pitting the expression of emotion against the use of words and paring away anything that seemed superfluous to communicating the central impulse were to become enduring aspects of Nielsen's acting style. Sir Johnston Forbes-Robertson, it will be recalled, had specifically chafed against the capped nature of the wordless performance he was asked to give in his screen Hamlet of 1913. Nielsen, by contrast, was an actress who, from a strikingly young age, found words a cumbersome impediment to an actor's potential nuance. She was, that is, an actress naturally suited to the silent screen.

The story about miming Ibsen for a theatre audition in her teens may, of course, be a piece of autobiographical revisionism, sculpted, or re-remembered, to invest the trajectory of her later life with neat teleology. However, her intuitive understanding and crafted subtlety in communicating the vicissitudes of energetic fun, erotic desire (and desirability), high comedy, grand pathos, tragic weight, wry amusement, willed repressions and divided interior worlds in her screen work, do suggest that mime might always have been her instinctively preferred performance mode. As the celebrated 'Silent Muse' she was later to become, her capacity to receive the intimately searching attention of the camera with an intellectual and emotional range won for her an enthusiastic and international following. She had first come to prominence for her work with the Nordisk Film Company in Denmark during the 1910s. By 1920, when she made *Hamlet*, however, she had already been enthusiastically appropriated by the star machinery of the German film industry. Here, her popularity reached the point where mounted police attended each of her premières to hold back the crowds.[6] Asta Nielsen had become a phenomenon: an icon of the silent screen and an international celebrity beyond it.

The Svend Gade/Asta Nielsen *Hamlet* now has a popular profile unsurpassed by any other Shakespeare film of the era. Not only is the film built upon a central conceit memorable for its daring but Nielsen's unmannered

---

[5] Asta Nielsen, *Die Schweigende Muse* (Munich: Wilhelm Heyne Verlag, 1979), p. 68. Translated from the German.
[6] *Ibid.*, p. 226.

performance at its heart, and the eloquent use of its expressionist sets that so strikingly showcase that performance, also ensure that the imagery and resonances linger in the mind long after the film's end. It is these two aspects of the production that will principally absorb us here.

The film's narrative drive, devised by screenwriter Erwin Gepard in discussion with Nielsen, drew upon the twelfth-century Danish history recorded by Saxo-Grammaticus and on *Fratricide Punished* (a 1704 German drama reputedly based on an earlier, lost play of *Hamlet*), and explicitly sought validation from Edward P. Vining's academic credentials.[7] Its eyebrow-raising central premise is a racy departure from Shakespeare: Hamlet is recast as a girl who at birth is publicly declared a boy in an attempt to safeguard the line of succession to the threatened Danish throne. Having grown up in this duplicity, Hamlet is obliged to sustain the pretence of maleness until her death when her 'tragic secret' is finally discovered. Hamlet finally dies in Horatio's arms, and in a moment of dramatic and entertaining epiphany, Horatio's hand runs unsuspectingly down the chest of the dead 'prince', thereby accidentally discovering the secret of her anatomy and so of her vexed identity.

The premise is extravagant but, needless to say, once it is granted, other interpretive possibilities line up obligingly to lend plausibility to it. Understanding Hamlet as a woman disguised as a man can, for example, shed new light upon Hamlet's harsh brush-off to Ophelia, freshly inflect Hamlet's concern to rein in Gertrude's sexuality and add heightened colour to the peculiar warmth of Hamlet's affection for Horatio. In fact, seen in its most sympathetic light, *Hamlet* as a whole can be rendered unsettlingly more explicable by being read in these re-gendered terms. Even as it seems to explain, however, it also complicates, and the processes of gender suppression that characterise the Hamlet of Vining's imagination and, as a consequence, of the Gade/Schall film, invest an already notoriously intricate dramatic figure with yet more layers of complexity. Nielsen's visually striking, intellectually thoughtful and emotionally burdened Hamlet makes bravely tortured efforts to deny her womanhood to the world while acknowledging it keenly in her own private self through the tormenting knowledge of her illicit love for Horatio and resultant jealousy of Horatio's

---

[7] Edward P. Vining, *The Mystery of Hamlet* (Philadelphia, 1881). The film's use of these sources has been well documented elsewhere. See, for example, Jill Edmonds, 'Princess Hamlet', in Viv Gardner and Susan Rutherford (eds.), *The New Woman and Her Sisters: Feminism and Theatre 1850–1914* (Ann Arbor: University of Michigan Press, 1992), pp. 59–76; Ann Thompson, 'Asta Nielsen and the Mystery of Hamlet', in Lynda E. Boose and Richard Burt (eds.), *Shakespeare the Movie: Popularizing the Plays on Film, TV and Video* (London: Routledge, 1997), pp. 215–24.

love for Ophelia. Part of the effect of the re-gendering, therefore, is to add
to the existing drama a story of ardent but thwarted desire.

Rethinking Hamlet as a woman intersected with a long-standing theatrical fashion for the role to be played by women. Hamlet's thoughtfulness, sensitivity, capriciousness, vulnerability and indecision were all
thought to render him ripe for feminising and the list of actresses who
had already taken up the challenge is extensive, including Sarah Siddons,
Julia Glover, Charlotte Cushman, Alice Marriott, Julia Seaman, Millicent
Bandmann-Palmer, Sarah Bernhardt, Gwendoline Lally, Janette Steer and
Suzanne Desprès.[8] Nor was Nielsen even the first female Hamlet on film.
Bernhardt had scooped these honours in 1900 as she parried and thrust at
Pierre Magnier's Laertes in the fencing bout that Clément Maurice had
filmed to memorialise Bernhardt's iconic stage Hamlet. The resulting picture, with synchronised sound recorded onto wax cylinders, was shown
as part of a varieties programme at the 1900 Paris Expo.[9] It was subsequently suggested that Bernhardt might follow up this brief film appearance as Hamlet with a compressed fuller version of the drama to be filmed
in situ at Elsinore.[10] Similarly, it was rumoured in 1912 that the flamboyant
Russian émigré actress, Alla Nazimova (who had already taken Broadway
by storm), might make *her* screen debut as Hamlet. Sadly, neither the
fuller Bernhardt film nor the Nazimova version was ever made. However,
the will to see a female screen Hamlet persisted.

In 1913, *MPW* announced that the popular American film actress Helen
Gardner (celebrated for her Becky Sharp in the Vitagraph *Vanity Fair* (1911)
and her Cleopatra in a six-reel *Cleopatra* first released in 1912) was to play
Hamlet in a five-reel production for her own company, Helen Gardner
Picture Players.[11] Some scenes were filmed but, for reasons unknown, the
picture itself was never completed and the footage that had been shot was
either lost or destroyed. Ball thought Gardner's *Hamlet* plans 'ill considered' and was dismissive of her abilities.[12] I, however, find her grace and
beauty beguiling and regret not being able to see her Hamlet. Her resting

---

[8] The succession of most of these female Hamlets is economically documented by Edmonds. For
a book-length exploration of the subject, see Tony Howard, *Women as Hamlet: Performance and
Interpretation in Theatre, Film and Fiction* (Cambridge University Press, 2007). On Bernhardt's
Hamlet, see G. Taranow, *The Bernhardt Hamlet: Culture and Context* (NY: Peter Lang, 1996).

[9] Ball, *Shakespeare on Silent Film*, pp. 24–8.   [10] *Ibid.*, pp. 108–9.

[11] The resulting 5,000-foot film was to have been distributed by the Fuller Company. See *MPW* v.16,
n.9 (31 May 1913), 923.

[12] Ball, *Shakespeare on Silent Film*, pp. 148, 151.

expression was marked by a keen intelligence and a hint of sadness that might have served her well as the prince.

A tantalisingly brief film fragment featuring another female screen Hamlet from the early cinema period has also come to light (Figures 7.1a and b). Since I have been unable to identify either the appealing actress or the production, I am as baffled by this fragment as I am pleased to add a new entrant to the list of screen Hamlets – albeit a currently unidentified one.[13]

In 1919, a Hamletian character not simply played by a woman but who was a woman appeared in a five-reel Italian offshoot entitled *Amleto e il suo Clown* (*On With The Motley* in its English release). In this film, a modern-day heroine, Alexandra (Soave Gallone), provocatively stage-manages the play-within-the-play from *Hamlet* in her mother's garden specifically to monitor the reaction of the man who married her mother following her own father's murder.[14] Believing her stepfather's response implicates him in that murder, she kills him.[15] Although the rest of the plot is largely un-Shakespearean, in this section of the action, Alexandra self-consciously constructs herself as an avenging Hamlet and plays out that role in her female self.

Even unmade, unfinished, unidentified or not fully Shakespearean in character as these five female *Hamlet* films were, they collectively helped to fuel the industry rumour mill on both sides of the Atlantic, keeping alive the idea of a female screen Hamlet and so contributing to a cumulative expectation that Nielsen would finally fulfil. Once she did, the well-populated line of female Hamlets preceding her performance inevitably informed the critical reception of the film. On its first release in America, for example, a reviewer for *MPW* wrote:

Mme Nielsen in playing the "melancholy Dane" is supported by numerous precedents established by such great actresses as Bernhardt, Charlotte Cushman ... Sarah Bernhardt, in being brought to task for essaying Hamlet, replied: "I cannot

[13] In March 2008, Zoran Sinobad of the LOC sent me two frames from the unidentified 16mm film fragment that the LOC had received (inventoried only as 'Hamlet') from the collection of film historian Gordon Hendricks. The footage is clearly from the early cinema period and, having matched the likeness against star cards of Helen Gardner, I thought (gleefully) it was from the 1913 unfinished, unreleased Gardner film. However, in a helpful correspondence on the subject, Gardner's granddaughter, Dorin Gardner Schumacher (who is currently writing a biography of her grandmother), assures me this is not Gardner. The puzzle therefore remains. The fragment is less than fifteen feet long (a few seconds projection time only). LOC call no.: FAC 2426. I would be interested to hear from anyone who can identify the actress or production.
[14] *Amleto e il suo Clown* (Italy: dir. Carmino Gallone, 1919). Written by Lucio D'Ambra.
[15] Ball, *Shakespeare on Silent Film*, p. 266.

Figure 7.1a and b. Stills from an unidentified early film fragment inventoried only as 'Hamlet'. A female Hamlet sits by an ornamental fountain in a black velvet tunic and hat where she is joined by (presumably) Claudius and Polonius. Courtesy of the Motion Picture, Broadcasting and Recorded Sound Division of the LOC.

see Hamlet as a man. The things he says, his impulses, his actions entirely indicate to me that he was a woman and it is recorded that the story from which Shakespeare drew his inspiration made this character a woman."[16]

Nielsen herself was uncowed by this considerable tradition and certainly cast aside the womanly-man that Bernhardt detected in Shakespeare: rather than a male Hamlet tempering the social codes of masculinity, she played a female Hamlet performing 'male', thus approaching the question of androgyny from the other side of a gender divide.

Previous roles

Stanley Cavell argues that an audience interest that keeps the film star fully in focus while temporarily allowing a fictional character to be mapped onto his or her screen presence colludes with the implicit dictates of the cinematic image:

The [stage] actor's role is his subject for study, and there is no end to it. But the screen performer is essentially not an actor at all: he *is* the subject of study, and a study not his own ... "Bogart" *means* "the figure created in a given set of films." His presence in those films is who he is, not merely in the sense that if those films did not exist, Bogart would not exist, the name "Bogart" would not mean what it does.[17]

In this, Cavell is indebted to Erwin Panofsky, who in 1934 formulated the relationship between actor and role in the cinema, as opposed to the theatre, in the following terms:

Othello or Nora are definite, substantial figures created by the playwright. They can be played well or badly, and they can be "interpreted" in one way or another; but they most definitely exist, no matter who plays them or even whether they are played at all. The character in a film, however, lives and dies with the actor. It is not the entity "Othello" interpreted by Robeson or the entity "Nora" interpreted by Duse, it is the entity "Greta Garbo" incarnate in a figure called Anna Christie or the entity "Robert Montgomery" incarnate in a murderer who ... will never cease to haunt our memories.[18]

In considering the 'entity [Asta Nielsen] incarnate in a figure called [Hamlet]', I follow Panofsky and Cavell's argument about how the

---

[16] 'Asta Nielsen is Supported by Precedent in Playing "Hamlet"', *MPW* v.53, n.3 (19 November 1921), 327.

[17] Stanley Cavell, *The World Viewed: Reflections on the Ontology of Film* (NY: The Viking Press, 1971), pp. 27–8.

[18] Panofsky, 'Style and Medium in the Moving Pictures' (1934). Reproduced in Panofsky, *Three Essays on Style* (ed.) Irving Lavin (Cambridge, Mass. and London: MIT Press, 1997), pp. 91–126 (118).

appreciation of star presence works to the following extent: that in the cinema, yet more so than on the stage, we read character through the determining filter of the specificity of the star who intimately and self-exposingly inhabits a role. The mechanisms of cinematic presentation and cinematic spectatorship conspire to render such stars potently present and visible within their screen performances.

However, neither Panofsky's nor Cavell's writing can fully account for the effect of Nielsen or Jannings in these films. While Garbo's Anna Christie, or Montgomery's 'murderer' may pale into insignificance beside the dimensions of the actor incarnating them, the same cannot be said of a character with the dimensions and legacy of a Hamlet or Othello: in a cinematic rendering of a Shakespearean role, both screen actor *and* character have a prior existence. Therefore, when screen star 'Asta Nielsen' plays Shakespearean character 'Hamlet', there is a collision and coalescing of *two* prior known 'entities' – that of the player with that of the part played. One of the pleasures such films afford is observing how actor and character accommodate themselves to the other's previous identities and help to mould each other's current and future ones. When we 'read' a Shakespearean performance given by any actor with a known stage or screen history, part of what we do intuitively is assess what emerges from those processes of encounter, collision and mutual accommodation.

The Nielsen we see within this Hamlet is one significantly inflected by the considerable screen history she was already trailing at that point. A simpering femininity had never been part of her repertoire whereas an energetic androgyny frequently had. Even when playing women, she had frequently exhibited traits more usually associated with male characters – riding, playing cards, drinking, overcoming adversity through vigorous action and political activism. In *Die Suffragette* (1913), for example, she played a militant Englishwoman who adopts violent means to achieve her liberationist ends, including planting a bomb in Parliament. More directly germane to *Hamlet*, she had played several previous 'breeches' roles (*Hosenrolle*): in, for example, *Wenn die Maske fällt* (1912), *Jugend und Tollheit* (1912) (playing a woman who slicks back her hair, dons black tie, passes herself off as a gentleman and woos a lady), *Zapatas Bande* (1914) (as a highway robber) and *Das Liebes-ABC* (1916) (playing a woman who pretends to be a man in order to take her own less-than-resolute boyfriend out on the town to educate him as a 'proper' man).[19]

---

[19] On Nielsen's previous *Hosenrolle*, see the illustrated (Dutch) article in *Skrien* n.181 (Dec–Jan 1991–1992), 34–5. A further double-page spread of stills of Asta playing men (being shaved at

Of these, it was her roles as a woman disguised as a man in *Jugend und Tollheit* of 1912 and *Das Liebes-ABC* of 1916 that she was most clearly revisiting in Hamlet. She was, that is, well practised not just in assuming a male gait but in performing the assumption of a male gait, and, moreover, in embracing women on screen in a way that communicated both a degree of anxious duplicity on the part of the character and an awareness of the *frisson* that the performed suggestion of a same-sex love could carry for spectators in the know (Figure 7.2).

However, while some of the playful mischief of the gender role play from the earlier films is still present in Nielsen's Hamlet (as fans of her earlier work would have recognised), to that mischievous energy has now been added an exquisitely tuned degree of both anguish and overarching gravitas. In part this reflects the shift from a game of gender transgression that her previous characters *en travestie* had *elected* to play for entertaining, enlightening or self-serving purpose, to a life of gender transgression forcibly visited upon this character. Drawing, as it does, upon points of continuity with her previous screen work, and devised as the flagship first release for her own production company, Art-Film, *Hamlet* is a definitive Nielsen star vehicle.[20] However, it does not simply reiterate the interests and iconographies of her previous work; rather, as the best star vehicles do, it references these in part to develop them. A significant proportion of her screen career is engaged in a witty and detailed investigation into the constructed nature, and social expectations, of a gendered identity. Her role within the exploration is frequently to challenge the received behavioural norms (as she did also in her own unconventional private life).[21] The Gade *Hamlet* acknowledges its place in this line-up of Nielsen pictures that interrogate gender stereotypes. However, the addition to the existing repertoire of a set of more complex resonances as the central protagonist agonises about her own trans-gendering makes an influential intervention into that cumulative exploration.

---

the barber's, embracing a lady on a bench, etc.) is included in Renate Seydel, Allan Hagedorff and Bernd Meier, *Asta Nielsen: Ihr Leben in Fotodokumenten* (Berlin: Henschelverlag, 1981), unpaginated.

[20] On the continuities of character presentation, cinematographic treatment, narrative role and performance style in star vehicle projects, see, for example, Richard Dyer, 'Stars as Images' in Joanne Hollows, Peter Hutchings and Mark Jancovich (eds.), *The Film Studies Reader* (London: Hodder Arnold, 2000), pp. 121–4 (partic. 123).

[21] Nielsen was, for example, a convention-defying young single mother. On her unorthodox private life, see Elsa Gress, 'Die Asta: A Personal Impression', *Sight and Sound* v.42, n.4 (Autumn 1973), 209.

Asta Nielsen - Film

HAMLET

Figure 7.2 A 1920 star card of Asta Nielsen as Hamlet
with Lilli Jacobsson as Ophelia, promoting the all-female
embrace as part of the film's market appeal.
Author's private collection.

In his recent monograph *Women as Hamlet*, Tony Howard has
given an illuminating discussion of the film as part of a broader legacy of female and politically contextualised Hamlets. For a detailed,
persuasive and enjoyable account of the sweep of the film, I defer to
Howard.[22] However, the two specific areas of investigation I have

---

[22] Howard, *Women as Hamlet*, pp. 137–59.

proposed – into Nielsen's own performance and its relationship to the set – merit further analysis and it is these selective areas of enquiry that I now pursue.

Nielsen's Hamlet

Asta Nielsen's fame as a screen actress was in part justly derived from her huge, expressive eyes. As Hamlet, she deftly maximises the dramatic impact both of her eyes and of her languid bodily grace to produce a hauntingly memorable performance finely poised between grand pathos and wry comedy. She wears a figure-denying short straight tunic, has short, straight hair and adopts self-consciously manly poses to delude her on-screen (and entertain her off-screen) public. Part of the delight an audience takes in these manly poses comes from observing how charmingly compromised they are by the elegance of the long legs that adopt them and by the discernible counter-impulses that have to be fought down within this Hamlet to sustain them. In the extra-cinematic world of 1920, however, a collection of character traits that suggestively signified 'male' as traditionally understood no longer represented the complete renunciation of socially acceptable womanhood that it is ostensibly offered as meaning within the story. In the context of 'liberated', boyish flappers, curve-minimising shift dresses and burgeoning debates about emancipation, the social constructions and presentation of gender were on the move; this film, therefore, draws upon and exaggerates some of the moment's existing ambivalences on this score.[23]

Against this background, Nielsen offers us androgyny as an appealing, and discreetly sexualised aesthetic. As Patrice Petro has argued, it was Nielsen's destabilising of the 'polar opposition between masculine and feminine', in this film and elsewhere, that 'paved the way for the popular acceptance of female androgyny in the cinema'.[24] Renouncing a version of femininity that was merely 'pretty' played well to American critics: they declared themselves tired of the colourless screen glamour models that, they said, had become Hollywood's stock in trade. In the *New York Times*,

---

[23] Weimar films of the 1920s started to celebrate women's intrusion into male workspace as white-collar workers (though typically ones whose gendered codes became not compromised but enhanced as displayed in such an environment). See Richard W. McCormick, *Gender and Sexuality in Weimar Modernity: Film, Literature and 'New Objectivity'* (NY: Palgrave, 2001).

[24] Patrice Petro, *Joyless Streets: Women and Melodramatic Representation in Weimar Germany* (Princeton University Press, 1989), p. 153.

James O. Spearing celebrated the unconventional beauties of Nielsen that challenged feminine cinematic norms:

One cannot speak of the work of Miss Asta Nielsen without enthusiasm. There will be discussion as to her physical charms. Some undoubtedly will call her beautiful, while others, preferring a different type of wife or sweetheart or sister, will say she is merely striking in appearance. But what does all this matter? The woman can act. She acts. That's the thing. She does not just pose before the camera, nor does she rant and tear around violently. She impersonates a character, she makes it live and have a meaning, a hundred meanings. Her mouth is not simply something to paint a Cupid's bow on. It is an organ to express the thoughts and feelings of the woman within. And her other features are not merely facial adornments or fixtures to be adorned, but human parts that reveal a human being. Miss Nielsen has grace, too, and the control of her body that permits her to use it to beautify her character and make its movements and postures significant.[25]

As others also attested, this was an actress who persuaded an audience she had a rich inner life rather than simply offering them an appealing visual confection. Indeed, so precisely did her performance communicate emotional state and turn of thought that, in remembering her mouth as 'not simply something to paint a Cupid's bow on', Spearing seems instead to remember that mouth as having actually 'express[ed] the thoughts and feelings of the woman within'. Unconsciously, therefore, he seems to believe he remembers her speaking. Nielsen would have been delighted to evoke the illusory memory of speech through mime alone. In her autobiography, she reports that she 'studied ways of reducing miming expressions and movements to a minimum, in a way that could not be seen by the naked eye, only captured by the camera'.[26] As she attuned her performance precisely to the particularities of the screen, she gave privileged access to the intellectual energy and wit of her implied thought life through a range of gestures and facial flickers that, though sometimes scarcely perceptible, nevertheless communicated impulses that were precisely felt and thought. The reviewer for *Exceptional Photoplays* was rhapsodic about the subtlety Nielsen brought to the screen in comparison with the standard fare from US actresses of the time:

Rare it is indeed to see so complete a subjection of all physical means – appearance, gesture, even the movement of an eye-lid – to the sheer art of showing forth the soul of a character as that which Asta Neilsen [sic] accomplishes in her role of Hamlet. This is what will be most acclaimed – and it will deserve any amount

---

[25] James O. Spearing, *NYT* (9 November 1921), 20 col. 3.
[26] Nielsen, *Die Schweigende Muse*, p. 227.

of acclamation – in this picture out of Denmark [sic]. For here is a woman whose like we have not on our own screen. Asta Neilsen's [sic] art is a mature art that makes the curly-headed girlies and painted hussies and tear-drenched mothers of most of our native film dramas seem as fantastic for adult consumption as a reading diet restricted to Elsie books and Mother Goose.[27]

Her performance was greeted as accessible without being anodyne and popular without being populist. A few refuseniks subsequently expressed caution along the lines of Maurice Bardèche and Robert Brasillach's suggestion that she was 'over-intellectual'.[28] Most, however, were significantly impressed by the nuance and variety she was able to achieve without resort to extravagant histrionics. Specifically, she was commended for giving her audiences a cinematic 'reading diet' that – unlike many Hollywood releases of the day – did not infantilise them by making them 'consume' cheaply generated stereotypes delivered with patronising emphasis. In 1917, Ruggero Ruggeri had offered his highly impassioned, gesticulatory Hamlet to the movie-going public. Just three years later, the disciplined naturalism and conspicuous modernity of Nielsen's Hamlet make that Italian performance look antiquated.

Nielsen's shaded vitality and stylishly minimalist performance stand out the more in the context of the film's other performances. Eduard von Winterstein gives a one-note lascivious and conspicuously iniquitous Claudius. When he is offered the crown by Polonius at the marriage banquet, with almost comically villainous eyes and puffed up chest he seizes it greedily to place it deliberately upon his own head. The cinematography colludes in emphasising his unremitting villainy. When in the closet scene, he discovers the body behind the arras, a grotesque and sustained close-up records his ugly horror. There is no hint of sorrow for the death of his counsellor, only a transparently self-interested fear and it is on this that the camera dwells unsparingly. The next shot pulls back to show the King staggering extravagantly towards the throne in the left foreground. As he collapses into it with heightened self-pity, Mathilde Brandt's self-serving and fully complicit Gertrude attempts to comfort him. The exaggerated performance style that both adopt coupled with the revealingly attentive cinematography render the sequence pure cartoon melodrama. Alongside these two villains, Hans Junckermann plays a silly, frail caricature of Polonius as a dizzy, lightweight, interfering muddle-head; Lilli Jacobsson, a fetching

---

[27] *Exceptional Photoplays* v.2, n.1 (Jan-Feb 1922), 8.
[28] Maurice Bardèche and Robert Brasillach, *The History of Motion Pictures* (trans. and ed.) Iris Barry (NY: W. W. Norton and the Museum of Modern Art, 1938), p. 194.

but largely dull Ophelia in love with Hamlet but wooed by Horatio; Heinz Steida, a dandified Horatio in fancy brocade tunic and wide sleeves, noticeably more ornate in coiffure and dress than either the modestly attired Ophelia or the sartorially minimalist Hamlet. Steida is, in fact, doubly outclassed in the film, dwarfed by the over-decorative character of his own wardrobe, and unworthy, in his lumbering obviousness, of the profound affection which this Hamlet bears him. Overall, this extensive assembly of rather heavy-handed or colourless performances acts as flattering foil to the scope, control and delicacy of the prince(ss) in their midst.

For all her naturalism, Nielsen is not averse to employing an extravagant gesture when occasion demands: these always, however, form part of her character's self-conscious repertoire of performative excess, deployed specifically to disconcert the unimaginative court functionaries that surround her. Thus it is, for example, that when visited by the King's mild-mannered, dullard phrenologist, she turns the pages of a large tome with vigorous abandon, consulting individual words alternately at arm's length and in satiric close-up. She performs this exaggerated act of 'reading' to sustain the illusion of madness. While indicating troubling eccentricity to her suggestible on-screen audiences, to her off-screen audience such moments chiefly communicate the delight she is taking in her own behavioural excesses.

The heightened performance lexicon for which Nielsen reaches at such moments is, however, assumed for studied effect as part of Hamlet's self-projections: when her Hamlet is not performing, Nielsen's own performance is understatedly contained. When instructing the players in an appropriate acting style, Nielsen's Hamlet, unlike Ruggeri's self-subverting air-sawing, merely taps her head and her heart with an offhand insouciance to indicate the places where emotion is to be felt. When Horatio tells her (via an intertitle) that his love for Ophelia exceeds his love for his friend because it is 'that of a man for a woman', Nielsen looks away with merely the exquisite suggestion of a quiet, pained resignation on her face: this brave suppression of the profundity of her hurt is more affecting than any grand gesture could have been. When Claudius hands the scroll addressed to the King of Norway (replacing England as Hamlet's destination in this version) straight across Hamlet's expectant hands and into those of Guildenstern instead, a brief cut-in to a close-up shows Hamlet looking down to follow this surprising transaction: she registers the oddity of being passed over and left empty-handed by the merest movement of her eyes. The effect of the snub and Hamlet's cognisance of its import are then emphasised not, as they might have been, by enhancing the performance dimensions, but rather simply by changing the shot. Thus the shot cuts to a wider angle on the same scene to show how pointedly slowly Hamlet withdraws her still outstretched but conspicuously empty hand while Guildenstern, meanwhile, receives the proffered scroll. When, during the night at the inn, she subsequently steals this same scroll, breaks its seal and reads its contents, a tightly framed mid-shot shows her contemplating in weighty silence the news that Claudius has instructed Norway to kill her. An iris slowly closes upon her, excluding all contextualising background in its incrementally narrowing focus on her face as she contemplates the enormity of the threat now facing her; her still but minutely expressive face alone, irradiated by candle-light, is required to carry both the narrative and emotional import of the scene. Despite a lack of noticeable facial movement, her performance persuades us that what we are witnessing is a sustained focus on a troubled but resourceful mind at work. The results of that resourcefulness are felt the next day in the scene at the Norwegian court. And it is characteristic of the modulations in pace and tonal character across the whole film that out of one of the most tense, reflective and conspicuously static moments of the film should emerge one of its wittiest and most dynamic.

Being despatched by Claudius not to England but to Norway gives this Hamlet a distinct advantage. Notwithstanding the ancient enmity between their fathers, in this version Hamlet and young Fortinbras (Fritz Achterberg) became good friends while at school together in Wittenberg. On arrival at the Norwegian court, therefore, the young Danish 'prince' is warmly reunited with 'his' friend of old. An existing bond, and a visibly warm one, between young Fortinbras and Hamlet was not what Rosencrantz and Guildenstern had been prepared for, as a brief two-shot of their surprised exchange of looks demonstrates. Fortinbras reads the newly doctored scroll and turns to Hamlet quizzically seeking explanation for the uncompromising request contained in it. Hamlet gives an extravagant shrug, seen in attentive close-up, to suggest that she knows nothing of such matters, being merely the (ostentatiously) innocent companion to the King's emissaries on this particular embassy. Accordingly, Fortinbras rolls up the scroll and declares (via an intertitle): 'Off with these two – *to the scaffold!*' As Rosencrantz and Guildenstern are seized and led from the chamber, looking understandably aghast at the unexpected turn events are taking, they shoot a glance back over their shoulders at Hamlet, implicitly appealing for a princely intervention to be made on their behalf. The shot cuts to Hamlet, seen once again in close-up, arms folded, observing their discomfiture as they are escorted from the chamber, her eyes lightly dancing and the hint of a smile playing at the corners of her mouth. In response to their appeal, she cocks an eyebrow and offers a mockingly respectful little bow in lightly pastiched imitation of the ceremonial bows they have been giving her while simultaneously colluding in plans for her death. It is a performance moment whose well-turned comedy depends on the strategically differentiated ways in which Hamlet's gesture plays, and is designed to play, to its two separate on-screen audiences: to Rosencrantz and Guildenstern it exposes the delight that Hamlet is taking in the poetic exactitude with which their treachery is now rebounding upon them; to Fortinbras and the rest of the assembled Norwegian court, however, her assumed innocence is persuasive and so, to them, her bow to her departing companions communicates merely the courteous but regretful acknowledgement of her powerlessness to intervene in matters between Heads of State. It is a moment in the film at which, in my experience, contemporary audiences laugh out loud at the wry knowingness of Nielsen's performance.

Mise-en-scène as dramatic commentary

It was not only Nielsen's performance itself, however, but also the way in which the production as a whole frames that performance that garnered praise from critics at the time. One American reviewer was particularly struck by the collaborative integration of mise-en-scène, cinematography and performance:

Director Sven Gade, the actors and the scene-makers have worked in effective harmony. The sets subtly but forcefully reinforce the action and the acting. And the photography realizes, at times superbly, the mood of the story. In this last regard, one is left to wonder if the picture's grim, tragic atmosphere could have been achieved by the soft effect that seems to be the present ideal of the best camera work.

Taken all in all, 'Hamlet' reaches a level not often seen in our motion picture theatres.[29]

The intimacy of the collaboration between set, cinematography and acting must have been helped by the fact that Gade, who directed, also designed the sets. He was, therefore, uniquely well placed to draw out their potential import as part of the overall interpretive conception.

The capacity for a film's visual design to become, in effect, a player in the drama was recognised early in the development of the medium. Writing in 1915, Vachel Lindsay claimed that in photoplays, 'non-human tones, textures, lines, and spaces take on a vitality almost like that of flesh

---

[29] *Exceptional Photoplays* v.2, n.1 (Jan-Feb 1922), 8.

and blood'.[30] German expressionist cinema of the late 1910s and 1920s emphasised that vitality, becoming known for the significance it attached to the 'tones, textures, lines, and spaces' of cinematic design (the films of F.W. Murnau and Fritz Lang acquiring the highest international profile in this respect). The Gade *Hamlet* does not stylise its expressionist architecture and design to the extent that either Robert Wiene's 1920 *Das Cabinet des Dr Caligari* (*The Cabinet of Dr Caligari*) or Nielsen's own 1923 film *Der Absturz* (*The Crash*) would so strikingly do. Nevertheless, the film's scenography is allowed its own articulacy about both character and plot. The dramatic stone arches plunge characters in and out of shadow while repeatedly drawing attention to implicitly demarcated spaces and to the ways in which characters linger on thresholds, or to the moments when they cross them.[31] The serpentine twists and turns of the castle through which Gertrude winds her duplicitous way for a clandestine and adulterous tryst with Claudius are suggestive not just of an architecturally labyrinthine landscape but also of a morally anfractuous one. The high angle down on the grand banqueting chamber becomes an animated *tableau* of lascivious indiscipline and bibulous consumption in a decadently permissive space. The dramatic taper-lit grand staircase seems plucked from a fairytale world, ironically highlighting how far removed from a world of romance is the grandly and sensitively tragic Hamlet who descends it. Casement windows feature frequently as the filter through which Hamlet observes others' pleasures in the carefree world beyond the literally and emotionally circumscribed spaces that she inhabits. Details of both Elsinore's and Wittenberg's architecture seem to draw her irresistibly into positions – in particular by windows looking out – in which the fettered quality of her life may find suggestive representation, the production's visual scheme working both in illustration of and sympathy with her plight. Most forcibly, therefore, the film's sets do not only frame Nielsen's delicate and dignified form: they also point up her story by underscoring her emotional and political separation from those around her.

Shakespeare's Hamlet is, by natural predisposition, set apart. His introspective questioning removes him from the flux of humanity.[32] The extraordinary circumstances foisted upon him further intensify this natural

---

[30] Lindsay, *The Art of the Moving Picture*, p. 161.

[31] See Monika Seidl, 'Room for Asta: Gender Roles and Melodrama in Asta Nielsen's Filmic Version of *Hamlet* (1920)', *Literature/Film Quarterly* v.30, n.3 (2002), 208–16.

[32] On Hamlet's temperamental isolation, see Leah Marcus, *Unediting the Renaissance: Shakespeare, Marlowe, Milton* (London and NY: Routledge, 1996), pp. 135–6.

propensity.[33] Tony Howard argues that casting a woman in the role of Hamlet serves, if anything, to exaggerate the profundity of this isolation, most female Hamlets (yet more so than their male counterparts) proving to be 'inassimilable figures alien to the norms around them'.[34] Of the raft of female Hamlets, Nielsen's is as desolately cut off from a synergy with the world as any of her sister Hamlets: in addition to the normal temperamental and circumstantial burdens of the Hamlet legacy, Nielsen's Hamlet is additionally propagating a lie about her own (gender) identity – and one, moreover, against which she is privately in angst-ridden revolt. She makes touching attempts to assimilate socially – in particular while at school in Wittenberg – but unsurprisingly, given the plot's foundational premise, is defined by the depth of her emotional isolation. This isolation is persistently reinforced by a sensitively conceived relationship between central performance and mise-en-scène.

It is in the emotionally fraught scenes between Horatio and Hamlet that set, characters and cinematography work most closely together to generate a shared discourse about identity, desire and isolation. Two such scenes will serve as illustration. The first follows on immediately from the closet scene. Horatio, in elaborate, pale, brocade tunic, leans against a castle post in left of frame. Hamlet, stylistically adrift from Horatio in her conspicuously plain black tunic, sits wearily fingering her sword in right of frame. An off-camera light source beyond Hamlet throws a large shadow of Hamlet onto the wall between them. Hamlet's double presence in the scene (as both substance and shadow) reminds us of the divided self that centrally characterises this Hamlet, while also alluding incidentally to the German cinematic interest in *Doppelgänger* themes.[35] Like a pale and partial imitation of the student of Prague's reflection that takes on a troublingly independent life, Hamlet's projected silhouette here acquires an identity distinct in emphasis from Hamlet's own – though in this case without recourse to mysticism.[36] Firstly, the shadow's bald outline of her assumed male form is more unambiguously 'male' than her real self,

---

[33] On Hamlet's circumstantial isolation, see A. D. Nuttall, *Shakespeare the Thinker* (New Haven and London: Yale University Press, 2007), p. 194.

[34] Howard, *Women as Hamlet*, p. 5.

[35] This had already been expressed through films such as the early *Der Student von Prag* (1913), *Das Wandernde Bild* (1920), *Der Januskopf* (1920) and *Das Cabinet des Dr Caligari* (1920). It would recur in films such as *Nosferatu* (1922), the remade *Der Student von Prag* (1926) and *Metropolis* (1927). The film's *Doppelgänger* themes are contextually related to Freudian psychoanalysis in Lisa S. Starks, ' "Remember me": Psychoanalysis, Cinema and the Crisis of Modernity', *SQ* v.53, n.1 (2002), 181–200.

[36] See *Der Student von Prag* (*The Student of Prague*, 1913) and its 1926 remake.

which, through the discernible flicker of anxiety about her projections, constantly equivocates about her gendered identity. The fact that it is the less equivocal silhouette that stands between her and the man she loves is graphically suggestive of the very obstruction (her supposed maleness) that keeps them apart. While an intertitle reports her as saying, 'My dear Horatio – Unburden thy heart', the frame composition therefore reinforces the impossibility of any reciprocal unburdening by her: the gender-simplified, intervening shadow of the 'prince' symbolically configures the impediment to their love, making any emotional disclosure on Hamlet's part unthinkable. Horatio accedes (again by intertitle) to Hamlet's plea for disclosure ('I will to you – good Hamlet'), and unburdens himself with unwelcome candour: *'I love Ophelia* – And her grief is mine.' In response to Horatio's evident distress, Hamlet rises, intending, perhaps, to comfort him. Inevitably, her shadow rises too, proportionally enhanced, and reaches Horatio first, apparently to envelop him in uninhibited shadowy intimacy. But the substantial Hamlet checks herself and the shadow is left suspended between them. Appropriately and effortfully in check, Hamlet does not then wrap up Horatio in an embrace as her shadow had seemed inclined to do but rather, by sheer force of self-restraining will, simply collects him and brings him back to sit with her where he then makes further, torturing disclosures of his love for Ophelia. In close-up we see Hamlet, having heard his confession, close her eyes in emotional exhaustion as if unwilling to look any longer upon the thing she cannot have. She has effectively lived out the scene doubly and in contesting modes: her shadow first graphically accentuating the doubleness of her public self and then symbolically hinting at her unspoken desires in relation to Horatio as a tormenting reminder of an intimacy she is debarred from claiming. In sympathy with Hamlet's wearied closing of her eyes, the film too now cuts away, altering the emotional tempo by moving to Claudius' conspiratorial meeting with Rosencrantz and Guildenstern.

Once Rosencrantz and Guildenstern's guilty complicity has been established, however, the film is drawn back once again to the painfully impeded interactions between Hamlet and Horatio. A generously framed two-shot (she now in left of frame, he in right) reveals them now waiting in the lobby space outside Claudius' study for the summons that will in due course send Hamlet to Norway. The acuteness of the emotional distance between them established in the previous scene now finds graphic expression in the conspicuous divisions of the set.

Though in a shared frame, they occupy starkly differentiated space. Horatio sits, slightly crumpled, in front of a heavy and ornate curtain decorated by elliptical ovals, each of which encases its own further complex pattern. The intricately worked design in heavily ornamented fabric is an appropriate counterpart to Horatio's own sartorial elaborateness: character and environment belong to the same world that gestures back to the fussier style of a former age. Hamlet, by contrast, though literally adjacent, nevertheless seems to inhabit a separate world – a space characterised by sharp, clean, modernist lines, the wall behind her almost courting the appearance of neat, vertical corrugation (Figures 7.3a–c). If Horatio blends harmoniously with *his* background, she too provides the perfect stylistic complement to hers, the angularity of her long thin arm forming a crisp triangle as she leans her protruding elbow against the wall, hand on head. Her thin body, precision in posture and angular pose seem perfectly, and modishly, attuned to the clarity and severity of her avant-garde surroundings. This striking clash of aesthetic styles, and, by association, of character types between the abruptly juxtaposed sections of the set is in keeping with the 'overly emphatic visual style and … propensity for violent contrast in both tone and style' that Lotte H. Eisner finds characteristic of Weimar cinematic convention more generally.[37] In this respect, the scene lives out the Weimar conventions conspicuously: the clean lines of her space, the heavy ornateness of his; her plain black tunic, high black neck and straight hair, his conspicuously fancy garb and crimped curls; her taut angularity, his hunchedness; her crisp, progressive modernism, his genteel historicity.

The stark polarity of the visual and emotional encounter between Hamlet's modernity and Horatio's periodicity catches something suggestively Shakespearean in their relationship. When, for example, Shakespeare's Horatio repeatedly exhorts Hamlet not to go with the ghost, Hamlet casts aside such timid objections with 'My fate cries out' (I.iv.58). When subsequently Shakespeare's Horatio tries to prevent his friend endangering himself in the fencing match, Hamlet once again refuses the offered exit, and replies, 'We defy augury' (V.ii.165). In both cases, there is a retrograde conservatism in Horatio's desire to eschew and defend and a forward thinking positivism in Hamlet's desire to move forward and confront. Aligning Hamlet with modernist aesthetics and progressive modes of thinking and Horatio with a more antiquated, conservative style from a former age, therefore, finds expression for one of the emotional undercurrents of the play. Hamlet's modernism in the 1920 production is unable, like all expressions of modernism perhaps,

---

[37] Eisner, quoted in Petro, *Joyless Streets*, p. 29.

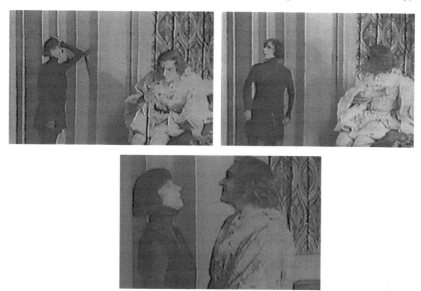

Figure 7.3a, b and c. Crisp, minimalist verticals and elaborate brocade: Hamlet's (Nielsen) modernist sensibilities are pitted against Horatio's (Steida) ornate periodicity in *Hamlet* (Art-Film: Gade, 1920).

to 'disentangle itself from the world it opposes', as Michael Wood puts it, and so needs a point of resistance in order properly to know itself.[38] Horatio constitutes an anachronism: he points to a more gracious world insulated from the emotional imperatives, moral angularities and political machinations of the present. In both his caution and his conspicuous outmoded-ness, he provides the foil that Hamlet craves. In those moments when they are shown occupying the same notional space while being dramatically removed from each other in it, the film graphically confirms Horatio's remoteness from everything that Hamlet is and, simultaneously, the heart-rending appeal to her of that very otherness. Unsurprisingly, perhaps, Horatio's decorous abstraction from the demands of the present holds a particular draw for the character most dangerously mired in the intensity of those demands.

---

[38] Michael Wood, 'Modernism and Film', in Michael Levenson (ed.), *The Cambridge Companion to Modernism* (Cambridge University Press, 1999), pp. 217–32 (218).

Un-Shakespearean Shakespeare

The 1920 *Hamlet* draws our attention repeatedly to the ways in which it departs from, or rewrites, Shakespeare. Not only, therefore, is this *Hamlet* without the 'prince', there are also no grave-diggers, no Yorick's skull and no ghostly apparitions.[39] In a production of *Hamlet*, such omissions obtrude. Moreover, it is not Hamlet but Horatio who initially rushes forward to challenge Laertes in affection for the dead Ophelia, and not Claudius but a demonised Gertrude who envenoms the foil, enlists Laertes in the conspiracy and drops poison in the cup. In addition, it is a production almost distractingly cluttered with events, not all of which are Shakespearean. Some are drawn from Saxo-Grammaticus, some from *Fratricide Punished* and others are apparently of the film-makers' own devising. The non-Shakespearean action includes two separate visits to a subterranean pit filled with poisonous snakes, the incriminating discovery of a dagger, an orgy, an unseemly tussle for possession of Ophelia's veil and a drinking bout between uncle and 'nephew'. Furthermore, a burning room is sealed to kill its occupants by smoke inhalation, the Queen throws herself dramatically across Claudius' asphyxiated body and then shows it to Laertes to sharpen his appetite for revenge. In fact, so many and so decided are the departures from the conventionalised sequence of iconic *Hamlet* moments we know – the equivalents of those pictorial moments from *Lear* whose shared iconicity Orwell celebrates[40] – that the production effectively exempts itself from the canonical legacy of *Hamlet* performances. It is a production that reflects thoughtfully and humorously on selected aspects of the Elsinore and central protagonist of Shakespeare's *Hamlet*. Even as it invokes the play, though, it also repeatedly liberates itself from too close an adherence to the specificity of Shakespeare's dramatic vision.

Paradoxically, however, the film is equally insistent that it should not be cut loose *entirely* from a Shakespearean frame of reference. As if to counterbalance its departures from Shakespeare, therefore, it intermittently asserts a superficial attachment to its genealogy through the use of direct quotation. The film's usual strategy in relation to its intertitles is to use plot-summaries, character introductions and snippets of non-Shakespearean dialogue: 'And so HAMLET Prince of Denmark

---

[39] Hamlet does, however, believe she hears a voice 'that seems to speak from out the tomb' and later claims to have seen her father 'in [her] dreams'.

[40] Orwell, 'Lear, Tolstoy and the Fool'. Discussed in the Preface.

Grew into a Goodly Youth'; 'Hamlet distrusts – his uncle'; 'LAERTES. Impetuous son of Polonius Court Chamberlain of Denmark'; 'Compelled to act the man – but in lonely wistful moments still a woman'; 'Hamlet's hidden love for Horatio – burns within him'; 'An orgy of the King'; 'Death reveals thy tragic secret!' Against the backdrop of this dominantly non-Shakespearean word-scape, the occasional appropriation of a Shakespearean phrase on the title cards is the more striking. Examples include: 'O my prophetic soul – Mine uncle!'; 'to sleep perchance to dream'; 'We are arrant knaves, all! Believe none of us – Get thee to a nunnery!'; 'Thou wretched – rash intruding fool – I took thee for thy better!'; 'Hold off the earth a while – Till I have caught her once more in mine arms!' The inclusion of such phrases anchors the production in the semblance of an authenticating relationship to the Shakespearean source. In practice, however, the specific uses of these Shakespearean lines frequently qualify, or even subvert, the nature of that advertised relationship. The film does not, for example, quote 'to sleep perchance to dream' to punctuate Hamlet's consideration about the appeal or otherwise of death, as Shakespeare has it. Rather the line, divorced from its poetic and semantic context as part of the 'To be or not to be' soliloquy, is used instead as the textual accompaniment to an image of Hamlet waking from dreaming of her father. Equally, when Hamlet tells Ophelia to get to a nunnery, it now sounds either like advice from the sorority to avoid treacherous men or the attempt of a jealous woman to remove her rival from the scene. Either way, though the words may be Shakespearean, their meaning has been transformed by the context of their citing.

In sum, the re-attributed or contextually transformed quotations serve less as the advertisement of a respectful intimacy with a Shakespeare source and, frequently, more as a means of illustrating this production's resistance to it. By economically referencing well-known poetic detail from the play, these snippets of quotation help us acknowledge, and so map, the distance between the two. For a 'version' of *Hamlet* that includes snake-pits, arson attacks, smoke inhalation, a Hamlet who is secretly female and a Horatio unknowingly in love with Hamlet, an occasional line from Shakespeare severed from its semantic and sometimes also its dramatic context cannot, that is, but highlight how vibrantly and interestingly *un*-Shakespearean most of the production is.

It was not, however, on its proximity to or distance from Shakespeare that the film's first audiences primarily judged it. If the surviving reviews are symptomatic, the production was received not so much as a heterodox oddity, but as a film that was funny and touching, visually striking and breathtakingly performed. While we cannot now 'unknow' the history of Hamlet performances that has intervened since this film's release, it is striking that, in its occasional screenings, the drama, pathos and well-turned comedy of the Asta Nielsen *Hamlet* still catch audiences today.

THE JANNINGS/KRAUSS *OTHELLO* (1922)

Whereas Asta Nielsen embraced the silent screen with a will, Emil Jannings was, by natural inclination, vehemently opposed to it. In his autobiography, he reports that he considered the whole thing nothing more than 'eine ausgesprochene Schaubudenangelegenheit' (a downright, low-life fairground booth).[41] When, in 1914, it was first suggested that he might himself work in the industry, he retorted that film held no interest for him because, as he announced, 'Ich bin Schauspieler … !'[42] Ever self-conscious about actorly identity, Jannings thought it impossible to be 'an actor' (*Schauspieler*) in film since the medium effectively turned everyone into marionettes.[43] For all his elitist protestations, however, Jannings eventually succumbed to the considerable financial incentives and supplemented his celebrated stage work by becoming the thing he had claimed to despise – a film actor. In the process, he reports having to learn a new set of performance codes particular to the new medium in order to ensure his screen performances did not look 'exaggerated' (*übertrieben*) and 'unspeakably overplayed' (*unaussprechlich gewollt*).[44]

By the time Jannings played Othello to Werner Krauss's Iago for Dmitri Buchowetzki's six-reel 1922 *Othello*, he had already made over forty films. Some of that experience had even been accrued specifically in collaboration with Krauss and Buchowetzki. Both Jannings and Krauss had, for example, appeared in *The Brothers Karamazov* (1918) under Buchowetzki's co-direction with Carl Frölich, and, the year before *Othello* was made, Jannings had taken the title role as the doomed Danton to Krauss's dictatorially evil Robespierre in *Danton* (1921), Buchowetzki's adaptation of Georg Büchner's play *Dantons Tod*. Both films were serious-minded, reputable projects – high profile adaptations that vaunted their association with a theatrical and literary heritage both through their subject matter and, importantly, in their casting of Jannings and Krauss with their weighty theatrical reputations in tow.

[41] Jannings, *Theater-Film – Das Leben und ich* (Berchtesgaden: Verlag Zimmer & Herzog, 1941), p. 115.
[42] *Ibid.*, p. 95. [43] *Ibid.*, p. 121. [44] *Ibid.*

Jannings's Othello and Krauss's Iago

Despite knowing in theory that he should temper his acting codes for the screen, nevertheless, in *Othello*, Jannings's blacked-up performance mostly emerges as a piece of eye-popping, nostril-flaring, furniture-chewing (and at one point literally handkerchief-munching) excess – *übertrieben* at every turn. Even in his calm moments, it would be a stretch to consider Jannings's Othello noble, and in his fits of passion he becomes a crude caricature of the wild and stary. Such an ungoverned performance was certainly not Jannings's only register, as other screen performances of greater nuance attest – most celebrated of which is his Professor Immanuel Rath in von Sternberg's *The Blue Angel* (1930).[45] His performance of Othello, however, sadly lends credibility to *The Bioscope* reviewer's opinion, published back in 1909, that it is all but impossible 'for any actor to invest Othello with due dignity and greatness by gesture alone'.[46] Difficult for any tragic character, this is particularly so for Othello whose rhetorical power is, perhaps, his chief bulwark against caricature. Robbed of poetic rhetoric, as he is in a silent film, Othello's poor judgement and increasingly unchecked responses to the world around him are disproportionately exposed. The transaction wrought upon this dramatic character by silent cinema is, therefore, as discussed in Chapter 3, particularly harsh. And whereas a gifted mime artist might nonetheless be able to rescue something of the character's dignity even without words, Jannings's performance in this film lacks the nuanced physical eloquence needed to counteract the character's linguistic deficit. What he offers instead is heightened theatricality and a 'tiresomely weighty' over-compensation in gestural and facial emphasis for not being the worded Othello he had played to acclaim on the stage.[47]

If Jannings's 'unspeakably overplayed' performance at the heart of the film is its chief disappointment, one of its principal delights is Werner Krauss's memorably vicious Iago. Krauss's screen persona was already well established as a darkly sinister force before he played Iago. Parts such as 'the evil cripple' luring men to their deaths in *The Dance of Death* (*Totentanz* written by Fritz Lang, directed by Otto Rippert, 1919) and, famously, the mysterious Dr Caligari in *The Cabinet of Dr Caligari*

---

[45] He played low-key, touching roles as well as grandiose ones during his film career and was awarded the first ever Oscar for *The Way of All Flesh* and *The Last Command* (1928).

[46] *The Bioscope* (11 November 1909), 45.

[47] Charles Ford, 'Emil Jannings', supplément à *l'Avant-Scène du Cinéma* 93 (June 1969), 295. Translated from the French.

(Wiene, 1920) had already left an indelible mark on his screen presence even before he played Jannings's powerful *bête noir* as the vicious Robespierre in *Danton* (1921). His casting as Iago, and its recapitulating of his role as Jannings's tormenter, therefore, ran with the grain of his screen career to date and Krauss was able to trade economically for colour and emphasis upon the accumulated associations of the previous archmanipulators he had played.[48]

It was a role that Krauss clearly relished. Clad in tight-fitting sleek black, with greased-down hair, a small, twirly moustache, one piratical hooped earring and heavy eye make-up, he creeps insect-like and with a half-limp swiftly through courtyards, halls and galleys to listen and to spy in pursuit of his dastardly schemes. His disturbingly psychotic tendencies express themselves in the sudden movement that explodes from nowhere – the startlingly abrupt overturning of his bowl of food to frighten Roderigo (Ferdinand von Alten), the fiercely sudden, sexualised assault on Emilia (Lya de Putti),[49] the hand brutally clapped over Roderigo's mouth, the percussively sharp twist of the head to look directly at Othello after 'Ha – I like not that.' These eruptions are not the mark of a character out of control, but rather the theatrically executed demonstrations of a character strategically in control of himself and of his projections. Krauss's Iago is not, however, only chillingly sinister: he is also comic – part cartoon villain, part scuttling beetle. Although physically repulsive, he appealingly combines the spirited and the precise. What makes him particularly winning – and often entertainingly so – is the irresistible delight he takes in his own villainy. The stylishly understated nonchalance with which he pockets a stream of Roderigo's coins as part of his ongoing extortion racket, for example, makes it difficult for a spectator not to applaud him. Certainly it is easier to take pleasure in the self-conscious villainy of this Iago than it is to feel pity for the film's histrionic Othello.

---

[48] Given Krauss's many film roles, it is noteworthy that his screen work is often downplayed in accounts of his career. See, for example, Alfred Mühr, *Die Welt des Schauspieler Werner Krauss* (Berlin: Brunnen-Verlag, 1928); Herbert Ihering, *Werner Krauss: Ein Schauspieler und das Neunzehnte Jahrhundert* (Berlin: Verlag Vorwerk 8, 1997) and Wolfgang Goetz, *Werner Krauss* (Hamburg: Hoffmann und Campe Verlag, 1954). *Othello* gets only a one-line mention in Krauss's autobiography, *Das Schauspiel meines Lebens* (Stuttgart: Henry Goverts Verlag, 1958), p. 80. Following *Othello*, Krauss, unlike Jannings, was cast again in Shakespearean films, playing Mordecai (Shylock equivalent) in the 1923 *Der Kaufmann von Venedig* (*The Jew of Mestri* in its English release) and Bottom in the 1925 *Ein Sommernachtstraum* (*A Midsummer Night's Dream*).

[49] Emilia appears as 'Lucia' in some (but not all) advertisements. See *Der Film* 6 (1922), 7. For clarity, I refer to her as Emilia.

The self-conscious humour of Iago's engagements with the general he is gulling is particularly evident at the end of the scene of Othello's fit. The sequence is worth attending to both for the particularity of the encounter between the two central characters and for its broader interpretive interest.

Exhausted by the suspicions by which he has been assailed, Othello lies down on a daybed to rest. There, however, his tortured imaginings take on graphic form in a cameo that appears projected onto the curtain behind his bed, seen first in long shot and then in tormenting close-up.[50] The cameo shows Desdemona (Ica von Lenkeffy) in Cassio's (Theodor Loos) arms (Figure 7.4a). Converting verbal accusation into a publicly accessible, vividly conjured image of supposed infidelity in this way cannot but influence the spectator's sense of Desdemona. In the play, an adulterous version of Desdemona is powerfully conjured by the extensive chicanery. So potently evocative is the slander that in response to the stage-play we, like Othello, sometimes need to see her actual presence on stage to recall the other version of Desdemona, the innocent one, who is more real than the adulterer of Iago's graphic descriptions. If, however, we have *seen* an image of her infidelity as well as hearing about it, as we do in this film, the slander inevitably assumes a degree of quasi-photographic truth that is harder entirely to dismiss. From our point of view, both Desdemonas – the innocent one and her fictional adulterous counterpart – are now cinematic 'fictional truths' on a broadly equal representational footing. Even knowing that the sight of Desdemona's infidelity has been conjured by a subjective mind-world is not in itself sufficient to dismiss its claim to having in some sense *happened*. The scene projected onto the curtain behind Othello's bed, therefore, cannot but subtly tarnish Desdemona – even though, as if in an attempt to temper exactly this effect, the scene cuts away to show the other Desdemona, the innocent one, kneeling at her *prie-dieu* throughout her husband's sullying dream of her (Figure 7.4b).

Writhing at his horrific fantasy, Othello's torment reaches such a pitch that he falls clumsily from the bed. Iago finds him on the floor and tenderly cradles his head in his arms, stroking his brow soothingly with his own hand. As he removes his hand, he looks with interested surprise and slight distaste at what comes off on it (Figure 7.5a).[51] This understated gesture

---

[50] Othello's destructive fantasy world has been graphically depicted in many filmed *Othellos* since. See, for example, Oliver Parker's 1995 film and Andrew Davies's 2001 made-for-television adaptation.

[51] He subsequently applies the handkerchief to Othello's forehead as a palliative compress and waves it around nonchalantly as evidence of Desdemona's supposed treachery.

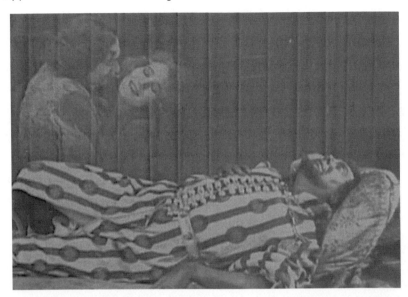

Figure 7.4 Stills from *Othello* (Wörner-Filmgesellschaft, 1922).
a. Othello's (Jannings) tormented imaginings of the supposed infidelity of Desdemona
(von Lenkeffy) take on damningly graphic form via a back projection.
b. The sequence cross-cuts to an image of the virtuous Desdemona praying, to reassert
her innocence in spite of the damning visuals.

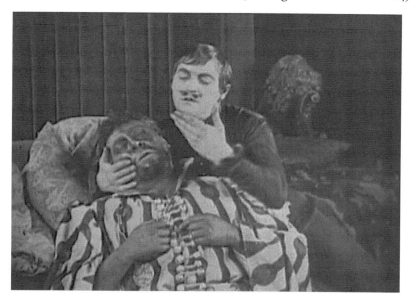

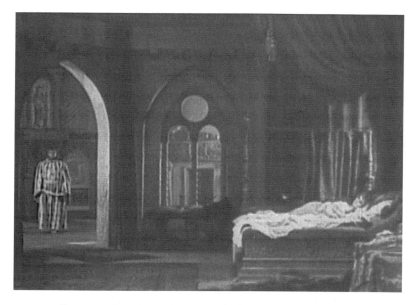

Figure 7.5a. Iago (Krauss) examines his hand having wiped Othello's forehead and b. Othello approaches the cathedral-like bedchamber where Desdemona sleeps.

might simply indicate disgust at coming into contact with his general's feverish sweat. In the context of Jannings's blacked-up performance, how-ever, Krauss's expression of interest in the impression left on his own hand here also registers the fact that in their *performance* of this scene at least, what he wipes from his general's brow is very probably boot polish.

Both in the particularity of Jannings's performance as a wild, wide-eyed and passionate Moor and in the film's meta-cinematic allusion to his status as a blacked-up performer, the film remembers a British Anson Dyer animated cartoon of two years previously. This one-reel burlesque had specifically pastiched the practice of blacking up to play the Moor by showing Othello applying his own burnt cork to 'become' black causing his girlfriend (familiarly known as 'Mona) to be comically and exagger-atedly smeared with black during an embrace as his artificially applied colour rubs off on her.[52] The cartoon was wryly topical in its lampooning of performance practices in relation to this play, dependent as they almost exclusively were on the blacking-up convention: the Jannings/Krauss film, released so soon after, seemed to illustrate its points of parody with satis-fying neatness. In Iago's gesture of surprise at the residue he finds on his own hand, however, the Buchowetzki film momentarily shifts from being a target of parody, to itself parodying the very performance tradition of which it forms part.

Set and cinematography

As a product of a national industry that valued the expressionist poten-tial of architectural design, the set for *Othello* is tremendous: it includes a grand set of courtyards, arches, staircases and balconies that allow the Duke of Venice to sit in pomp, Iago to hop triumphantly across expanses of space, and the sprightly Emilia to run frantically from place to place, seeking a stolen handkerchief or responding to the disquieting cry of her mistress.[53] Crucially, it can accommodate a series of crowd scenes that con-textualise the domestic drama within a larger social and political frame-work. Othello is sent to Cyprus not merely on the say-so of the Senate, but partly because the Venetian populus on the streets calls for him to be sent in their cause. Similarly, near the end of the film, there is a popular uprising

[52] The 1920 Dyer *Othello* is held at the BFI National Archive.

[53] The set's dimensions and solidity may be instructively compared with the cramped character of the Cypriot world in the 1909 FAI *Othello* (discussed in Chapter 3) as a gauge of the industry's progress in set design, lighting in depth of field and camera sensitivity for deep-focus photogra-phy since the transitional era.

on the streets of Cyprus to lament Othello's arrest. In a series of brief but frequent cut-aways from the intensity of the domestic drama throughout the film, the crowds in both places are shown following the news, gossiping, being partisan and constituting a collective social pressure.

Moreover, the Turk in this version of the drama has not been as thoroughly routed at the arrival on Cyprus as he is in Shakespeare's rendering of events. Throughout the film, reports come that he is pressing to attack, and these reports become more urgent as the climax approaches, reinforcing the claustrophobic pressure of life on Cyprus and adding a political and military dimension to the mounting crescendo. The introduction of reports of the advancing Turk in effect *Hamletises* the usually far more domestically focused *Othello*, mimicking the rhythms of Fortinbras's advance as the background to the more familial events playing out at Elsinore. Though the Turk does not actually arrive to look upon the tragic loading of the bed at the end of the film, the repeated announcements of his increasing proximity do contribute to the rising pressure upon Othello, forcing events towards the crisis.

The climax, when it comes, is played out in a high key. Othello is glimpsed in depth of field through an archway in left of shot. Also in deep space, in an alcove above Othello's head, stands a statuette of the Virgin Mary. Simultaneously visible in shot, brightly, almost spiritually, lit on the bed in the right foreground, is Desdemona's sleeping form (Figure 7.5b). It is a bravura piece of cinematography that showcases the ambition of the mise-en-scène and the crispness of the shot's engagement with deep staging. The set for this bedchamber scene resembles a cathedral with Gothic arched windows, fluted columns, a high round window through which light floods and a raised, decoratively carved stone bed overhung by a high, richly draped canopy – altar and pulpit rolled into one composite image. In the midst of this lighting, set and statuary, Othello's painfully deliberate advance through the arch into the bedroom is akin to that of a priest processing slowly through the chancel towards the sanctuary to perform a liturgical rite. Jannings's exaggerated performance elsewhere in the film makes the studied discipline of this walk the more noticeable.

Even when Othello finally reaches the altar-bed, the moment of the murder is then further delayed by a series of dialogue cards (about whether Desdemona has prayed tonight, about the handkerchief, about Cassio). These interrupt a sequence of alternating close-ups of Othello's anger and Desdemona's fear. Characteristically, the film does not fight shy of sustaining its close-ups for an almost uncomfortable length of time. The effect of this here is both to generate a sense of embarrassing intrusion into the grotesque intimacy of these particular exchanges and to hold the poise of the pre-climactic moment for a daringly long period of time. When the moment finally comes, it is desperate and violent. Even the noise it generates is evoked by a repeated cut to the running figure of Emilia, who has clearly been alerted to some danger by hearing cries.

The murder of Desdemona has often tempted film-makers into shooting indulgently sensationalised action. In the 1914 Italian four-reel *Othello* made by Ambrosio, however, this scene is treated with a discipline scarcely seen before or since. The camera follows the central action of the scene as Othello throws Desdemona onto the bed prior to killing her. Then, however, at the very moment we would expect it to move in to view the lurid action from close quarters, it eschews any prurient interest in the details of that encounter by panning away right. Unusually, therefore, the murder takes place teasingly out of shot, frame left. Meanwhile the camera reveals instead, with clear metaphorical significance, a lit candle illuminating a painting of the Virgin Mary. As we watch, the candle is suddenly extinguished, releasing a little trail of smoke that winds upwards past the painting. The inference is clear: in Othello's own phrase, the light has been 'put out'. In leaving Desdemona's fate principally at the level of suggestion, the film resists the temptation to exploit the opportunity for histrionic spectacle. The fact that the camera *could* show so much (and in grisly close-up if it chose to) makes its decision to show almost nothing the more striking and the more welcome.

In the Buchowetzki film, however, there is no coy panning away or searching for a suggestive metaphor to evoke Desdemona's death: the scene only cuts to Emilia to add an implied realistic dimension – sound – to the horrific sensory specifics of the murder. In its final image, Othello grips Desdemona's throat with both hands forcing her head to dangle backwards over the edge of the bed, now seen upside down, brilliantly lit and centre frame (Figure 7.6). In the context of the cathedral-bedroom, the priestly advance, and the altar-like architecture of the bed, the image is infused not only with a sensationalised pathos but also with a clear sense of the sacrilegious character of this sacrament-violating act. In having set Othello on to desecrate the sanctity of his marriage bed in such symbolically telegraphed ways, the seal is set on Iago's triumph over Othello.

*

Both the 1920 *Hamlet* and the 1922 *Othello* make eloquent use of their impressive sets, provide some stunning visual drama and include moments that take one back to the play to consider anew its cadences, sympathies,

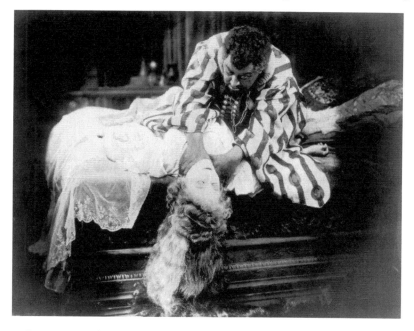

Figure 7.6 Desdemona as sacrificial lamb, murdered on her altar-bed in *Othello* (Wörner-Filmgesellschaft, 1922). The act of strangulation, unlike a Shakespearean smothering, heightens the sensational impact of the scene by keeping Desdemona's face visible throughout. Publicity still, courtesy of Photofest, NYC.

poetry and performance possibilities. Where they differ most strikingly as viewing experiences is in the nature of their central performance. In *Hamlet*, Asta Nielsen is a screen star in her element: in *Othello*, Emil Jannings presents as a classical stage actor out of his.[54]

In *Practical Hints on Acting for the Cinema*, published the year before Jannings's *Othello* was made, Agnes Platt specifically compared effective screen acting techniques with those suitable for the stage:

In film work, exaggeration of any sort is a mistake … [A]ll unnecessary movements [should be] eschewed … It is a great mistake to suppose that when acting for the cinema you must be constantly employing gesture … [A] mobile face, which would be expressive on the stage, is apt on [sic] the cinema to take the leap from the sublime to the ridiculous. It is hardly too much to say that the less facial contortion you use for the cinema the better … The expression of the eyes

---

[54] Since his other film performances were not all overblown, it may simply be that he made an unfortunate calculation about what was required specifically for playing Shakespeare on screen.

is the one thing needful ... The dramatic actor who riots in facial play and rapid gesticulation is like a caricature of himself when his work is reproduced upon the screen.[55]

By the 1920s, as one contemporary critic wrote:

the actors no longer plant themselves in front of the lens; instead it shifts with and for them, it turns around them, it puts itself before or behind them, above or below them, seizing upon their smallest expressions at the fraction of a second that is the most significant.[56]

Whereas, therefore, for the 1913 *Macbeth*, Arthur Bourchier had been commended on having 'broadened his style, amplified his gesture, and developed increased facial expression',[57] by 1920, with the camera's willingness to 'seiz[e] upon the[] smallest expressions' with intimate and mobile attentiveness, it was no longer amplification but containment that suited the narrative tendencies of the medium. The screen actors of the 1920s that light up the screen, holding our rapt gaze, are not those who assail the camera with a series of prepared attitudes, but rather those who allow it to read them and discern their mysteries. Such actors can register emotion by allowing the merest shadow to pass across their face, can communicate embarrassment or desire by a momentary, barely perceptible, check in their step, express tension, curiosity, suspicion or hurt by the slightest change in the tilt of the chin or angle of the brow, and, crucially, they can animate each emotional vicissitude through the thought just discernible behind the eyes. Screen stars from this era are not actors working on this occasion without words, but mime artists working *with* their own communicative tools. And the particularities of their craft may not coincide precisely with those of classical actors from the legitimate stage.

The predilection to cast Shakespearean actors for Shakespeare films of the silent era sprang from an assumption that Shakespearean acting was a transmediatable skill – that being able to give a powerful performance in a worded medium would necessarily equip one to do so also in an unworded medium. It did not, of course, automatically do so. Though, in the 1920s, Jannings's reputation as a classical stage actor was enormous in Germany (principally through his work with Max Reinhardt at Berlin's Deutsches Theater), for his screen Othello, he opts for more, not less,

[55] Platt, *Practical Hints on Acting for the Cinema*, pp. 23, 26, 27, 29.
[56] Review of *Variety* (1925). Quoted in Bordwell, *On the History of Film Style*, p. 33.
[57] *KLW* (9 October 1913), 2555.

'facial contortion', becomes indeed 'a caricature of himself' and is a very long way from the 'sublime'.

A fêted classical actor from the legitimate stage, such as Herbert Beerbohm Tree, Johnston Forbes-Robertson or Emil Jannings, certainly brought significant benefits to a film in terms of cultural profile and artistic gravitas. However, part of the on-screen performance of each is – almost inevitably – an act of compensation for the absence of the expressive voice on which that actor had previously relied in his stage work. On screen, they chafe against the constraints of the medium – and it shows. By contrast, the performances of screen actors such as Elena Makowska, Theda Bara, Francis X. Bushman, Lya de Putti (who was also a dancer) or Asta Nielsen are entire in themselves, unmarred by a sense of cap or compromise. It is the nuanced delights on offer from such silent era Shakespearean mime artists that point up with unsparing clarity the *übertrieben* nature of the performance given by some of the less versatile theatrical imports. And it is these same artists who have passed on the tradition in Shakespearean mime that, as the Afterword discusses, is still alive today.

'No tongue, all eyes! Be silent':
performing wordless Shakespeare today

It is one of the ironies of this history that the unbearably tongue-less Lavinia from *Titus Andronicus*, that 'map of woe' who talks 'in signs' with such touching grace (III.ii.12), never graced the silent screen.[1] To compound the irony, Hamlet, who talks not in signs but in abundant supplies of words, underwent the awkward business of accommodating his word-heavy self to the silent screen with striking regularity.[2]

Once commercial sound film reached the screens in 1927, the few years that followed saw silent film production necessarily cede, and with unseemly haste, to the swiftly established market supremacy of the talking picture. Silent pictures became passé and, from a film historian's point of view, the material results of the industry's decisive shift in attention were grim: cans of silent film were systematically cleared out of studio vaults to make shelf space for the talkies. But though so many prints were binned and burned, depriving the future of some unrecoverable treasures in the process, some things from the era survived – not all of them material. There may, as Paul Auster suggests, be a 'great chasm of forgetfulness' yawning between then and now, but not all the impulses that animated that time have been lost in the chasm.[3] Some dramatic possibilities – imprinted deep upon a cultural memory, but dismissed as naïve or ridiculous in the proselytising enthusiasm of the early days of the talkies[4] – simply

---

[1] Lavinia, however, is not just silent, she has *been* silenced and the horrific particularity of her wordlessness would have needed to be distinguished from the merely conventional silences of all around her in such a medium. Moreover, *Titus Andronicus* was then out of favour: until revived in 1923, it appeared only in Edward Ravenscroft's 1687 adaptation *Titus Andronicus: or, the Rape of Lavinia*. Lavinia does not appear on screen in the silent era, therefore, partly because the play had no currency at the time (having previously given offence). Other Shakespeare plays never made into silent films include many of the histories, *Coriolanus*, *Troilus and Cressida* and *Pericles*.

[2] *Hamlet* was the most frequently cinematically adapted work of any in the era, Shakespearean or otherwise.

[3] Paul Auster, *The Book of Illusions* (London: Faber, 2002), p. 15. The full quotation appears at the front of this book.

[4] See, for example, the Vitagraph Chairman's dismissive sound era reflections on the silent Shakespeare films he had himself made. Albert E. Smith, *Two Reels and a Crank*, p. 263.

temporarily went to ground to await the moment when they could find renewed expression and a more receptive audience.

The touchingly eccentric will to perform *Hamlet* without the words was one such impulse. Like a rogue movement biding its time, it lay mostly dormant in the intervening years. But then in 2002, it found its moment to re-emerge and burst back onto the cultural landscape – not now on the screen but, in its reawakened, remade form, on the stage.

The central interest of this book has been the workings of the silent film industry in its engagements with Shakespeare. By way of tangential conclusion, however, I finish by considering the work of one contemporary theatre company, which has revivified the practice of performing mimed, wordless Shakespeare. The popularity of these recent wordless stage productions testifies to the particularity of their imaginative choreography and finely tuned performances. However, it also incidentally suggests a willingness on the part of audiences to rediscover and reconnect with Shakespeare's plays as repositories for and communicators of narrative rhythm, social impulses, states of mind, iconic images and emotional springs not exclusively dependent on words for their effects (though often incidentally summoning them in arresting ways). It is these very attributes that silent Shakespeare films, at their best, also offered.

The Synetic Theater Company is based in Arlington, Virginia. Its artistic director is Paata Tsikurishvili, its principal choreographer, Irina Tsikurishvili – a husband and wife team from the Republic of Georgia, trained in a variety of classical theatre, physical theatre, movement and dance forms.[5] In 2002, Synetic mounted a wordless stage version of *Hamlet* at the Stanislavsky Theater Studio in Washington DC, entitled *Hamlet… the rest is silence* (in which Paata Tsikurishvili himself played the lead).[6] In 2007, the company followed it up with a wordless *Macbeth* and in early 2008, a wordless *Romeo and Juliet*, both at the Rosslyn Spectrum, Arlington. There have been several revivals of *Hamlet* and *Macbeth*, including at the Kennedy Center, Washington DC. The company's production of *A Midsummer Night's Dream* will open at the Kennedy Center in May 2009 and they also plan to mount a wordless *Tempest* in the future. Its goal in relation to these Shakespeare productions, as, for example, articulated in the programme for *Macbeth*, is to 'blend movement, dance, text

---

[5] For company details, see www.classika.org/Synetic/about.html.
[6] *Hamlet … the rest is silence* won three Helen Hayes Awards in 2002, for Best Resident Play, Best Director and Best Choreography.

and drama in new and arresting ways', and, by doing so, to understand Shakespeare on the 'almost imperceptibly subconscious level of dreams and nightmares'.[7] The 'text' included in the blend forms part of the rehearsal process but has no presence in the final performances.

In 2007, Synetic's wordless Shakespeare productions prompted a discussion about silent Shakespeare on Hardy M. Cook's international Shakespeare discussion group *Shaksper* (sic). Responses were varied. Norman D. Hinton, for example, asked caustically whether after Shakespeare without words, Beethoven without the music, and Monet in the dark might not be next.[8] Such responses echoed the starting position of some theatre critics also: in response to Synetic's *Macbeth*, for example, Nicholas F. Benton had asked whether performing Shakespeare without the words might not be akin to asking Michael Jordan to play basketball without a ball.[9] Others, however, were less dismissive. On the *Shaksper* discussion list, Peter Holland suggested that the partial Shakespeare that a silent production represents is broadly comparable to the partial Shakespeare that a radio production also constitutes: neither may be whole but both are full of dramatic possibility.[10] Unsurprisingly, my own interest in what wordless dramatisations of Shakespeare can bring to an understanding not only of film history but also of Shakespeare – what submerged cadences can be released, well-springs of feeling tapped, cultural forces revealed and even nuances of poetry analogically explored – aligns me fully with Holland on this question. Despite missing a key dramatic element, either wordless or imageless Shakespeare can, done well, challenge and refresh our engagements with the plays through the jostling processes of defamiliarisation and necessarily selective concentration required of us.

Innately provocative though presenting Shakespeare without the words has proved, Synetic's Shakespeare productions have attracted sell-out audiences and garnered extraordinary reviews. Writing in *The Washington Post*

---

[7] Paata Tsikurishvili, 'Director's Notes', *Macbeth* Synetic programme (2007), p. 2. Author's collection.

[8] Norman D. Hinton, 'Wordless Macbeth' discussion thread, *Shaksper: The Global Electronic Shakespeare Conference* (online posting, 18 January 2007). Consulted at: www.shaksper.net/archives/2007/0044.html.

[9] Nicholas F. Benton, 'A "Macbeth" With All the Moves, None of the Words', *Falls Church News-Press* (Thursday, 18 January 2007). After this cautious opening about the project *per se*, Benton was won over by the production which he then reviewed enthusiastically. Review consulted at: www.fcnp.com/news/a_macbeth_with_all_the_moves_none_of_the_words_20070118.html.

[10] Peter Holland, 'Wordless Macbeth' discussion thread, *Shaksper: The Global Electronic Shakespeare Conference* (online posting, 18 January 2007). Consulted at: www.shaksper.net/archives/2007/0044.html.

in 2002 in response to *Hamlet*, William Triplett wrote that although this is not the play 'as most of us have probably ever seen it', it is, nevertheless, the *Hamlet* that we know 'in our bones'.[11] For the 2007 revival at the Kennedy Center (part of the 'Shakespeare in Washington' Festival), another reviewer for the *Post* reached again for the idea of a production that 'works in a primal way': 'You don't understand this "Hamlet" – you feel it in your gut'.[12] Its elemental force seemed to reconnect its audiences with a primordial version of *Hamlet* about love, loss, introspection, isolation and revenge. It is the version, critics imply, whose pulse we find we know (with some kinship to the commonly owned, consensually recognised pictorial version of *Lear* to which Orwell alerts us).[13] There has, moreover, been no shortage of review phrases relating the particular eloquence of Synetic's performances to that of words. Michael Toscano's headline for his review of the 2003 *Hamlet* revival – 'Body Language Speaks Volumes in Silent "Hamlet"' – is symptomatic in its ascription of quasi-linguistic attributes to the performances.[14] The productions are 'read' as discursive as well as narrative, inquisitive in their detail as well as powerful in their drift. In response to the Synetic *Macbeth*, Peter Marks wondered at how surprisingly 'pliantly' Shakespearean tragedy yielded to a wordless dramatisation.[15] The following year he was, if anything, yet more impressed with the company's *Romeo and Juliet*, the production's 'waves of pure and emphatic gesture' causing him to conclude that its 'sophisticated melding of sensuality, musicality and [silent] storytelling, lifts the company to another magnitude (sic) of accomplishment'.[16] In sum, Synetic has successfully carved out for itself an extremely well respected East Coast niche with an international profile as nuanced and imaginative interpreters of 'silent Shakespeare'.

The writers, actors, directors, producers and even accompanying moving picture lecturers who have appeared in this book are unable now to tell us what they were hoping to achieve in silent Shakespeare films, how they

[11] William Triplett, 'Synetic's "Hamlet": The Rest Is Silence'. *The Washington Post* (8 April 2002), CO1.

[12] Sarah Kaufman, 'Silent "Hamlet", Felt in the Bones: Synetic Theater Mounts a Mesmerizing Revival at the Kennedy Center', *The Washington Post* (5 June 2007), CO8.

[13] On Orwell and the Shakespeare we carry within us, see Preface, pp. xix–xxi.

[14] Michael Toscano, 'Body Language Speaks Volumes in Silent "Hamlet"', *The Washington Post* (23 October 2003). Consulted at: www.georgiaemb.org/DisplayMedia.asp?id=234.

[15] Peter Marks, 'The Unquiet Silence of Synetic's "Macbeth"', *The Washington Post* (20 January 2007), CO1.

[16] Peter Marks, ' "Romeo and Juliet": Such Sweet Sorrow', *The Washington Post* (29 January 2008), CO1.

arrived at an interpretive approach, what prejudices they had to combat, what sort of pleasure the films gave on exhibition and to whom. However, in tracing the ongoing dramatic legacy left by silent Shakespeare films, it is instead now possible to speak to contemporary practitioners of wordless Shakespeare to discuss the challenges and possibilities inherent in the project. The approach of these contemporary performers does not replicate those employed by film production companies in the silent era: in many respects, it diverges from them decisively. But it is these practitioners who have picked up the baton of this particular performance tradition, enabling us to catch the flow of the ongoing dramatic current in its thoughtfully remade contemporary expression.

In April 2007 I sat in on Synetic rehearsals in Arlington, Virginia and discussed his silent productions of *Hamlet* and *Macbeth* with artistic director and principal actor Paata Tsikurishvili. As a codicil to this study, a transcript of excerpts from that conversation follows.[17]

JB: *Hamlet* is a very wordy play with an unrivalled theatrical status. Did it take a particular sort of courage to take this one on as your first venture into wordless Shakespeare, as opposed to one of the comedies, for example?

PT: Yes, and we attracted a lot of criticism for it. How dare I touch Shakespeare's words? How could I do that? And *Hamlet* – some people were outraged. But I already had experience of doing Shakespeare without words at college in Georgia and Shakespeare is not only the words of course. I wanted to catch Shakespeare's thoughts, Shakespeare's imagery, the archetypes, the hidden agendas and find a way of showing them. So we do this through another language, an international language that allows in more people. And it really touched people in deep places, in their souls.

JB: Sometimes in your Shakespeare productions there seems to be almost a line-for-line transcription of the poetry through the detail of the gestural choreography and at other times the reading is much freer. How do you use the text in your preparation, and at what point do you leave that behind?

PT: In the beginning, we always read and argue and think with and from the text. We exchange thoughts: who catches what images? Which phrases, which images seem pivotal? We look for the archetypes. We find that actions speak louder than words – actions are not better, they're just louder. So we look for 'the loud way' of telling the story and of showing thought. I have a vocabulary to tell a story through the body, through dance, through

---

[17] I met with Paata Tsikurishvili and Nathan Weinberger, Synetic's literary adaptor, on 18 April 2007. Nathan Weinberger was part of the broader conversation, but did not contribute to the section included here.

movements, so I tell stories that way. For *Macbeth*, I recorded some voice-over, used it in rehearsal and then jettisoned it. So yes, we had text as part of the process in rehearsal to help us find the meanings that we then drama-tised with our bodies.

JB: Is there for you something primal about the body and its ways of commu-nicating, whereas words are on some level always a mediated expression of feeling?

PT: That's it: working without words can reach people in a different way, and sometimes a more profound way. The reviewer from *The Washington Post* said he thought people felt our *Hamlet* in their bones. I understand that. We're trying to find the thing Shakespeare *felt* for which he then found words. It's the pre-lingual bit we're after, the psychology that the poetry comes from. What was going on in Shakespeare's head *before* he wrote 'To be or not to be'? We like guessing at that, trying to recapture its essence, its emotional centre. So, partly, we try to *translate* the poetry through move-ment, finding equivalent images in translated form, and partly we try to capture the thought the poetry came *from*.

JB: Your Hamlet enters with a skull which is many things to him – his friend, lover, toy, prop, dance partner, tool for tormenting others, oddly consoling proxy version of himself (Figures 8.1a and b). The tortured intimacy of that relation-ship with death, and with the dead, seems to inform much of the production that follows. Was this consciously the mainspring for the production?

PT: Yes, absolutely. Of course, the skull's a transplant in some ways from a later point in the play. Shakespeare does not have Hamlet entering with a skull – but Hamlet carries the *thought* with him, so we gave the thought form, to make it visible. My Hamlet needs to *show* his intimacy with death and with the dead since he can't tell us about it. So when Ophelia wipes a tear from Hamlet's eye, he wipes a tear from the skull's eye. He feels part of it and he filters his experiences through it. So he makes sense of Ophelia's gesture of compassion to him by repeating it with the skull. It's where things are anchored for him...

We found having a symbol useful in the adaptation. We let the play give us the symbol though. *Hamlet* gave us the skull: one of the things *Macbeth* gave us is the crown, and we do something similar with the torturing temp-tation the crown represents. It's seductive and Lady Macbeth, for example, uses it to make Macbeth want it completely. But we like to use something that can become different things.

JB: And equally, you often work without props, and without scenery, and the actors' bodies then become the exclusive focus in communicating the emo-tional turns of the play. I am thinking, for example, of the dance-encounter between Hamlet and Ophelia in which they so nearly, and yet never quite, touch fingers in that exquisite poise of 'nearly-ness'.

PT: And Hamlet repeats a version of that dance with Ophelia's corpse later in the production when their hands are entwined but again without quite

Figure 8.1a and b. Paata Tsikurishvili as Hamlet. Publicity stills for *Hamlet… the rest is silence* (Synetic Theater, 2002). Photographer Raymond Gniewek. Images courtesy of Synetic Theater Company.

touching and together they form wings and we allow Hamlet to think he has recovered her. But then her hand drops and he is reminded that it was only his *desire* to bring her back that has temporarily re-conjured her.

JB: And she then seems so *very* dead – more dead even than she had before he half-summoned her back to life. It's a cruel moment for Hamlet.

PT: There are lots of cruel moments for Hamlet. It's not a kind play.

JB: I found the detail of that ghost-dance brought the text to mind in suggestive ways – anticipating the flights of angels that will be asked to 'wing' Hamlet to his rest in due course, for example.

PT: Well everything in the play wheels back to thoughts of death, and in particular, yes, to thoughts of Hamlet's own death. Even when the skull is not physically on stage, we wanted its influence to be felt. So thoughts of death are never very far away. But there are definitely light moments, and funny moments, within that too.

JB: Which makes me think of your version of the dumb show. Was it a problem to decide what to do with that in an entirely wordless production, to distinguish it somehow from all the other wordlessness around it?

PT: The dumb show: why did Shakespeare write that most delicate moment in a 'dumb' way? Visually, Hamlet assaults the King and Queen with the sight of what they have done. They have to see it without verbal distraction and that's difficult to stomach. I use the moment to accuse them, of course, but also to bring some lightness to the register and some colour. I use a different performance note to allow people to catch their breath in the middle of a painful drama. So we do it skittishly, with colourful skirts, silly crass tricks, and some ironic playing. Our performance of 'The Mousetrap' is heightened, played big, exaggerated. We give it a cartoonish charge because yes: it needs to feel different from the rest of the drama around it. We changed the tone of the performances to signal that, but without lessening the force of the accusation it dramatises...

JB: Do you have detractors who are opposed in principle to stripping Shakespeare of his dramatic language?

PT: Yes, but their objections tend to be 'in principle' objections which disappear when they actually see the show. Then they stop writing about all the things wordless Shakespeare isn't and start talking about what it is.

Filmography

COMMERCIALLY AVAILABLE SILENT SHAKESPEARE FILMS

At the time of writing, there are four commercially available DVDs featuring silent Shakespeare films.

(1) *SILENT SHAKESPEARE*

Produced by the BFI, this release includes seven silent Shakespeare films:

i. *King John* (BMBC: dir. W.K.-L. Dickson, 1899), starring Tree.
ii. *The Tempest* (Clarendon: dir. Percy Stow, 1908), cast unknown.
iii. *A Midsummer Night's Dream* (Vitagraph: dirs. J. Stuart Blackton and Charles Kent, 1909), starring Ranous, Costello, Swayne Gordon and Turner.
iv. *King Lear/Re Lear* (FAI: Gerolamo Lo Savio, 1910), starring Novelli and Bertini.
v. *Twelfth Night* (Vitagraph: dir. Charles Kent, 1910), starring Turner, Kent, Swayne Gordon.
vi. *The Merchant of Venice/Il Mercante di Venezia* (FAI: dir. Gerolamo Lo Savio, 1910), starring Novelli and Bertini.
vii. *Richard III* (Co-operative Film Company: dir. F.R. Benson, 1911), starring F.R. Benson and Constance Benson.

(2) *OTHELLO* (WÖRNER-FILMGESELLSCHAFT: DIR. DIMITRI BUCHOWETZKI, 1922)

Produced by Kino Video, in addition to the Buchowetzki/Jannings *Othello*, this release also includes four supplementary short silent Shakespeare films from the Library of Congress archives:

i. Duel Scene from *Macbeth* (AMBC, 1905).

ii. *The Taming of the Shrew* (Biograph: dir. D.W. Griffith, 1908), starring Florence Lawrence and Arthur V. Johnson.

iii. *Romeo Turns Bandit/Roméo se fait bandit* (Pathé: dir. Romeo Bosetti, 1910), starring Max Linder.

iv. *Desdemona* (Nordisk: dir. August Blom, 1911), starring Valdemar Psilander and Thyra Reimann.

(3) THE THANHOUSER COLLECTION VOL. 7: 'THANHOUSER PRESENTS SHAKESPEARE'

Produced by Thanhouser Company Film Preservation Inc., this release includes three Thanhouser silent Shakespeare films:

i. *The Winter's Tale* (dir. Barry O'Neil, 1910), starring Martin Faust.

ii. *Cymbeline* (dir. Frederick Sullivan, 1913), starring Florence LaBadie.

iii. *King Lear* (dir. Ernest Warde, 1916), starring Frederick Warde.

(4) *RICHARD III* (SHAKESPEARE FILM COMPANY: DIR. JAMES KEANE, 1912)

Produced by Kino Video in association with the American Film Institute, this release starring Frederick Warde features a specially commissioned score by Ennio Morricone.

GENERAL FILMOGRAPHY

All films mentioned in the book (Shakespearean and non-Shakespearean) are listed below. This is not, however, an exhaustive list of all Shakespeare films from the silent era. For a non-selective list of silent Shakespeare films, including full technical specifications, running times and locations of surviving prints, I defer to The British Universities Film and Video Council's online, open-access 'Shakespeare on film, television and radio' database – part of whose brief is to be both comprehensive and regularly updated as new material comes to light. At the moment of writing, the site is scheduled for full launch within months. This being the case, and given word count constraints for this project, to duplicate that list here also would be otiose.[1] Where, therefore, additional filmographic information is sought, readers are referred to:

An International Database of Shakespeare on Film, Television and Radio (BUFVC): www.bufvc.ac.uk/databases/shakespeare/

For the reader's reference, helpful, hard-copy Shakespearean filmographies may also be found in:

Robert Hamilton Ball, *Shakespeare on Silent Film* (NY: Theatre Arts, 1968).
Kenneth S. Rothwell and Annabelle Henkin Melzer, *Shakespeare on Screen: An International Filmography and Videography* (London: Mansell; NY: Neal-Schuman, 1990).
Luke McKernan and Olwen Terris (eds.), *Walking Shadows: Shakespeare in the National Film and Television Archive* (London: BFI, 1994).
Kenneth S. Rothwell, *A History of Shakespeare on Screen* (Cambridge University Press, 1999).

Films listed here are arranged chronologically by year, and alphabetically by title within each single year. Archive details are given for those surviving films not commercially available. Where commercially available copies exist, it is presumed expedient for most readers to consult these first, before accessing archival prints. In such cases, therefore, the release details of the relevant DVD are supplied (or simply the fact of the availability of a DVD for easily locatable titles). Where multiple film prints exist but no commercially available version, archive listings here are not exhaustive. Film archival holdings are available for researchers to view by prior appointment at BFK, CSC (Rome), Cineteca di Bologna, Cineteca Italiana (Milan), Deutsche Kinemathek, DIF, Folger (not a film archive

---

[1] This ambitious and very welcome database is scheduled to go live in March 2009. I have been able to observe its pre-launch progress from a position on its steering group.

but holds accessible copy-prints of some films), GEH, LOC, and the BFI National Archive (formerly the NFTVA). Availability details supplied are, to the best of my knowledge, correct at the time of writing. I have attempted, where possible, to give the year of release for the country in which the film was first released: release dates for international distribution may, of course, vary.

Year	Title and production company	Director (or other production personnel)	Principal cast	Availability / status
1896	*Black Diamond Express, The* (Edison)	James H. White	none	BFI National Archive
1896	*Trilby and Little Billee / The Kissing Scene Between Trilby and Little Billee* (AMBC)	unknown	unknown	presumed lost
1897	*Haunted Castle, The* (George Albert Smith Films)	George Albert Smith	unknown	presumed lost
1898	*Photographing a Ghost* (George Albert Smith Films)	George Albert Smith	unknown	presumed lost
1898	*Tearing Down the Spanish Flag* (Vitagraph)	J. Stuart Blackton	Blackton's hand	presumed lost
1898/ 1899	*Studio Troubles / Wicked Willie* (BMBC)	unknown	unknown	presumed lost
1899	*King John* (BMBC)	William K-L Dickson Walter Pfeffer Dando	H. Beerbohm Tree Dora Senior	*Silent Shakespeare* BFI DVD
1899	*Haunted House, The* (Lubin)	unknown	unknown	presumed lost
1900	*Duel d'Hamlet, Le / The Duel Scene from Hamlet* (Phono-Cinéma-Théâtre)	Clément Maurice	Sarah Bernhardt Pierre Magnier	Deutsche Kinemathek (Berlin)
1901	*Countryman and the Cinematograph, The* (Paul's Animatograph Works)	Robert W. Paul	unknown	*Early Cinema: Primitives and Pioneers* BFI DVD
1901	*Diable et la Statue, Le / Le Diable Géant / Le Miracle de la Madonne / The Devil and the Statue* (Méliès)	Georges Méliès	Georges Méliès	*Georges Méliès: First Wizard of Cinema (1896–1913)* DVD
1902	*Burlesque on Romeo and Juliet* (Edison)	unknown	unknown	presumed lost
1902	*Uncle Josh at the Moving Picture Show* (Edison)	Edwin S. Porter	Charles Manley	*Film Classics: The Origins of Cinema* Vol. 1 (Video)

1902 (& re-made 1904)	*Vie et la Passion de Jésus Christ, La* (Pathé)	Lucien Nonguet/ Ferdinand Zecca	Madame Moreau Monsieur Moreau	*The Life and Passion of Jesus Christ* Image Entertainment DVD
1905	*Duel Scene from Macbeth* (AMBC)	Billy Bitzer	unknown	*Othello* (1922) Kino Video DVD
1905	*Miroir de Venise, Le / Une Mésadventure de Shylock / The Venetian Look-glass* (Méliès)	Georges Méliès	unknown	presumed lost
1905	*Seven Ages of Man* (Edison)	unknown	unknown	BFI National Archive
1905	*Tempest, The* storm scene (Urban)	Charles Urban	Tree's company	presumed lost
1906	*Dream of a Rarebit Fiend, The* (Edison)	Wallace McCutcheon Edwin S. Porter	Jack Brawn John P. Brown	*Early Cinema: Primitives and Pioneers* BFI DVD
1906	*Midwinter Night's Dream, A / Little Joe's Luck* (Vitagraph)	unknown	unknown	presumed lost
1906	*Modern Oliver Twist, A* (Vitagraph)	J. Stuart Blackton	unknown	presumed lost
1907/ 8/9 (?)	*Death of Othello / Desdemona* (Messter)	Franz Porten	Henny Porten Franz Porten	presumed lost
1907	*Hamlet* (Méliès)	Georges Méliès	Georges Méliès	presumed lost
1907	*Haunted Hotel, The* (Vitagraph)	J. Stuart Blackton	Paul Panzer Billy Ranous	GEH
1907	*Othello / Otello* (Cines)	Mario Caserini Gaston Velle	Mario Caserini Maria Caserini	presumed lost
1907	*Shakespeare Writing Julius Caesar / Le Rêve de Shakespeare / La Mort de Jules César* (Méliès)	Georges Méliès	Georges Méliès	presumed lost

Year	Title and production company	Director (or other production personnel)	Principal cast	Availability / status
1907	*Washerwoman's Revenge, The* (Vitagraph)	unknown	unknown	presumed lost
1907	*Wrong Flat, The; or A Comedy of Errors* (Vitagraph)	unknown	Leo Delaney	presumed lost
1908	*Antony and Cleopatra* (Vitagraph)	Charles Kent	Maurice Costello Florence Lawrence	presumed lost
1908	*As You Like It* (Kalem)	Kenean Buel	Gene Gauntier	presumed lost
1908	*Barbara Fritchie: The Story of a Patriotic American Woman* (Vitagraph)	J. Stuart Blackton	Julia Arthur, Edith Storey, Earle Williams	presumed lost
1908	*Hamlet / Amleto* (Cines) Remade in 1910 – see below.	Mario Caserini	Amleto Novelli Fernanda Negri Pouget	BFI National Archive/ CSC
1908	*Hamlet / Amleto* (Milano)	Luca Comerio	unknown	presumed lost
1908	*Julius Caesar* (Lubin)	unknown	unknown	presumed lost
1908	*Julius Caesar* (Vitagraph)	William V. (Billy) Ranous J. Stuart Blackton	Billy Ranous Charles Kent Florence Lawrence	BFI National Archive
1908	*Macbeth* (Vitagraph)	Billy Ranous	Billy Ranous	presumed lost
1908	*Merchant of Venice, The* (Vitagraph)	J. Stuart Blackton	Billy Ranous Julia Swayne Gordon	presumed lost
1908	*Othello* (Nordisk)	unknown	Carl Alstrup	presumed lost
1908	*Othello* (Pathé) NB: some filmographies list this film as extant, with Russian titles. That film is actually FAI's 1909 version.	unknown	The Erik Schmedes singers	presumed lost

Year	Title	Director	Cast	Archive/Status
1908	*Othello* (Vitagraph)	Billy Ranous	Billy Ranous, Julia Swayne Gordon, Hector Dion	presumed lost
1908	*Richard III* (Vitagraph)	J. Stuart Blackton, Billy Ranous	Billy Ranous, Florence Auer, Maurice Costello	presumed lost
1908	*Romeo and Juliet / Giulietta e Romeo* (Cines)	Mario Caserini	unknown	presumed lost
1908	*Romeo and Juliet* (Gaumont)	unknown	Godfrey Tearle, Mary Malone	presumed lost
1908	*Romeo and Juliet* (Vitagraph)	J. Stuart Blackton	Florence Lawrence, Paul Panzer, Charles Kent	Folger
1908	*Salome* (Vitagraph)	J. Stuart Blackton	Florence Lawrence, Maurice Costello	BFI National Archive
1908	*Taming of the Shrew, The* (Biograph)	D.W. Griffith	Florence Lawrence, Arthur Johnson, Linda Arvidson	*Othello* (1922) Kino Video DVD
1908	*Tempest, The* (Clarendon)	Percy Stow	unknown	*Silent Shakespeare* BFI DVD
1908	*Western Courtship: A Love Story of Arizona* (Vitagraph)	J. Stuart Blackton	unknown	presumed lost
1909	*For Her Country's Sake* (Vitagraph)	unknown	unknown	presumed lost
1909	*Hamlet* (Lux)	Gérard Bourgeois	Jean Mounet-Sully	presumed lost
1909	*Jephthah's Daughter: A Biblical Tragedy* (Vitagraph)	unknown	Annette Kellerman	BFI National Archive
1909	*Kenilworth* (Vitagraph)	unknown	Maurice Costello, Florence Turner	presumed lost
1909	*King Lear* (Vitagraph)	Billy Ranous	Billy Ranous, Florence Auer	BFI National Archive

Year	Title and production company	Director (or other production personnel)	Principal cast	Availability / status
1909	*Lancelot and Elaine* (Vitagraph)	Charles Kent	Charles Kent Florence Turner	presumed lost
1909	*Life of George Washington, The* (Vitagraph)	unknown	unknown	presumed lost
1909	*Life of Moses, The* (Vitagraph)	J. Stuart Blackton	Pat Hartigan	GEH
1909	*Macbeth / Macbett* (Cines)	Mario Caserini	Dante Capelli Maria Caserini Gasperini	LOC Folger
1909	*Midsummer Night's Dream, A* (Vitagraph)	Charles Kent J. Stuart Blackton	Billy Ranous, Maurice Costello, Florence Turner, Julia Swayne Gordon	*Silent Shakespeare* BFI DVD
1909	*Oliver Twist* (Vitagraph)	J. Stuart Blackton	Edith Storey William Humphrey Elita Proctor Otis	*Dickens Before Sound* BFI DVD
1909	*Othello / Otello* (FAI)	Gerolamo Lo Savio	Ferruccio Garavaglia Cesare Dondini Vittoria Lepanto Alberto Nepoti	LOC
1909	*Princess Nicotine / The Smoke Fairy* (Vitagraph)	J. Stuart Blackton	Gladys Hulette Paul Panzer	LOC
1909	*Saul and David* (Vitagraph)	J. Stuart Blackton	Maurice Costello Billy Ranous Florence Lawrence	BFI National Archive
1909	*Trovatore, Il* (FAI)	Louis J. Gasnier	Francesca Bertini Gemma Farina	presumed lost

Year	Title	Director	Cast	Availability
1909	*Way of the Cross, The* (Vitagraph)	J. Stuart Blackton	Rose Tapley Maurice Costello William Humphrey	BFI National Archive
1910 (1911?)	*Brutus* (Cines)	Enrico Guazzoni	Amleto Novelli ?	BFI National Archive/ Folger
1910	*Cupid and the Motorboat* (Vitagraph)	J. Stuart Blackton	John Bunny	presumed lost
1910	*Elektra* (Vitagraph)	J. Stuart Blackton	Maurice Costello Mary Fuller	presumed lost
1910	*Hamlet* (Barker)	William George Barker	Charles Raymond	presumed lost
1910	*Hamlet / Amleto* (Cines) (A reissue of the 1908 version)	Mario Caserini	Amleto Novelli Fernanda Negri Pouget	BFI National Archive/ CSC
1910	*Hamlet* (Nordisk)	August Blom	Alwin Neuss, Aage Hertel	presumed lost
1910	*King Lear / Re Lear* (FAI)	Gerolamo Lo Savio	Francesca Bertini Giannina Chiantoni	*Silent Shakespeare* BFI DVD
1910	*Lucrezia Borgia* (FAI)	Gerolamo Lo Savio	Vittoria Lepanto	presumed lost
1910	*Lunatic at Large, A* (Vitagraph)	unknown	Kenneth Casey	presumed lost
1910	*Merchant of Venice, The / Il Mercante di Venezia* (FAI)	Gerolamo Lo Savio	Francesca Bertini Olga Giannini Novelli Ermete Novelli	*Silent Shakespeare* BFI DVD
1910	*Romeo Turns Bandit / Roméo se fait bandit* (Pathé)	Romeo Bosetti	Max Linder Romeo Bosetti	*Othello* (1922) Kino Video DVD
1910	*Saved by the Flag* (Vitagraph)	Laurence Trimble	Ralf Ince, Edith Storey	presumed lost
1910	*Twelfth Night* (Vitagraph)	Charles Kent	Florence Turner Charles Kent Julia Swayne Gordon	*Silent Shakespeare* BFI DVD

Year	Title and production company	Director (or other production personnel)	Principal cast	Availability / status
1910	Winter's Tale, A (Thanhouser)	Barry O'Neil	Martin Faust Alfred Hanlon Amelia Barleon	Thanhouser DVD Vol.7 (Thanhouser Presents Shakespeare)
1911	Battle Hymn of the Republic, The (Vitagraph)	J. Stuart Blackton	Ralph Ince, Maurice Costello, Edith Storey	BFI National Archive
1911	Desdemona (Nordisk)	August Blom	Valdemar Psilander Thyra Reimann	Othello (1922) Kino Video DVD
1911	Henry VIII / Scenes from Shakespeare's King Henry VIII (Barker)	William George Barker	H. Beerbohm Tree Arthur Bourchier	destroyed
1911	Jealousy (Vitagraph)	unknown	Florence Turner	presumed lost
1911	Lady Godiva (Vitagraph)	J. Stuart Blackton	Julia Swayne Gordon	BFI National Archive
1911	Macbeth (Co-operative Cinematograph Company)	unknown	Constance Benson Frank Benson	presumed lost
1911	One Flag at Last (Vitagraph)	unknown	Earle Williams Rose Tapley	presumed lost
1911	Richard III (British Co-operative Cinematograph Company)	Frank Benson	Frank Benson	Silent Shakespeare BFI DVD
1911	Romeo and Juliet / Giulietta e Romeo (FAI)	Ugo Falena Geralmo Lo Savio	Gustavo Serena Francesca Bertini Ferruccio Garavaglia	LOC Folger
1911	Romeo and Juliet (Thanhouser)	Barry O'Neil	George Lessey Julia M. Taylor	Folger

Year	Title	Director	Cast	Status
1911	Subduing of Mrs Nag, The (Vitagraph)	George D. Baker	John Bunny, Flora Finch	presumed lost
1911	Tale of Two Cities, A (Vitagraph)	William Humphrey	Maurice Costello Florence Turner John Bunny	BFI National Archive
1911	Tempest, The (Thanhouser)	Edwin Thanhouser	Ed Genung Florence La Badie	presumed lost
1911	Tested by the Flag (Vitagraph)	unknown	Leo Delaney Edith Storey	presumed lost
1911	Vanity Fair (Vitagraph)	Charles Kent	Helen Gardner Harry Northrup	BFI National Archive
1911	Village King Lear, A / Le Roi Lear au Village (Gaumont)	Louis Feuillade	René Carl, Alice Tissot, Suzanne Grandais	LOC Folger
1912	Aida (FAI)	unknown	Bianca Lorenzoni Vigilio Frigerio	presumed lost
1912	As You Like It (Vitagraph)	J. Stuart Blackton Charles Kent	Maurice Costello, Rose Coghlan, Charles Kent	Folger
1912	Cardinal Wolsey (Henry VIII) (Vitagraph)	Laurence Trimble	Hal Reid Julia Swayne Gordon	BFI National Archive/ Folger
1912	Cleopatra (Helen Gardner Picture Players)	Charles L. Gaskill	Helen Gardner	presumed lost
1912	Illumination, The (Vitagraph)	Charles L. Gaskill	Tom Powers Helen Gardner	BFI National Archive
1912	Indian Romeo and Juliet, An (Vitagraph)	Laurence Trimble	Wallace Reid Florence Turner	presumed lost
1912	Jugend und Tollheit	Urban Gad	Asta Nielsen Hans Mierendorff Fritz Weidemann	presumed lost

Year	Title and production company	Director (or other production personnel)	Principal cast	Availability / status
1912	*Merchant of Venice, The* (Thanhouser)	Lucius Henderson	William Bowman Florence LaBadie	presumed lost
1912	*Musketeers of Pig Alley, The* (Biograph)	D. W. Griffith	Elmer Booth Lillian Gish	*D.W. Griffith – Years of Discovery* DVD
1912	*Richard III* (Shakespeare Film Company)	James Keane	Frederick Warde	*Richard III* Kino Video DVD
1912	*Sheriff Jim's Last Shot* (Vitagraph)	Rollin S. Sturgeon	unknown	presumed lost
1912	*Tempest, The* (Éclair)	Émile Chautard (?)	unknown	presumed lost
1912	*Too Much Wooing of Handsome Dan* (Vitagraph)	Rollin S. Sturgeon	George Stanley	presumed lost
1912	*Way of a Man with a Maid, The* (Vitagraph)	unknown	Maurice Costello Leah Baird	presumed lost
1912	*Wenn die Maske fällt* (Deutsche Bioscop)	Urban Gad	Asta Nielsen Fritz Weidemann	BFK
1913	*Cymbeline* (Thanhouser)	Frederick Sullivan	Florence LaBadie James Cruze	Thanhouser DVD Vol.7 (*Thanhouser Presents Shakespeare*)
1913	*Hamlet* (Gaumont-Hepworth)	Hay Plumb	Johnston Forbes-Robertson Gertrude Elliott	BFI National Archive/ Folger
1913	*He Fell in Love with His Mother-in-Law* (Vitagraph)	Bert Angeles	James Morrison Norma Talmadge	presumed lost

Year	Title	Director	Cast	Archive
1913	*Julius Caesar* (Edison Kinetophone)	unknown	unknown	presumed lost
1913	*Macbeth* (Film Industrie Gesellschaft)	Arthur Bourchier	Arthur Bourchier, Violet Vanbrugh	presumed lost
1913	*Student von Prag, Der* (Deutsche Bioscop)	Paul Wegener	Paul Wegener, John Gottowt	presumed lost
1913	*Suffragette, Die* (Bioscop-Union)	Urban Gad	Asta Nielsen	BFK/Deutsche Kinemathek (Berlin)
1913	*Winter's Tale, A / Una tragedia alla Corte di Sicilia* (Milano)	Baldassare Negroni	V. Cocchi, Pina Fabbri	BFI National Archive
1914	*Cabiria* (Itala Film)	Giovanni Pastrone	Carolina Catena, Lidia Quaranta	Kino Video DVD
1914	*Istruttoria, L'* (Cines)	Enrico Guazzoni	Mario Almirante, Ruggero Ruggeri	presumed lost
1914	*Julius Caesar / Cajus Julius Caesar* (Cines)	Enrico Guazzoni	Amleto Novelli, Gianna Terribili-Gonzales, Augusto Mastripietri	BFI National Archive/ LOC/Folger
1914	*Leone di Venezia, Il* (Ambrosio)	Luigi Maggi	Paolo Colaci, Lena Lenard	Cineteca Italiana (Milan)
1914	*Othello / Otello* (Ambrosio)	Arturo Ambrosio, Arrigo Frusta	Paolo Colaci, Riccardo Tolentino, Léna Lenard, Ubaldo Stefani	Cineteca di Bologna
1914	*Two Little Dromios* (Thanhouser)	unknown	Mignon Anderson, Riley Chamberlin	presumed lost
1914	*Zapatas Bande* (Projektions-AG, 'Union')	Urban Gad	Asta Nielsen	BFK
1915	*Battle Cry of Peace, The* (Vitagraph)	J. Stuart Blackton, Wilfrid North	Charles Richman, L. Rogers Lytton, James Morrison	presumed lost

Year	Title and production company	Director (or other production personnel)	Principal cast	Availability / status
1915	*Carmen* (Fox)	Raoul Walsh	Theda Bara, Einar Linden	presumed lost
1915	*Devil's Daughter, The* (Fox)	Frank Powell	Theda Bara, Paul Doucet	presumed lost
1915	*Fool There Was, A* (Fox)	Frank Powell	Theda Bara, Edward José	DVD
1915	*Hilda of the Slums* (Vitagraph)	Unknown	William Burke Natalie De Lonton	presumed lost
1915	*Lulu* (Monopol)	Augusto Genina	Ruggero Ruggeri Tilde Teldi	presumed lost
1915	*Seashore Romeo, A* (Rex)	Ben F. Wilson	Ben F. Wilson Dorothy Phillips	presumed lost
1915	*Sin* (Fox)	Herbert Brenon	Theda Bara William E. Shay	presumed lost
1915	*Siren of Hell* (Fox)	Raoul Walsh	Theda Bara	presumed lost
1915	*Sottomarino 27, Il* (Cines)	Nino Oxilia	Ruggero Ruggeri	presumed lost
1915	*When Hungry Hamlet Fled* (Thanhouser)	Unknown	Harry Benham Claude Cooper	BFI National Archive
1916	*Freddy versus Hamlet* (Vitagraph)	Frank Currier	William Dangman Daisy Devere	presumed lost
1916	*Hamlet Made Over* (Lubin)	Earl Metcalfe	Clarence Elmer Billie Reeves	presumed lost
1916	*King Lear* (Thanhouser)	Ernest Warde	Frederick Warde Ernest Warde	Thanhouser DVD Vol.7 (*Thanhouser Presents Shakespeare*)

Year	Title	Director	Cast	BFI National Archive/Deutsche Kinemathek (Berlin)
1916	*Liebes-ABC, Das* (Neutral-Film)	Magnus Stifter	Asta Nielsen	
1916	*Macbeth* (Éclair)	unknown	Séverin-Mars, Georgette Leblanc	presumed lost
1916	*Macbeth* (Triangle-Reliance)	John Emerson	Herbert Beerbohm Tree, Constance Collier	presumed lost
1916	*Master Shakespeare, Strolling Player* (Thanhouser)	Frederick Sullivan	Florence La Badie, Robert Vaughn	presumed lost
1916	*Merchant of Venice, The* (Broadwest) [2 reels out of the original 5 survive]	Walter West	Matheson Lang, Hutin Britton, J.R. Tozer	BFI National Archive/Folger
1916	*Pimple as Hamlet* (Piccadilly)	Fred Evans	Fred Evans	presumed lost
1916	*Real Thing at Last, The* (Bushey Heath Co.)	James Barrie, L.C. MacBean	A.E. Matthews, Edmund Gwenn, Godfrey Tearle, Nelson Keys, Gladys Cooper	presumed lost
1916	*Romeo and Juliet* (Fox)	J. Gordon Edwards	Theda Bara, Harry Hilliard	presumed lost
1916	*Romeo and Juliet* (Metro)	John W. Noble	Beverly Bayne, Francis X. Bushman	presumed lost
1916	*Romeo of the Coal Wagon* (Kalem)	William Beaudine	Freddie Fralick, Gus Leonard	presumed lost
1916	*To Be or Not to Be* (Beauty)	Ed Watt	John Gough, Orral Humphrey	presumed lost
1916	*Tugboat Romeo, A* (Keystone)	William Campbell	Chester Conklin, Marie Manley	presumed lost

Year	Title and production company	Director (or other production personnel)	Principal cast	Availability / status
1916	*Villainous Villain, A* (Vitagraph)	Larry Semon	Patsy De Forest William Shea	presumed lost
1917	*Barnyard Hamlet, The* (Powers)	W. E. Stark	unknown	presumed lost
1917	*Bullies and Bullets* (Vitagraph)	Larry Semon	Hughie Mack Patsy De Forest	presumed lost
1917	*Hamlet / Amleto* (Rodolfi-Film)	Eleuterio Rodolfi	Ruggero Ruggeri Elena Makowska	Cineteca di Bologna
1917	*Masks and Faces* (Ideal)	Fred Paul	Johnston Forbes-Robertson Irene Vanbrugh	BFI National Archive
1917	*Noisy Naggers and Nosy Neighbors* (Vitagraph)	Larry Semon	Larry Semon Florence Curtis	presumed lost
1917	*Womanhood, the Glory of the Nation* (Vitagraph)	J. Stuart Blackton	Alice Joyce Harry T. Morey	presumed lost
1918	*Passing of the Third Floor Back, The* (First National Pictures)	Herbert Brenon	Johnston Forbes-Robertson Molly Pearson	presumed lost
1919	*Dance of Death, The/ Der Totentanz* (Helios Film)	Fritz Lang Otto Rippert	Werner Krauss Sascha Gura	presumed lost
1919	*Oh 'Phelia* (Hepworth)	Anson Dyer	[Animation]	BFI National Archive
1919	*On with the Motley / Amleto e il suo Clown* (Lucio D'Ambra)	Carmino Gallone	Soave Gallone	presumed lost

Year	Title	Director	Cast	Availability
1920	Cabinet of Dr Caligari, The / Das Cabinet des Dr Caligari (Decla-Bioscop)	Robert Wiene	Werner Krauss, Conrad Veidt	DVD
1920	Hamlet: Drama of Vengeance (Art-Film)	Svend Gade, Heinz Schall	Asta Nielsen, Heinz Stieda, Eduard von Winterstein	BFI National Archive/ Folger/ DIF (colour print)
1920	Januskopf, Der (Lipow)	F. W. Murnau	Conrad Veidt, Magnus Stifter	presumed lost
1920	Othello (Hepworth)	Anson Dyer	[Animation]	BFI National Archive
1920	Taming of the Shrew, The (Pickford Corp. and Elton Corp. – Released by United Artists)	Sam Taylor	Douglas Fairbanks, Mary Pickford	DVD
1920	Wandernde Bild, Das (May)	Fritz Lang	Mia May, Hans Marr	presumed lost
1921	Brothers Karamazov, The / Die Brüder Karamasoff (Maxim-Film)	Dimitri Buchowetzki, Carl Frölich	Emil Jannings, Werner Krauss	presumed lost
1921	Danton (Wörner-Filmgesellschaft)	Dimitri Buchowetzki	Emil Jannings, Werner Krauss	presumed lost
1922	Merchant of Venice, The (Masters Films)	Challis Sanderson	Sybil Thorndike, Ivan Berlyn	presumed lost
1922	Nosferatu (Jofa-Atelier Berlin-Johannisthal)	F.W. Murnau	Max Schreck, Gustav von Wangenheim, Greta Schröder	DVD
1922	Othello (Wörner-Filmgesellschaft)	Dimitri Buchowetzki	Emil Jannings, Werner Krauss, Ica von Lenkeffy	Kino Video DVD
1923	Jew of Mestri, The / Der Kaufmann von Venedig (Peter Paul Felner-Film)	Peter Paul Felner	Werner Krauss, Hans Brausewetter, Carl Ebert	BFI National Archive/ Folger

Year	Title and production company	Director (or other production personnel)	Principal cast	Availability / status
1925	*Midsummer Night's Dream, A* / *Ein Sommernachtstraum* / *Wood Love* (Neumann-Filmproduktion)	Hans Neumann	Tamara Geva Werner Krauss Theodore Becker	presumed lost
1926	*Student von Prag, Der* (Sokal-Film)	Henrik Galeen	Conrad Veidt Werner Krauss	DVD
1927	*Metropolis* (Universum Film)	Fritz Lang	Alfred Abel, Theodor Loos, Brigitte Helm	DVD
1930	*Blue Angel, The* / *Der Blaue Engel* (Universum Film)	Josef von Sternberg	Emil Jannings Marlene Dietrich	DVD
1936	*As You Like It* (Inter-Allied)	Paul Czinner	Laurence Olivier	DVD
1940	*Jud Süß* (Terra-Filmkunst)	Veit Harlan	Ferdinand Marian Werner Krauss	DVD
1995	*Othello* (Castle Rock)	Oliver Parker	Laurence Fishburne Kenneth Branagh Irène Jacob	DVD
1996	*William Shakespeare's Romeo + Juliet* (Bazmark Films)	Baz Luhrmann	Leonardo DiCaprio Claire Danes	DVD
2001	*Othello* (Canadian Broadcasting Corporation)	Geoffrey Sax (script Andrew Davies)	Eamonn Walker Christopher Eccleston Keeley Hawes	DVD
2004	*Merchant of Venice, The* (Spice Factory in association with the UK Film Council)	Michael Radford	Al Pacino Jeremy Irons Joseph Fiennes	DVD

Bibliography

SELECTED UNPUBLISHED MATERIALS

Archive of the Bethlem Royal Hospital
Line-drawn magic lantern slides (Box A07/1).

Folger Shakespeare Library (Washington DC)
The Robert Hamilton Ball Collection including Ball's extensive hand-written card catalogue and miscellaneous correspondence and notes.
Annotated prompt copies of Charles Kean and Herbert Beerbohm Tree stage productions.

George Eastman House (Rochester, NY)
Line-drawn and artistically coloured magic lantern slides, many from the Louis Walton Sipley Collection.

Interview transcript
Transcript of author's interview with Paata Tsikurishvili and Nathan Weinberger of Synetic Theater, 18 April 2007, Arlington, Virginia.

The Magic Lantern Society's Slide Readings Library
Nineteenth-century lantern scripts for *The Seven Ages of Man* and *Romeo and Juliet*.

The Motion Picture, Broadcasting and Recorded Sound Division of the Library of Congress (Washington DC)
Many copyright deposit materials for silent films, including:
- *Romeo and Juliet* (Fox, 1916): typed continuity script (77 loose pages). 'Romeo and Juliet. A Photoplay in Seven Parts. Adapted for the Screen by Adrian Johnson. Directed by J. Gordon Edwards for the Fox Film Corporation. William Fox President'. Copyright registered LP 9376 (23 October 1916).
- *Richard III* (1912) copyright deposit file. Copyright registered CIL 1299 (9 September 1913).

The Palace Theatre Archive (London)
The Palace Theatre of Varieties Programme (25 September 1899). ('Theatre Programmes: American Biograph 1897–1902'.)

PhD dissertation
Barber, Xenophon Theodore, *Evenings of Wonders: A History of the Magic Lantern Show in America* (Unpublished PhD dissertation, New York University, 1993).

Private collections
  Postcards, star cards, theatre programmes, moving picture programmes, lantern slides, photographs, stills, trade papers and miscellaneous film memorabilia from the collections of private individuals, named in the appropriate places in the book.

The Theatre Museum, Covent Garden (London)
  Stage production and theatre files, including:
  – Tree *King John* production file
  – Tree *The Tempest* production file
  – The Princess's Theatre file

The Tree Archive, University of Bristol Theatre Collection (Bristol)
  Materials related to Herbert Beerbohm Tree's stage productions of *King John* and *The Tempest*, including the Fly Plot for *King John*.

WEB RESOURCES

(availability confirmed, March 2008)

Conversion tables of 'the Fed'
  (for equivalents contemporary sums) from the Federal Reserve Bank of Minneapolis: http://woodrow.mpls.frb.fed.us/research/data/us/calc/.

Photographic images of works of art
  Hans Makart's painting 'Romeo and Juliet' (late 1860s?): www.photographersdirect.com/buyers/stockphoto.asp?imageid=657464
  Jean-Léon Gérôme's painting 'The Death of Caesar' (1867): www.zazzle.com/the_death_of_caesar_by_jean_leon_gerome_print-228564908681002278
  Carl Ludwig Friedrich Becker's steel engraving 'Othello Before the Senators' (1892): www.thelostleaf.com/detail.asp?artID=119

Reviews posted online, including:
  Chris Hastings and Catherine Milner, 'Hollywood rivals battle to bring The Merchant of Venice to screen', *Telegraph* (16 August 2003). Consulted online at: www.telegraph.co.uk/news/main.jhtml?xml=%2Fnews%2F2003%2F08%2F17%2Fwshakes17.xml
  Nicholas F. Benton, 'A "Macbeth" With All the Moves, None of the Words', *Falls Church News-Press* (Thursday, 18 January 2007). Consulted online at: www.fcnp.com/news/a_macbeth_with_all_the_moves_none_of_the_words_20070118.html.
  Michael Toscano, 'Body Language Speaks Volumes in Silent "Hamlet"', *The Washington Post* (23 October 2003). Consulted online at: www.georgiaemb.org/DisplayMedia.asp?id=234.

SHAKSPER [sic] postings:
  'Wordless Macbeth' Postings from Normal D. Hinton and Peter Holland on *SHAKSPER [sic]: The Global Electronic Shakespeare Conference* (online postings, 18 January 2007). www.shaksper.net/archives/2007/0044.html

Synetic Theater Company
www.classika.org/Synetic/about.html
Terry Borton's forthcoming book
  Cinema before Film: Victorian Magic Lantern Shows and America's First Great Screen Artist, Joseph Boggs Beale. Excerpts posted at: www.magiclanternshows. com/filmhistory.htm.

BOOKS

Abel, Richard (ed.), *Encyclopedia of Early Cinema* (Abingdon and NY: Routledge, 2005).
  and Altman, Richard (eds.), *The Sounds of Early Cinema* (Bloomington: Indiana University Press, 2001).
Anthony, Barry, *The Kinora: Motion Pictures for the Home, 1896–1914* (Hastings: The Projection Box, 1996).
Anzi, Anna Cavallone, *Shakespeare Nei Teatri Milanesi Del Novecento (1904–1978)* (Bari: Adriatica Editrice, 1980).
Archer, William and Lowe, Robert, *The Fashionable Tragedian* (Edinburgh: Thomas Gray and Company, 1877).
Aubert, Charles, *L'Art Mimique Suivi d'un Traité de la Pantomime* (Paris: Meuriot, 1901). *The Art of Pantomime*, trans. Edith Sears (NY: Henry Holt, 1927).
Auster, Paul, *The Book of Illusions* (London: Faber, 2002).

Ball, Robert Hamilton, *Shakespeare on Silent Film: A Strange Eventful History* (NY: Theatre Arts Books, 1968).
Bardèche, Maurice and Brasillach, Robert, *The History of Motion Pictures,* trans. and ed. Iris Barry (NY: W. W. Norton and the Museum of Modern Art, 1938). Original French edn., *Histoire du Cinéma* (Paris, 1935).
Barry, Iris, *Let's Go to the Pictures* (London: Chatto and Windus, 1926).
Bartholomeusz, Dennis, *The Winter's Tale in Performance in England and America 1611–1976* (Cambridge University Press, 1982).
Bartalotta, Gianfranco, *Amleto in Italia Nel Novecento* (Bari: Adriatica Editrice, 1986).
Bate, Jonathan and Jackson, Russell (eds.), *Shakespeare: An Illustrated Stage History* (Oxford University Press, 1996).
Beerbohm, Max, *Herbert Beerbohm Tree* (London: Hutchinson, n.d.). The Bodleian lists the first edition as '1920'.
Bingham, Madeleine, *The Great Lover: The Life and Art of Herbert Beerbohm Tree* (London: Hamish Hamilton, 1978).
Blackton Trimble, Marian, *J. Stuart Blackton: A Personal Biography by his Daughter* (Metuchen, New Jersey and London: Scarecrow Press, 1985).
Booth, Michael R., *Victorian Spectacular Theatre 1850–1910* (London: Routledge, 1981).
Bordwell, David, *On the History of Film Style* (Cambridge, Mass. and London: Harvard University Press, 1997).
  Staiger, Janet and Thompson, Kristin, *The Classical Hollywood Cinema: Film Style and mode of Production to 1960* (NY: Columbia University Press, 1985).

Boose, Lynda E. and Burt, Richard (eds.), *Shakespeare the Movie: Popularizing the Plays on Film, TV and Video* (London: Routledge, 1997).

Bowser, Eileen, *The Transformation of Cinema 1907–1915* (NY: Scribner, 1990).

Bragaglia, Leonardo, *Ruggero Ruggeri in sessantacinque anni di storia del teatro rappresentato* (Roma: Trevi Editore, 1968).

Brewster, Ben and Jacobs, Lea, *Theatre to Cinema* (Oxford University Press, 1997).

Bristol, Michael, D., *Shakespeare's America/America's Shakespeare* (London and NY: Routledge, 1990).

Brown, Richard and Anthony, Barry, *A Victorian Film Enterprise: The History of the British Mutoscope and Biograph Company, 1897–1915* (Trowbridge: Flicks Books, 1999).

Browne, Van Dyke, *Secrets of Scene Painting and Stage Effects* (London: Routledge, 1913).

Buchanan, Judith, *Shakespeare on Film* (Harlow: Longman-Pearson, 2005).

Bulman, James C. (ed.), *Shakespeare, Theory and Performance* (London and NY: Routledge, 1996).

Burrows, Jon, *Legitimate Cinema: Theatre Stars in Silent British Films 1908–1918* (University of Exeter Press, 2003).

Cardullo, Bert, Gottesman, Ronald and Woods, Leigh (eds.), *Playing to the Camera: Film Actors Discuss Their Craft* (NY and London: Yale University Press, 1998).

Cavell, Stanley, *The World Viewed: Reflections on the Ontology of Film* (NY: The Viking Press, 1971).

Chanan, Michael, *The Dream that Kicks: the Pre-History and Early Years of Cinema in Britain* (London and NY: Routledge, 1996).

Christie, Ian, *The Last Machine: Early Cinema and the Birth of the Modern World* (London: BBC/BFI, 1994).

Coleridge, S. T., *Shakespeare Criticism*, 2 vols (ed.) T. M. Raysor (London: J.M. Dent, 1960).

Collick, John, *Shakespeare, Cinema, and Society* (Manchester University Press, 1989).

Cook, Olive, *Movement in Two Dimensions* (London: Hutchinson, 1963).

Cosandey, R., Gaudreault, A. and Gunning, T. (eds.), *Une Invention du Diable? Cinéma des Premiers Temps et Religion* (Sainte-Foy: Les Presses de l'Université Laval, 1992).

Cran, Mrs George, *Herbert Beerbohm Tree* (London: John Lane, The Bodley Head, 1907).

Crompton, Dennis, Henry, David and Herbert, Stephen (eds.), *Magic Images: The Art of Hand-Painted and Photographic Lantern Slides* (London: MLS, 1990).

Darley, Felix Octavius Carr, *The Darley Gallery of Shakespearean Illustrations* (NY, Philadelphia: J. M. Stoddart, 1884).

Davies, Anthony and Wells, Stanley (eds.), *Shakespeare and the Moving Image* (Cambridge University Press, 1994).

Dickson, William Kennedy-Laurie and Dickson, Antonia, *History of the Kinetograph, Kinetoscope and Kineto-phonograph* (NY: Albert Bunn, 1895). Facsimile edition (NY: Museum of Modern Art, 2000).

Dobson, Michael, *The Making of the National Poet: Shakespeare, Adaptation and Authorship, 1660–1769* (Oxford: Clarendon, 1992).

Donohue, Joseph, *Theatre in the Age of Kean* (Oxford: Basil Blackwell, 1975).

Downer, Alan S., *The Eminent Tragedian: William Charles Macready* (Cambridge, Mass.: Harvard University Press, 1966).

Eckert, Charles W. (ed.), *Focus on Shakespearean Film* (Englewood Cliffs: Prentice-Hall, 1972).

Elliston, Robert William, *The History, Murders, Life, and Death of Macbeth: and a full description of the scenery, action, choruses, and characters of the Ballet of Action, of that name, as performed with enthusiastic Applause, to overflowing Houses, a Number of Nights, at the Royal Circus, St. George's Fields, London; with the Occasional Address, spoken by Mr. Elliston; And every Information, to simplify the Plot; and enable the Visitors of the Circus, to comprehend this matchless Piece of Pantomimic and Choral Performance* (London, 1809).

Elsaesser, Thomas (ed.), *Early Cinema: Space, Frame, Narrative* (London: BFI, 1990).

Fitzgerald, Percy H., *Principles of Comedy and Dramatic Effect* (London: Tinsley Brothers, 1870).

Fitzsimmons, Linda and Street, Sarah (eds.), *Moving Performance: British Stage and Screen, 1890s–1920s* (Trowbridge: Flicks Books, 2000).

Forbes-Robertson, Johnston, *A Player Under Three Reigns* (Boston: Little, Brown, 1925).

Hamlet by William Shakespeare as arranged for the stage by Forbes Robertson and presented at the Lyceum Theatre on Saturday, September 11, 1897 (London: Nassau Press, 1897).

Foulkes, Richard (ed.), *Shakespeare and the Victorian Stage* (Cambridge University Press, 1986).

Performing Shakespeare in the Age of Empire (Cambridge University Press, 2002).

Fullerton, John (ed.), *Celebrating the Centenary of Cinema, 1895* (Sydney and London: John Libbey and Co. Ltd, 1998).

Garcia, Gustave, *The Actors' Art: A Practical Treatise on Stage Declamation, Public Speaking and Deportment, for the Use of Artists, Students and Amateurs* (London: T. Pettitt, 1882).

Gardner, Viv and Rutherford, Susan (eds.), *The New Woman and Her Sisters: Feminism and Theatre 1850–1914* (Ann Arbor: University of Michigan Press, 1992).

Garrett, John (ed.), *Talking of Shakespeare* (NY: Hodder and Stoughton, 1954).

Gaudreault, André, *Du Littéraire au filmique: système du récit* (Paris: Meridians Klinksieck, 1988).

Goetz, Wolfgang, *Werner Krauss* (Hamburg: Hoffmann und Campe Verlag, 1954).

Gollancz, Israel (ed.), *A Book of Homage to Shakespeare* (Oxford University Press, 1916).

Graham, Arthur, *Shakespeare in Opera, Ballet, Orchestral Music and Song: An Introduction to Music Inspired by the Bard* (Lampeter: Edwin Mellen Press, 1997).

Grieveson, Lee and Krämer, Peter (eds.), *The Silent Film Reader* (London and NY: Routledge, 2004).

Grillo, Ernesto, *Shakespeare and Italy* (Glasgow University Press, 1949).

Gunning, Tom, *D. W. Griffith and the Origins of American Narrative Film* (Urbana and Chicago: University of Illinois Press, 1991).

Halio, Jay L., *A Midsummer Night's Dream: Shakespeare in Performance* (Manchester University Press, 1994).

Hammerton, J. A., *Barrie: The Story of a Genius* (NY: Sampson Law, 1929).

Harbage, Alfred, *Shakespeare Without Words and Other Essays* (Cambridge, Mass.: Harvard University Press, 1972).

Hazlitt, William, *Characters of Shakespeare's Plays* (Cambridge University Press, 1915).

Heard, Mervyn, *Phantasmagoria: The Secret Life of the Magic Lantern* (Hastings: The Projection Box, 2006).

Henderson, Diana E. (ed.), *A Concise Companion to Shakespeare on Screen* (Oxford: Blackwell, 2006).

Henson, Leslie, *My Laugh Story. The Story of My Life: Up to Date* (London: Hodder and Stoughton, n.d.). The Bodleian catalogue lists '1926?' as publication date.

Hepworth, Cecil, *Came the Dawn: Memories of a Film Pioneer* (London: Phoenix House, 1951).

Herbert, Stephen and McKernan, Luke (eds.), *Who's Who of Victorian Cinema* (London: BFI, 1996).

Hertogs, Daan and de Klerk, Nico (eds.), *Disorderly Order: Colours in Silent Film* (Amsterdam: Stichting Nederlands Filmmuseum, 1996).

Hill, Aaron, *The Art of Acting; in which the dramatic passions are properly defined and described . . . to which is prefixed The Actor's Epitome, a poem by the above author* (London: J. Smelton, 1801).

Hoenselaars, A. J. (ed.), *Reclamations of Shakespeare* (Amsterdam and Atlanta: Rodopi, 1994).

Hollows, Joanne, Hutchings, Peter and Jancovich, Mark (eds.), *The Film Studies Reader* (London: Hodder Arnold, 2000).

House, M., Storey, G., Tillotson, K. et al. (eds.), *The British Academy Pilgrim Edition of the Letters of Charles Dickens*, vol. III (Oxford: Clarendon Press, 1974).

Howard, Camille Cole, *The Staging of Shakespeare's 'Romeo and Juliet' as a Ballet* (Lampeter: Edwin Mellen Press, 1992).

Howard, Tony, *Women as Hamlet: Performance and Interpretation in Theatre, Film and Fiction* (Cambridge University Press, 2007).

Hughes-Hallett, Lucy, *Cleopatra: History, Dreams and Distortions* (London and NY: Harper and Row, 1990).

Ihering, Herbert, *Werner Krauss: Ein Schauspieler und das Neunzehnte Jahrhundert* (Berlin: Verlag Vorwerk 8, 1997).

Irace, Kathleen O., *The First Quarto of Hamlet* (Cambridge University Press, 1998).

Jackson, Russell (ed.), *The Cambridge Companion to Shakespeare on Film* (Cambridge University Press, 2000).

Jannings, Emil, *Theater-Film – Das Leben und ich* (Berchtesgaden: Verlag Zimmer & Herzog, 1941).

Jorgens, Jack, *Shakespeare on Film* (Bloomington: Indiana University Press, 1977).

Kean, Charles, *Shakespeare's Play of The Tempest, Arranged for Representation at the Princess's Theatre ... by Charles Kean, F.S.A. ...* (London, 1857).

Keil, Charlie, *Early American Cinema in Transition: story, style and filmmaking, 1907–1913* (University of Wisconsin Press, 2001).

Kennedy, Dennis, *Looking at Shakespeare: A Visual History of Twentieth Century Performance* (Cambridge University Press, 1993).

Kitchin, Laurence, *Drama in the Sixties: Form and Interpretation* (London: Faber, 1966).

Klein, Holger and Daphinoff, Dimiter (eds.), *Hamlet on Screen* Shakespeare Yearbook v. 8 (Lancaster: Edwin Mellen Press, 1997).

and Marrapodi, Michele (eds.), *Shakespeare and Italy* Shakespeare Yearbook v. 10 (Lancaster: Edwin Mellen Press, 2001).

Kliman, Bernice W., *Hamlet: Film, Television and Audio Performance* (Rutherford: Farleigh Dickinson University Press, 1988).

Knight, Joseph, *Theatrical Notes* (London: Lawrence and Bullen, 1893).

Krauss, Werner, *Das Schauspiel meines Lebens* (Stuttgart: Henry Goverts Verlag, 1958).

Latham, Robert and Matthews, William (eds.), *The Diary of Samuel Pepys*, v.VII '1666' (London: G. Bell and Sons, 1972).

Leisegang, Franz Paul, *Dates and Sources: A Contribution to the History of the Art of Projection and Cinematography* (London: MLS, 1988).

Levenson, Michael (ed.), *The Cambridge Companion to Modernism* (Cambridge University Press, 1999).

Levine, Lawrence W., *Highbrow/Lowbrow: The Emergence of Cultural Hierarchy in America* (Cambridge, Mass.: Harvard University Press, 1988).

Lindsay, Vachel, *The Art of the Moving Picture* first published 1915, revised edition 1922 (NY: Liveright, 1970).

Lippman, Max (ed.), *Shakespeare im Film* (Wiesbaden: Deutsches Institut für Filmkunde, 1964).

Lowrey, Carolyn, *The First One Hundred Noted Men and Women of the Screen* (NY: Moffat, Yard and Company, 1920).

McCormick, Richard W., *Gender and Sexuality in Weimar Modernity: Film, Literature and 'New Objectivity'* (NY: Palgrave, 2001).

Mackail, Denis, *The Story of J. M. Barrie: A Biography* (London: Peter Davies, 1941).

McKernan, Luke and Terris, Olwin (eds.) *Walking Shadows: Shakespeare in the National Film and Television Archive* (London: BFI, 1994).

McKernan, Luke and Tempel, Mark van den (eds.), *The Wonders of the Biograph*, special issue Griffithiana (2000).

Macleod, Mary, *The Shakespeare Story-book* (London: Wells, Gardner, Darton & Co., 1902).

Macready, William Charles, *Reminiscences and Selections from his Diary and Letters*, 2 vols., edited by F. Pollock (London, 1875).

Mannoni, Laurent, *The Great Art of Light and Shadow: Archaeology of the Cinema* (University of Exeter Press, 2000).

Manvell, Roger, *Shakespeare and the Film* (London: J.M. Dent and Sons, 1971).

   Theater and Film: A Comparative Study of the Two Forms of Dramatic Art, and the Problems of Adaptation of Stage Plays into Film (Rutherford: Farleigh Dickinson University Press, 1979).

Manzini, Amerigo, *Gli uomini del giorno* n. 35, 'Ruggeri' (Milan: Casa Edittrice Italiana, 1920).

Marcus, Leah, *Unediting the Renaissance: Shakespeare, Marlowe, Milton* (London and NY: Routledge, 1996).

Martineau, Jane (ed.), *Victorian Fairy Painting* (London: Royal Academy of Arts, 1997).

   et al., *Shakespeare in Art* (London and NY: Merrell, 2003).

Matthews, A. E., *Matty: An Autobiography* (London: Hutchinson, 1952).

Mills, John A., *Hamlet on Stage: The Great Tradition* (Westport, Connecticut and London: Greenwood, 1985).

Moncrieff, William Thomas, *Rochester; or King Charles the Second's Merry Days. A Musical Comedy* (London, 1828).

   Tom and Jerry; or Life in London, 2nd edn. (London: Richardson, 1828).

Moody, Jane, *Illegitimate Theatre in London, 1770–1840* (Cambridge University Press, 2000).

   and O'Quinn, Daniel (eds.), *The Cambridge Companion to British Theatre, 1730–1830* (Cambridge University Press, 2007)

Morley, Sheridan, *Tales from the Hollywood Raj: The British, the Movies, and Tinseltown* (NY: Viking, 1983).

Mühr, Alfred, *Die Welt des Schauspieler Werner Krauss* (Berlin: Brunnen-Verlag, 1928).

Musser, Charles, *The Emergence of Cinema: The American Screen to 1907* (NY: Simon Schuster and Prentice-Hall, 1990).

   High-Class Moving Pictures (Princeton University Press, 1991).

Nagler, A. M., *A Source Book in Theatrical History* (NY: Dover, 1952).

Newton, H. Chance, *Cues and Curtain Calls, Being the Theatrical Reminiscences of H. Chance Newton* (London: John Lane, 1927).

Nichol, Allardyce, *Film and Theatre* (London: George G. Harrap, 1936).

Nicholson, Watson, *The Struggle for a Free Stage in London* (Boston and NY: Houghton, Mifflin and Co., 1906).

Nielsen, Asta, *Die Schweigende Muse*, German edn. (Munich: Wilhelm Heyne Verlag, 1979).

Niver, Kemp R. (ed.), *Biograph Bulletins 1896–1908* (Los Angeles: Locare Research Group, 1971).

Nuttall, A. D., *Shakespeare the Thinker* (New Haven and London: Yale University Press, 2007).

Odell, George C. D., *Shakespeare from Betterton to Irving*, 2 vols (London: Constable, 1921).

Orwell, George, *Collected Essays, Journalism and Letters* v.4 (1945–1950), Sonia Orwell and Ian Angus (eds.) (London: Secker and Warburg, 1968).

Panofsky, Erwin, *Three Essays on Style* (ed.) Irving Lavin (Cambridge, Mass. and London: MIT Press, 1997).

Park, James, *British Cinema: the Lights that Failed* (London: Batsford, 1990).

Patterson, Richard S. and Dougall, Richardson, *The Eagle and the Shield: A History of the Great Seal of the United States* (Honolulu, Hawaii: University Press of the Pacific, 2005).

Pearson, Hesketh, *Beerbohm Tree: His Life and Laughter* (London: Methuen, 1956).

Pearson, Roberta E., *Eloquent Gestures: The Transformation of Performance Style in the Griffith Biograph Films* (Berkeley, Los Angeles and Oxford: University of California Press, 1992).

and Uricchio, William, *Reframing Culture: the Case of the Vitagraph Quality Films* (Princeton University Press, 1993).

Pecor, Charles Joseph, *The Magician and the American Stage* (Washington D.C.: Emerson and West, 1977).

Petro, Patrice, *Joyless Streets: Women and Melodramatic Representation in Weimar Germany* (Princeton University Press, 1989).

Platt, Agnes, *Practical Hints on Acting for the Cinema* (London: Stanley Paul, 1921).

Prothero, Rowland E. (ed.), *The Works of Lord Byron: Letters and Journals* vol.II (London: John Murray, 1898).

Rainey, Lawrence (ed.), *Modernism: An Anthology* (Oxford: Blackwells, 2005).

Raymond, George, *Memoirs of Robert William Elliston, Comedian* (London, 1857).

Rees, Terence, *Theatre Lighting in the Age of Gas* (London: Society for Theatre Research, 1978).

Robinson, David (ed.), *The Lantern Image* (London: MLS, 1993).

From Peepshow to Palace: the Birth of American Film (NY: Columbia University Press, 1996).

Rothwell, Kenneth S., *A History of Shakespeare on Screen* (Cambridge University Press, 1999).
'Early Shakespeare Movies: How the Spurned Spawned Art,' ISA Occasional Paper No.8 (Chipping Campden: Clouds Hill Printers, 2000).
and Annabelle Henkin Melzer, *Shakespeare on Screen: An International Filmography and Videography* (London: Mansell, NY: Neal-Schuman, 1990).

Sadoul, Georges, *Le Cinéma Devient un Art: L'Avant-Guerre* (Paris: Denoël, 1951), vol. III of Sadoul, *L'Histoire Générale du Cinéma* 6 vols (Paris: Denoël, 1950–1975).
Seydel, Renate, Hagedorff, Allan and Meier, Bernd, *Asta Nielsen: Ihr Leben in Fotodokumenten, Selbstzeugnissen und zeitgenössischen Betrachtungen* (Berlin: Henschelverlag, 1981).
Shakespeare, William, *Hamlet by William Shakespeare: As Arranged for the Stage by Forbes-Robertson and Presented at the Lyceum Theatre on Saturday September 11, 1897* (London: Nassau Press, 1897).
Shakespeare, William, *Hamlet* (Shakespeare in Production) (ed.) Robert Hapgood (Cambridge University Press, 1999).
Shakespeare's Hamlet: The Story of the Play Concisely Told. Produced in Conjunction with the Cinematograph Film Showing Sir J. Forbes-Robertson and Miss Gertrude Elliott and their Full Company from Drury Lane Theatre with 55 Illustrations Taken from the Film (London: Stanley Paul and Co, 1913).
Shapiro, James, *1599: A Year in the Life of William Shakespeare* (London: Faber, 2005).
Shattuck, Charles H., *Shakespeare on the American Stage: from Booth and Barrett to Sothern and Marlowe* vol.II (Washington DC: Folger Shakespeare Library, 1987).
Showalter, Elaine, *The Female Malady: Women, Madness, and English Culture, 1830–1980* (London: Virago, 1987).
Slide, Anthony, *The Big V: A History of the Vitagraph Company* (Metuchen, N.J.: The Scarecrow Press, 1976).
Smith, Albert E., *Two Reels and a Crank: From Nickelodeon to Picture Palace* (Garden City, NY: Doubleday, 1952).
Sillars, Stuart, *Painting Shakespeare: the Artist as Critic 1720–1820* (Cambridge University Press, 2006).
Stam, Robert and Raengo, Alessandra (eds.), *A Companion to Literature and Film* (Oxford: Blackwell, 2004).
Summers, Montague, *Shakespeare Adaptations* (London: J. Cape, 1922).

Taranow, G., *The Bernhardt Hamlet: Culture and Context* (NY: Peter Lang, 1996).
Taylor, Gary, *Reinventing Shakespeare: A Cultural History from the Restoration to the Present* (London: Vintage, 1991).
Taylor, George, *Players and Performances in the Victorian Theatre* (Manchester University Press, 1989).

Tosi, Virgilio, *Cinema before Cinema: The Origins of Scientific Cinematography* (London: BUFVC, 2005).

Tree, Herbert Beerbohm, *Hamlet from an actor's prompt book: the substance of a lecture delivered by Herbert Beerbohm Tree to the Wolverhampton Literary Society, October 1895, and published in the 'Fortnightly Review', December 1895* (London: Nassau Press, 1897).

The Tempest: As Arranged for the Stage by Herbert Beerbohm Tree, Souvenir Edition of The Tempest for the 50th performance in the run (London, 1904).

The Tempest: A Descriptive Theatre Programme, His Majesty's Theatre (London, 1904).

Some Notes on A Midsummer Night's Dream, produced at His Majesty's Theatre (for the second time) on Easter Monday, April 17th, 1911, by Sir Herbert Beerbohm Tree (London, 1911).

Thoughts and Afterthoughts, 3rd edn. (London: Cassell, 1915).

Trewin, J.C., *Shakespeare on the English Stage: 1900–1964* (London: Barrie and Rokcliff, 1964).

A Tribute to the Genius of William Shakespeare being the programme of a performance at Drury Lane Theatre on May 2, 1916, the tercentenary of his death (London: Macmillan, 1916).

Usai, Paolo Cherchi, *Vitagraph Company of America: il cinema prima di Hollywood* (Pordenone: Edizioni Studio Tesi, 1987).

Burning Passions: An Introduction to the Study of Silent Cinema (London: BFI, 1994).

Vardac, A. Nicholas, *Stage to Screen: Theatrical Method from Garrick to Griffith* (Cambridge, Mass.: Harvard University Press, 1949).

Vaughan, A.T. and Vaughan, V.M., *Shakespeare's Caliban: A Cultural History* (Cambridge University Press, 1991).

(eds.), *Shakespeare in American Life* (Washington DC: Folger Shakespeare Library, 2007).

Vining, Edward P., *The Mystery of Hamlet* (Philadelphia, 1881).

Waller, Gregory, A., *The Stage/Screen Debate: A Study in Popular Aesthetics* (NY: Garland, 1983).

Warde, Frederick, *Fifty Years of Make-Believe* (NY: International Press Syndicate, 1920).

Wells, Stanley (ed.), *The Cambridge Companion to Shakespeare Studies* (Cambridge University Press, 1986).

and Taylor, Gary (eds.), *William Shakespeare: The Complete Works* (Oxford: Clarendon, 1988).

and Stanton, Sarah (eds.), *The Cambridge Companion to Shakespeare on Stage* (Cambridge University Press, 2002).

Wilson, Edwin (ed.), *Shaw on Shakespeare* (London: Cassell, 1962).

Wyke, Maria, *Projecting the Past: Ancient Rome, Cinema and History* (NY and London: Routledge, 1997).

BOOK CHAPTERS, ARTICLES AND REVIEWS
in trade papers, newspapers, journals and edited collections

Allen, Robert C., 'Asta Nielsen: The Silent Muse', *Sight and Sound* v.**42**, n.4 (Autumn 1973), 205–9.

'Association's All-Star Picture a Winner', *MPW* v.**33**, n.9 (1 September 1917), 1351.

'Asta Nielsen is Supported by Precedent in Playing "Hamlet"', *MPW* v.**53**, n.3 (19 November 1921), 327.

Aumont, Jacques, 'Griffith: the Frame, the Figure', in Thomas Elsaesser (ed.), *Early Cinema: Space, Frame, Narrative* (London: BFI, 1990), pp. 348–59.

'B. Nichols Talks', *MPW* v.**18**, n.7 (15 November, 1913), 721.

Ball, Robert Hamilton, 'The Shakespeare Film as Record: Sir Herbert Beerbohm Tree', *SQ* v.**3** (July 1952), 227–36.

'Tree's King John Film: An Addendum', *SQ* v.**24** (1973), 454–9.

Bara, Theda, 'How I Became a Film Vampire', *Forum* **62** (July 1919), 83–93.

Bioscope, The (8 March 1908), 993; (10 December 1908), 14; (25 February 1909), 3; (11 November 1909), 5, 45; (3 March 1910), 47; (21 November 1912), 319; (12 June 1913), 773; (25 September 1913), 982; (8 March 1917), 993.

Blaisdell, George, 'Review of the Metro *Romeo and Juliet*', MPW v.**30**, n.5 (4 November 1916), 685.

Brownlow, Kevin, 'Silent Films – What Was the Right Speed?', in Thomas Elsaesser (ed.), *Early Cinema: Space, Frame, Narrative* (London: BFI, 1990), pp. 282–92.

Buchanan, Judith, '"Orgies of Gesticulation"? Pedigree and Performance Codes in Sir Johnston Forbes-Robertson's and Ruggero Ruggeri's Silent Films of *Hamlet*', *Shakespeare* v.**2**, n.1 (June 2006), 24–46.

Introduction to 'Silent Shakespeare' Special Issue, *Shakespeare* v.**3**, n.3 (December 2007), 283–92.

'"In Mute Despair": Early Silent Films of *The Tempest* and their Theatrical Referents', *Shakespeare* v.**3**, n.3 (December 2007), 315–36.

'Shakespeare and the Magic Lantern', *Shakespeare Survey* **62** (2009, forthcoming).

Bush, W. Stephen, 'Lecture on Moving Pictures', *MPW* v.**3**, n.8 (22 August 1908), 136–7.

'Shakespeare in Moving Pictures', *MPW* v.**3**, n.23 (5 December 1908), 446–7.

'Signs of a Harvest', *MPW* v.**9**, n.4 (5 August 1911), 272.

'Classics and the Screen: Lessons Drawn from the Recent Filming of "Romeo and Juliet" – Evils of Unjustified Criticism', *MPW*, v.**30**, n.6 (11 November 1916), 863.

Bushman, Francis X., 'A Moving Picture *Romeo and Juliet*: The Restrictions and Latitudes of the Screen in Presenting the Greatest Lovers of All', *Motion Picture Magazine* v.**12**, n.8 (September 1916), 111–15.

'Bushman and Bayne at Broadway: Stars of Metro's *"Romeo and Juliet"* Address Big House and Are Given Ovation', *MPW* v.**30**, n.6 (11 November 1916), 870.

'Can Shakespeare be "Filmed"?', *The Bioscope* (29 June 1916), 1290.

Cinema News and Property Gazette, The v.11, n.215 (23 November 1916), p16.

Cinema News and Property Gazette, The v.11, n.216 (30 November 1916), xxvi.

'Competition in Juliets Pays Managers', *MPW* v.**30** n.7 (18 November 1916), 1047.

de Cordova, Rudolph, 'Twenty Years After', *The Picturegoer Weekly* (7 November 1936).

Crangle, Richard, ' "Next Slide Please": The Lantern Lecture in Britain, 1890–1910', in Richard Abel and Rick Altman (eds.). *The Sounds of Early Cinema* (Bloomington: Indiana University Press, 2001), pp. 39–47.

Dallas, E. S., 'The Drama', *Blackwood's Magazine* **79** (February 1856), 227–31.

Danson, Lawrence, 'Gazing at *Hamlet*, or the Danish Cabaret', *Shakespeare Survey* **45** (1992), 37–51.

Dehn, Paul, 'The Filming of Shakespeare', in John Garrett (ed.), *Talking of Shakespeare* (NY: Hodder and Stoughton, 1954), pp. 49–72.

'Demoralizing Moving Pictures', *The Times* (3 August 1899), **12** col. 5.

Dench, Ernest A., 'Stage Stars on the Screen', *Pictures and Picturegoers* v.**9**, n.102 (29 January 1916), 400–2.

Dent, Alan, 'The World of the Cinema: Speculations and Regrets', *Illustrated London News* (14 May 1960). Unpaginated clipping on file at the Theatre Museum.

Donohue, Joseph, 'Burletta and the Early Nineteenth-Century English Theatre', *Nineteenth-Century Theatre Research* **1** (1973), 29–51.

Duey, Helen, 'Shakespeare in the Films: An Interview with Sir Herbert Beerbohm Tree', *Woman's Home Companion* (June 1916), 91.

Duffy, Robert A., 'Gade, Olivier, Richardson: Visual Strategy in *Hamlet* Adaptation', *Literature/Film Quarterly* **4** (1976), 141–52.

Dyer, Richard, 'Stars as Images' in Joanne Hollows, Peter Hutchings and Mark Jancovich (eds.), *The Film Studies Reader* (London: Hodder Arnold, 2000), pp. 121–4.

Dyer, T. F. T., 'Foresters at Home', *Art Journal* (October 1885), 301.

'Editorial Chat', *CNPG* v.**10** n.179 (16 March 1916), 3.

Edmonds, Jill, 'Princess Hamlet', in Viv Gardner and Susan Rutherford (eds.), *The New Woman and Her Sisters: Feminism and Theatre 1850–1914* (Ann Arbor: University of Michigan Press, 1992), pp. 59–76.

Ellison, James, 'Beerbohm Tree's *King John* (1899): A *fin-de-siècle* Fragment and its Cultural Context', *Shakespeare* ('Silent Shakespeare' special issue), v.**3**, n.3 (December 2007), 293–314.

Era, The (29 March 1913), 19.

Exceptional Photoplays v.**2**, n.1 (Jan-Feb 1922), 8.

Film, Der 6 (1922), 7.

'The Filming of "Hamlet": Interview with Mr. Cecil Hepworth', *The Bioscope* (24 July 1913), 275.

Findon, B. W., 'Farewell of Forbes-Robertson', *The Play Pictorial* v.**21**, n.129 (June 1913), 110–11.

Ford, Charles, 'Emil Jannings', supplément à l' *Avant-Scène du Cinéma* **93** (June 1969), 295.

Forsyth, Neil, 'Shakespeare the Illusionist: Filming the Supernatural', in Russell Jackson (ed.), *The Cambridge Companion to Shakespeare on Film* (Cambridge University Press, 2000), pp. 274–94.

'Shakespeare and Méliès: Magic, Dream and the Supernatural', *Études Anglaises* v.**55**, n.2 (April/May/June 2002), 167–80.

'400 Stand in Rain to Pay Honor to Shakespeare', *New York Herald* (24 April 1916), 6.

Gates, Harvey H., 'Florence Turner Talks About Acting', *The New York Dramatic Mirror* (30 October 1912), 28.

Gianetto, Claudio, 'The Giant Ambrosio, or Italy's Most Prolific Silent Film Company', *Film History* v.**12**, n.3 (2000), 240–9.

Goldie, Albert, 'Subtlety in Acting', *The New York Dramatic Mirror* (13 November 1912), 4.

Graham, Charles, 'Acting for the Films in 1912', *Sight and Sound* v.**4**, n.15 (Autumn 1935), 118–19.

Grau, Robert, 'High Grade Exploitation of Photoplays', *Motion Picture Story Magazine* (May 1913), 115.

Graves, George W., '"Romeo and Juliet". William Fox's Screen Interpretation Features Theda Bara', *Motography* v.**16**, n.19 (4 November 1916), 1042.

'Green Room Jottings', *Motion Picture Classic* v.**3**, n.4 (December 1916), 63.

Gress, Elsa, 'Die Asta: A Personal Impression', *Sight and Sound* v.**42**, n.4 (Autumn 1973), 209.

Guneratne, Anthony R., '"Thou Dost Usurp Authority": Beerbohm Tree, Reinhardt, Olivier, Welles, and the Politics of Adapting Shakespeare', in Diana E. Henderson (ed.), *A Concise Companion to Shakespeare on Screen* (Oxford: Blackwell, 2006), pp. 31–53.

Gunning, Tom, 'The Cinema of Attractions: Early Film, Its Spectator and the Avant-Garde', *Wide Angle* v.**8**, n.3–4 (1986), 63–70.

'The Intertextuality of Early Cinema: A Prologue to Fantômas', in Robert Stam and Alessandra Raengo (eds.), *A Companion to Literature and Film* (Oxford: Blackwell, 2004), pp. 127–43.

'"Now you See it, Now you Don't": the Temporality of the Cinema of Attractions', in Lee Grieveson and Peter Krämer (eds.), *The Silent Film Reader* (London and NY: Routledge, 2004), pp. 41–50.

Gunter, Lawrence J., 'Expressionist Shakespeare: The Gade/Nielsen Hamlet (1920) and the History of Shakespeare on Film', *Post Script: Essays in Film and Humanities* (Winter/Spring 1998), 90–102.

Hapgood, Robert, 'Shakespeare on Film and Television', in Stanley Wells (ed.), *The Cambridge Companion to Shakespeare Studies* (Cambridge University Press, 1986), pp. 273–86.

Hankin, John, '*The Tempest* in a Teacup', *Punch* (9 May 1900), 330.

Harrison, Louis Reeves, *MPW* v.**10**, n.5 (4 November 1911), 357.

Higson, Andrew, 'Heritage Discourse and British Cinema Before 1920', in John Fullerton (ed.), *Celebrating the Centenary of Cinema, 1895* (Sydney and London: John Libbey, 1998), pp. 182–9.

Hoffman, H. F., 'The Murder of Othello', *MPW* v.**9**, n.2 (22 July 1911), 110.

Hooker, Brian, 'Shakspere (sic) and the Movie', *Century* v.**93**, n.2 (December 1916), 298–304.

Howard, Tony, 'The Rest Is Silence. Asta Nielsen As Hamlet', *Women and Theatre* Occasional Papers 2 (1992), 28–92.

Imrie, Thos. S., 'Australian Notes', *MPW* v.**31**, n.7 (17 February 1917), 994.

Jackson, Russell, 'Actor-Managers and the Spectacular', in Jonathan Bate and Russell Jackson (eds.), *Shakespeare: An Illustrated Stage History* (Oxford University Press, 1996), pp. 112–27.

'Shakespeare's Fairies in Victorian Criticism and Performance', in Jane Martineau (ed.), *Victorian Fairy Painting* (London: Royal Academy of Arts, 1997), pp. 38–45.

'Staging and Storytelling, Theatre and Film: "Richard III" at Stratford, 1910', *New Theatre Quarterly* **62** (May 2000), 107–21.

'Jean-Leon Gérôme Dead; French Painter and Sculptor Found Lifeless in Bed', *NYT* (11 January 1904), 7.

'Jolo', Review of *King Lear*, *Variety* v.**45**, n.6 (5 January 1917), 25.

Judson, Hanford C., '*Hamlet* with Forbes Robertson: The Knickerbocker Film Company Offers in Three Reels a Great Play With a Great Star and a Great Cast Supporting Him', *MPW* v.**25**, n.2 (10 July 1915), 317–18.

Kachur, B. A., 'Shakespeare Polticized: Beerbohm Tree's *King John* and the Boer War', *Theatre History Studies* **12** (1992), 25–44.

Kahn, Coppélia, 'Remembering Shakespeare Imperially: The 1916 Tercentenary', *SQ* v.**52**, n.1 (2001), 456–78.

Kaufman, Sarah, 'Silent "Hamlet", Felt in the Bones: Synetic Theater Mounts a Mesmerizing Revival at the Kennedy Center', *The Washington Post* (5 June 2007), C08.

Keil, Charles, 'From the Manger to the Cross: The New Testament Narrative and the Question of Stylistic Retardation', in R. Cosandey, A. Gaudreault and T. Gunning (eds.), *Une Invention du Diable? Cinéma des Premiers Temps et Religion* (Sainte-Foy: Les Presses de l'Université Laval, 1992), pp. 112–20.

Kennedy, Dennis, 'Shakespeare Without the Language', in James C. Bulman (ed.), *Shakespeare, Theory and Performance* (London and NY: Routledge, 1996), pp. 133–48.

KLW (28 January 1909), 759; (13 May 1909), 12; (1 July 1909), 349; (16 March 1911), 1339; (9 October 1913), 2555.

'"King John" in the Mutoscope. A Glimpse at Mr. Tree for a Penny', *The Westminster Gazette* (21 September 1899), 4.

King, Norman, 'The Sound of Silents', *Screen* v.**25**, n.3 (May–June 1984), 2–15.

Kitchin, Laurence, 'Shakespeare on the Screen', *Shakespeare Survey* **18** (1965), 70–74.

Kleine, George, 'Progress in Optical Projection in the Last Fifty Years,' *Film Index* (28 May 1910), 10.

Koebner, Thomas, 'Hamlet as a Woman: Asta Nielsen's Shakespeare Film of 1921' in Holger Klein and Dimiter Daphinoff (eds.), *Hamlet on Screen* Shakespeare Yearbook v.**8** (Lancaster: Edwin Mellen Press, 1997), pp. 125–32.

L.J.S., Review of *The Real Thing at Last*, *CNPG* v.**10**, n.181 (30 March 1916), 13.

'London Letter', sub-headed 'Few Prominent Actors in Pictures' (16 March 1912), *MPW* v.**12**, n.2 (13 April 1912), 124.

'"Macbeth" Pruned in Chicago', *MPW* v.**2**, n.24 (13 June 1908), 511.

McKernan, Luke, 'Beerbohm Tree's King John rediscovered', *SB* v.**11**, n.1 (Winter 1993), 35–6.

'Further News on Beerbohm Tree's *King John*', *SB* v.**11**, n.2 (Spring 1993), 49–50.

'A Scene – King John – Now Playing at Her Majesty's Theatre', in Linda Fitzsimmons and Sarah Street (eds.), *Moving Performance: British Stage and Screen, 1890s–1920s* (Trowbridge: Flicks Books, 2000), pp. 56–68.

'Percy Stow', in Richard Abel (ed.), *Encyclopedia of Early Cinema* (Abingdon and NY: Routledge, 2005), p. 613.

'"A Complete and Fully Satisfying Art on its Own Account": Cinema and the Shakespeare Tercentenary of 1916', *Shakespeare* ('Silent Shakespeare' special issue) v.**3**, n.3 (December 2007), 337–51.

McManus, John T., 'Matthews of the Movies', *NYT* (17 January, 1937). Clipping on file at NYPL.

McQuade, James S., '"Brutus". Kleine's First Cines Release – Extraordinary One-Reel Picture Based on Shakespeare's "Julius Caesar"', *MPW* v.**11**, n.3 (20 January 1912), 193.

Marinetti, F.T., 'The Founding and the Manifesto of Futurism' (1909) in Lawrence Rainey (ed.), *Modernism: An Anthology* (Oxford: Blackwells, 2005), pp. 3–6.

Marker, Frederick J., 'The First Night of Charles Kean's *The Tempest*, from the Notebook of Hans Christian Andersen', *Theatre Notebook* v.**25**, n.1 (1970), 20–3.

Marks, Peter, 'The Unquiet Silence of Synetic's "Macbeth"', *The Washington Post* (20 January 2007), c01.

'"Romeo and Juliet": Such Sweet Sorrow', *The Washington Post* (29 January 2008), c01.

Metro Picture News 'Romeo and Juliet' One-Page Special Number (19 October 1916). LOC call number LP 9354.

Moody, Jane, 'Writing for the Metropolis: Illegitimate Performances of Shakespeare in Early Nineteenth-Century London', *Shakespeare Survey* **47** (1994), 61–9.

——'"Dictating to the Empire": Performance and Theatrical Geography in Eighteenth-century Britain', in Jane Moody and Daniel O'Quinn (eds.), *The Cambridge Companion to British Theatre, 1730–1830* (Cambridge University Press, 2007), pp. 21–42.

Morning Leader, The (21 September 1899), 4.

Motion Picture Classic, v.**3**, n.1 (September 1916), 49–52.

Motion Picture Classic v.**3**, n.2 (October 1916), 29–33.

Motion Picture Magazine v.**12**, n.11 (December 1916), 123.

MPW v.**2**, n.19 (9 May 1908), 413; v.**2**, n.24 (13 June 1908), 511; v.**3**, n.13 (26 September 1908), 245; v.**6**, n.7 (19 February 1910), 257; v.**6**, n.17 (30 April 1910), 690; v.**8**, n.17 (29 April 1911), 943; v.**8**, n.26 (1 July 1911), 1506; v.**8**, n.28 (15 July 1911), 49; v.**10**, n.10 (9 December 1911), 818; v.**11**, n.7 (17 February 1912), 581; v.**16**, n.9 (31 May 1913), 923; v.**21**, n.1 (4 July 1914), 21; v.**25**, n.1 (3 July 1915), 18; v.**28**, n.6 (6 May 1916), 997; v.**28**, n.8 (20 May 1916), 1342; v.**29**, n.1 (1 July1916), 19; v.**29**, n.2 (8 July 1916), 258; v.**29**, n.7 (12 August 1916), 1086; v.**29**, n.11 (9 September 1916), 1711; v.**30**, n.2 (14 October 1916), 178; v.**30**, n.3 (21 October 1916), 340–1, 418; v.**30**, n.4 (28 October 1916), advertising supplement inserted between 490 and 491; v.**30**, n.5 (4 November 1916), 766, 840, 952–3; v.**30**, n.6 (11 November 1916), 825, 829, 837, 870, 892; v.**30**, n.7 (18 November 1916), 1040, 1041, 1044, 1047; v.**30**, n.8 (25 November 1916), 1204, 1198; v.**33**, n.9 (1 September 1917), 1351.

Mullin, Michael, 'Strange Images of Death: Sir Herbert Beerbohm-Tree's *Macbeth, 1911*', *Theatre Survey* (November 1976), 125–42.

Musser, Charles, 'The Nickelodeon Era Begins: Establishing the Framework for Hollywood's Mode of Representation', in Thomas Elsaesser (ed.), *Early Cinema: Space, Frame Narrative* (London: BFI, 1990), pp. 256–73.

New York Dramatic Mirror (4 June 1910), 32; (6 November 1912), 36.

Newton, H. Chance, 'About Town: "King John" at Her Majesty's', *The Sketch* (20 September 1899), 388.

Nickelodeon, The (September 1909), 71.

'Observations by our Man About Town', *MPW* v.**16**, n.1 (5 April, 1916), 51.

'The Old Lady in the Audience: Mother Squeers Gossips About the Film Makers', *Motography* (May 1911), 77–8.

'Ordinary Movie Presentation of Famous Old Tragedy', *Wid's Film Daily* v.**2**, n.50 (14 December 1916), 1170.

Orwell, George, 'Lear, Tolstoy and the Fool' (first published Polemic 7 (March 1947)) in Orwell, *Collected Essays, Journalism and Letters* v. **4** (1945–1950), Sonia Orwell and Ian Angus (eds.) (London: Secker and Warburg, 1968), pp. 287–302.

Panofsky, Erwin, 'Style and Medium in the Moving Pictures' (1934). Reproduced in Panofsky, *Three Essays on Style* (ed.) Irving Lavin (Cambridge, Mass. and London: MIT Press, 1997), pp. 91–126.

Pearson, Roberta E. and Urrichio, William, 'How Many Times Shall Caesar Bleed in Sport? Shakespeare and the Cultural Debate about Moving Pictures', *Screen* v.**31**, n.3 (1990), 243–61.

'"Shrieking From Below the Grating": Sir Herbert Beerbohm Tree's *Macbeth* and His Critics', in Hoenselaars (ed.), *Reclamations of Shakespeare* (Amsterdam and Atlanta: Rodopi, 1994), pp. 249–71.

'The Bard in Brooklyn: Vitagraph's Shakespearean Productions', in McKernan and Terris (eds.), *Walking Shadows: Shakespeare in the National Film and Television Archive* (London: BFI, 1994), pp. 201–6.

Pictures, The (21 October 1911), 1.

Pictures and the Picturegoer v.9, n.105 (19 February 1916), 483–4.

Photoplay 13 (May 1918), 23–4.

'The Playhouses', *ILN* (30 September 1899), 451.

'Review of New Films', *New York Dramatic Mirror* (12 December 1908), 6.

'*Romeo and Juliet* (Fox Cor.).' *Variety* **44** (27 October 1916), 28.

'Romeo and Juliet (Metro)', *Variety* **44** (27 October 1916), 28.

Sargent, Epes Winthrop, 'Technique of the Photoplay', *MPW* v.**9**, n.2 (22 July 1911), 108.

Schoch, Richard W., 'Pictorial Shakespeare', in Stanley Wells and Sarah Stanton (eds.), *The Cambridge Companion to Shakespeare on Stage* (Cambridge University Press, 2002), pp. 58–75.

Seidl, Monika, 'Room for Asta: Gender Roles and Melodrama in Asta Nielsen's filmic version of *Hamlet* (1920)', *Literature/Film Quarterly* v.**30**, n.3 (2002), 208–16.

'Shakespeare Movie Way. Romeo and Juliet Make Love in the Tomb for Fox production', *NYT* (23 October 1916), 10.

'Shakespeare's Name rings Through St. John's Cathedral: Sir Johnston Forbes-Robertson and Sir Herbert Beerbohm Tree Principal Speakers at Tercentenary Celebration of the Actors' Alliance', *New York Herald* (24 April 1916), 6.

Shaw, George Bernard, 'Bernard Shaw and the Heroic Actor', *The Play Pictorial* v.**21**, n.129 (June 1913), 124.

'Silent Film of 1913 Brings Back a Great Hamlet', *ILN* (14 May 1960). Unpaginated clipping available to view on microfiche at the BFI.

Silvester, Richard, 'The Shakespearean Stage and the Stage of To-day', *Review of Reviews*, May 1916, 591.

"Sir J. Forbes Robertson in Knickerbocker Production", *MPW* v.**25**, n.2 (10 July 1915), 312.

Sketch, The, King John: review and stills (27 September 1899), 413.

Skrien n.181 (Dec–Jan 1991–1992), 34–5.

Smith, Emma, "'Remember Me": The Gaumont-Hepworth Hamlet – 1913', in Holger Klein and Dimiter Daphinoff (eds.), *Hamlet on Screen* Shakespeare Yearbook vol. VIII (Lancaster: Edwin Mellen Press, 1997), pp. 110–24.

'"Sir J. and Lady Forbes-Robertson left for America on Saturday": Marketing the 1913 *Hamlet* for Stage and Screen', in Linda Fitzsimmons and Sarah Street (eds.), *Moving Performance: British Stage and Screen, 1890s–1920s* (Trowbridge: Flicks Books, 2000), pp. 44–55.

Sothern, E. H., '"The New Art" as Discovered by E. H. Sothern', *The Craftsman* v.**30** (September 1916), 572–643.

Southern, Richard, 'The Picture-Frame Proscenium of 1880', *Theatre Notebook* v.**5**, n.3 (1951), 59–61.

Spearing, James O., Review of the Nielsen *Hamlet*, *NYT* (9 November 1921), 20 col. 3.

Spehr, Paul C., 'Throwing Pictures on a Screen: The Work of W.K-L. Dickson, Filmmaker', in Luke McKernan and Mark van den Tempel (eds.), *The Wonders of the Biograph*, special issue Griffithiana (2000), 66–70.

Stage, The, King John: a review, (21 September 1899), 13; (27 March, 1913), 19.

Standard, The (23 September, 1913), 8.

Starks, Lisa S., '"Remember me": Psychoanalysis, Cinema and the Crisis of Modernity', *SQ* v.**53**, n.1 (2002), 181–200.

Summers, Rollin, 'The Moving Picture Drama and the Acted Drama: Some Points of Comparison as to Technique', *MPW* v.**3**, n.12 (19 September, 1908), 213.

Sutcliffe, J. B., 'British Notes', *MPW* v.**32**, n.11 (16 June 1917), 1771.

Tatler, The, Review of Granville Barker's *A Midsummer Night's Dream*, 660 (18 February 1914), 197.

'The Thanhouser Triumph', *MPW* v.**6**, n.21 (28 May 1910), 876.

'Le Théâtre À Londres: *King John* de Shakespeare au Her Majesty's Theatre', *Le Théâtre* (20 September 1899), 19.

Thompson, Ann, 'Asta Nielsen and the Mystery of *Hamlet*', in Lynda E. Boose and Richard Burt (eds.), *Shakespeare the Movie: Popularizing the Plays on Film, TV and Video* (London: Routledge, 1997), pp. 215–24.

Toddle, Timothy, 'A Magic Lantern Entertainment', in Dennis Crompton, David Henry and Stephen Herbert (eds.), *Magic Images: The Art of Hand-Painted and Photographic Lantern Slides* (London: MLS, 1990), pp. 47–53.

Tomadjoglou, Kimberly, 'Rome's Premiere Film Studio: Società Italiana Cines', *Film History* v.**12**, n.3 (2000), 262–75.

Tree, Herbert Beerbohm, 'Impressions of America. Part I: "Not Bad for a Young Country"', *The Times* (8 September 1916), 11.

'A Tragic "Movie": Sir J. M. Barrie's Cinema Burlesque', *The Times* (8 March 1916), 11.

Triplett, William, 'Synetic's 'Hamlet': The Rest Is Silence', *The Washington Post* (8 April 2002), C01.

Vaughan, Virginia Mason, 'Making Shakespeare American: Shakespeare's Dissemination in Nineteenth-Century America', in Virginia Mason

Vaughan and Alden T. Vaughan (eds.), *Shakespeare in American Life* (Washington DC: Folger Shakespeare Library, 2007), pp. 23–33.

'Vitagraph Notes', *MPW* v.**8**, n.28 (15 July 1911), 49.

Weitzel, Edward, 'Obituary for Herbert Beerbohm Tree', *MPW* v.**33**, n.3 (21 July 1917), 430.

Welsh, James M., 'Shakespeare With – and Without – Words', *Literature/Film Quarterly* v.**1** (1973), 84–88.

Wiggins, Jack, 'Peepshow', *The Cine-Technician* v.**4**, n.17 (Sept.–Oct. 1938), 76.

'William Fox's Greatest Production: Theda Bara as "Juliet": An Artistic and Dramatic Triumph', *The Bioscope* (23 November 1916), 741.

Wolf, Steffen, 'Geschichte der Shakespeare-Verfilmungen (1899–1964)', in Max Lippman (ed.), *Shakespeare im Film* (Wiesbaden: Deutsches Institut für Filmkunde, 1964), pp. 15–32.

Wood, Michael, 'Modernism and Film', in Michael Levenson (ed.), *The Cambridge Companion to Modernism* (Cambridge University Press, 1999), pp. 217–32.

Index

Bold type indicates a central-case reference; bold italics indicates reference to a figure; the suffix n indicates reference to a note.

Abel, Richard, 40n, 82n
Achterberg, Fritz, German film actor, 231
acting editions, 47, 86, 156, 159, 161
acting manuals, 46, 174–75, *176*, *177*
acting styles, in transition, 174
    considered characteristic of particular
        nations, 174, 178, 187–89
    facial expressivity, 139–41, 144, 231–32, 241,
        249–50
    histrionic or excessive, xxii, 62, 63, 64, 166,
        167, 172–74, 178–80, 181, 183–85, 229,
        230, 240, 241, 242, 246
    'mugging' (the mouthing of inaudible words
        for the camera), 63, 171, 172, 198–99
    naturalistic/verisimilar/minimalist, 164, 170,
        174, 181, 183, 228–32, 242, 249–51
    pantomimic codes, 19, 46, 49, **173–78**, *176*,
        177, 181
advertising, *see* marketing strategies
Ambrosio-Film, Italian film production
    company
    company and its distribution, 126, 186
    Otello/Othello (Frusta, 1914), 21, 90–91, 94, 248
American film industry – institutional struc-
    tures, exhibition conventions and national
    self-consciousness, 105–09, 112–15,
    190–96, 217; satirised, 192–98, 212–13,
    see also individual American production
    companies AMBC, Edison, Essanay,
    Fox, Kalem, Lubin, Metro, Rex, Sam
    Taylor, Selig, Shakespeare Film Company,
    Thanhouser, Triangle-Reliance, Vitagraph
American Mutoscope and Biograph Company
    (AMBC), film production company, also
    known as Biograph
    company attributes and exhibition
        conventions, 57n, 105, 106, 107, 109
    company logo, 116; the 'Biograph Girl',
        Florence Lawrence, 3, 143
    *The Kissing Scene Between Trilby and Little
        Billee* (1896), 61
    duel scene from *Macbeth* (Bitzer, 1905),
        74–75n
    Americanism, of production company, films
        and approach to Shakespeare, 112–18
    anachronisms, 193, 197, 237
    androgyny, 20–21, 224–26, **226**, 227
    Angeli, Diego, Italian translator of
        Shakespeare, 70n
    Angiers, battle of, *tableau* interpolated in Tree's
        stage *King John* (1899), 64, 70n
    Angus, Ian, xixn
    Anthony, Barry, 58n, 59n, 62n, 64–65n, 67n,
        68n, 69n, 70n
    Antony and Cleopatra, Shakespeare play
        Antoine et Cléopatre, ballet (1761), 49n
        Antony and Cleopatra, Vitagraph film (Kent,
            1908), 75, 108, 119n, 130
    Anzi, Anna Cavallone, 164n, 166n, 178n
    Archer, William, 'pamphleteer', 175n, 178n
    archives and libraries
        American Film Institute (AFI), 203n;
        BFI National Archive (formerly
            the National Film and Television
            Archive): 79n, 80n, 106n, 149–50n,
            187, 217n, 246n; British Library (BL),
            London, 43n, 45n; Bodleian, The,
            Oxford, 160n, 175–76n; Cinématèque
            de Toulouse: 150n; Cineteca di
            Bologna: 150n; Il Centro Sperimentale
            di Cinematographia, Rome (CSC):
            80n; Deutsches Institut für Film,
            Frankfurt: 217n; Folger Shakespeare
            Library, Washington DC (Folger): 33n,

archives and libraries (*cont.*)
8on, 106n, 198n, 201n, 217n; George
Eastman House, Rochester, New York
(GEH), 31, 33n; MOMA, New York,
185–86n; Motion Picture and Recorded
Sound Division, Library of Congress,
Washington DC (LOC), 52n, 77n,
8on, 91n, 97, 128, 170n, 198n, 202n,
203, 221n, 222; National Archives, 64n;
Nederlands Filmmuseum, 72n; New
York Public Library (NYPL), 193n;
Palace Theatre Archive, 66n; Russian
State Film Archive, 91n; Theatre
Museum, Covent Garden, London,
6on, 7on, 152n; University of Bristol
Theatre Collection, 7on
archives/archiving priorities, xxii, 2n, 29n, 31,
40, 64n, 66n, 7on, 71n, 252
artistic representations, of Shakespearean
scenes, **xxn**, 146, **156–57n**
Shakespearean paintings used in lantern
sequences, 35–38
art works appearing in, or animated by,
films, **121–24**, 141, 146, 156–57, 248
see also 'Death of Caesar', 'King Lear in
the Storm' and entries under Ophelia,
Hamlet, Othello and *Romeo and Juliet*
Art-Film, Asta Nielsen's German film
production company
Hamlet, Drama of Vengeance (Gade, 1920), 5,
7, 135, 185–86n, **217–40**
As You Like It, Shakespeare play
E.W.Godwin's open-air production (1885),
50–51
lantern slide sequences, 30, 31, 74n
Seven Ages of Man, Edison film (director
unknown, 1905), 74n
As You Like It, Kalem film (Buel, 1908), 75
As You Like It, Vitagraph 3-reel film
(Blackton and Kent, 1912), 108, 130, 133
As You Like It, Inter-Allied film (Czinner,
1936), 217n
Aubert, Charles, 175, *177*, 178
Aumont, Jacques, 163

Baines, Richard Manwaring, lanternist and
slide collector, 27n
Ball, Robert Hamilton, xviiin, 2n, 4, 6, 15n, 52n,
61, 69, 70–72, 74–75n, 77–78, 90n, 94n,
119n, 126n, 127n, 130n, 131n, 132n, 148n,
149n, 186n, 187, 191, 198n, 199n, 201n, 203n,
205, 206n, 210n, 211n, 217n, 220, 221n
ballet, 9, 46, 49, 56
'ballet of action', speechless stage production
with recitative, 43–45
Bancroft, Squire, theatre manager, 53

Bandmann-Palmer, Millicent, stage actress (as
Hamlet), 220
Bangs, John Kendrick, 192
'banners', *see* 'scrolls'
Bara, Theda, screen actress (as Juliet), 2, 4, 20,
203–12, *204*, *209*, 251
Barber, Xenophon Theodore, 26n
Bardèche, Maurice, 229
Barker, Harley Granville, British actor and
theatre director, 136
Barker, William G, film director and producer,
2, 72, 149, 184
Barker Motion Photography, British film
production company
Hamlet (Barker, 1910), 149
King Henry VIII (Barker, 1911), 2, 72, 184, 197n
Barleon, Amelia, American screen actress, 128
Barnes, J.H., stage and screen actor, 156
Barrie, James (J.M.), writer/director of *The Real
Thing at Last* (Bushey Heath co., 1916),
2–3, 19–20, 77, **190–98**, 202, 212, 213;
scenarist for *As You Like It* (1936), 217n
Barry, Iris, xviin, 229n
Bartalotta, Gianfranco, 168n
Bate, Jonathan, 53
Battle Hymn of the Republic, The, non-
Shakespearean film, *see* Vitagraph
Bayne, Beverly, screen actress, 20, 202, 205–11,
208, 215–16
Becker, Carl Ludwig Friedrich, artist, 37, 38n
Benjamin, Walter, 2on
Benson, Frank, British stage and screen actor
(as Richard III), 4, 77
Berg, Irene and Samuel, arrangers of musical
scores, 211n, 216
Bernhardt, Sarah, French stage and screen
actress, 3, 15n, 41, 72, 74n, 77, 148, 220,
221, 223
Bertini, Francesca, Italian screen actress, 3,
90, 125
biblical subjects, in lantern slides, 27, 28;
in films, 17, 108, 170n
Biograph, shortened form of The American
Mutoscope and Biograph Company
(AMBC) *q.v.*, and of its daughter
company, The British Mutoscope and
Biograph Company (BMBC), *q.v.*
Birtwhistle, Richard, collector, 113n
Black Castle, The, play in unpatented
theatre, 45
Black Diamond Express, The, early Edison film,
145–46
blacking-up, 241, 243–46, *244*, *245*
Blackton, J. Stuart, Vitagraph director/
production manager, 113, 115, 130, 146–47
Blaisdell, George, 9n, 203n, 207n

Blood-Red Knight, The, play in unpatented theatre, 45
Bogart, Humphrey, 223
'boomer', category of lecturer, *q.v.*
Boose, Lynda E., 219n
Booth, Michael, 50n, 52n
Bordwell, David, 2n, 7n, 20n, 156n, 250n
Borton, Terry, American lanternist and lantern historian, 26n, 36
Bourchier, Arthur, English stage and screen actor, 184, 197, 250
Bowser, Eileen, 18n
Bragaglia, Leonardo, 164n
Brandt, Mathilde, German film actress (as Gertrude), 229
Brasillach, Robert, 229
Brecht, Berthold, 20n
Brewster, Ben, 24n
Bristol, Michael, 114
British Actors' Film Company, 192n, 196
British film industry, 57, 79
  acting compared with continental styles, 187–89
  output morally condemned, 57–60
  preference for word-driven film-making, in comparison with Hollywood, 199
  satirised, in comparison with American film industry, 190–98
  its Shakespeare films critically preferred to Italian ones, 185–87
  stops making Shakespeare feature films, 217
  see also individual British production companies Barker, British Mutoscope and Biography Company, Broadwest, Bushey Heath, Clarendon, Co-operative Cinematograph Company, Gaumont, Inter-Allied, Masters, Piccadilly, Walderaw; and individual British films, in partic. *King John* (1899), *The Tempest* (1908), *Richard III* (1911), *Hamlet* (1913), *The Real Thing at Last* (1916)
British Film Institute (BFI), London
  DVD *Silent Shakespeare*, 4, 62, 71n, 77n, 79n, 91n, 106n, 198n, 260
  BFI National Archive, 79n, 80n, 106n, 150n, 155n, 187, 214n, 217n
British Mutoscope and Biograph Company (BMBC), also known as 'Biograph' company attributes and exhibition conventions, 62n, 105, 106, 107, 109
  King John (Dickson and Dando, 1899), 23, 40, **61–72, 65,** 74, 77
  Studio Troubles/Wicked Willie (1898/9), 57–60
Broadwest, British film production company
  Merchant of Venice (Walter West, 1916), 77, 201

Brothers Karamazov, The (Buchowetzki, 1921), non-Shakespearean film, 240
Brown, Richard, 58n, 59n, 62n, 64–66n, 68n, 69n, 70n
Browne, Gordon, artist, 156–57n
Brownlow, Kevin, 22n, 75n
Brutus, Cines film (1910), *see Julius Caesar*
Buchanan, Judith, xxii, 2–3, 29n, 35n, 38n, 60n, 62, 127n, 137n, 149n, 152n, 201n
Büchner, Georg, German playwight, 240
Buchowetzki, Dimitri, Russian film director in German film industry, 21, 217, 240–49
Bunyan, John, 28
Burbage, Richard, 166–67
Burrows, Jon, xviiin, 72n, 160n, 161n, 175n, 189n, 201n
Burt, Richard, 219n
Bush, W. Stephen, moving picture lecturer and writer for *MPW*, xxi, 10–11, 15, 42, 121n, 206n
Bushey Heath Co, British film production company
  The Real Thing at Last, lampooning comparative productions of *Macbeth* (Barrie and MacBean, 1916), 2–3, 19–20, 77, **190–201,** 202, 212–13
Bushman, Francis X., American screen actor, 4, 20, 202, 207, **208,** 209, 215–16

Caesar and Cleopatra, play by Bernard Shaw, 155
Calvert, Louis, actor, 64
Capelli, Dante, actor, 3, 80, 198n
'Carados', *see* H. Chance Newton
Cardinal Wolsey, Vitagraph film from *Henry VIII* (Trimble, 1912), 108
Cardullo, Bert, 111n
Carmen, two non-Shakespearean films, subject of rival releases, 203n
Caserini, Mario, Italian film director, 80n, 198n
casting, 79, **85,** 86n, 110, 133, 135, 137, 138–39, 144, 152, 190, **192–94,** 198, **202–04,** 207, 234, 240, 242, 250–51
Cavell, Stanley, 223–24
censors, 3, 57, 59–60, 108n, 124n, 197
Chanan, Michael, 23n
Christie, Anna, film actress, 223–24
Christie, Ian, 118n
cinematograph, xxi, 20, 23, 40, 42, 66, 146
'Cinematographe', 106
cinematography, 76, 82, 96, 99, 137, 141, 151, 164, 166, 188, 201, 229, 232, 234–35, 246, 247
Cines, Rome-based film production company, 5, 77, 186
Otello/Othello (Caserini and Velle, 1907), 75

Cines (*cont.*)
  Ameleto/Hamlet (Caserini, 1908, reissued 1910), 75, 80, 149
  Giulietta e Romeo/Romeo and Juliet (Caserini, 1908), 75–76
  Macbett/Macbeth (Caserini, 1909), 4, 80, 170n, 198n
  Brutus, film offshoot of *Julius Caesar* (Guazzoni, 1910), 19, 105, 106, 125–26n
  Gajus Julius Caesar/ Julius Caesar (Guazzoni, 1914), 105, 106n, 115, 116, *123*, 126
Clarendon, British film production company
  The Tempest (Stow, 1908), 18, **74–88**, 94–95, 103–04
Coghlan, Rose, American film actress, 133
Collick, John, 23n, 60n, 71n
Colman, George, theatre manager, 16
colour, hand-colouring, stencilling, tinting (slides and films), xxii, 26, 29n, 30, 31, 33, 36, 91n
comedy, comic effects and comedians (deliberate and inadvertent), 13, 20, 27, 28, 66, 75, 102–03, 106, 111, 121–30, 173–74n, 192–97, 200–01, 214, 227, 229, 231–32, 240, 242, 243, 246, 259
Comedy of Errors, The, Shakespeare play
  Two Little Dromios, Thanhouser film (1914), 127n
  The Wrong Flat; or A Comedy of Errors, non-Shakespearean Vitagraph film (1907), 108
Cook, Olive, 27
Cookson, S.A., British stage and screen actor, 62, 64, **65**
Cooper, Gladys, British stage and screen actress, 193, 200n
Co-operative Cinematograph Company, 77
  Macbeth (director unknown, 1911), 197–98
  Richard III (Benson, 1911), 197, 198n
Corbin, John, 181
Coriolanus, Shakespeare play, of which no silent film made, 252n
Cornely, Edouard, 156–57n
Cosandey, R, 104n
Costello, Maurice, American screen actor, 3, 130, 144, 145
costume
  historical accuracy on stage, 50; of Shakespearean characters in lantern slides, 33–34; *King John* (1899), 62n, 64n; Tree's and Stow's Calibans, 85; Vitagraph's lavish and historical costumes, 110, 112; *Julius Caesar*

(Vitagraph, 1908); 116; *A Winter's Tale* (Thanhouser, 1910), 127; *A Midsummer Night's Dream* (Vitagraph, 1909), 132; Penelope (*q.v.*) in *A Midsummer Night's Dream* (Vitagraph, 1909), 133, *134*; Florence Turner (*q.v.*) (as Viola/ Cesario for Vitagraph), 142, *142*; Julia Swayne Gordon (as Olivia for Vitagraph), 139, 140, *142*; Caesar in *Brutus* (Cines, 1910); 126; Ophelia in *Hamlet* (1913), 156, 157; Edmund Gwenn in *The Real Thing at Last* (1916), 195; Francis X. Bushman's 'scanted garb' in *Romeo and Juliet* (Metro, 1916), 207; in *Romeo and Juliet* (Metro, 1916), 211n; in unidentified film of *Hamlet*, *222*; in *Hamlet* (1920), 227, 230, 234, **236–37**, *237*; in *Othello* (1922), 242, *244*, *245, 249*
Countryman and the Cinematograph, The, non-Shakespearean film (Paul, 1901), 129n
Cran, Mrs George, 64n, 85n
Crocombe, Leonard, 143n
Crompton, Dennis, 29n
cross-dressing/cross-casting/transgendering (*travestie* roles)
  Hamlet, 20–21, 219–23, 224–26, **226;** Oberon, 135n; Lady Macbeth, 194
crowd scenes, 115, 207, 210, 211, 246–47
Cushman, Charlotte, American stage actress (as Hamlet), 220, 221
Cymbeline, Shakespeare play
  Briggs' lantern slide sequence (early 1890s), 31
Cymbeline, Thanhouser film (Sullivan, 1913), 127n

Daggerwood, Sylvester, character in 18th-century drama, 16
Dali, Salvador, 20n
Dallas, E.S., 22n
Daly, Augustin, 135
D'Ambra, Lucio, Italian scenarist/screenwriter, 221n
Dando, Walter Pfeffer, film-maker, 57, 62
Danes, Claire, American screen actress, 216n
Danish film industry, 149, 218, *see also* Nordisk, Svend Gade, Asta Nielsen
Dante, in Pathé advertising poster, *89*
Danton, played by Jannings, 240
Darley, Felix Octavius Carr, ink-wash drawing 'King Lear in the Storm', 37; *The Darley Gallery of Shakespearean Illustrations*, 38n

de Cordova, Rudolph, film scenarist/screen-
  writer, 203
de Klerk, Nico, 91n
de Putti, Lya, film actress and dancer (Emilia
  in *Othello*), 251
'Death of Caesar', painting by Gérôme *q.v.*,
  'quoted' in Vitagraph's *Julius Caesar*
  (1908), 121–24, 146, *see also* artistic
  representations
Death of Othello, film from Verdi's opera,
  see Othello
Defoe, Daniel, 28
Dehn Paul, xviin
Dench, Ernest A., 172
Dent, Alan, 152
Desdemona, offshoot films by Messter and
  Nordisk, 77
Desprès, Suzanne, actress (as Hamlet), 220
di Caprio, Leonardo, screen actor, 216n
Dickens, Charles, 17, 26n, 28; in Pathé
  advertising poster, **89**
Dickson, William Kennedy-Laurie,
  film-maker, 23, 25, 56, 57, 62, 68, 69
Dion, Hector, film actor, 201
distribution
  distributors' aspiration in relation
    to Shakespeare films, 214; films
    advertised by distributors, 90,
    151; films branded by production
    company in distribution, 105, 106–07;
    film exchanges (federated film
    markets), 106n; distribution handled
    by separate company, 74, 220n;
    international distribution, 68, 89, 90,
    101–02, 135, 143, 154, 185, 186, 205,
    206–07; international distribution
    withheld, 197; production companies'
    and distributors' monopolising
    engagements with exhibitors, 106,
    206; typical speed of film through
    production and distribution
    cycle, 132
Dondini, Cesare, Italian stage and screen actor
  (Iago in 1909 *Othello*), 91–92, **92, 93**
Donohue, Joseph, 43n, 50n, 174n
Doppelgänger themes, 234
Dougall, Richardson, 113n
Duey, Helen, 63n
Dumas, Alexander, in Pathé advertising poster,
  89
Duse, Eleonora, Italian stage actress, 223
Dyer, Anson, cartoonist, illustrator, director,
  21, 149, 217n, 246
Dyer, Richard, 225n
Dyer, T.F.T., 50–51

eagle, Vitagraph company logo, 113–23, *117, 120,*
  122, 145
Éclair, French film production company
  The Tempest (1912), 52, 80
  Macbeth (director unknown, 1916), 198n
Edison, Thomas, early film pioneer, 25, 62
Edison Manufacturing Company, American
  film production company, 107, 109, 141,
  143, 145
  Shakespearean films
    Burlesque on Romeo and Juliet (1902),
      74n
    Seven Ages of Man (1905), 74n
    single scene from *Julius Caesar* (1913),
      15n
  non-Shakespearean films
    The Black Diamond Express (1896),
      145–46
    of assassination of President McKinley
      (1901), 118
    Uncle Josh at the Moving Picture Show
      (Porter, 1902), 131n
    The Dream of a Rarebit Fiend
      (McCutcheon and Porter, 1906),
      170n
Edmonds, Jill, 219n, 220n
Edwards, J. Gordon, film director for Fox *q.v.*,
  203n, 205
Eisner, Lotte. H., 236
Elizabeth I, portrait of in a slide, 32
  played by Florence Turner, 143
Elliott, Gertrude, British stage and screen
  actress (Ophelia in 1913 *Hamlet*), 152, 156,
  158, 160, 172, **182,** 183
Ellison, James, 61n, 67n, 70n
Elliston, Robert William, 43–44
Elsaesser, Thomas, xxiin, 11n, 75n, 163n
Elsinore, setting of *Hamlet*, directly used by
  Nordisk (1910), 149; imitated by Hepworth
  (1913), 153, 163; location intended for a film
  not made, 220; dramatised by Art-Film
  (1920), 233, 238, 247
Embankment, London, scene of BMBC's
  open-air studio, 61, 70
Emerson, John, film director, 198–99
Esenwein, J. Berg, 158
Essanay, American film production company,
  107
Euripides, Greek tragedian, 6
exhibition conventions in silent cinema
  lecturers in early cinema, 10–13, 15, 28,
    102–03, 145, 195
  musical accompaniment, xviin, xxii, 28, 66,
    125, 195, 211, 216
  speakers behind the screen, 13n

exhibition conventions in silent cinema (*cont.*)
  published programmes, 13n, 52n, 66n, 67,
    68–69, 107n, 115–16, *123*
  variety programming, 40, 66, 67, 68–69, 75,
    103, **106–07**, 111, 220
  feature-film programming, 202, 206, 215
  venues (music halls, penny-gaffs, shop-
    front theatres, vaudeville theatres,
    nickelodeons, picture palaces), 10, 13,
    41, 57, 62, **66–69**, 102–03, 106–07,
    107n, 112, 145, 160, 195, 203n, 206,
    213–14

Fairbanks, Douglas, screen actor, 217n
Falena, Ugo, Italian screen actor and director,
    91–92, *92*, *93*
Famous Players-Lasky, American film produc-
    tion company, *Carmen* (1915), 203n
Farrar, Geraldine, screen actress, 203n
Faust, Martin, screen actor, 128
Felton, Cornelius, 26n
Film d'Arte Italiana (FAI), Italian film
    production company, 5, 77, **88–90**, 186
  films of Verdi operas, *Il Trovatore* (1909) and
    Aida (1911), 89
  Otello/Othello (Lo Savio, 1909), 4, 18, 74, 77,
    88–104, *92*, *93*, *97*
  Re Lear/King Lear (Lo Savio, 1910), 90, 91,
    105, 106, **125**
  *Il Mercante di Venezia / The Merchant of
    Venice* (Lo Savio, 1910), 90, 91
  Giulietta e Romeo/ Romeo and Juliet
    (Geralmo and Lo Savio, 1911), 90, 91
Film Industrie Gesellschaft, German film
    production company, *Macbeth* (Bourchier,
    1913), 184, 197
film industry development stages,
    16–20, **18n**
  pioneering era (c.1895–1906), 17, 57–73, 74,
    74–75n, 145–46
  transitional era (c.1907–1913), 18–19, **75–104**,
    105–46
  early cinema, incorporating both pioneering
    and transitional phases (1895–1913),
    19, 105
  feature-film era (1913–1927), 147–251
  sound era (post-1927), 213, 216n, 217n
Findon, B.W., 152
First World War, effects on international film
    distribution, 186, 206
Fitzgerald, Percy H., 43n, 46, 47, 54, 181, 183
Fitzsimmons, Linda, 71n, 158n
focal lengths, *see also* cinematography
  close-up, 76, 162, 163, 169, 170, 173, 179, 229,
    230, 231, 235, 243, 247, 248
  mid-shot, 76, 139, 231

long-shot, 98, 99, 162, 169, 231; use of depth-
    of-field, 141–42, 211
Fool, The, character in *King Lear*, xix, 127, 201;
    interpolated character in Thanhouser's *A
    Winter's Tale* (1910), 127–29, *128*
Forbes, Norman, British stage and screen actor,
    194
Forbes-Robertson, Johnston, British stage and
    screen actor, xvii, 4, 5, 19, 77, 190; screen
    Hamlet, xvii, 5, 19, 147, **149–64**, *153*,
    154, 169–72, 179–89, *182*, 199, 218; stage
    Hamlet, 150, 151–52, 156, 160–61, 179n,
    180; non-Shakespearean films, 184
Forestier, A., illustrator, 174n
Forrest, Edwin, American stage actor, 210
Forsyth, Neil, 77n
Foulkes, Richard, 71n
Fox Film Corporation (Fox), American film
    production company, *see also* Bara
  Romeo and Juliet (Edwards, 1916), 2, 8–9, 20,
    190, 191, **201–16**, *204*, *209*
  continuity script ('Fox continuity script'),
    203, 204n, 206n, 207n, 211–12
  courted competition with simultaneous
    Metro release, 203–16
  non-Shakespearean Fox films starring Bara,
    Carmen (Walsh, 1915), 203n, 205; *Siren
    of Hell* (Walsh, 1915), 205; *A Fool There
    Was* (Powell, 1915), 205; *Sin* (Brenon,
    1915), 205; *The Devil's Daughter* (Powell,
    1915), 205
Francis, David, 3n
Freddy Versus Hamlet, skittish appropriation,
    see Vitagraph
French film industry, *see* individual film
    production companies Éclair, Gaumont,
    Méliès, Pathé
Frölich, Carl, German film director, 240
Fuller Company, film distributors, 220n
Fullerton, John, 28n
Fuseli, Henry, artist, 30, *see also* artistic
    representations

Gade, Svend (also Sven), Danish film director
    working in German film industry, 186n,
    217, 218–20, 232–33, 237
Gallone, Carmino, Italian film director, 221n
Gallone, Suave, Italian film actress, 221
Garavaglia, Ferruccio, Italian film actor, 91,
    94n, 95–96, 100
Garbo, Greta, Swedish film actress, 223–24
Garcia, Gustave, 174–76, *176*, 178
Gardner, Helen, American film actress,
    220, 221n
Gardner, Viv, 219n
Garrett, John, xviin

Gasperini, Maria Caserini, Italian film actress, 80, 198n

Gates, Harvey H., 144n

Gaudreault, André, 13n, 103n

Gaumont, French film production company which spawned a British division, 109, 126

Romeo and Juliet (unknown, 1908), 75–76

Le Roi Lear au Village/ A Village King Lear (Feuillade, 1911), 77

Hamlet (Plumb, 1913), 19, **149–65**, **184–89**, 199

Othello (Anson Dyer, 1920), burlesque animation, 21, 217n, 246

Oh'Phelia (Anson Dyer, 1919), burlesque animation, 149, 217n

Gepard, Erwin, scenarist/screenwriter, 219

German expressionism, 219, 233, 246

German film industry, 2, 20, 217–49; *Doppelgänger* German films, 234n

see also individual film production companies Art-Film, Film Industrie Gesellschaft, Messter, Neumann-Filmproduktion, Peter Paul Felner-Film, Wörner-Filmgesellschaft

Gérôme, Jean-Léon, painter of 'The Death of Caesar' *q.v.*

ghosts, in *Hamlet*, 236; in lantern slide sequences (including Hamlet's ghost), 28, 29, 33; Hamlet's ghost on film, 80, 149, 157, 167–70; and absent from film, 238; Banquo's ghost on film, 132; non-Shakespearean film ghosts, 170n

'giddy', animated picture with risqué subject, *Studio Troubles*, 57–60

Gielgud, John, 152

Glover, Julia, stage actress (as Hamlet), 220

Glulick, J., artist, 152, **153**

Godwin, E.W., theatre producer, 50–51

Goethe, Johann Wolfgang von, in Pathé advertising poster, **89**

Goetz, Wolfgang, biographer of Krauss, 242n

Goldie, Albert, 181n

Gollancz, Israel, 190n

Gordon, Julia Swayne, American screen actress for Vitagraph, 3, **124**, 130, 139, **142**

Gorky, Maxim, 20n

Gottesman, Ronald, 110n

Gounod, Charles, composer, 211

Graham, Arthur, 49n

Graham, Charles, 163

Gramsci, Antonio, Italian political theorist and cultural critic, 166, 185

Grau, Robert, 12n

Graves, George W., 205n

Gress, Elsa, 225n

Griffith, D.W., American film director, 163, 198

Grillo, Ernesto, 164n, 179n

Guazzoni, Enrico, 125

Guneratne, Anthony, xviiin

Gunning, Tom, 17, 18n, 68n, 74, 76n, 103n

Gwenn, Edmund, British stage and screen actor, 194–95

Hamilton, Clayton, xxi

Hamlet, Shakespeare play
ballet, 49n

lantern slide sequences, 29, 31, **32–39**, **37, 38**

stage productions, Burbage, 165–66; Tree (1895) 168n; Forbes-Robertson (1897), 19, 152; Forbes-Robertson (1913), 150, 151–52, 156, 160–61, 179n, **180**; various, 150, 155 Ruggeri (1915 in Italy), 164, 166, 168n; Ruggeri (1926 European tour), 165–66; Synetic's wordless production (2002 with revivals), 253–59

novelisation of 1913 film (*Shakespeare's Hamlet, The Story of the Play concisely told*), 160–62, 183

variant texts, Q1 and Q2, 161

overview of *Hamlet* films, 147–51

Le Duel d'Hamlet / The Duel Scene from Hamlet, Phono-Cinéma-Théâtre film (Maurice, 1900), 15n, 41, 72, 74n, 220

Hamlet, Méliès film (Méliès, 1907), 75

Amleto/Hamlet, Cines film (Caserini, 1908, reissued 1910), 75, 80n, 149

Hamlet, Barker film (Barker, 1910), 149

Hamlet, Gaumont-Hepworth film (Plumb, 1913), xvii, 5, 19, 147, **149–64**, **153**, **154**, 169–72, 179–89, **182**, 199, 218

Amleto/Hamlet, Rodolfi film (Rodolfi, 1917), 5, 19, 149–50, **164–70**, **172–79**, **181**, **185–89**, 229, 230

Hamlet, Drama of Vengeance, Art-Film film (Gade, 1920), 5, 7, 185–86n, **217–40**, 248–49

Hamlet, Nordisk film (Blom, 1910), 149

Hamlet, Lux film (Bourgeois, 1909), 185–86n

offshoots

When Hungry Hamlet Fled, Thanhouser film (director unknown, 1915), 148n, 149

Freddy versus Hamlet, Vitagraph film (Currier, 1916), 107, 148n, 149, 200

Pimple as Hamlet, Piccadilly film (Evans, 1916), 149, 200

Hamlet, Shakespeare play *(cont.)*
 To Be or Not To Be, Beauty film (Watt,
  1916), 149, 200
 Hamlet Made Over, Lubin film (Metcalfe,
  1916), 149, 200
 The Barnyard Hamlet, Powers film (Stark,
  1916), 149
 Oh'Phelia, Hepworth animation film
  (Anson Dyer, 1919), 149, 217n
 Amleto e il suo Clown / On with the Motley,
  D'Ambra film (Gallone, 1919), 221
Hammerton, J.A., biographer of Barrie, 192,
 195n, 196n
Hankin, John, satirist, 48–49
Hanlon, Alfred, film actor, 128
Hann, Walter (incorrectly given elsewhere as
 Hamm), designer of stage *tableaux,*
 69–70
Hapgood, Robert, 6
Harrison, Louis Reeves, 189n
Hastings, Chris, 213n
Haviland, William, British stage actor, 86
Hazlitt, William, 175
Heard, Mervyn, lanternist and lantern
 historian, 29n, 30n
Heard, Mo, lantern historian, 35n
Helen Gardner Picture Players, 220
Hendricks, Gordon, 221n
Henry VIII, Shakespeare play
 staging principles, 51
 Scenes from Shakespeare's King Henry VIII,
  Barker offshoot film (Barker, 1911), xvii,
  2, 72, 77, 184, 197n
Henry, David, 29n
Henson, Leslie, 193n, 194
Hentschel, C., artist, 156n, *see also* Ophelia *and*
 artistic representations
Hepworth, Cecil, British film director and pro-
 ducer, 19, 149–64, 169–70, 188
Herbert, Stephen, lantern historian, 25n, 29n,
 35n, 116n
Hertogs, Daan, 91n
Higson, Andrew, 18n
Hill, Aaron, 174
Hilliard, Harry, American screen actor,
 207, **209,**
*History, Murders, Life and Death of Macbeth,
 The,* stage-production, *see Macbeth*
Hoenselaars, A.J., 72n, 192n
Hoffman, H.F., 103
Hollows, Joanne, 225n
Hosenrolle, 'breeches roles', 224, *see also* cross-
 dressing
House, M., 26n
Howard, Camille Cole, 49n

Howard, Tony, 220n, 226, 234
Howe, Julia Warde, 109
Hughes, Arthur, artist, his painting 'Ophelia'
 used as a lantern slide (1890s), 35, 37–39,
 156n, *see also* artistic representations
Hughes-Hallett, Lucy, 205n
Hugo, Victor, in Pathé advertising poster, **89**
Hulette, Gladys, American child screen actress,
 131, 132
Hutchings, Peter, 225n

Ibsen, Henrik, playwright, 6, 218
Ihering, Herbert, biographer of Krauss, 242n
Imrie, Thos. S., 207n
Indian Romeo and Juliet, An (Trimble, 1912),
 Vitagraph offshoot, *see Romeo
 and Juliet*
intertitles (also known as title cards), 13, 15,
 45, 55, 77n, 80n, 81, 95, 102, 103, 115,
 116, **117,** 135, 144, 150n, 157, 158–59,
 162, 171, 173, 193–94, 207, 211, 230,
 231, 235, 238–39
Irace, Kathleen O., 161n
Irving, Henry, actor-manager, 48, 152, 156–57n,
 175–78, 183n
Italian film industry, 2; non-Shakespearean
 films made in the spectacular style, 186;
 performance styles (compared with
 British and American), 187–89; Ruggeri's
 compared with Nielsen's, 229, *see also*
 individual film production companies
 Ambrosio, Cines, Film d'Arte Italiana,
 Milano, Rodolfi

Jackson, Russell, xviiin, 53, 86n, 135n
Jacobs, Lea, 24n
Jacobsson, Lilli, screen actress (plays Ophelia
 with Nielsen), **226,** 229
Jancovich, Mark, 225n
Jannings, Emil, stage and screen actor, 4, 7–8,
 20, 21, 77, 94, 217, 224, 240–51, **244, 245,**
 249
'Jingle', journalist for *Pick-Me-Up,* 67n
Johnson, Adrian, scriptwriter, 203n, 204
Johnson, Tefft, American screen actor, 140
'Jolo', pseudonymous reviewer for *Variety,* 9
Jorgens, Jack, 6
Jud Süß (Veit Harlan, 1940), 21
Judson, Hanford C., 155n, 164n, 170n,
 171n, 211n
Julius Caesar, Shakespeare play, 118
 *Le Rêve de Shakespeare/ La Mort de Jules
  César/ Shakespeare writing Julius Caesar,*
  Georges Méliès offshoot film (Méliès,
  1907), 2, 75, 106, 119

Julius Caesar, Vitagraph film (Ranous and Blackton, 1908), 4, 16, 19, 105, 106, 108, **115–26, 117, 122,** 132, 139, 146

Brutus, only partly Shakespearean Cines film (Guazzoni, 1910), 19, 105–06, **125–26**

Scene from *Julius Caesar*, Edison Kinetophone film (director unknown, 1913), 15n

Gajus Julius Caesar/ Julius Caesar, Cines film (Guazzoni, 1914), 105, 115–16, **123, 126**

Junckerman, Hans, German screen actor, 229

Kachur, B.A., 70n
Kahn, Coppélia, 113n, 190n
Kalem, American film production company, 107

As You Like It (Buel, 1908), 75

Romeo of the Coal Wagon, offshoot film (Beaudine, 1916), 200

Kean, Charles, theatrical actor-manager, 29, 47–48, 70n, 85

Kean, Edmund, theatrical actor-manager, 28, 175, 178

Keil, Charlie, 18n, 104
Kemble, Charles, actor-manager, 50
Kennedy, Dennis, 48n, 53n, 78n
Kent, Charles, stage and screen actor, film director for Vitagraph, 4, **120,** 130, 131, 138–41, **140**

Keys, Nelson, British stage and screen actor, 194

Keystone, American film production company

A Tugboat Romeo, Shakespeare offshoot film (Campbell, 1916), 200

King, Norman, 10n

King John, Shakespeare play
stage productions
Coburg Theatre, *Magna Charta, or, The Eventful Reign of King John* (1823), 70n
Kemble's production at Covent Garden (1824), 50
Tree's production at Her Majesty's Theatre (1899), 17
films
King John, BMBC film from Tree's stage production (Dickson and Dando, 1899), 4, 23, 40, 41, 57–73, **65,** 74n, 77

King Lear, Shakespeare play, 99, 127, 143, 238
Orwell's visual recollection of the play, xix-xx, 238, 255
Edmund Kean's stage production (1821), 28
lantern slide sequences, 29, 31
'King Lear in the Storm', drawing by Darley, used as lantern slide, 37, 38n

other artistic representations, xxn

King Lear, Vitagraph film (Ranous, 1909), 19, 105, 106, 108, **124,** 125, 127, 131, 132, 139, 143

Re Lear/ King Lear, FAI film (1910), 90, 91, 105–06, 125

Le Roi Lear au Village/ A Village King Lear, Gaumont updated film (Feuillade, 1911), 77

King Lear, Thanhouser film (Ernest Warde, 1916), **front cover,** 9, 13, 32–33, 77, 96–97, 127n, 201

Kino, DVD/video production company, 4, 217n, 260–61

Kitchin, Laurence, 6
Klauber, Adolph, 155n
Kleine Optical Company, American film production company and distributor, 107, 186

Kleine, George, 27n
Kliman, Bernice W., 155n, 185n
Knight, Joseph, 47n
Krauss, Werner, stage and screen actor (as Iago), 21, 217, **240–46,** 248, **245**

Kuleshov, Lev, 7

Lady Godiva, non-Shakespearean film, *see* Vitagraph

Lake, Fred, 79n
Lally, Gwendoline, British actress (as Hamlet), 220

Lamb, Charles and Mary, 54–55, 56
Lang, Fritz, German film director, 233, 241
Lang, Matheson, British actor, 201
lantern, *see* magic lantern
Latham, Robert, 26n
Launcelot and Elaine, non-Shakespearean film, *see* Vitagraph

Lawrence, Florence, American screen actress, 'the Biograph Girl', 3, 143, 144, 211n

Lawrence, Gerald, British stage and screen actor, 64

leaders, alternative name for intertitles, 158–59, *see also* intertitles

Le Diable et la Statue, offshoot film with loose connections to *Romeo and Juliet* (Méliès, 1901), 74n

lecturers, live, for early moving pictures, xviin, 10–13, 15, 28, 102–103, 145, 195
'boomer', category of lecturers, 12–13
for lantern shows, 29–30
see also exhibition conventions

Leeds, Arthur, 158
Leisegang, Franz Paul, 23n

Lepanto, Vittoria, Italian screen actress, 91, 94n, 95, **97,**
Levenson, Michael, 237
Levine, Lawrence W., 15, 114n, 210n
Licensing Act of 1737, 43; repealed 1843, 46
Lindsay, Vachel, 6, 77, 232–33
Lippman, Max, 12n
Lo Savio, Gerolamo, Italian film director, 74, 88, 91, 92
logos, company logos exhibited within films, 95, 96, 112–13, 116–18, *117*, *120 see also* eagle
Lonergan, Lloyd, 127n
Longfellow, Henry, poet, 28
Lowe, Robert, 'pamphleteer', 175n, 178n
Lowrey, Caroline, 215n
Lubin, American film production company, 107, 109
Julius Caesar (director unknown, 1908), 75
Hamlet Made Over, offshoot (Metcalfe, 1916), 149, 200
The Haunted House, non-Shakespearean film (1899), 170n
Luhrmann, Baz, film director, 216n
Lumière brothers, film pioneers, 23, 57; as slide manufacturers, 28n, 56
Luzzi, Eusebio, eighteenth-century ballet producer, 49n

MacBean, L.C., co-director with J.M.Barrie of *The Real Thing at Last* (1916), 191
Macbeth, Shakespeare play
 ballet, 49n
 Elliston's wordless 'ballet of action', *The History, Murders, Life and Death of Macbeth* (1809), 43–45
 Forrest's and Macready's rival stage productions (1849), 210
 lantern slide-sequences, 29, 30, 31
 films, compared 197–200
 duel scene from *Macbeth,* AMBC film (Bitzer, 1905), 74–75n
Macbeth, Vitagraph film (Ranous, 1908), 19, 75, 105, 106, 108, 119–21, *120,* 131–32, 139, 143, 170n, 197
Macbeth/Macbeth, Cines film (Caserini, 1909), 4, 80, 170n, 198n
Macbeth, Co-operative Cinematograph Company film (F.R.Benson, 1911), 197–98
Macbeth, Film Industrie Gesellschaft film (Bourchier, 1913), 184, 197
Macbeth, Éclair film (director unknown, 1916), 198n

Macbeth, Triangle-Reliance film (Emerson, 1916), 2, 20, 72–73, 77, 190, 191, 192n, **198–202,** 213
The Real Thing at Last, Bushey Heath Company's film lampooning comparative productions of *Macbeth* (Barrie and MacBean, 1916), 2–3, 19–20, 77, **190–201,** 202, 212–13
McCormick, Richard W., 227n
Mackail, Denis, biographer of Barrie, 191, 194n
McKernan, Luke, xviiin, 25n, 64n, 71, 79n, 81n, 82n, 116n, 187n, 192n, 201n, 213–14n
McKinley, American President, 118
Macleod, Mary, 54, 156–57n
McManus, John T., 193n
McQuade, James S., 126n
Macready, William Charles, actor-manager, 47, 210
magic lantern, 10, **23–42,** 56, 74n, 146,
 lantern lectures and exhibition conventions, 28–31, 41n, 42
 lantern technology, 26–27
 slide manufacturing production companies
  Alfred Pumphrey, 30n; Bamforth, 28n; Briggs and Company, 28n, **30–39;** Carpenter and Westley, 28n; Eastman Kodak Company, 28n; Keystone, 28n; Lancaster, 28n; Lumière brothers, 28n, 56; Newton, 28n; Riley brothers, 28n; Theobald and Company, 28n, 30; Unger und Hoffmann, 28n; York and Sons, 30n
 non-Shakespearean subjects, 27, 28
 Shakespearean subjects (images of stage actors in role, satirical slides, exemplary slides, compressed plots (*Hamlet* case-study), painterly quotations, use of Shakespeare's image), 28–42
Magic Lantern Society, The (MLS), 29n, 30n
Magna Carta, signing of, not in Shakespeare's *King John,* 69; interpolated *tableau* in Tree's 1899 stage production, 69–72
Magna Charta, Henry Milner's play (1823), 70n
Magnier, Pierre, French stage and screen actor, 220
Makart, Hans, artist of balcony scene from *Romeo and Juliet,* 38
Makowska, Elena, Polish film actress (Ophelia in 1917 *Hamlet*), 173, 185, 251
Mannoni, Laurent, 27n, 28n
Manvell, Roger, 6, 71n
Manzini, Amerigo, 164n, 165, 166

Marcus, Leah, 233n
Marescalchi, Luigi, eighteenth-century ballet
    producer, 49n
Marinetti, F.T., 25n
Marker, Frederick J., 48n
marketing strategies, xviiin, 10, 19, **89**, **226**
    advertisements, 67, **89**, 90, 107–08, 109, 110,
        112, 131–32, 137–38, 149–50n, 154–55,
        158n, 202, 207, 209, 242
    authentic locations, 90–91, 149; billboards,
        107
    commercial tie-ins/analogue productions
        (novelisations, glossy programmes,
        published stories), 54–55, 115–16, 123,
        160–62
    company branding and logos, 95, **105–13**,
        116–21
    competition between rival releases, 203n,
        208–11, 213
    film used to advertise stage production,
        68, 69
    limited exhibition runs, 2
    mass markets, 56, 160–62, 164, 187, 206,
        213–14
    minimising scurrility, 57
    Shakespeare used as improving influence,
        and to denote corporate quality, 18n,
        89, 108, 110, 138
    stars
        films showcasing stars, 142–43, 143–45,
            152, 183, 187, 198–99, 202, 203–05,
            204, 206–12, **208**, **209**, 214, 216,
            226, 251
        in-person appearances, 144–45, 215–16, 218
        star cards, 79n, **180**, **182**, **226**
Marriott, Alice, British stage actress
    (as Hamlet), 220
Marshall, Frank A., 156–57n
Martineau, Jane, xxn, 86n
Masters, British film production company
    The Merchant of Venice, part of 'Tense
        Moments from Great Plays' one-reeler
        series (Sanderson, 1922), 217n
Matthews, A.E., stage and screen actor, 192,
    193n, 194, 195n, 196n, 197n, 200n
Matthews, William, 26n
Maurice, Clément, French film-maker, 15n,
    220, *see also Hamlet* duel scene (1900)
Méliès, Georges, French film pioneer
    Hamlet (Méliès, 1907), 75
    *Le Rêve de Shakespeare/ La Mort de Jules
        César/ Shakespeare writing Julius Caesar*
        (Méliès, 1907), 2, 105–06, 119
    Le Diable et la Statue, offshoot of *Romeo and
        Juliet* (Méliès, 1901), 74n

'double exposure' non-Shakespeare films,
    170n
Melzer, Annabelle Henkin, 185–86n, 262
Merchant of Venice, The, Shakespeare play
    nineteenth-century realist stage production,
        50
    lantern slide sequence, 31
    *Le miroir de Venise / Une Mésadventure
        de Shylock/ The Venetian Look-glass*,
        offshoot film (Méliès, 1905), 75n
    The Merchant of Venice, Vitagraph film
        (Blackton, 1908), 75, 105–06, 108,
        119–21, 139, 143
    *Il Mercante di Venezia / The Merchant of
        Venice*, FAI film (Lo Savio, 1910),
        90, 91
    The Merchant of Venice, Broadwest film
        (Walter West, 1916), 77, 201
    The Merchant of Venice, Thanhouser film
        (Henderson, 1912), 127n
    The Merchant of Venice, Masters film
        (Sanderson, 1922), 217n
    *Der Kaufmann von Venedig/ The Jew of
        Mestri* (Felner, 1923), 242n
    The Merchant of Venice, Spice Factory sound-
        era film (Radford, 2004), 213
    The Merchant of Venice, (as yet) unmade film
        to have starred Patrick Stewart, 213
Merry Wives of Windsor, The, Shakespeare play,
    lantern slide sequence, 31
Messter, German film production company
    Death of Othello / Desdemona,
        Shakespearean offshoot (Porten, 1907),
        74–75n
Metro, American film production company
    Romeo and Juliet (Noble, 1916), 7, 9, 20,
        54–55, 190, 191, **201–16**, **209**
Midsummer Night's Dream, A, Shakespeare
    play, 15
    ballet, 49n; lantern slide sequence, 31
    trends in performance history, 136–37
    Daly's stage production (1895), 135
    Tree's stage production (1900), 135
    Tree's revival production (1911), 137
    Harley Granville Barker's stage production
        (1914), 136
    A Midsummer Night's Dream, Vitagraph film
        (Kent and Blackton, 1909), 19, 105, 106,
        108, **130–37**, **134**, 139, 141, 143
    *Ein Sommernachtstraum / A Midsummer
        Night's Dream*, Neumann-
        Filmproduktion film (Neumann, 1925),
        135n, 242n
Midwinter Night's Dream, A, or Little Joe's Luck,
    non-Shakespearean film, *see* Vitagraph

Milano, Italian film production company
 Hamlet (Comerio, 1908), 75
 *Una tragedia alla Corte di Sicilia/ A Winter's
 Tale* (Negroni, 1913), 32
Millais, John Everett, artist, 156n, *see also*
 artistic representations
Mills, John A., 171n, 179n
Milner, Catherine, 213n
Milner, Henry, nineteenth-century playwright,
 70n
Milton, John, 28
*Miroir de Venise, Le/ Une Mésadventure de
 Shylock* (Méliès, 1905), Shakespearean
 offshoot film, *see The Merchant of Venice*
Molière, playwright, 6
Mollison, William, stage and screen actor, 64
Moncrieff, William Thomas, nineteenth-
 century playwright, 43n, 45
Montgomery, Robert, American screen actor,
 223–24
Moody, Jane, 16n, 43n, 44, 45n, 175n, 178n
Morley, Sheridan, 191n, 199n, 200n
Mortimer, John, artist, xxn
Morton, Mr, manager of the Palace Theatre, 67,
 see also Theatres
'Mother Squeers', fictional commentator on
 early film production companies, 109–10,
 112, 138, 145
Motion Picture and Recorded Sound Division,
 Library of Congress, Washington DC
 (LOC), 52n, 77n, 80n, 91n, 97, 128, 170n,
 198n, 202n, 203, 221n, 222
Motion Picture Patents Company, 107
Mounet-Sully, Jean, stage and screen actor, 149
Much Ado About Nothing, Shakespeare play,
 stage production, 48, 183n
'mugging', the mouthing of words on silent
 film, *see* acting styles
Mühr, Alfred, 242n
Mullin, Eugene, script-editor for Vitagraph, 131
Murnau, F.W., German film director, 233
music halls, 22, 46–47, 66, 67; production of
 Shakespeare, 24
musical accompaniment to films, xviin,
 28, 66, 195, 211; to lantern shows, 28,
 31; to wordless stage productions, 43;
 synchronised sound, 15n, 74–75n, 220
Musketeers of Pig Alley, The, Biograph film
 (1912), 76n
Musser, Charles, 10–11n, 13n
mutoscope cards, 66n
Muybridge, Eadweard, film pioneer, 56

National Association of the Motion Picture
 Industry, 215

Nazimova, Alla, Russian stage actress, 220
Neilson, Julia, stage and screen actress, 64
Nepoti, Alberto, Italian film actor, 91, 95
Neumann-Filmproduktion, German film
 production company
 *Ein Sommernachtstraum / A Midsummer
 Night's Dream / Wood Love* (Neumann,
 1925), 135n, 242n
Neuss, Alwin, German stage and screen actor,
 149
Newton, H. Chance ('Carados'), 61–62
Nichols, B., 171n
Nicholson, Watson, 43n
nickelodeons, 107n, *see also* exhibition
 conventions, venues
Nielsen, Asta, Danish screen actress, 4, 5, 7, 20,
 77, 135, 185–86n, 217–40, **226**, **237**, 249,
 251; personal life, 225; in non-Shakespear-
 ean films, 224–25, 233
Niver, Kemp R., 68n
Noble, John W., American film
 director, 202
Nordisk, Danish film production company
 Asta Nielsen's early film career, 218
 Othello (unknown, 1908), 75
 Hamlet (Blom, 1910), 149
 Desdemona, offshoot from *Othello* (Blom,
 1911), 77
Norton, Freddie, composer, 195
novelisation of film *Hamlet* (1913), *see Hamlet*
Novelli, Amleto, Italian stage and screen actor,
 125
Novelli, Ermete, Italian stage and screen actor,
 3, 125, 164
Noverre, Jean-Georges, eighteenth-century
 French ballet choreographer, 49n
Nuttall, A.D., 234n

Olivier, Laurence, actor, 217n
O'Mahoney, Lt Col C.C.S., real name of actor
 Charles Sefton, 71n
O'Neil, Barry, film director for Thanhouser,
 127n
Ophelia, character in *Hamlet*, subject of
 paintings, lantern slides and film
 interpretations, xx, 33–39, **37**, **38**, 80n,
 156–57n, 156–58, 160–61, 164, 168, 173, 174,
 178, 179, **180**, 185, 218–20, **226**, 230, 235,
 238, 239
optical toys, 23, 24n, 57
O'Quinn, Daniel, 16n
Orwell, George, xix-xxi, 238, 255
Orwell, Sonia, xixn
Othello, Shakespeare play
 lantern slide sequences, 37

Death of Othello/ Desdemona, Messter offshoot film from Verdi's opera (Porten, 1907), 75n

Othello, Vitagraph film (Ranous, 1908), 75, 90, 105, 108, 119, 201

Otello/Othello, FAI film (Lo Savio, 1909), 4, 18, 74, 77, **88–104**, *92*, *93*, *97*

Desdemona, Nordisk offshoot film (Blom, 1911), 77

Othello, unidentified version exhibited in Berlin with live lecture (1912), 12, 104n

Otello/Othello, Ambrosio film (Frusta, 1914), 21, 90–91, 94, 248

Othello, Wörner-Filmgesechellschaft film (Buchowetski, 1922), 7–8, 20, 21, 77, 94, 217, 224, **240–51**, *244*, *245*, *249*

Othello, Castle Rock sound-era film (Parker, 1995), 243n

Othello, Andrew Davies' updated version for LWT (Geoffrey Sax, 2001)

Pacino, Al, screen actor, 213

paintings, *see* artistic representations

Paget, F.M., stage and screen actor, 62n

Panofsky, Erwin, 223

pantomime, established theatrical convention for wordless performance, 43, 46, 49, 55; associated performance codes, 19, 46, 49, 173–78, *176*, *177*, 181

Park, James, 189n

Paster, Gail Kern, 114n

patents, royal, 42–43

Pathé, Charles, 88

Pathé, French film production company, 88, 91n, 107, 109; with rooster as logo, 95, 96, 116

Othello (unknown, 1908), 75

Roméo se fait bandit/ Romeo Turns Bandit, updated offshoot (Bosetti, 1910), 197n

La Vie et la Passion de Jésus Christ, episodic Passion play (Nonguet and Zecca, 1902 & 1904), 170n

Patterson, Richard S., 113n

Paul, Robert W., film pioneer, 56, 57; director of non-Shakespearean *The Countryman and the Cinematograph*, 129n

Pearson, Roberta, author, 15n, 16n, 72n, 107n, 108n, 110, 115n, 121n, 124n, 137n, 174n, 181n, 192n, 212n, 213n

Pecor, Charles Joseph, 26n

Penelope, interpolated character replacing Oberon in Vitagraph's *A Midsummer Night's Dream*, 133–36, *134*

Pepys, Samuel, diarist, 26n

Pericles, Shakespeare play, of which no silent film made, 252n

Peter Paul Felner-Film, German film production company

Der Kaufmann von Venedig/ The Jew of Mestri (Felner, 1923), 242n

Petro, Patrice, 227n, 236n

Pezzaglia, A, Italian film actor, 94n

Piccadilly, British film production company

Pimple as Hamlet, Shakespeare offshoot film (Evans, 1916), 149, 200

Pickford, Mary, film actress, 217n

'pictures', held stage *tableaux*, 53, 69–70

Pike, Benjamin Jr., 27n

pioneering era (1895–1906), *see* film industry development stages

piracy, of film prints, 116, *see also* logos

Planché, James Robinson, theatre designer, 50

Platt, Agnes, 172, 249–50

Plumb, Hay, British film director, 19, **149–64**, 169, 188

Plumpton, Alfred, orchestra manager at the Palace Theatre, 66n

Poel, William, theatre director, 78

Pollock, F., 47n

Porter Edwin S., American film director, 129n, 143

Pound, Ezra, 20n

Poussin, artist, xxn, *see also* artistic representaitons

premières (opening of a run), 60, 66, 132, 149n, 150n, 160, 195, 200, 203, 216n, 218

President Lincoln portrayed on Vitagraph film, 109

programmes from theatres, xviiin, 13, 47–48, 54, 66n, 67n, 70, 152, *153*

programmes for films, 13n, 52n, 66n, 67, 68–69, 107n, 115–16, *123*

programming of films, *see* exhibition conventions

Pudovkin, Vsevelod, 20

Pushkin, Alexander, 17

Q1, Q2 and Quarto, *see Hamlet* and *King Lear*

Queen Mary, at Royal Command Performance (1916), 200

Queen Victoria, on film, 66

Racine, 17

Radford, Michael, film director, 213

Raengo, 18n, 74n

Rainey, Lawrence, 25n

Ranous, William ('Billy') V., film actor and director for Vitagraph, 115, *120*, 130

Raymond, Charles, screen actor, 149

Raymond, George, 43n
Real Thing, The, stage farce, 192
Real Thing at Last, The (1916), spoof film of
    Macbeth, see Macbeth
Rees, Terence, 28n
Reinhardt, Max, German theatre director and
    producer, 20n, 250
religious imagery, 35–36, *245,* 247, 248
Rex, American film production company
    A Seashore Romeo, Shakespearean offshoot
    (Wilson, 1915), 197n
Richard III, Shakespeare play
    in lantern slides, 29
    Richard III, Vitagraph film (Blackton and
        Ranous, 1908), 75, 108, 115n
    Richard III, Co-operative Cinematograph
        Company film (Benson, 1911), 197–98n
    Richard III, Shakespeare Film Company
        film (Keane, 1912), 4, 12–13, *14,* 52, 77
Ringham, Walter, British stage and screen
    actor, 156
Robeson, Paul, American stage and screen
    actor, 223
Robinson, David, 10n, 26n, 40n, 105n, 158n
Rock, William T. ('Pop'), co-director of
    Vitagraph, 113
Rodolfi, Eleuterio, Italian film director and
    founder of Rodofi-Film
    Amleto/Hamlet, Rodolfi film (Rodolfi, 1917),
        5, 19, 149–50, *164–70, 172–79,* 181,
        185–89, 229, 230
Roi Lear au Village, Le, Shakespearean offshoot,
    see King Lear
Romeo and Juliet, Shakespeare play, xx; in ballet,
    49n; lantern slide sequences, 30, 31, 38
Romeo and Juliet, Gaumont film (director
    unknown, 1908), 75–76
Romeo and Juliet, Vitagraph film (Blackton,
    1908), 75, 105, 106, 108, *120,* 121, 139,
    143, 144, 211n
Giulietta e Romeo/ Romeo and Juliet, Cines
    film (Caserini, 1908), 75
Giulietta e Romeo/ Romeo and Juliet, FAI
    film (Falena and Lo Savio, 1911), 90, 91
Romeo and Juliet, Thanhouser film (O'Neil,
    1911), 127n
Romeo and Juliet, Fox film (Edwards, 1916),
    2, 8–9, 20, 190, 191, *201–16, 204, 209*
    courted competition with simultaneous
    Metro release, 203–16
Romeo and Juliet, Metro film (Noble, 1916),
    7, 9, 20, 54–55, 190, 191, *201–16, 209*
William Shakespeare's Romeo + Juliet,
    Bazmark film (Luhrmann, 1996), 216n
Le Diable et la Statue, Méliès offshoot
    (Méliès, 1901), 74n

Burlesque on Romeo and Juliet, Edison
    offshoot (director unknown, 1902), 74n
Roméo se fait bandit/ Romeo Turns Bandit,
    Pathé updated offshoot (Bosetti, 1910),
    197n
An Indian Romeo and Juliet, Vitagraph
    offshoot (Trimble, 1912), 2, 77, 108, 144
A Seashore Romeo, Rex film (Wilson, 1915),
    197n
Romeo of the Coal Wagon, Kalem film
    (Beaudine, 1916), 200
A Tugboat Romeo, Keystone film (Campbell,
    1916), 200
Rothwell, Kenneth, xviiin, 13n, 78, 186n
Ruggeri, Ruggero, Italian stage and screen actor
    (in 1917 *Hamlet),* 5, 19, 149–50, *164–70,*
    165, 172–79, 181, 185–89, 229, 230
running speeds for silent film, 75n, 79n
Rutherford, Susan, 219n

Sadoul, Georges, 88n
Sargent, Epes Winthrop, 159
satire, 48–49, 122–29, 129n, 192–98, 200–01
Saxo-Grammaticus, 219, 238
scenery and set dressing, 78, 115–16, 141, *142,*
    207, 232–33, 235–37, *237,* 242, 243, *244,*
    245, 246–48
Schall, Heinz, German film director, 217
Schoch, Richard W., 183n
Schoenberg, Arnold, 20n
Schumacher, Helen Gardner, granddaughter of
    Helen Gardner, 221n
Scott-Gatty, Alexander, British stage and
    screen actor, 156
'scrolls' (also known as 'banners'), slogans car-
    ried on stage by actors, 44–45, 55
Seaman, Julia, stage actress (as Hamlet), 220
Sefton, Charles (stage name of
    C.C.S.O'Mahoney), 71
Seidl, Monika, 233n
Selig, American film production
    company, 107
Sellmann, Professor Dr, German linguistician, 12
Senior, Dora, stage and screen actress, 62, 64
Seven Ages of Man, Edison film (1905), 74n;
    slide-sequences, 30, *see also As You Like It*
Shakespeare, William, playwright, *see also*
    individual play titles *Antony and Cleopatra,*
    As You Like It, The Comedy of Errors,
    Coriolanus, Hamlet, Henry VIII, Julius
    Caesar, King John, King Lear, Macbeth,
    The Merchant of Venice, The Merry Wives
    of Windsor, A Midsummer Night's Dream,
    Much Ado About Nothing, Othello, Pericles,
    Richard III, Romeo and Juliet, The Taming
    of the Shrew, The Tempest, Timon of Athen,

Titus Andronicus, Troilus and Cressida, Twelfth Night, The Winter's Tale
represented in person on lantern slide, 31–32; on nineteenth-century stage curtain, 114; on Pathé advertising poster, 89; on film, in Méliès *Le Rêve de Shakespeare* (1907), Milano's *Una tragedia alla Corte di Sicilia* (1913), Bushey Heath's *The Real Thing at Last* (1916), *see under Julius Caesar, The Winter's Tale and Macbeth*

his authorship examined on film, *see* Thanhouser *Master Shakespeare, Strolling Player* (1916)

his works widely cited in nineteenth-century America, 15–16

his mind known to Tree, 51; and imagined by Albert E. Smith, 130

his statue beflagged in New York, 1916, 190

Shakespeare Film Company, The, American production company

Richard III (Keane, 1912), 4, 12–13, *14*, 52, 77

'Shakespeare Illustrated', lantern slide series, 30–39

Shakespeare Writing Julius Caesar, Méliès film (1907), *see Julius Caesar*

Shapiro, James, 118n

Shattuck, Charles H., 155n, 181n

Shaw, George Bernard, 19, 78, 152, 155

Showalter, Elaine, 35

Siddons, Sarah, British stage actress, on lantern slide, 29; as Hamlet, 220

Silent Shakespeare, BFI DVD, 4, 62, 77n, 91n, 106n, 140n, *260*

Sillars, Stuart, xxn

Simoni, Renato, 164, 165, 166

Sinobad, Zoran, 221n

Slide, Anthony, 107n, 143n, 144n

Smedley, William Thomas, chairman of BMBC, 60

Smith, Albert E., Vitagraph chairman, 107n, 111, 113, 130, 144n, 145–46

Smith, Emma, xviiin, 158n, 160n

Smith, George Albert, film pioneer
The Haunted Castle (1897), 170n
Photographing a Ghost (1898), 170n
see also ghosts

Smith, Samuel, MP, 59

Sothern E.H., stage and screen actor, 110–11

Southern, Richard, 53n

Spearing, James O., 228

speech ban at unpatented theatres, *see* wordless productions

Speht, Paul, 25n

sport on film
Cambridge rowing 'bumps', 66; polo at Hurlingham, 66; hurdle race at the

Queen's Club, 66; Yale football team, 68–69

Staiger, Janet, 20n

Stam, Robert, 18n, 74n

Stanton, Sarah, 183n

Starks, Lisa, xviiin, 234n

stars, *see under* marketing strategies

Steere, Janette, stage actress (as Hamlet), 220

Steida, Hans, German screen actor, 230, 236–37, *237*

Stewart, Patrick, stage and screen actor, 213

Storey, G., 26n

Stow, Percy, film director, 74, 78–79, 82, 85–87, *see also The Tempest* (1908)

Stratford-upon-Avon Shakespeare Festival, 215

Street, Sarah, 71n, 158n

Stuart, Violet, stage actress, *14*

Studio Troubles, also known as *Wicked Willie*, a BMBC short film (1899) *58–60*

Summers, Rollin, 174n

Sutcliffe, J.B., 215n

Swift, Jonathan, 27, 28

synchronised sound, 15n, 74–75n, 220, *see also* musical accompaniment

Synetic Theater Company, 21, 253–59, *258*

tableaux, see 'pictures'

Talmadge, Norma, screen actress, 144

Tales from Shakespeare, 54–55

Tamara, Russian dancer, 135n

Taming of the Shrew, The, Shakespeare play lantern slide sequences, 31
The Taming of the Shrew, Biograph film (Griffith, 1908), 75
The Taming of the Shrew, Sam Taylor film (Taylor, 1929), 217n

Taranow, G., 220n

Taylor, Gary, 1n

Tchaikovsky, composer, 211

Tearle, Godfrey, British stage and screen actor, 194

Tempest, The, Shakespeare play
Macready's stage production (1838), 47
Charles Kean's stage production (1857), 47–48
Tree's stage production (1904), 54; and resulting storm scene on film (1905) 72, 74–75n, 85–88
satirical appropriation, 48–49
in lantern slide sequences, 31
The Tempest, Clarendon film (Stow, 1908), 18, 74, 77–88, *94–95*, 98, 103–04
The Tempest, Thanhouser film (Thanhouser, 1911), 86n, 127n
The Tempest, Éclair film (Chautard [?], 1912), 52

Tennyson, Alfred Lord, 28, 107
tercentenary year of Shakespeare's death,
    1916, associated committees, cultural
    commemorations and satirical
    interventions, 19, 77, 113n, **190–216**, 217
Terris, Olwen, 79n, 187n, 213–14n, 262
Thackeray, William, 17
Thanhouser, Edwin, founder of film
    production company, 127n
Thanhouser, Gertrude, Thanhouser, 127n
Thanhouser, Ned, grandson of Edwin
    Thanhouser scenarist, 127n
Thanhouser, American film production com-
    pany, 5, 77, 116, 127n, 148
DVD, *Thanhouser presents Shakespeare
    1910–1916*, 4, 106n, 201n, **261**
A Winter's Tale (O'Neil, 1910), 19, 105, 106,
    126–29, *128*
The Tempest (Edwin Thanhouser, 1911), 86n,
    127n
Cymbeline (Sullivan, 1913), 127n
King Lear (Ernest Warde, 1916), *front cover*,
    9, 13, 33, 77, 96–97, 127n, 201
Romeo and Juliet (O'Neil, 1911), 127n
The Merchant of Venice (Henderson, 1912),
    127n
Two Little Dromios [ie *The Comedy of Errors*]
    (director unknown, 1914), 127n
Master Shakespeare, Strolling Player
    (Sullivan, 1916), 127n
When Hungry Hamlet Fled, Shakespeare
    offshoot (director unknown, 1915), 148n
Theatres, movie theatres and music halls,
    see also exhibition conventions, venues
Academy Theater, The, New York, 206;
    Alhambra, The, London, 46; Broadway
    Theater, The, New York, 203n, 215–16;
    Coburg Theatre, The, London, 70n;
    Coliseum, The, London, 195; Covent
    Garden, London, 42, 50; Daly's
    Theatre, 135; Deutsches Theater,
    Berlin, 250; Drury Lane, London,
    28, 42, 150, 152, 160, *180*, 191n; Fifth
    Avenue Theater, Brooklyn, 145; George
    Steiner's Playhouse, New York, 206;
    Globe Playhouse, The, London, xxii;
    Haymarket Theatre, The, 42, 53;
    Her Majesty's Theatre, London, 49,
    60–62, 66–69, 70n, 71n, 135; becomes
    His Majesty's Theatre after accession
    of Edward VII, 85, 137; Kennedy
    Arts Center, Washington DC, 22;
    London Coliseum, 195; Lyceum, The,
    London, 48, 156, 183n; National Film
    Theatre, The, London: 72n; The New

Gallery Kinema, London: 149n, 160;
    Poli Wonderland Theater, The, New
    Haven, 68; Prince Theater, 13n; New
    Gallery Kinema, London, 149n, 160,
    162; Palace Theatre of Varieties, The,
    London, xvii-xvii, 66–68; Princess's
    Theatre, London, 47; Royal Circus,
    The, London, 43, 44; Royal Theatre
    of Copenhagen, 217n; Sadler's Wells,
    London, 50; St Charles Theater, New
    Orleans, 114, 119; Savoy Theatre,
    London, 136; Strand Theatre, Sydney,
    207n; Teatro Lirico, Milan, 150, 164;
    Teatro Vittioria, Turin, 150n; Olympic
    Theatre, Broadway, 13n, 52n; Tivoli
    Theatre, The, London, 62n
Thompson, Ann, 219n
Thompson, Kristin, 20
Thorndike, Sybil, stage and screen actress, 217n
Tillotson, K., 26n
Timon of Athens, Shakespeare play
    lantern slides, 31
title cards, *see* intertitles
Titus Andronicus, Shakespeare play, 1, 252
Toddle, Timothy, lanternist-showman, 29–31
Tolstoy, Leo, xixn, 238, 255
Tosi, Virgilio, 23–24
trade papers, film periodicals, journals and
    newspapers (trades listed xviiin)
Art Journal, The, 31n, 35; *Athenaeum, The*,
    journal, 48n; *Augusta Chronicle*,
    American local newspaper, 13; *Avanti*,
    Italian newspaper, 166; *Biograph, The*,
    xviiin, 148, 201; *Bioscope, The*, 11, 79n,
    80n, 100–01, 116, 135, 147n, 150, 151,
    152, 169n, 184n, 199, 212n; *Blackwood's
    Magazine*, journal, 22n, 136n; *Cinema
    News and Property Gazette, The*
    (*CNPG*), xviiin, 8, 192, 193n, 196; *Cine-
    Technician, The*, journal, 58; *Craftsman,
    The*, journal, 111n; *Daily Chronicle,
    The*, newspaper, 64; *Daily Mail, The*,
    newspaper, 136; *Daily News, The*,
    newspaper, 68; *Eckart – Ein Deutsches
    Literaturblatt*, journal, 12; *Era, The*,
    xviiin, 152; *Études Anglaises*, journal,
    77n; *Exceptional Photoplays*, 228–29,
    232; *Film Daily*, xviiin, 211n; *Forum*,
    journal, 2n, 203n; *Griffithiana*, 25n;
    Illustrated Films Monthly, The, xviiin,
    161; *Illustrated London News, The*
    (*ILN*), journal, xviiin, 64, 152n, 155n;
    Kinematograph and Lantern Weekly, The
    (*KLW*), xviiin, 41, 52n, 91n, 170n, 185,
    187, 188, 197n, 198n, 250n; *Literature/*

Film Quarterly, xviiin, 233n; *London Graffic*, journal, 155n; *London News*, journal, 155n; *Metro Picture News*, production company publicity paper, 202n, 205, 207n, 208n, 211n; *Motion Picture Classic, The*, xviiin, 54, 55n, 203n; *Motion Picture Magazine, The (MPM)*, xviiin, 204n, 207n; *Motion Picture Story Magazine, The*, xviiin, 161; *Motography* (incorporating *The Nickelodeon*), xviiin, 109, 138n, 145n, 205; *Moving Picture World, The (MPW)*, xviiin, xxi, 9, 11, 12, 41, 75n, 86n, 90, 101, 103, 108n, 109n, 110n, 115n, 126n, 127n, 138, 144, 145n, 154, 155n, 159n, 163n, 174, 188, 189n, 197n, 198n, 202n, 203n, 205n, 206n, 207n, 208, 209, 210n, 213n, 214n, 215, 216n, 220n, 223n; *New York Dramatic Mirror, The*, 109n, 110n, 143, 181n; *Nickelodeon, The, see Motography*; *Optical Lantern and Cinematic Journal, The*, xviiin; *Optical Magic Lantern Journal, Almanac*, 40 (re-launched as *Kinematograph and Lantern Weekly (KLW)*); *Photographic News, The*, 68; *Photoplay*, 207n; *Picturegoer Weekly, The*, 203n; *Pictures, The* , xviiin, 161–62; *Pictures and the Picturegoer*, 72–73, 143n, 172n, 198; *Play Pictorial, The*, 151n, 154, 155n; *Saturday Review, The*, journal, 152n; *Screen*, journal, 10n; *Shakespeare*, journal, 192n; *Shakespeare Bulletin (SB)*, 71n; *Shakespeare Quarterly (SQ)*, 71n, 113n, 191n, 234n; *Shakespeare Yearbooks*, 185–86n; *Sight and Sound*, 163n, 225n; *Skrien*, Dutch journal, 224n; *Stage, The*, journal, 152, 155; *Standard, The*, journal, 160; *Southport Visiter, The*, 58; *Telegraph, The*, newspaper, 213n; *Times, The*, newspaper, 191, 200n; *Variety*, journal, 205, 207n, 211, 212, 250n; *Wide Angle*, 17n; *Wid's Film Daily*, 98n
transgendering, *see* cross-dressing
transitional era, *see* film industry development stages
Tree, Herbert Beerbohm, theatre actor-manager, film actor, xvii, 2, 3, 4, 17, 20, 23, 41, 48–49, 51, 54, 58, 60–73, 74–75, 77, 78, 85–88, 135, 137, 163n, 168n, 190, 191, 192n, 197n; 198–202, 251
Tree, Mrs Herbert Beerbohm, stage actress, 67
Tree, Viola, stage actress, 85–86
Triangle-Reliance, American film production company

Macbeth (Emerson, 1916), 2, 20, 72–73, 77, 190, 191, 192n, **198–202**, 213
Trilby, Tree's stage production, 60–61
Troilus and Cressida, Shakespeare play, of which no silent film made, 252n
Turner, Florence, film actress ('the Vitagraph Girl'), 3, 105, 130–31, *134*, 139, 142–45, *142*
Twelfth Night, Shakespeare play lantern slide sequence, 31
Twelfth Night, Vitagraph film (Kent, 1910), 19, 105–06, 108, 131
Two Little Dromios, see The Comedy of Errors
Tyler Film Company, British film production and distribution company, 52

Uncle Josh at the Moving Picture Show, Edison non-Shakespearean film (Porter, 1901), 129n
Uricchio, William, xviiin, 15n, 16n, 72n, 107n, 108n, 110, 115n, 121n, 124n, 137n, 192n, 212n, 213n
Urban-Eclipse, American film production company, 109
Usai, Paulo Cherci 102n, 107n

van den Tempel, Mark, 25n
Vanbrugh, Irene, stage and screen actress, sister of Violet Vanburgh, 194, 195
Vanbrugh, Violet, stage and screen actress, wife of Arthur Bourchier, 197
Vardac, A.Nicholas, 24n, 50n, 56
Vaughan, Alden T., 85n, 114n
Vaughan, Virgina Mason, 85n, 114
Verdi, composer of opera *Othello*, 74–75n; source of FAI films, 89
Vestris, Madame Eliza, stage actress, 135
Vining, Edward P., 219
Vitagraph, American film production company, 5, 18–19, 77, 105–46
 eagle as company logo,113–23, *117*, *120*, *122*, 145
 the 'Vitagraph Girl', Florence Turner, 3, 105, 130–31, *134*, 139, 142–45, *142*
 publications, *Vitagraph Pictures Annual Studio Yearbook*, 112; *Vitagraph Bulletin*, 137n, 138
Vitagraph repertory company, 138–39
Antony and Cleopatra (Kent, 1908), 75, 108, 119n, 130
Julius Caesar (Ranous and Blackton, 1908), 4, 16, 19, 75, 105, 106, 108, 115–26, *117*, *122*, *123*, 132, 139, 146
Macbeth (Ranous, 1908), 19, 75, 105, 106, 108, 119–21, *120*, 131–32, 139, 143, 170n, 197

Vitagraph, American film production company
(*cont.*)
The Merchant of Venice (Blackton, 1908), 75,
105–06, 108, 119–21, 139, 143
Othello (Ranous, 1908), 75, 90, 105, 108, 119,
139, 201
Richard III (Blackton and Ranous, 1908), 75,
108, 115n
Romeo and Juliet (Blackton, 1908), 75, 105,
106, 108, *120*, 121, 139, 143, 144, 211n
King Lear (Ranous, 1909), 19, 105, 106, 108,
124, 125, 127, 131, 132, 139, 143
A Midsummer Night's Dream (Kent and
Blackton, 1909), 105, 106, 108, **130–37**,
134, 139, 141, 143
Twelfth Night (Kent, 1910), 19, 105–07, 108,
131, **137–42**, *140*, *142*, 146
As You Like It (Blackton and Kent, 1912),
108, 130, 133
Hamlet (projected but never made), 149
Shakespeare offshoots
An Indian Romeo and Juliet
(Trimble, 1912), 2, 77, 108
Cardinal Wolsey, offshoot of Henry VIII
(Trimble, 1912), 108
*A Midwinter Night's Dream; or Little Joe's
Luck* (unknown, 1906), 108
The Wrong Flat; or A Comedy of Errors
(unknown, 1907), 108
Freddy Versus Hamlet (Currier, 1916), 108,
149n, 200
non-Shakespeare films
Salome (Blackton, 1908), 108; *Oliver
Twist* (Blackton, 1909), 108; *A Tale
of Two Cities* (Humphrey, 1911), 108,
130; *Launcelot and Elaine* (Kent,
1909), 108, 139, 143; *Vanity Fair*
(Kent, 1911), 108, 220; *A Modern
Oliver Twist* (Blackton, 1906),
108; *Elektra* (Blackton, 1910), 108,
130; *The Life of Moses* (Blackton,
1909), 108; *Jephthah's Daughter, A
Biblical Tragedy* (unknown, 1909),
108; *Saul and David* (Blackton,
1909), 108; *The Way of the Cross*
(Blackton, 1909), 108; funeral
of King Edward VII (1910), 109;
Illumination (Gaskill, 1912), 108; *The
Life of George Washington* (unknown,
1909), 109, 113; *The Battle Hymn of
the Republic* (Blackton, 1911), 109;
Lady Godiva, 112; *Princess Nicotine
or The Smoke Fairy*, 131; *Kenilworth*
(unknown, 1909), 143; *Jealousy*

(unknown, 1911), 144; *The Haunted
Hotel* (Blackton, 1907), 170n; other
non-Shakespearean films, listed by
title, 111, 113
'Vitascope', 106
von Alten, Ferdinand, German screen actor,
242
von Lenkeffy, Ica, German screen actress,
243–50, *244*, *245*
von Winterstein, Eduard, German screen actor,
229

Walderdaw, British film production company,
217n
Warde, Ernest, film actor and director, *front
cover*, 13, 201
Warde, Frederick, stage and screen film actor
and lecturer, *see also Richard III* (1912) and
King Lear (1916), **front cover**, 4, 9, 13, *14*,
32–33, 52, 77, 96–97, 127n, 201
Waterhouse, John William, artist of painting
of Ophelia, 157–58n, *see also* artistic
representations
Weitzel, Edward, 164
Wells, Stanley, 1n, 182n
White, James Fisher (sometimes credited as
James Fisher), stage and screen actor, 62n,
64
Wicked Willie, alternative title of BMBC 'giddy'
Studio Troubles q.v., 58
Wiene, Robert, German film director, 233
Wiggins, Jack, 58n
Wilkie, Edmund H, 40
Wilson, Edwin, 78n, 152n
Winter's Tale, The, Shakespeare play
in lantern slides sequences, 31
A Winter's Tale, Thanhouser film
(O'Neill, 1910), 4, 19, 105–06, 126–29,
128
*Una tragedia alla Corte di Sicilia / A
Winter's Tale*, Milano film (Negroni,
1913), 32
Wolf, Steffen, 12n
Wood, Michael, 237
Woods, Leigh, 111n
Woolf, Virginia, 20n
wordless stage productions, 42–50, 55, 253–59,
see also pantomime
Wörner-Filmgesellschaft, German film
production company
Othello (Buchowetzki, 1922), 7–8, 20, 21, 77,
94, 217, 224, 240–51, *244*, *245*, *249*
Wrong Flat, The, or A Comedy of Errors,
non-Shakespearean film, see Vitagraph

3901947R00189

Printed in Great Britain
by Amazon.co.uk, Ltd.,
Marston Gate.